# ANNALS of DYSLEXIA

VOLUME 51                                                    2001

*Annals of Dyslexia* is listed in *Current Contents/Social and Behavioral Sciences* (CC/ S&BS), the Social Sciences Citations Index ©(SSCI™), and *Chicoral Abstracts to Reading and Learning Disabilities*. Microfilm and photocopies are available from University Microfilms International.

The journal is annotated and indexed by the ERIC Clearinghouse on Handicapped and Gifted Children for publication in the monthly print index; *Current Index to Journals in Education* (CIJE); and the quarterly index, *Exceptional Child Education Resources* (ECER).

The International Dyslexia Association®
Chester Building/Suite 382
8600 LaSalle Road
Baltimore, MD 21286-2044

Printed in the United States of America

### Notice

Members of The International Dyslexia Association® receive *Annals of Dyslexia*
without charge. Additional copies of this issue are available from The
International Dyslexia Association® at $15.00 each for members and $18.50
each for nonmembers plus 20% for postage and handling. Send orders prepaid
to the address above.

Cover design: Joseph M. Dieter, Jr.
Compositor: Type Shoppe II Productions, Ltd.
Printer: Port City Press

ISSN 0736-9387

# ANNALS OF DYSLEXIA

Volume 51                                                    2001

## Contents

# FOREWORD

*Annals of Dyslexia* is an interdisciplinary, peer-reviewed journal published annually by The International Dyslexia Association. Its focus is on the understanding, prevention, and remediation of written language difficulties (reading, writing, spelling, handwriting) and related areas, giving primary consideration to original research papers and including significant reviews and well-documented reports of effective practices. We encourage and often solicit submissions from members of IDA and other researchers, educators, and clinicians concerned with language disabilities.

Before introducing this volume, on behalf of The International Dyslexia Association, we express our condolences to the family and friends of Candace S. Bos who passed away on August 13, 2001. Candace is first author of an article in Part III.

Part I, *Distinguished Addresses,* has two papers that are based on highlights from invited presentations at the 51st IDA conference in November, 2000. G. Reid Lyon, recipient of the Samuel T. Orton award, pays tribute to leading figures in the field, reviews converging evidence about how reading develops and how to teach it, and makes suggestions for future research and practice. Robert Brooks, the Samuel T. and June Lyday Orton distinguished lecturer, defends the important role of classroom teachers in nurturing the emotional lives of their students.

Part II, *Understanding Dyslexia: IQ-Discrepancy and Other Definitional Issues,* features two articles on definition and identification. Virginia Berninger challenges us to rethink our ideas about identifying and diagnosing dyslexia. Flowers and her colleagues examine the efficacy of the achievement discrepancy hypothesis.

Many *Annals* readers have an interest in the translation of research into practice. In Part III, *Research into Practice: Instruction and Intervention,* there are four papers that have implications for practitioners. Hook and her colleagues describe findings of a two year study they conducted with a small number of students to determine the efficacy of Fast ForWord, a training program involving acoustically modified speech. Candace Bos, et al. examine teachers' knowledge and perceptions about early reading instruction. The last two articles are on spelling. Post and her colleagues describe an intervention study they conducted on explicit vs. implicit instruction of spelling patterns. Schlagel summarizes historical and current research and thinking on approaches to spelling.

Part IV, *Relating Oral Language Abilities to Reading,* is a tribute to the research of Samuel T. Orton. The four articles in Part IV are on aspects of speech/language processing difficulties as they relate to reading. In combination, the papers provide further support for this intricate relationship.

In the last section, *Dyslexia and Math* (Part V), both C.K. Leong and his colleague and T.R. Miles and his colleagues use structured interviews as a way of examining the reasoning processes that children go through in math problem-solving.

As outgoing Acting Editor, I would like to express my special appreciation to Associate Editor Hollis Scarborough for assisting me in obtaining outstanding reviewers, providing critical reviews, and making numerous editorial suggestions. I also appreciate the judicious editing and editorial advice of Associate Editor Susan Brady. I am grateful to the Editorial Advisory Board members and to this year's ad hoc reviewers: G. Backhouse, M. Bruck, L. D. Compton, L. Cutting, P. Gerber, D. Gilroy, N. Gregg, B. Levy, S. Petrill, L. Siegel, and S. Stage. Thanks to the IDA staff and especially Cindy Ciresi, Director of Conferences, for her support these past two years. Special thanks also go to Type Shoppe II for their superb editorial assistance and for facilitating the production of the journal.

Editor

To submit a manuscript to the *Annals of Dyslexia,* you must do so by January 10 to receive consideration for publication in the following year. For information about submitting a manuscript to the *Annals of Dyslexia,* contact The International Dyslexia Association, Chester Building Suite 382, 8600 LaSalle Rd., Baltimore, MD 21286-2044; FAX 410/321-5069; PH: 410-296-0232; e-mail: info@interdys.org; *Guidelines for Contributors* are available online at http://www.interdys.org. Individual copies of papers in the current or prior issues (including those from the *Bulletin of the Orton Society*) are available at the same address. The cost of an individual paper is $4.00, including postage and handling.

# PART I
## Two Distinguished Addresses

In Part I, G. Reid Lyon and Robert B. Brooks, two educators who have made substantial contributions to our understanding of dyslexia, present highlights from their distinguished addresses at the 51st Annual Conference of The International Dyslexia Association in Washington, D.C., November 8-11, 2000. Dr. Lyon was the Samuel T. Orton award recipient and Dr. Brooks, the Samuel Torrey and June Lyday Orton memorial lecturer.

## THE 2000 SAMUEL T. ORTON AWARD PRESENTED TO REID LYON

Each year the International Dyslexia Association presents an award to an individual who has made outstanding and far-reaching contributions to the field. This past year's 2000 Samuel T. Orton award recipient was G. Reid Lyon, a research psychologist and Chief of the Child Development and Behavior Branch of the National Institute of Child Health and Human Development (NICHD) at NIH. Dr. Lyon is responsible for the direction, development, and management of research programs in developmental psychology, cognitive neuroscience, behavioral pediatrics, reading, and human learning and learning disorders. He has authored, co-authored, and edited over 100 journal articles, books, and book chapters on learning differences and disabilities. He currently serves as an advisor to President George W. Bush on child development and education research and policies and is responsible for translating NIH scientific discoveries relevant to the health and education of children to the White House, the United States Congress, and other governmental agencies.

Largely through Dr. Lyon's efforts in this important governmental position, he has supported and overseen funding for research on dyslexia. Those of us affiliated with IDA thank Dr. Lyon for the impact he has made on the field by helping educators to achieve a better understanding of the causes and treatment of dyslexia.

**The Citation:**
**The International Dyslexia Association**
**The Samuel T. Orton Award**
**Presented to**
**G. Reid Lyon, Ph.D.**
*Chief, Child Development and Behavior Branch*
*National Institute of Child Health and Human Development,*
*National Institute of Health*

In recognition of your tireless effort on behalf of those at-risk of reading failure and to inform reading instruction through research based knowledge.
*November 10, 2000*

## THE SAMUEL TORREY AND JUNE LYDAY ORTON MEMORIAL LECTURER: ROBERT B. BROOKS

We are honored to introduce our readers to Robert B. Brooks, this past year's Samuel T. and June Lyday Orton Memorial Lecturer. Dr. Brooks serves on the faculty of the Harvard Medical School and lectures nationally and internationally on topics pertaining to motivation, resilience, self-esteem, family relationships, and the qualities of effective leaders. He received the Gubernatorial Award for Distinguished Public Service for his work with the Governor's Alliance against Drugs; the "Hall of Fame" awards from CH.A.D.D. and the Connecticut Association for Children with Learning Disabilities; a Special Recognition and Media Award from the Massachusetts Psychological Association; and the "Friends of Families Award" from the Family Place. He has written and coauthored a number of books and articles on self-esteem, education, resilience, psychotherapy, and sex education. Teachers, in particular, may be interested in his book, *The Self-Esteem Teacher*, published by Treehaus Communications.

We pay special tribute to Dr. Brooks for his belief that "every child who enters school needs to be special" and for his valuable advice on how to be an effective educator through nurturing optimism and hope in individuals with learning disorders.

# Acceptance of the
# Samuel Torrey Orton Award
# November 2000, Washington, D.C.

*G. Reid Lyon*

National Institute of Child Health and Human Development

It is a privilege for me to express my deep gratitude for this wonderful honor. I am humbled by your kindness and your recognition. In accepting the Samuel Torrey Orton Award from the International Dyslexia Association, however, I must give credit where credit is due. The work that is being recognized through this award would not even have been thought about if it were not for the tremendous contributions made by Dr. Orton and his colleagues as they pushed the scientific and clinical envelope over 50 years ago to understand and treat this complex and debilitating disorder called dyslexia. The contributions you are recognizing through this award also stand squarely on the shoulders of my predecessors who have received it, including, for example, Dorothy Whitehead, Lucia Karnes, Rosa Hagin, Jeannette Jansky, Jeanne Chall, Wilson Anderson, Priscilla Vail, and Howard Gardner. And please forgive me for leaving some recipients out. It is not by design but due to failing memory. But even more specifically, this award must be shared with Dr. Duane Alexander, Director of the National Institute of Child Health and Human Development

Annals of Dyslexia, Vol. 51, 2001
ISSN 0736-9387

within the National Institutes of Health. Dr. Alexander's vision and courage laid the programmatic foundation for contributions made to our understanding and treatment of dyslexia by scientists within the NICHD Reading Research Program. And it is to these scientists that this award really belongs. While I do not have time to name them all, I would not be standing before you today if Jim Kavanagh, David Gray, Sally Shaywitz, Ben Shaywitz, Jack Fletcher, Barbara Foorman, David Francis, Joe Torgesen, Rick Wagner, Marilyn Adams, Isabelle Liberman, Al Liberman, Susan Brady, Anne Fowler, Benita Blachman, Carol Fowler, Don Shankweiler, Mike Studdert-Kennedy, Ken Pugh, Hollis Scarborough, Frank Wood, Becky Felton, Lynn Flowers, Keith Rayner, Dennis Molfese, Victoria Molfese, Martha Denckla, Frank Vellutino, Donna Scanlon, Ginger Berninger, Guinevere Eden, Dick Olson, John DeFries, Bruce Pennington, Louisa Moats, Robin Morris, Maryanne Wolf, Maureen Lovett, Roscoe Dykman, Chris Lonigan, Josh Breyer, Barbara Wise, Deborah Waber, Al Galaburda, Gordon Sherman, Glen Rosen, George Hynd, Frank Manis, Shelly Smith, and all of the scientists on their teams had not brought their intellectual gifts and dedication to the study of reading, dyslexia, and other types of learning disabilities. Their tremendous dedication to children and adults with dyslexia, and their enormous commitment to applying the best scientific thinking to the study of dyslexia, has enabled so many individuals with the disorder to alleviate the pain that comes from its consequences. The only way that I can feel comfortable accepting this award is to accept it on their behalf.

Indeed, we have come a very long way. Because of the efforts of countless teachers, parents, and scientists, many of whom are identified above, we now have a much greater understanding of what it takes to develop skilled reading abilities, why some children and adults do not learn to read, and what we can do about fixing that. Along the way, we have also been able to forge a respected science and psychology of reading development and reading instruction. This is a long time in coming. Recall that in 1967, Jeanne Chall, after interviewing textbook authors, reading specialists, and teachers for her analysis of the "great debate" in reading wrote " . . . their language was often more characteristic of religion and politics than of science and learning" (Chall, 1967, p. 3). While many in the reading community continue to debate the "reading wars" from a philosophical and ideological perspective, it is the science of reading that is guiding the development and implementation of prevention and early intervention programs for children at-risk for reading failure in many states. It is also the science of reading that provides the foundation for federal legislation and funding for reading programs and the preparation of reading teachers throughout the country.

Over the past decade in particular, we have been able to bring science to the teaching of reading and to base both classroom and clinical practices on evidence-based instructional approaches that have proven effective in well-designed studies (see The Report of the National Reading Panel, 2000). Fortunately, we are moving away from simplistic and polarized ideas about how reading develops and how best to teach it. On the basis of extensive converging evidence from a substantial number of studies, we know that while phonics instruction is necessary, it is not sufficient to produce skilled readers. Reading requires a knowledge of letters and sounds as a foundation and also requires the ability to read fluently, to spell accurately, to deploy a strong knowledge of vocabulary, and to apply systematically strategies to enhance comprehension of a wide variety of text formats and types of literature. Thus, evidence-based reading approaches and programs emphasize phonics as only one component of a comprehensive program.

No doubt, it is one thing to accumulate substantial evidence to support this conclusion, but it is another to ensure that teachers can apply the research evidence to their selection and implementation of instructional strategies, approaches, and programs. And it is in this area that we have let our teachers and their students down. It remains the case that the majority of our kindergarten and elementary school teachers, as well as many reading specialists and special educators, continue to rely on unproven instructional reading programs and approaches to the detriment of many of their students. It is also clear that many teachers continue to have a difficult time determining if the reading programs that are used in their particular schools and districts actually address the complex range of skills necessary to learn to read and whether they offer evidenced-based strategies and instructional routines that have proven beneficial to well-defined students.

The reading community in general, and the International Dyslexia Association in particular, must take the lead to ensure that reading instruction in our nation's schools adheres to the best scientific evidence available. This means that our future and veteran teachers must know how reading skills develop, why some children have difficulty, and how to identify and implement the most effective instructional armamentarium on the basis of specific student characteristics. While it may be difficult to change the culture within many departments of education at our colleges and universities, strong and courageous leadership can bring about significant change in others. Where this seems impossible, we have seen that bold leadership within governors' offices, state legislatures, and local districts can help teachers in training, as well as veteran teachers, circumvent the mediocrity and sometimes the malpractice of education departments that refuse to adhere to evidence-based standards by offering alternative preparation and continuing education programs that lead to certification.

We cannot bring about these necessary changes unless there is a solid and universal commitment to making sure our teachers understand what constitutes scientific evidence and how to apply these standards to their selection and implementation of programs and interventions. Within this context, we must realize that we undermine this commitment to evidence and quality when we, ourselves, recommend or defend interventions or programs on the basis of experience, anecdotal evidence, or dogma rather than on data. It is now time for all reading approaches to adhere to the same high standards of evidence and proven effectiveness. Let us be clear: these standards must apply as much to the Orton-Gillingham method and other structured multisensory language-based reading programs and interventions as they do to programs like Reading Recovery or philosophical literature-based approaches. Let us not kid ourselves. We will not see genuine lasting change and reading improvement in all of our students until this consistency of proven effectiveness for all reading approaches, methods, and programs is achieved. Our children deserve no less.

Address correspondence to G. Reid Lyon, Child Development and Behavior Branch, National Institute of Child Health and Human Development. e-mail: rl60a@nih.gov

## References

Chall, J. S. (1967). *Learning to read: The great debate.* New York: McGraw-Hill.

National Reading Panel. (2000). *Teaching children to read: An evidenced-based assessment of the scientific research on reading and its implications for reading instruction.* Bethesda, MD: The National Institute of Child Health and Human Development, The National Institutes of Health.

# Fostering Motivation, Hope, and Resilience in Children with Learning Disorders

*Robert B. Brooks, Ph.D.*

Harvard Medical School
Cambridge, Massachusetts

*I have had the opportunity to work with many children and adolescents with learning disorders during the past 30 years. In conducting therapy with these youths, I became increasingly aware that most were burdened by feelings of low self-worth and incompetence and that many believed that their situation would not improve. Not surprisingly, this sense of hopelessness served as a major obstacle to future success. Once children believe that things will not improve, they are likely to engage in self-defeating ways of coping such as quitting or avoiding tasks, blaming others for their difficulties, or becoming class clowns or bullies. Thus, a negative cycle is often set in motion, intensifying feelings of defeat and despair.*

As I listened closely to children with learning disorders, I came to understand that if we were to help them be more motivated and learn more effectively, we must ensure that our interventions address not only their specific learning needs but their feelings of low self-worth as well and that we must provide them with opportunities to experience realistic accomplishment that nurtured optimism and hope.

In my discussions with countless educators and parents, I began to appreciate another major dimension determining whether or not these youngsters with learning disorders would be successful. All of us who work with or raise children, whether teachers, clinicians, or parents, possess certain assumptions about why children behave the way they do. These assumptions, which I often refer to as a mindset, subtly or not so subtly guide our interactions with children. Frequently, we are not even aware of the components of this mindset although they direct much of our behavior.

If we examine the school environment, I have found that educators have many different assumptions about the process of education and about students with learning disorders. Given this, a question can be raised, namely, "What is the mindset of an effective educator?" or worded somewhat differently, "What are the assumptions and behaviors of an educator who will touch the mind, heart, and spirit of children with learning disorders and infuse them with realistic hope?"

In attempting to answer this question in this article, I will rely on the many interactions I have had with educators as well as my own experiences as a principal of a school in a locked-door unit of a psychiatric hospital, and as a consultant to both public and independent schools. My journeys have introduced me to teachers and school administrators who are skilled in touching both the minds and hearts of students, who recognize the importance of focusing not only on developing the intellectual lives of students but also their emotional lives, and who, through word and deed, demonstrate a deep commitment to creating school climates in which *all* students will thrive.

These talented educators possess a mindset that guides their teaching style and their interaction with students, and reinforces a zest for learning, even in those children struggling with learning disorders. I believe that the ingredients of this mindset are predicated on common sense and an adherence to basic principles of human dignity and respect. I know that many educators are already engaged in practices that follow from the tenets of this mindset so that what I highlight will hopefully serve as a validation of their existing teaching style.

## THE MINDSET OF EFFECTIVE EDUCATORS

The following are several of the key components that I believe represent the mindset of the effective educator. Space limitations do not permit a lengthier discussion of each of these components nor the inclusion of other components. However, it is my hope that this relatively brief description will provide the reader with a sense of the mindset that I believe should be learned, embraced, and incorporated by all educators in their teaching activities because the end result will be many more students with learning disorders who are saved from future failure and who are helped to lead more productive, fulfilling lives.

## ADDRESSING THE SOCIAL-EMOTIONAL NEEDS OF A STUDENT IS NOT AN EXTRA CURRICULUM ACTIVITY

At one of my workshops, I was discussing the significant impact that educators have on the social-emotional life of students. A high school science teacher in the audience challenged the emphasis I was placing on social-emotional factors by contending, "I am a science teacher. I know my science and I know how to convey science facts to my students. Why should I have to spend time thinking about the student's emotional or social life? I don't have time to do so and it will distract me from teaching science."

I know that there are many teachers and school administrators who would take issue with the views expressed by this science teacher, who believe as I do that addressing a student's social and emotional development may be as vital as teaching specific academic skills and content. However, I am also aware that there are many educators who would concur with her opinion. I believe it is unfortunate that a dichotomy has emerged prompting some educators to perceive that nurturing a student's emotional and social well-being is mutually exclusive of the task of teaching academic skills. I am convinced, based on my own experiences as well as the feedback I have received from many educators, that strengthening a student's self-worth is not an "extra" curriculum; if anything, a student's sense of belonging, security, and self-confidence in a classroom provides the scaffolding that supports the foundation for increased learning, motivation, self-discipline, responsibility, and the ability to deal more effectively with mistakes.

## EMPATHY IS ONE OF THE MOST IMPORTANT SKILLS OF AN EFFECTIVE TEACHER

If you were to ask me, "What do you consider to be one of the most vital skills for a teacher to possess?" I would respond, "Empathy." Translated to the school arena, empathy is the capacity of teachers to place themselves inside the shoes of their students and to see the world through the student's eyes. Goleman (1995) highlights empathy as a major component of emotional intelligence.

Being empathic encourages us to ask, "Whenever I say or do things with students, am I saying or doing these things in a way that my students will be most responsive to my message?" "For example, a teacher may wish to motivate a student with learning problems by exhorting the student to "just try harder." While the teacher may be well-intentioned, such a comment is frequently experienced in a negative, accusatory way. When students feel accused, which is not uncommon among children and adolescents with learning disorders, they are less likely to be cooperative. Consequently, the teacher's comment will not produce the desired results. However, if the teacher had been empathic, he or she might have wondered, "If I were having difficulty in my role as a teacher, would I want another teacher or my principal to say to me, 'If you just tried harder you wouldn't have this problem'?"

To highlight the importance of empathy, I have asked educators in my workshops to think of a teacher they liked and one that they did not like when they were students. I then ask them to think of words that they would use to describe each of these teachers. Finally, I say, "Just as you have words to describe your teachers, your students have words to describe you. What words would you hope they used to describe you? What words would they actually use?" Teachers who appreciate the importance of empathy constantly ask these questions of themselves. Most important, their interactions are guided by thoughts about how they wish to be perceived and described by their students.

## EDUCATORS HAVE A LIFELONG IMPACT
## ON STUDENTS AND ON THE DEVELOPMENT OF RESILIENCE

As noted earlier, many students with learning disorders are beset with feelings of doubt about their future. Effective educators appreciate that what they say and do in the classroom each day can have a lifelong influence on their students (Brooks, 1991; Brooks & Goldstein, 2001). This appreciation of their impact adds meaning and purpose to their work, empowering them and lessening feelings of stress and burnout. In the past 15 to 20 years, there has been an increased effort to delineate those factors that help at-risk youth to overcome adversity and become resilient. Schools especially have been spotlighted as environments for nurturing self-esteem, hope, and resilience. For example, psychologist Julius Segal (1988), in describing resilient youth, writes:

> From studies conducted around the world, researchers have distilled a number of factors that enable such children of misfortune to beat the heavy odds against them. One factor

turns out to be the presence in their lives of a charismatic adult--a person with whom they can identify and from whom they gather strength. And in a surprising number of cases, that person turns out to be a teacher (p. 10).

A basic belief that resides within the mindset of effective educators is that they have the power to be the charismatic adult in a student's life and they actively seek opportunities to do so. These educators recognize that all of their actions in the classroom can have an impact on students, an impact that goes far beyond today, next week, or next month. While this impact is true for all students, it has special relevance for students with learning problems who are burdened by feelings of vulnerability and hopelessness.

## WE MUST AVOID ACCUSATIONS, BLAME, AND LABELS

At the beginning of my career, when children did not improve in therapy with me or in the school at which I was principal, I was quick to call them "resistant," "oppositional," "unmotivated," and "manipulative." The use of such pejorative labels basically blamed the very youngsters I was supposedly helping. One of the most significant changes in my own mindset was to begin to accept the notion that whether or not a child benefited from therapy or school had as much, if not more, to do with the style and behavior of the therapist or educator than what the child brought into the situation. This was a major shift in my thinking since I had been taught initially that resistance was for all intents and purposes a part of one's inner character and would be displayed in all situations. Yet it was difficult for me to continue to subscribe to this belief as I observed so-called "resistant" and "unmotivated" students who were very cooperative and motivated with some teachers but not with others.

I am not implying that we should blame ourselves when we are confronted with a challenging student, but instead of blaming the student through the use of accusatory labels, we should ask what it is that we can do differently so that this student might be more responsive and willing to learn. For instance, I worked with one student with learning problems who disliked school but loved taking care of pets. When he was given the job of being the "pet monitor" of the school, which entailed his ensuring that the pets were cared for, writing a short book with the assistance of his teacher about pet care (the book was bound and placed in the school library), and lecturing in each class of his elementary school about taking care of pets, his motivation to be in school, to write, and to learn increased markedly. He was fortunate to have a teacher and principal who had the courage to change their approach or script rather than expecting him to make the first move. Once they offered opportunities for this student to shine, his seeming "resistance" disappeared.

## ALL STUDENTS ARE DIFFERENT AND LEARN DIFFERENTLY, AND WE MUST TEACH THEM IN WAYS IN WHICH THEY LEARN BEST

There is a plethora of research in the fields of education, developmental psychology, and the neurosciences that have taught us about how every child is different from birth, that children have different temperaments, learning styles, and kinds of intelligence. Yet, even with this research, I often hear teachers say, "We must treat all children the same. If we make an accommodation for this student, how will the other students feel? We must be fair."

I would not want any student to feel a teacher is not fair, but we must appreciate that fairness does not imply expecting the same amount of work from each student. It has been my experience that if at the beginning of the school year, school teachers openly explain to their students that we all learn differently and that these differences require the implementation of a variety of accommodations, students will not develop the feeling that the teacher is unfair. What is unfair, and a prescription for frustration and failure, is to require students to learn and perform in identical fashion although they possess different learning and temperamental styles.

Some educators have expressed concern that making accommodations will be very time-consuming. However, when I describe the most common types of accommodations I have requested for students with learning disorders, most educators have remarked that these are realistic and achievable and do not require significant changes in the classroom routine. Some of these accommodations include, but are not limited to:

1.  Permitting students to take untimed tests.
2.  Establishing a maximum time for homework each night (the child's parent can verify this).
3.  Allowing students with attentional and learning problems to have two sets of books, one at home and one at school, to lessen the pressure they experience about the possibility of losing books.

4.  Providing assignments for the entire week on Monday (or at the end of the previous week) so that parents can help their children organize their time and work.

5.  Permitting students with writing difficulties to use computers for all written work (surprisingly, some teachers still require homework assignments to be handwritten).

## STUDENTS WILL BE MOST RESPONSIVE AND MOTIVATED TO LEARN FROM US WHEN WE MEET THEIR BASIC NEEDS

Effective educators recognize that before they attempt to teach a child academic skills or content, their first task is to create a safe and secure environment in which all students feel comfortable and motivated to learn. This is an issue that requires even more diligence when working with students with learning disorders. One of the foremost researchers in the area of motivation has been psychologist Edward Deci at the University of Rochester. Deci's model suggests that students will be more motivated to learn when particular needs have been met (Deci & Flaste, (1995). Deci articulates three such needs.

1.  To belong and feel connected to the school (I would also add the words "to feel welcome").

2.  To feel a sense of autonomy and self-determination.

3.  To feel competent.

An appreciation of these needs can serve as guideposts, leading educators to ask such questions as: How do I help each student feel welcome in my classroom? What choices do I provide my students so that they develop a sense of ownership? Do I incorporate and teach problem-solving skills in all of my activities so that students can learn to make informed decisions? Do I use discipline more as a form of punishment or as a way of teaching self-discipline? That is, do I involve students in helping create some of the rules and consequences in the classroom? Do I identify and reinforce the strengths of students so that they feel more competent? Do I convey the message from the first day of class that mistakes are part of the learning process and that we can learn from mistakes and not fear them?

Effective teachers constantly consider these and related questions. They reflect on whether they are assisting students to feel welcome in the classroom, whether they are promoting a sense of ownership or autonomy, and whether they are helping students feel competent. I use a metaphor to capture the need for competence, namely, "islands of competence." I often ask educators to identify, reinforce, and display each student's "islands of competence" as a concrete way of demonstrating that we all have strengths. One of the most effective ways to display the strengths of students is by ensuring that each student has a responsibility at school (e.g., tutoring a younger child, helping in the office, painting murals) that highlights the student's competencies. Success begets success. Self-esteem and dignity are based on authentic accomplishments, and each new accomplishment increases the child's motivation to learn and take realistic risks.

## PARENTS ARE OUR PARTNERS, NOT OUR ADVERSARIES

The mindset of the effective teacher recognizes that we must develop close working relationships with parents. I have witnessed far too many situations in which educators and parents have become adversaries, more so when a child has a learning disorder. I realize that it is not always an easy task to develop positive parent-teacher relationships, especially when a youngster is having difficulty in school, but it is a very important goal to achieve. I visited one elementary school in which teachers called each parent the day before the new school year began to express their desire to work closely together. They encouraged the parents to feel free to call them with any questions or concerns, and they conveyed the wish for a positive relationship during the year.

The teachers at the school told me that they implemented this practice of contacting parents before school began because typically, the first time they called most parents was when there was a problem. They said that initiating contact with parents in a more positive way enhanced their relationship with parents and, very important, had a beneficial effect on the learning and motivation of the students.

## DEVELOPING AN ORIENTATION SESSION AT THE BEGINNING OF THE YEAR (BUT IT'S NEVER TOO LATE) HELPS CREATE A POSITIVE MINDSET FOR BOTH EDUCATORS AND STUDENTS

In order to reinforce the mindset of the effective educator, I recommend an "orientation period" at the beginning of the school year, a period during which educators are made more aware of this mindset and the ways in which it can be used to create a positive school climate in which all members of the school community feel safe and secure.

The "orientation period" I envision is divided into two phases. The first takes place a day or two before students arrive and involves exercises that nurture a positive mindset. During this phase, educators can share with each other why they became educators as a way of recalling the purpose of their work.   In addition, I have asked teachers to revisit their past when they were students and to describe a teacher they had whom they really liked and a teacher they did not like. I then state that just as they have words to describe their teachers, their students will have words to describe them. I ask them to think about what words they hope their students will use to describe them, emphasizing that the words students use to describe a teacher will determine how respectful, cooperative, motivated, and self-disciplined students will be, and how much they will learn from their teachers. As these descriptive words are recorded, educators can discuss what they might say and do during the year to maximize the probability that their students will, in fact, use favorable rather than unfavorable words to describe them.

Closely linked to this exercise of positive and negative descriptions of our teachers is an exercise related to specific memories we have of school. I ask educators to share one of their most positive memories of school, a memory that involved something a teacher or school administrator said or did that boosted their confidence. I also ask them to describe a negative memory involving an educator that diminished their confidence and self-worth. It is impressive to observe the wide spectrum of emotions that are triggered as teachers recall these memories, some of which go back decades, and as they reflect on how these memories continue to influence their lives years after the events occurred.

I observe that given the indelible nature of these memories, and the fact that their students will develop memories of them during the upcoming school year, they should think actively about and rely on their childhood experiences to guide what they do with their students. For example, a fourth grade teacher should think, "When I was in the third, fourth, or fifth grade, what did a teacher say or do that strengthened my self-esteem, motivation, and ability to learn? Am I providing the same experiences for my current students?" or "What did a teacher say or do that was hurtful, and compromised my ability to feel comfortable and to learn in the classroom? Am I making certain I do not do any of these things with my students?" The next question for the staff to consider and discuss is, "What can we do this year to ensure that almost all of the memories of our students will be positive and enhance motivation for learning?"

I have been fortunate to work with teachers during this initial phase of the "orientation period" and have witnessed first-hand the excitement that emerges as educators recognize the significant role that their teachers played in their lives and how they can do the same for their students. These exercises set a truly positive tone for the new school year.

The second part of the "orientation period" that I advocate is implemented during the first two or three days of school, but it is essential to refine and reinforce the activities that transpire during these initial days throughout the school year. During these first few days, I actually recommend that educators not feel compelled to engage in teaching academic content. Instead, I believe the time should be devoted to create a classroom climate in which all students will feel safe, secure, and motivated to learn. I have found this to be especially important for children with learning problems, many of whom are intensely anxious about school.

Although some may question this kind of orientation period and say it is a waste of several days of classroom teaching time, it has been my experience that by structuring the first few days to address the needs of students, the students will be more comfortable, more receptive to learning, more involved as active participants in their own education, more capable of dealing with frustration and mistakes, and more respectful and self-disciplined. Just as effective educators must approach their responsibilities with a positive mindset, we must help develop a positive mindset for learning in our students.

What are some of the actual activities that can be scheduled during the first few days of school? If we use Deci's framework, we can ask, "How do we begin to meet a student's needs to feel welcome, autonomous, and competent?" Teachers quickly learning the names of their students helps to establish a sense of feeling welcome. One fourth grade teacher reported bringing in her class photo when she was in fourth grade and using it as a way of discussing what it was like for her. Seeing her as a fourth grader immediately created a more personal touch in the classroom environment.

In addition, as noted earlier, students will feel more welcome when we teach them in ways they learn best. Therefore, during the first couple of days of class, educators can openly discuss the different ways we all learn and the importance of accommodations. This open discussion will help students be more tolerant toward each other and lessen possible feelings that accommodations are unfair.

To promote a sense of ownership or autonomy, teachers can enlist students in helping create class rules and consequences, especially once a teacher has reviewed nonnegotiable rules. Not only are students more likely to follow rules that they have helped to create, but in the process, teachers can reinforce problem-solving and decision-making skills and, very importantly, nurture self-discipline or self-control, another crucial feature of emotional intelligence. Teachers can begin to discuss with students with learning disorders strategies that will help these students to learn more effectively.

Since the fear of making mistakes and feeling humiliated is one of the most significant obstacles to learning and is especially pronounced in children with learning disorders, I have proposed during the second phase of the "orientation period" that teachers ask their class, "Who in this class thinks that they will make mistakes and not understand something the first time it is taught this year?" Before any student can respond, teachers can raise their own hand and share memories of their anxieties when they were students. They can generate a class discussion about the best ways to guarantee that students will not be worried about being called on, of giving a wrong answer, of making mistakes on a test, or of not understanding certain material. Verbalizing directly the fear of making mistakes typically serves to minimize its potency, thereby creating a classroom environment that feels safe and secure. Within this feeling of security, learning will flourish.

In addition to helping students feel more competent by lessening their fear of failure, teachers can ask students what they enjoy doing and what they think they do very well. Early in the school year, educators can begin to note a student's "islands of competence." Students who excel in art can be enlisted to produce work that can be displayed. Other students can be enlisted as buddies, mentors, or tutors for younger students. Various "jobs" can be assigned in the classroom. I have witnessed countless examples of students with learning problems who flourished when educators found opportunities to acknowledge and showcase their strengths.

It is obvious that there are many worthwhile activities that can take place during the first few days of school that will set the framework for a school climate in which all members of the school feel excited and motivated.

## IS IT MORE IMPORTANT FOR SOME STUDENTS TO BE LABELED "SPECIAL NEEDS" OR TO VIEW ALL STUDENTS AS NEEDING TO FEEL SPECIAL?

In ending this brief discussion of the mindset of the effective educator, there is one other ingredient I would like to emphasize that in many ways is interwoven with several of the others. I realize that for a variety of important reasons, not the least of which is to secure accommodations and funding, we use the label "special needs." In my discussions with educators who touch the minds and hearts of their students, I am left with the impression that it would be more in concert with their approach if we de-emphasized the term "special needs" and instead placed a banner in front of every school that read, "Every child who enters this school needs to feel special."

I believe that the mindset of the effective educator is motivated to help all students feel special and appreciated. We can accomplish this by being empathic, by treating students in the same ways that we would like to be treated, by finding a few moments to smile and make them feel comfortable, by teaching them in ways they can learn successfully, by taking care to avoid any words or actions that might be accusatory, by minimizing their fears of failure and humiliation, by encouraging them, and by recognizing their strengths. When we achieve these steps, we truly will become their "charismatic adults." We will have touched their hearts and minds, and in the process, they will learn from us and take the gifts of knowledge, acceptance, and resilience into their adult lives. What a wonderful legacy the effective educator bestows on the next generation.

Address correspondence to Robert B. Brooks, Ph.D., 60 Oak Knoll Terrace, Needham, MA 02492; e-mail: contact@drrobert brooks.com

### References

Brooks, R. B. (1991). *The self-esteem teacher*. Loveland, OH: Treehaus Communications.

Brooks, R. B., & Goldstein S. (2001). *Raising resilient children*. Chicago, ILL: Contemporary Books.

Deci, E., & Flaste, R. (1995). *Why we do what we do: Understanding self-motivation.* New York: Guilford.

Goleman, D. (1995). *Emotional intelligence*. New York: Bantam.

Segal, J. (1988). Teachers have enormous power in affecting a child's self-esteem. *The Brown University Child Behavior and Development Newsletter, 10*, 1–3.

# PART II
## Understanding Dyslexia: IQ-Discrepancy and Other Definitional Issues

Issues of definition and diagnosis continue to challenge educators as ongoing research helps us continue to refine our definition(s) of dyslexia. In the 1995 *Annals of Dyslexia*, G. Reid Lyon discussed the "working" definition of dyslexia that is currently used by the National Institutes of Child Health and Human Development, the National Center for Learning Disabilities, and the IDA Research Committee. Two articles in this year's *Annals* provide further support for this working definition and highlight the need to change the nation's current discrepancy-based definitions.

Virginia Berninger provides a concise review of definitional issues. She begins with an historical perspective on developmental dyslexia in the U.S. and examines research that supports IDA's "working definition," i.e., dyslexia as the dissociation between word reading skills and higher level processes. She then proposes that educators develop a Diagnostic and Treatment Manual for Educational Disorders, analogous to the Diagnostic and Statistical Manual of Mental Disorders (DSM) in psychiatry which, in her view, does not address academic difficulties (such as poor reading) sufficiently. In her view, a manual of this kind would provide a much needed classification scheme for better understanding of developmental and learning differences.

D. Lynne Flowers and her colleagues conducted a longitudinal study on the use of the ability-achievement discrepancy formula. Their findings support those of other studies showing that IQ-achievement discrepancy is not an appropriate method of determining which children need help learning to read. Findings also support a "deficit" rather than "developmental lag" model of reading disability. In their conclusions, the authors make recommendations for changes in public policy.

# Understanding the 'Lexia' in Dyslexia: A Multidisciplinary Team Approach to Learning Disabilities

*Virginia W. Berninger*

University of Washington
Seattle, Washington

*The historical roots of the IQ-achievement discrepancy definition of learning disability are discussed as a reference point for explaining why this definition came into being and why it is inadequate for dealing with the variety of learning and developmental disabilities that present in school settings. A proposal is offered and justified for defining learning disabilities on the basis of profiles for multiple developmental domains that affect learning. In this proposal, developmental dyslexia is differentiated from other learning disabilities. Developmental dyslexia is defined as uneven development (dissociation) between word reading and higher-level processes in the functional reading system. Dyslexics may struggle with word reading because of deficits in phonological processes, orthographic-phonological connections, and/or fluency (rate, automaticity, or executive coordination). The need for both national and international classification schemes for defining specific learning and developmental disabilities for the purposes of educational services and research is emphasized.*

Grant P50 33812-06 from the National Institute of Child Health and Human Development supported preparation of this article.

Annals of Dyslexia, Vol. 51, 2001

Not all learning disabilities are reading disabilities and not all reading disabilities are dyslexia. Dyslexia is a language disorder but not all language disorders are dyslexia. Unfortunately, current classification schemes do not clearly define what a learning disability is, what a language disability is, what a specific reading disability is, what dyslexia is, or what a specific writing disability is. This lack of clear definitions for learning disabilities is compromising both service delivery and research. In this invited article, I was asked to comment on definitional issues from the perspective of a psychologist. My views draw on my clinical training and experience as a psychologist on multidisciplinary teams in schools and hospitals and my knowledge of the research literature. The proposed definition of dyslexia—its hallmark features that define it and differentiate it from other learning disabilities—is restricted to developmental dyslexia in which a student struggles to learn to read; it does not apply to acquired dyslexia in which a previously normal reader loses reading function in specific ways. I conclude with a recommendation to develop a multidisciplinary manual for research, diagnosis, and treatment of developmental and learning disorders.

## HISTORICAL ROOTS

Currently, considerable concern and controversy exists over how to define learning disabilities (e.g., Frith, 1999; Henry, Ganschow, & Miles, 2000; Tønnessen, 1997). The following discussion of definitional issues is limited, by necessity, to historical developments in the United States that I have witnessed firsthand. However, historical accounts of how learning disabilities in other countries are identified, defined, and treated instructionally are desirable, and add to anthropological understanding of alternative ways of dealing with these same issues in different cultural settings in which languages vary along a variety of linguistic features (e.g., the special issue of the *Journal of Learning Disabilities*, Vol. 32, 1999), and schooling varies along a variety of sociological dimensions (Kame'enui, Simmons, & Coyne, 2000) and instructional practices (Thompson & Johnston, 2000).

The federal legislation in the United States that mandated a free and appropriate education for all students with educationally handicapping conditions was the result of the joint efforts of parents and professionals who advocated for students with diverse learning differences. At one extreme were students who were globally impaired in all areas of development. Parents of children with mental retardation were still being told, in many cases, to send their children away from home or at least not send them to school. At the other extreme were students who were not brain damaged or significantly impaired in any area of development but who had specific impairment in one or more academic skills. Many children with dyslexia were not being provided with adequate diagnostic and instructional services at school, and their parents were turning to the private sector for such services. In between these extremes were students who were neurologically impaired and had congenital or acquired selective damage to certain neural systems in the context of cognition in the normal range, students who had rare genetic conditions, and slow(er) learning students who were in the lower limits of the normal range but below the population mean. However, parent advocacy groups for students with mental retardation and with dyslexia were the most visible in the 1960s and 1970s when the lobbying for the federal legislation for a free and appropriate education was taking place. As a result of historical happpenstance, the resulting federal definitions of educationally handicapping conditions are biased toward ruling between mental retardation and dyslexia in differential diagnosis. The middle groups who did not have as visible advocacy groups did not fare as well. Changes in providing special education services should remedy this situation.

The definitions in the original federal legislation were also more influenced by the prevailing assessment practices of the time than by scientific research knowledge. The major assessment tool of the school psychologist was the IQ test, and the major diagnostic question was whether a student was mentally retarded (IQ below the normal range) or was underachieving relative to IQ (considered a yardstick for potential or expected achievement). For nearly a quarter of a century, IQ retained its prominent role as a cutoff criterion for mental retardation or as a criterion for evaluating whether achievement was discrepant from expected performance. Then Siegel (1989) rocked the boat by questioning whether IQ is relevant to learning disabilities. The wake from that article is still having its impact.

## CURRENT SITUATION

*Mental Retardation.* Many parents whose children meet definitional criteria for mental retardation prefer the label "learning disabilities" that has less social stigma. For this reason, *some* school personnel started using the label learning disabilities instead of mental retardation. This use of the diagnosis of learning disability can be misleading. In this case, the label does not imply that the student has normal intelligence and can be expected to achieve at or near grade level or catch up in development if schools provide an appropriate education. Surprisingly, little research has focused on identifying evidence-based approaches for teaching reading and writing to students with overall cognitive development in the mentally retarded range. These children may have a variety of other developmental disorders that often occur along with mental retardation and affect how they learn written language.

*Slow(er) Learning.*    The law did not make provision for the slow(er) learners whose measured achievement is commensurate with their cognitive development but who struggle to keep up with faster learning peers.  To get around this oversight, in some school districts, children are qualified for learning disabilities services only on the basis of low academic achievement for age and grade without consideration of their overall profile across different developmental domains. There is no research evidence, however, that these children achieve significantly better in literacy skills if given pull-out services rather than general education. Little research attention has been directed to helping general education classroom teachers deal more effectively with students at the lower limits of the normal range or establishing reasonable levels of learning outcome for slower learners so that they are not unfairly penalized if they do not meet standards in state assessments that may be geared to the mean or even higher.

*Specific Language Disability or Impairment.*    The American Psychiatric Association (1994) estimates that about 6 percent to 11 percent of students may have specific language impairment at some time in their schooling (3 percent mixed receptive and expressive disorder; 3 percent to 5 percent expressive disorder). Specific language impairment means that overall development for understanding and/or producing language is significantly below overall level of cognitive development. Although these students may receive language therapy, they are unlikely to receive comprehensive and ongoing language-based instruction in academic subjects, even though they are more likely to be at risk for academic problems than peers without specific language impairment (e.g., Aram, Ekelman, & Nation, 1984; Bishop & Adams, 1990; Trauner, Wulfeck, Tallal, & Hesselink, 2000). Children who struggled in learning language also may struggle in learning how to use language to learn academic subjects, but little research exists on this topic; nor does existing special education law recognize their persisting learning difficulties once they learn language. Children who had specific language impairment during the preschool years, and who have continuing difficulty in using language to learn during the school age years, may be the most underidentified and underserved group at present.

*Dyslexia.* Of all the learning disabilities, dyslexia is the only one which an IQ-reading achievement discrepancy might identify appropriately at certain stages of reading development. However, IQ-achievement discrepancy does not capture the hallmark features of dyslexia. Dyslexia is a specific dissociation in the functional reading system of individuals whose overall motor, language, cognitive, and social/emotional development and sensory skills are in the normal range for age. Their written word skills develop more slowly than their higher level skills, such as text comprehension and verbal reasoning. Research has clearly established that individuals with dyslexia have more difficulty in pronouncing single words out of sentence context than in sentence context or have a history of having had this difficulty earlier in reading development (e.g., Stanovich, 1986). Thus, dyslexia—Greek for impaired (dys) and word (lexia)—is an aptly chosen diagnostic label.

A *functional system* is a set of component processes that are orchestrated to achieve a specific task or goal such as reading or writing (Luria, 1973). A *dissociation* is a pattern of uneven development in which two or more related skills do not develop at the same relative rate. In dyslexia, reading single words does not develop as easily as reading text (sentences embedded in discourse structures) or verbal reasoning. Typically, the various component processes of a functional system are developed to about the same level and can function in concert fairly well. If, however, one component is underdeveloped relative to the other components, the learner may struggle: it is hard to orchestrate components that are not developing in tandem. That is what happens in dyslexia. The learner has to work harder and exert more effort than unaffected peers to accomplish the same reading task because the components of the functional reading system are unevenly developed. Consider the analogy of a novice musician playing in an orchestra with expert musicians. The novice has to work harder to keep up with the experts. In dyslexia, readers' brains have to work harder and exert more effort when reading because their word reading component and related phonological skills are like the novice and not as efficient (Perfetti, 1985; Richards et al., 1999; Shaywitz et al., 1998) as their text comprehension and verbal reasoning skills, which are like the experts with better developed skills. Compared to the other learning disabilities, more research exists on how to teach reading to dyslexics.

*Summary.*   All in all, by the dawn of the 21st century, there is a growing consensus that IQ-achievement discrepancy is not a valid way to identify children with wide ranging learning disabilities who may need special instructional assistance in learning to read, write, and do math (Lyon & Fletcher, 2001). IQ-achievement discrepancy is not valid for identifying students for early intervention when it is easiest to prevent severe reading problems (e.g., Scarborough, 1989; Vellutino, Scanlon, & Lyon, 2000). Nor does this operational definition based on "one size fits all" capture the hallmark features of learning differences for specific kinds of academic skills (Berninger & Abbott, 1994). At the beginning of the 21st century, we need a classification system that is responsive to the needs of all students with learning differences.

## DEVELOPMENTAL AND ACADEMIC PROFILES

In my clinical training and professional experience as a psychologist at Boston's Children's Hospital, I learned a different approach to dealing with learning and developmental disabilities than is represented in the federal definition. This approach did not rely exclusively on any single assessment instrument or on any single developmental domain independent of the context of a profile of developmental domains. This approach was developmental in four ways. First, developmental assessment was organized around the five major domains of child development: motor (gross and fine), aural/oral language and communication (receptive and expressive), cognition (thinking and conceptual understanding), social/emotional, and executive functions (e.g., attention, self-regulation, and the like). Second, development was interpreted in the context of both biological and social factors within a nature-nurture interaction framework. Sensory (auditory, visual, and somatosensory) and motor systems were assessed in more than a cursory manner. Medical conditions were diagnosed, and family systems and community support networks were evaluated. Third, assessment was not restricted to a frozen moment in time but rather took into account change—quantitative and qualitative—over time. Baselines for evaluating development within a domain over time were obtained by repeatedly assessing children on at least three occasions (e.g. six months apart). And fourth, the emphasis was on current developmental status rather than future potential, but prognosis was discussed with parents when sufficient information from repeated assessments over time was available.

Development was assessed by multidisciplinary teams that synthesized assessment information specific to the disciplinary expertise of each team member within and across developmental domains. To the extent possible, this information was organized to address issues of etiology, treatment, and prognosis (probable course of events), all of which are issues of concern to parents. IQ tests were given as one index of cognitive development, along with other cognitive or neuropsychological measures relevant to the reason for referral. *Any single test score had diagnostic significance only in the context of the developmental profile within and across domains.* Test results were only one source of information and were combined with interview information, developmental and educational history, behavioral observations, and process assessment to test clinical hypotheses. Process assessment modified task requirements or compared performance across tasks with different stimulus inputs or requirements to analyze the source of breakdowns in processing.

This approach also had a model for thinking about normal development within as well as across domains. The normal range refers to the fact that within a developmenal domain, abilities tend to fall along a continuum of varying degrees of skill development. Sometimes, abilities fall at the lowest end of the continuum outside the normal range, and sometimes they fall at the lowest end within the normal range. The point along the continuum that divides the normal and the below normal range is arbitrary, but it is often defined on the basis of statistical frequency (e.g. two standard deviations below the mean or bottom 2.5 percent of the population). Although overall functioning in a developmental domain may be in the normal range, there may be selective impairment in one or more skills in that domain or sensory modality. The selective impairment may be *relative* to overall development in that domain or across all domains or may be *absolute* in that it falls below the normal range in that domain. The selective impairment also may be subtle and not observable without formal testing. In this model, normal functioning is defined both within each domain and across multiple domains in an individual's profile.

Five prototypical developmental profiles often occurred:

1.  Global impairment in which all domains fell in the below normal range.

2.   Atypical impairment in which two or more but not all domains fell in the below normal range.

3.   Specific impairment in only one developmental domain (e.g., aural/oral language).

4.   Selective impairment in one or more skills in a developmental domain that overall was in the normal range (i.e. did not have specific impairment).

5.   Performance at the lower end of the normal range in all domains of development (i.e. the slower learner) with or without a pattern of superimposed fluctuations, above and below, average performance in the lower limits of the normal range.

Each of these profiles is now discussed further to illustrate the point that a single psychometric test score for a skill has meaning for etiology, treatment, and prognosis only in the context of the overall developmental profile.

*Global Impairment.*   Mental retardation cannot be diagnosed solely on the basis of an IQ score. The diagnosis should be made only when all domains of development fall significantly below the normal range. Typically, it is assumed that a measure of adaptive function will assess development across domains, but even better is assessment by a multidisciplinary team, each member of which is an expert in a domain of development. After age six, many tests of developmental skills have better predictive validity than before. Using the term developmental delay prior to age six may give some parents false hope that their child will catch up to normal. At some point, it is important to clarify whether development is delayed or globally impaired. Sometimes, cultural differences result in IQ scores in the mildly retarded range, but significant impairment across all the developmental domains is unlikely to be due to cultural differences. About one-third of the individuals with mental retardation also have diagnosable conditions such as Down syndrome, fragile X syndrome, or autism. Although not all individuals with these medical conditions are mentally retarded, many are, and if they are, this pattern of development is relevant to their learning to read. They can learn but at a much slower rate, in a more concrete way, and with an earlier plateau than those with normal development. Their aural/oral language is delayed because of their cognitive delays (e.g., Aram et al., 1984; Silva, Williams, & McGee, 1987). Clinical folklore suggests that mildly retarded individuals may reach a fourth- to sixth-grade reading level and moderately retarded individuals may reach a second-grade reading level by the end of high school. However, research is needed on this issue, especially for individuals who have coexisting medical conditions, genetic syndromes, or diagnosable developmental disabilities. Although some autistic children are hyperlexic (Healy, Aram, Horwitz, & Kessler, 1982; Siegel, 1984), not all are. However, mentally retarded individuals who are also autistic should not be diagnosed as dyslexic; nor should it be assumed that they need the same educational treatments as individuals with dyslexia. Mental retardation and dyslexia are mutually exclusive conditions.

*Atypical Development.* Some children are not globally delayed in all areas of development but are not developing normally in all domains. Atypical development is characterized by abnormal development in two or more domains (e.g., expressive language and social/emotional) in the context of otherwise normal development. Skills in the normal domains may be "splinter" skills that have different significance than they would in a profile of normal development in all domains. For example, if one subtest score (e.g., in picture completion) falls in the lower limits of the normal range in the context of a profile that is otherwise overall in the mentally retarded range, parents should not be given false hope that their child has the potential to become fully normal if the school provides an appropriate education. The learning problems of atypically developing children need to be evaluated and treated to a large extent on the basis of their own unique developmental profiles. Hardly any research exists on reading development in children with specific profiles of atypical development and effective ways to teach them. Their other developmental problems may constrain how they learn, how fast they learn, and their learning outcome. They may benefit from special help in reading, make documentable gains in reading each year, but never read on grade level defined by the typical performance of age peers.

*Specific Developmental Impairment.* Sometimes, only one domain is impaired and develops more slowly or atypically. A relatively common example is specific language impairment or specific language disability in which aural/oral language development is not normal, but cognitive development (as assessed by a measure of nonverbal reasoning that assesses thinking independent of language skills) is normal. Children with specific language impairment also may have selected impairment in fine motor skills (e.g., in oral-motor planning) in the context of otherwise normal motor development. Specific language impairment should not be diagnosed on the basis of low aural/oral language skills alone because the low language may be due to low cognitive ability. Although dyslexia is a language disorder rather than a visual perceptual disorder (Vellutino, 1979), dyslexia and specific language disorder are not the same. In dyslexia, but not specific language disorder, overall aural/oral language development is in the normal range. However, dyslexics may have subtle, selective impairment in auditory language skills, as our brain imaging studies showed (Corina et al., 2001; Richards et al., 1999).

Another specific developmental impairment is attention deficit hyperactivity disorder (ADHD), inattention or hyperactivity or mixed subtypes. Although children with globally impaired or atypical developmental profiles may have poor attention and respond to psychopharmacological treatment of those symptoms of poor attention, the etiology, treatment, and prognosis for their attentional difficulties are not the same as for a child whose overall development in all areas is normal except for the specific impairment in attention/executive functions, with or without selective impairment in other domains (e.g., fine motor skills). Such children, whose development is basically normal except for attention/executive functions, also are very different from those who have specific impairment in social/emotional functioning as well as attention/executive functions and are at greater risk for developing psychopathology. It is important to tease apart whether the attentional problems are primary or the result of poor aural/oral language processing. Hardly any research has examined the most effective reading instruction for children with specific impairment in executive functions.

*Selective Impairment within a Developmental Domain.* During the school age years, the cognitive domain develops subdomains of procedural and informational knowledge related to academic curriculum. Dyslexia is a specific impairment in the functional reading system, one subdomain of the cognitive domain. It is specific in that the aural/oral, cognitive, fine motor, and executive function domains are normally developing, but dyslexics may have selective (subtle) impairment in these domains. They also may have specific impairments in other academic skills (writing and math). Other children may have specific impairments in reading that are not dyslexia (a problem specific to word reading). Some children have rate problems only (e.g., Lovett, 1987) or comprehension problems only (e.g., Oakhill & Yull, 1996). Other children have specific impairments in writing or math, but not in reading. Berninger and Abbott (1994) and Berninger (1998) proposed component reading and writing skills that should be assessed to diagnose specific reading and writing disabilities.

Many children have selective impairment in the motor, aural/oral language, cognition, social/emotional, or executive function domains in the context of development that is otherwise normal. This intraindividual variation is the normal variation that is found in most classrooms but is typically not identified or treated. For example, gifted learning disabled students fall at both tails of the normal distribution (cf. Robinson, Zigler, & Gallagher, 2000), in the upper end in intellectual ability and at the lower end in a specific lower-order reading or writing skill (e.g., Yates, Berninger, & Abbott, 1995). Children with profiles showing such uneven development can struggle considerably with specific aspects of the curriculum.

*Low End of Normal Range Across Developmental Domains.* Within a domain of development, individuals fall along a continuum that is referred to as the normal range. Some individuals consistently fall within the lower limits of the normal range across all domains of development. For example, they may tend to fall between one and two standard deviations below the mean (e.g., between the 16th and 3rd percentile) on all aural/oral language, cognitive, and academic measures. These students are sometimes called slow(er) learners because they can learn, but at a slower rate and lower learning outcome than age peers, and at a faster rate and higher learning outcome than students who are globally impaired across all areas of development. They often show progress consistent with their verbal reasoning ability. However, sometimes these students have coexisting medical, genetic, neurological, or developmental disorders that impose uneven development (dissociations) on their developmental profile. There is little research on effective reading instruction for students who have flat developmental profiles across domains or uneven developmental profiles across domains, but whose average development and verbal reasoning falls within the lower limits of the normal range. No research has ever shown that it is reasonable to expect that these students with verbal reasoning and average development in the lower limits of the normal range should develop reading comprehension skills at or above grade level (50th percentile).

No validated, criterion-referenced system for assessment of reading development, based on a national, representative sample, exists to chart reading development on the basis of milestones independent of age or grade norms for slow(er) learners or those with global or atypical development. Such criterion-referenced measures, based on national samples, may be more appropriate than norm-referenced measures for students with learning disabilities due to cognitive and language abilities in the lower limits of the normal range or in the mild, moderately, or severely impaired range.

## RESEARCH-SUPPORTED DEFINITIONS

Recent scientific research supports three conclusions that should inform definitional issues. First, just because IQ-achievement discrepancy is inadequate as a definition, it does not follow that IQ (a proxy for cognitive development) is irrelevant to learning differences. Second, there is empirical evidence for distinguishing among different kinds of learning disabilities. Third, it is now possible to define dyslexia on the basis of inclusion criteria: what it is rather than what it is not.

*Relevance of IQ.*   Olson and colleagues (e.g., Olson et al., 1999) have shown that IQ is relevant to the etiology and remediation of dyslexia. Reading disability is more likely to have a genetic basis in children with IQs over 100 than with IQs below 100 (Wadsworth, Olson, Pennington, & De Fries, 2000). Reading disability defined by IQ-achievement discrepancy is more likely to be heritable than reading disability defined without consideration of IQ (Olson, Datta, Gayan, & De Fries, 1999). Quantitative trait loci (QTL) analyses show that DNA markers on Chromosome 6 are associated with general cognitive ability (Chorney et al., 1998). Several research groups have replicated linkage of dyslexia to Chromosome 6 (Wood & Grigorenko, in press). A special region of the frontal lobes may be involved in intelligence and this is a distinct brain region from the areas known to be involved in language (Duncan et al., 2000). Demonstrating a biological basis for intelligence or language does not rule out the environmental influences on intelligence and language learning or nature-nurture interactions (see Eckert, Lombardino, & Leonard, 2001). Rather, it suggests that biological factors may cause dissociations in cognitive, language, and other skills; these dissociations create different profiles of learning differences that influence how and how well children learn academic subjects.

*Differential Diagnosis.*   A growing scientific literature provides evidence for distinguishing among three different kinds of learning profiles: specific language impairment (in which language is underdeveloped for nonverbal cognitive development); dyslexia (in which word reading is underdeveloped for verbal cognitive development); and low verbal ability (in which both reading and cognitive development fall in the lower limits of the normal range). Catts (2000) followed children with low language skills in kindergarten, second grade, and fourth grade. He identified four subtypes in second and fourth graders and an additional late emerging subtype in fourth graders using a measure of listening comprehension that was correlated with IQ: (a) dyslexics (good listening comprehension but poor word reading); (b) hyperlexics (poor listening comprehension but good word reading); (c) specific language impaired (poor listening comprehension and poor word reading); (d) other (good listening comprehension and good word reading); and (e) late emerging reading comprehension problems in fourth grade (listening comprehension in the low end of normal range and poor reading comprehension). Catt's "other" subtype may be explained by Bishop and Adams' (1990) finding that children whose preschool language problems resolve by age five and a half have normal literacy skills during the school years. However, children whose preschool language problems have not resolved by age five and a half continue to have persisting language and reading disabilities (Bishop & Adams, 1990), comparable to Catts' "specific language impairment" subtype. Catt's specific language impaired subtype is more at-risk for learning academic subjects, in general, and for social and behavioral problems during the school age years than are those with articulation only problems (Aram et al., 1984). The specific language impaired subtype has severe delays in speaking, mild delays in motor milestones, and neurological abnormalities and needs more than language therapy; this subtype also needs comprehensive academic programming (Trauner et al., 2000). Others have also observed Catts' "late emerging" subtype in specific reading disablility in comprehension (e.g., Oakhill & Yull, 1996; Scarborough, 2001).

The brain imaging literature also supports the distinction between dyslexia and specific language impairment. A deficit in the integration of rapidly changing acoustical events (e.g., Tallal, Merzenich, Miller, & Jenkins, 1998) may explain some kinds of specific language impairment, but not dyslexia (Mody, Studdert-Kennedy, & Brady, 1997). The frequently reported rightward asymmetry of the planum temporale appears to be a neuranatomical marker for specific language impairment rather than specific to dyslexia (Gaugher, Lombardino, & Leonard, 1997). The specific language impaired subtype also has an extra sulcus in the inferior frontal gyrus (Clark & Plante, 1998). Leonard and colleagues are finding distinctive neuroanatomical markers for the specific language impaired subtype and the dyslexic subtype (e.g., Leonard, 2001; Leonard et al., 2001a; Leonard, Eckert, Lombardino, Given, & Eden, 2001b). Other brain research supports the distinction between the slow(er) learner who has low verbal intelligence, and low reading skill and dyslexics who have average or better verbal intelligence and low reading skill. Molfese (2000; in press) found that new-borns' electrophysiological recordings to auditory language differentiated IQ-discrepant dyslexics and non IQ-discrepant poor readers at age eight.

*Defining Dyslexia on the Basis of Inclusion Criteria.* Dyslexia is specific in that overall functioning in all developmental domains falls within the normal range, and *significant* sensory, motor, or aural/oral impairment is absent. Because overall aural/oral language falls in the normal range, dyslexics do not have specific language impairment. However, they may have selective, subtle problems in some aspects of aural/oral language ranging from phonological skills (e.g., Catts, Fey, Zhang, & Tomblin, 1999; Liberman, Shankweiler, Fischer, & Carter, 1974; Wagner & Torgesen, 1987), to rapid naming of visual stimuli (e.g., Denckla & Rudel, 1976; Wolf, Bally, & Morris, 1986; Wolf & Bowers, 1999), to syntactic processing (e.g., Scarborough, 1990, 1991). There is a growing consensus that despite a core phonological deficit in dyslexia, other oral/language problems occur in the phenotype (behavioral expression of a disorder) (e.g., Catts et al., 1999; Lombardino, Riccio, Hynd, & Pinheiro, 1997; Morris et al., 1998; Scarborough, 2001; Wolf & Bowers, 1999). For example, in the Morris et al. study, four of the seven reading disability subtypes had a phonological problem, two had problems in language skills, and one had a rate problem. Another selective impairment in dyslexia that has been documented (Catts, 1989) but understudied (McCormick, 2000; Nicholson, 2000) is oral-motor planning problems (apraxia) that may account for the oral reading dysfluency of some dyslexics. Orthographic (visual word form) deficits (Berninger, Abbott, Thomson, & Raskind, 2001; Olson, Wise, & Forsberg, 1994) and problems in forming orthographic-phonological connections (Berninger & Traweek, 1991; Breznitz, in press; Raskind et al., 2000) also have been observed.

Whether individuals with developmental dyslexia also have selective, subtle impairments in sensory skills such as fast visual processing (Eden, van Meter, Rumsey, Masiog, Woods, & Zeffiro, 1996), and motor skills such as cerebellar fine tuning of motor skills (Nicholson & Fawcett, 1995; Nicholson, 2000), is still being investigated. It is premature to dismiss these possibilities, given the mounting supportive as well as occasional conflicting evidence (Skottun & Parke, 1999). More research is needed to link these possible subtle sensory and motor deficits to known phenotypes in disabled reading, namely orthographic coding of written words in short-term memory and word-specific orthographic representations in long term memory (Berninger et al., 2001), and the phonetic module for speech perception that codes articulatory features and is related to development of phonological awareness (Liberman, 1999). Clearly, separate sensory pathways for auditory and visual stimuli (including word forms) project to brain regions involved in reading (Booth & Burman, 2001). Because language has no end organs (Liberman, 1999), it forms connections with the mouth, hand, and eyes. It stands to reason that selective, subtle sensory and motor problems *may* interfere with dyslexics' reading and writing.

Dyslexics also may have difficulty with executive functions, especially in the self-regulation of their attentional processes during learning (e.g., Hsu, Berninger, Thomson, Wijsman, & Raskind, in press; Wood & Felton, 1994). Wood and Flowers (1999) demonstrated with Positron Emission Tomography (PET) that the same brain regions that underactivate in dyslexia also underactivate in the inattentive subtype of attention deficit hyperactivity disorder. Wolf and Bowers' (1999, figures 2, 3, and 4) model has an attentional mechanism feeding into rapid naming. Thomson et al. (1999) showed that a factor based on inattention ratings had a significant path to rapid naming and orthographic (written word form) factors, but not to a phonological factor (see Berninger, Abbott, Billingsley, & Nagy, 2001, for details). Attention ratings predict response to early intervention (e.g, Stage, Abbott, Jenkins, & Berninger, 2000; Torgesen et al., 1999) and later remediation (e.g. Torgesen et al., 2001). Dyslexics benefit from interventions that teach multiple strategies that help them self-regulate their attention to written words (Berninger, 2000; Hart, Berninger, & Abbott, 1997; Lovett, Lacerenza, & Borden, 2000; Lovett et al., 2000). Dyslexics' impaired motor timing control (Wolff, Cohen, & Drake, 1984) may be yet another indicator of their executive function problems. During functional magnetic resonance imaging (fMRI), dyslexics' brains activated differently than did good readers when they were supposed to attend to phonology and when they were supposed to ignore phonology, suggesting that they have difficulty in the executive coordination of the aural language codes (Corina et al., 2001). For these reasons, dyslexics may have difficulty learning literacy skills in the regular classroom (inclusion model). They learn best when a teacher closely monitors and provides assistance in regulating their attentional processes and delivers highly explicit instruction aimed at all the components of reading and writing.

Defining and diagnosing dyslexia is complicated by the fact that its phenotypic (behavioral) expression changes across reading development. Scarborough (1990; 2001) and Badian (1995) showed that different language processes contribute to reading disability at different stages of reading development. In addition, dyslexics may have difficulty with different components of the curriculum at different stages in their educational career. In kindergarten and first grade, their sublexical phonological impairment may interfere with learning to associate specific phonemes with specific letters or letter combinations for the purpose of phonological decoding. And their rapid lexical naming impairment may interfere with learning to name alphabet letters (e.g. associating the three phonemes in the name for x with that letter symbol) and to name written words as units (i.e., acquisition of a set of words recognized automatically after repeated exposures). Specific subtypes at this stage also fluctuate from year to year (Manis, Custodio, & Szeszulski, 1993). During the primary grades, their syntactic impairment may compromise fluency so that oral reading of text does not have the normal melody or intonation that accompanies the syntax of spoken language (Berninger et al., 2001). Later, when expected volume of reading increases, dyslexics who have learned sufficient phonological decoding skills to read accurately may not be able to keep up with assignments because of slow reading rate. Their word-level problems may affect spelling as well as word reading. As the curriculum increases expectations for written expression, dyslexics with residual spelling problems may find it increasingly difficult to express their ideas in writing. Reading comprehension, in contrast, does not seem to be as impaired as the other reading and writing skills once a certain proficiency in word reading is reached (e.g., Berninger, 2000; Goulandris, Snowling, & Walker, 2000; Paulesu et al., 2001; Torgesen et al., 2001).

In some cases, the reading problems persist into the adult years, but in other cases they do not, and the individual is said to have compensated (Gilger, Hanebuth, Smith, & Pennington, 1996). However, behavioral measures such as phonological awareness, rapid naming, and pseudoword reading often detect residual difficulties in adults with a history of reading problems who appear to be compensated (Felton, Naylor, & Wood, 1990). Problems in reading rate (e.g., Bruck, 1990; Torgesen et al., 2001) and spelling (e.g., Bruck, 1993; Lefly & Pennington, 1991) often persist long after accurate word reading is achieved. Harder to measure and often not visible to others is the amount of effort some compensated dyslexics exert during reading. Moreover, dyslexia may have an impact on the family system because of the psychosocial problems associated with it (Boetsch, Green, & Pennington, 1996) that affect more than one family member. One-fourth of children with dyslexia have a parent who is affected or compensated (Wood & Grigorenko, in press). Children with two affected parents are at greater risk for dyslexia than those with one affected parent, and the latter are at greater risk than those with no affected parents (Gilger et al., 1996; Wolff & Melngailis, 1994).

Dyslexia is treatable (Richards et al., 2000) but dyslexics are more likely to get appropriate reading instruction early in reading development (e.g., explicit instruction in alphabetic principle) which is effective for learning to read the one- and two-syllable words in the Anglo Saxon layer of the language that predominates in primary grade texts. Dyslexics are less likely to get explicit instruction in morphological awareness (e.g., Carlisle, 2000), structural analysis (e.g., Nagy, Osborn, Winsor, & O'Flahavan, 1994), and word origin (e.g., Balmuth, 1992; Henry, 1990) needed to decode intermediate grade texts in which words from the Romance and Greek layers of the language predominate. Moreover, IQ-achievement discrepancy is often based just on accuracy measures of reading achievement and not measures of reading rate (Compton, 2000a, 2000b; Kame'enui et al., 2000) or spelling that might tap the kinds of persisting problems dyslexics experience. Ironically, some school personnel tell parents that dyslexia does not exist; this failure to acknowledge this specific kind of learning disability is often upsetting to parents whose families are riddled with dyslexia.

In conclusion, dyslexia is a dissociation between word learning and verbal reasoning and text learning that is genetically constrained but treatable and that changes its phenotypic expression over the course of development. Initial difficulties in naming letters and attaching phonemes to them (i.e. orthographic—> phonological connections) give way to difficulties in learning phonological decoding and automatic word recognition (accuracy and then speed), oral reading fluency (intonation or melody of spoken language), and written spelling (phonological—> orthographic connections). Affected individuals have selective, subtle impairments in aural/oral language, especially in metalinguistic awareness (Mattingly, 1972), but have overall normal aural/language development and verbal reasoning that varies from average to superior. The causes of dyslexia are complex. Multiple genes are probably involved. However, most dyslexics have difficulty with phonological short-term memory, phonological decoding, and/or phonological awareness (Wagner & Torgesen, 1987).

**FUTURE DIRECTIONS**

If reading problems are diagnosed on the basis of only reading achievement out of the context of developmental profiles, as just described, confusion will result regarding etiology, treatment, and prognosis for reading disabilities that differ depending on the developmental context in which they occur. Defining reading disability as only low reading achievement ignores whether the reading problem occurs in the context of atypical development, specific language impairment, dyslexia, or low normal verbal ability. That approach to definition also fails to identify and serve the gifted learning disabled (Yates et al., 1995), and it fails to tailor intervention to a student's entire profile of developmental and academic skills. Depending on that entire profile, learners differ in the etiology of their learning differences, appropriateness of specific instructional practices, and prognosis if given appropriate instruction. Ignoring developmental profiles in which reader's disabilities occur also may lead to errors in generalizing results of research on effective instructional practices. Because schools are legally mandated to provide appropriate education for students with learning disabilities, they need a body of research on academic instruction that is based on well-defined samples in terms of students' developmental profiles.

During the last quarter of the 20th century, there was controversy over whether reading disability falls at the low end of the normal range or represents a non-normal hump in the lower tail. Either position presupposes that there is only one relevant distribution for reading. Wood and Grigorenko (in press) propose that this controversy be reframed in terms of variance-covariance matrices that acknowledge the multidimensional underpinnings of reading disabilities. Biological systems are characterized by complexity (Gallagher & Appenzeller, 1999), and functional reading and writing systems are no exception. Learning differences cannot be readily reduced to overly simplistic "one size fits all" definitions. A viable definitional scheme must facilitate meeting the needs of all learners.

Psychiatrists and clinical psychologists developed the various versions, including the current fourth edition, of the *Diagnostic and Statistical Manual for Mental Disorders* (American Psychiatric Association, 1994) to improve research and service delivery by reaching a consensus on defining specific mental disorders. Although originally devoted exclusively to mental health disorders, child psychologists and child psychiatrists use this manual to evaluate many children and youth with academic difficulties. Hence, developmental, learning, and educational disorders are now included, but the *DSM-IV* does not cover them in sufficient depth or breadth, or with sufficient understanding of schools as host settings (cf. Kame'enui et al., 2000). For example, it includes a definition for mental retardation, but not for intellectual giftedness, and shows a bias toward the lower tail of the normal distribution (Robinson et al., 2000). Nor does the *DSM-IV* give adequate coverage to assessment-intervention links, including effective, evidence-based instructional interventions for treating learning differences in school settings. Yet, practitioners who rely on the manual routinely generate educational recommendations that the legal system often imposes on schools.

A comparable "Diagnostic and Treatment Manual for Educational Disorders" is sorely needed. It may reference the *DSM-IV* but is developed independently of it by professionals in multiple disciplines who serve school age children and youth for the purposes of providing better research and research-supported services in and out of school settings for learning problems. A working group of expert scientist-practitioners might be convened to develop such a manual and then be re-convened periodically to revise it. Defining the developmental and individual differences that occur in school settings and influence how students learn is necessary for better understanding of the etiology, treatment, and prognosis of reading problems. A comprehensive classification scheme for developmental and learning differences would benefit from the multi-axis approach of the *DSM-IV*, but the axes should be uniquely tailored to school settings (Berninger, 1998). For example, the executive function domain (Lyon & Krasnegor, 1996), the social emotional domain (Boetsch et al., 1996), and the domain of necessary components of curriculum (Berninger, 1998) are as important as the language/communication, cognitive, and motor domains. Axes are also needed for concurrent medical and other physical conditions and for relevant family and community factors affecting student learning. This diagnostic scheme should be developed by professionals who rely on research evidence and not by government officials.

The overly exclusive reliance on IQ-achievement discrepancy in defining learning differences is not the only problem with currently existing federal definitions for educationally handicapping conditions. A major problem is that government officials translate federal law into procedures for their states and essentially write the definitions. Educational professionals drawing on scientific research are not the ones writing the definitions of learning disabilities. More emphasis is placed on monitoring the procedures by which students qualify for special education services and school systems qualifying for dollars than on monitoring student progress on a daily, weekly, monthly, and yearly progress to evaluate whether students are benefiting from special services. Schools are rewarded financially for identifying failing students rather than for preventing reading problems through early intervention programs and for transforming failing students into succeeding students. This situation is analogous in many ways to the managed health care in which business officials dictate procedures for medical practice rather than basing medical practice on scientific knowledge and professional standards of practice set by the physicians. The law guarantees a free, appropriate education rather than one based on scientifically supported instructional practices that result in measurable progress. The law has no provision for updating appropriate educational practices for diagnosis and intervention on the basis of scientific advances. Only when professionals from many disciplines come together to change this unfortunate situation will all students with developmental and learning disabilities be served well.

## ACKNOWLEDGMENTS

The author thanks anonymous reviewers, Joanne Carlisle, and Le Ganschow for helpful comments on prior drafts; Sally Shaywitz for helpful discussions on definitional issues; and Beverly Wolf, Bonnie Meyer, and Anita Nason for help in launching the University of Washington Learning Disabilities Center.

Address correspondence to 322 Miller, Box 353600, University of Washington, Seattle, WA 98195-3600, vwb@u.washington.edu

## References

American Psychiatric Association. (1994). *Diagnostic and statistical manual of mental disorders* (4th ed.) Washington DC: Author.

Aram, D., Ekelman, B., & Nation, J. (1984). Preschoolers with language disorders: 10 years later. *Journal of Speech and Hearing Research, 27*, 232–244.

Badian, N. (1995). Predicting reading ability over the long term: The changing roles of letter naming, phonological awareness, and orthographic processing. *Annals of Dyslexia, 45*, 79–96.

Balmuth, M. (1992). *The roots of phonics. A historical introduction.* Baltimore: York Press.

Berninger, V. (1998). *Process assessment of the learner (PAL): Guides for reading and writing intervention.* San Antonio, TX: The Psychological Corporation.

Berninger, V. (2000). Dyslexia, the invisible, treatable disorder: The story of Einstein's Ninja turtles. *Learning Disability Quarterly, 23*, 175–195.

Berninger, V., & Abbott, R. (1994). Redefining learning disabilities. Moving beyond aptitude-treatment discrepancies to failure to respond to validated treatment protocols. In G. R. Lyon (ed.), *Frames of reference for the assessment of learning disabilities: New views on measurement issues* (pp. 163–202). Baltimore: Paul H. Brookes Publishing Co.

Berninger, V., Abbott, R., Billingsley, F., & Nagy, W. (2001). Processes underlying timing and fluency of reading: Efficiency, automaticity, coordination, and morphological awareness. In M. Wolf (ed.), *Dyslexia, fluency, and the brain* (pp 384–414). Baltimore: York Press.

Berninger, V., Abbott, R., Thomson, J., & Raskind, W. (2001). Language phenotype for reading and writing disability: A family approach. *Scientific Studies of Reading, 5*, 59–105.

Berninger, V., & Traweek, D. (1991). Effects of two-phase reading intervention on three orthographic-phonological code connections. *Learning and Individual Differences, 3*, 323–338.

Bishop, D., & Adams, C. (1990). A prospective study of the relationship between specific language impairment, phonological disorders, and reading retardation. *Journal of Child Psychology and Psychiatry, 31*, 1027–1050.

Boetsch, E., Green, P., & Pennington, B. (1996). Psychosocial correlates of dyslexia across the life span. *Development and Psychopathology, 8*, 539–562.

Booth, J., & Burman, J. (2001). Development and disorders of neuro-cognitive systems for oral language and reading. *Learning Disability Quarterly, 24*, 205–215.

Breznitz, Z. (in press). Asynchrony of visual-orthographic and auditory-phonological word recognition processes: An underlying factor in dyslexia. *Journal of Reading and Writing.*

Bruck, M. (1990). Word-recognition skills of adults with childhood diagnoses of dyslexia. *Developmental Psychology, 26*, 439–454.

Bruck, M. (1993). Component spelling skills of college students with childhood diagnoses of dyslexia. *Learning Disability Quarterly, 16*, 171–184.

Carlisle, J. (2000). Awareness of the structure and meaning of morphologically complex words: Impact on reading. *Reading and Writing: An Interdisciplinary Journal, 12*, 169–190.

Catts, H. (1989). Speech production deficits in developmental dyslexia. *Journal of Speech and Hearing Disorders, 54*, 422–428.

Catts, H. (2000, November). Who are the poor readers: Answers from a longitudinal study. Paper presentation at International Dyslexia Association. Washington, DC.

Catts, H., Fey, M., Zhang, X., & Tomblin, B. (1999). Language basis of reading and reading disabilities: Evidence from a longitudinal investigation. *Scientific Studies of Reading, 3*, 331–361.

Chorney, M., Chorney, K., Seese, N., Owen, M., Daniels, J., McGuffin, P., Thompson, L., Detterman, D., Benbow, C., Lubinski, D., Eley, T., & Plomin, R. (1998). A quantitative trait locus associated with cognitive ability in children. *Psychological Science, 9,* 159–166.

Clark, M., & Plante, E. (1998). Morphology of the inferior frontal gyrus in developmentally language disordered adults. *Brain and Language, 61,* 288–303.

Compton, D. (2000a). Modeling growth of decoding skills in first-grade children. *Scientific Studies of Reading, 4,* 219–258.

Compton, D. (2000b). Modeling the response of normally achieving and at-risk first grade children to word reading instruction. *Annals of Dyslexia, 50,* 53–84.

Corina, D., Richards, T., Serafini, S., Richards, A., Steury, K., Abbott, R., Echelard, D., Maravilla, K., & Berninger, V. (2001). fMRI auditory language differences between dyslexic and able reading children. *Neuroreport, 12,* 1195–1201.

Denckla, M., & Rudel, G. (1976). Rapid "automatized" naming (R.A.N.): Dyslexia differentiated from other learning disabilities. *Neuropsychologia, 14,* 471–479.

Duncan, J., Seltz, R., Kolodny, J., Bor, D., Herzog, A., Newell, F., & Emslie, H. (2000). A neural basis for general intelligence. *Science, 289,* 457–460.

Eckert, M., Lombardino, L., & Leonard, C. (2001). Tipping the environmental playground: Who is at risk for reading failure? *Child Development, 72,* 988–1001.

Eden, G., van Meter, J., Rumsey, J., Masiog, J., Wood, F., & Zeffiro, T. (1996). Abnormal processing of visual motion in dyslexia revealed by functional brain imaging. *Nature, 382,* 66–69.

Felton, R., Naylor, C., & Wood, F. (1990). Neuropsychological profile of adult dyslexics. *Brain and Language, 39,* 485–497.

Frith, U. (1999). Paradoxes in the definition of dyslexia. *Dyslexia, 5,* 192–214.

Gallagher, R., & Appenzeller, T. (1999). Beyond reductionism. Introduction to special issue on complex systems. *Science, 284,* 79.

Gaugher, L., Lombardino, L., & Leonard, C. (1997). Brain morphology in children with specific language impairment. *Journal of Speech, Language, and Hearing Research, 40,* 1272–1284.

Gilger, J., Hanebuth, E., Smith, S., & Pennington, B. (1996). Differential risk for developmental reading disorders in the offspring of compensated vesus noncompensated parents. *Reading and Writing: An Interdisciplinary Journal, 8,* 407–417.

Goulandris, N., Snowling, M., & Walker, I. (2000). Is dyslexia a form of specific language impairment? A comparison of dyslexic and language impaired children as adolescents. *Annals of Dyslexia, 50,* 103–122,

Hart, T., Berninger, V., & Abbott, R. (1997). Comparison of teaching single or multiple orthographic-phonological connections for word recognition and spelling: Implications for instructional consultation. *School Psychology Review, 26,* 279–297.

Healy, J., Aram, D., Horowitz, S., & Kessler, J. (1982). A study of hyperlexia. *Brain and Language, 17,* 1–23.

Henry, M. (1990). Words. *Integrated decoding and spelling instruction based on word origin and word structure.* Austin, TX: PRO-ED.

Henry, M., Ganschow, L., & Miles, T. R. (2000). The issue of definition: Some problems. *Perspectives,* [The International Dyslexia Association] *26,* 38–43.

Hsu, L., Berninger, V., Thomson, J., Wijsman, E., & Raskind, W. (in press). Familial aggregation of dyslexia phenotypes: Paired correlated measures. *Neuropsychiatric Genetics.*

Johnson, E., & Breslau, N. (2002). Increased risk of learning disabilities in low birth weight boys at age 11 years. *Biological Psychiatry, 47,* 490–500.

Kame'enui, E., Simmons, D., & Coyne, M. (2000). Schools as host environments: Toward a school-wide reading improvement model. *Annals of Dyslexia, 50,* 33–51.

Lefly, E., & Pennington, B. (1991). Spelling errors and reading fluency in compensated adult dyslexics. *Annals of Dyslexia, 41,* 143–162.

Leonard, C. (2001). Imaging brain structure in children: Differentiating language disability and reading disability. *Learning Disability Quarterly, 24,* 158–176.

Leonard, C., Eckert, M., Lombardino, L., Oakland, T., Kranzler, J., Mohr, C., King, W., & Freeman, A. (2001a). Anatomical risk factors for phonological dyslexia. *Cerebral Cortex, 11,* 148–157.

Leonard, C., Eckert, M., Lombardino, L., Given, B., & Eden, G. (2001b). Two anatomical phenotypes for reading impairment. *Journal of Cognitive Neuroscience, 12*(abs).

Liberman, A. (1999). The reading researcher and the reading teacher need the right theory of speech. *Scientific Studies of Reading, 3,* 95–111.

Liberman, I., Shankweiler, D., Fischer, F., & Carter, B. (1974). Explicit syllable and phoneme segmentation in the young child. *Journal of Experimental Child Psychology, 18,* 201–212.

Lombardino, L., Riccio, C., Hynd, G., & Pinheiro, S. (1997). Linguistic deficits in children with reading disablities. *American Journal of Speech-Language Pathology, 6,* 71–78.

Lovett, M. (1987). A developmental approach to reading disability: Accuracy and speed criteria of normal and deficient reading skill. *Child Development 58,* 234–260.

Lovett, M., Lacerenza, L., & Borden, S. (2000). Putting struggling readers on the PHAST track: A program to integrate phonological and strategy-based remedial reading instruction and maximize outcomes. *Journal of Learning Disabilities, 33,* 458–476.

Lovett, M., Lacerenza, L., Borden, S., Frijters, J., Steinbach, K., & DePalma, M. (2000). Components of effective remediation for developmental reading disability: Combining phonological and strategy-based instruction to improve outcomes. *Journal of Educational Psychology, 92,* 263–283.

Luria, A. R. (1973). *The working brain.* New York: Basic Books.

Lyon, G. R., & Fletcher, J. M. (2001). Early warning system. *Education Matters,* Summer, pp. 22–29.

Lyon, G. R., Fletcher, J. M., Shaywitz, S. E., Shaywitz, B. A., Torgesen, J. K., Wood, F. B., Schulte, A., & Olson, R. (2001). Rethinking learning disabilities. In C. E. Finn, A. J. Rotherham, & C. R. Hokanson (eds.), *Rethinking special education for a new century* (pp. 259–288). Washington, DC: Thomas B. Fordham Foundation and the Progressive Policy Institute.

Lyon, G. R., & Krasnegor, N. (Eds.) (1996). *Attention, memory, and executive functions.* Baltimore: Paul H. Brookes.

Manis, F., Custodio, R., & Szeszulski, P. (1993). Development of phonological and orthographic skill: A 2- year longitudinal study of dyslexic children. *Journal of Experimental Child Psychology, 56,* 64–86.

Mattingly, I. (1972). Reading, the linguistic process, and linguistic awareness. In J. F. Kavanagh, & I. Mattingly (eds.), *Language by ear and by eye: The relationships between speech and reading* (pp. 133-147). Cambridge, MA: MIT Press.

McCormick, M. (2000). Dyslexia and developmental verbal apraxia. *Dyslexia. An International Journal of Research and Practice, 6,* 210–214.

Mody, M., Studdert-Kennedy, M., & Brady, S. (1997). Speech perception deficits in poor readers: Auditory processing or phonological coding? *Journal of Experimental Child Psychology, 64,* 199–231.

Molfese, D. (in press). Newborn brain responses predict language development skills that emerge eight years later. *Brain and Language.*

Molfese, D. (2000). Predicting dyslexia at 8 years using neonatal brain responses. *Brain and Language, 72,* 238–245.

Morris, R., Stuebing, K., Fletcher, J., Shaywitz, S., Lyon, G. R., Shankweiler, D., Katz, L., Francis, D., & Shaywitz, B. (1998). Subtypes of reading disability: Variability around a phonological core. *Journal of Educational Psychology, 90,* 347–373.

Nagy, W., Osborn, J., Winsor, P., & O'Flahavan, J. (1994). Structural analysis: Some guidelines for instruction. In F. Lehr & J. Osborn (eds.), *Reading, language, and literacy* (pp. 45–58). Hillsdale, NJ: Lawrence Erlbaum Associates.

Nicholson, R. (2000). Dyslexia and dysgraphia: Commentary. *Dyslexia: An International Journal of Research and Practice, 6,* 203–204.

Nicholson, R., & Fawcett, A. (1995). Dyslexia is more than a phonological disability. *Dyslexia: An International Journal of Research and Practice, 1,* 19–36.

Oakhill, J., & Yull, M. (1996). Higher order factors in comprehension disability: Processes and remediation. In C. Cornaldi, & J. Oakhill (Eds.), *Reading comprehension difficulties: Processes and interventions* (pp. 69–92). Mahwah, NJ: Lawrence Erlbaum Associates.

Olson, R., Datta, H., Gayan, J., & DeFries, J. (1999). A behavioral genetic analysis of reading disabilities and component processes. In R. M. Klein & P. A. McMullen (eds.), *Converging methods for understanding reading and dyslexia* (pp. 133–151). Cambridge, MA: MIT Press.

Olson, R., Datta, H., Gayan, J., Hulslander, J., Ring, J., Wise, B., DeFries, J., Pennington, B., & Wadsworth, S. (1999). Does IQ matter for the reading profile, etiology, and remediation of reading disability? Yes, yes, yes! Paper presented at Society for the Scientific Study of Reading. Montreal.

Olson, R., Wise, B., & Forsberg, H. (1994). Genes, environment, and the development of orthographic skills. In V. W. Berninger (ed.), *The varieties of orthographic knowledge. I. Theoretical and developmental; issues.* Oordrecht, The Netherlands: Kluwer.

Paulesu, E., Demonet, J., Fazio, F., McCrory, E., Chanoine, V., Brunswick, N., Cappa, F., Cossu, G., Habib, M., Frith, C., & Frith, U. (2001). Dyslexia: Cultural diversity and biological unity. *Science, 291,* 2165–2167.

Pennington, B., Gilger, J., Pauls, D., Smith, S., Smith, S., & DeFries, J. (1991). Evidence for major gene transmission of developmental dyslexia. *Journal of Medical Association, 266,* 1527–1534.

Perfetti, C. (1985). *Reading ability.* New York: Oxford University Press.

Psychological Corporation. (1991). *Wechsler intelligence scale for children, third edition.* San Antonio: The Psychological Corporation.

Raskind, W., Hsu, L., Thomson, J., Berninger, V., & Wijsman, E. (2000). Family aggregation of dyslexic phenotypes. *Behavior Genetics, 30,* 385–96.

Richards, T., Dager, S., Corina, D., Serafini, S., Heide, A., Steury, K., Strauss, W., Hayes, C., Abbott, R., Kraft, S., Shaw, D., Posse, S., & Berninger, V. (1999). Dyslexic children have abnormal chemical brain activation during reading-related language tasks. *American Journal of Neuroradiology, 20,* 1393-1398.

Richards, T., Corina, D., Serafini, S., Steury, K., Dager, S., Marro, K., Abbott, R., Maravilla, K., & Berninger, V. (2000). Effects of phonologically driven treatment for dyslexia on lactate levels as measured by proton MRSI. *American Journal of Radiology, 21,* 916–922.

Robinson, N., Zigler, E., & Gallagher, J. (2000). Two tails of the normal curve. Similarities and differences in the study of mental retardation and giftedness. *American Psychologist, 55,* 1413–1424.

Scarborough, H. (1989). Prediction of reading disability from familial and individual differences. *Journal of Educational Psychology, 81,* 101–108.

Scarborough, H. (1990). Very early language deficits in dyslexic children. *Child Development, 61,* 1728–1734.

Scarborough, H. (1991). Early syntactic development of dyslexic children. *Annals of Dyslexia, 41,* 207–220.

Scarborough, H. (2001). Connecting early language and literacy to later reading (dis)abilities: Evidence, theory, and practice. In S. Neuman & D. Dickinson (eds.), *Handbook for research in early literacy* (pp. 97–110). New York: Guilford Press.

Shaywitz, S., Shaywitz, B., Pugh, K., Fullbright, R., Constable, T., Menci, E., Shakweiler, D., Liberman, A., Skudlarski, P., Fletcher, J., Katz, L.,Marchione, K., Lacadie, C., Gatenby, C., & Gore, J. (1998). Functional disruption in the organization of the brain for reading in dyslexia. *Proceedings of the National Academy, 95,* 2636–2641.

Siegel, L. (1984). A longitudinal study of a hyperlexic child: Hyperlexia as a language disorder. *Neuropsychologia, 22,* 577–585.

Siegel, L. (1989). Why we do not need intelligence scores in the definition and analysis of learning disabilities. *Journal of Learning Disabilities, 22,* 514–518.

Silva, P., Williams, S., & McGee, R. (1987). A longitudinal study of children with developmental language delay at age three: Later intelligence, reading, and behavior problems. *Developmental Medicine and Child Neurology, 29,* 630–640.

Skottun, B., & Parke, L. (1999). The possible relationship between visual deficits and dyslexia: Examination of a critical assumption. *Journal of Learning Disabilties, 32,* 2–5.

Stage, S., Abbott, R., Jenkins, J., & Berninger, V. (2000). Predicting response to early reading intervention using Verbal IQ, reading-related language abilities, attention ratings, and Verbal IQ—word reading discrepancy. To appear in special issue of the *Journal of Learning Disabilities.*

Stanovich, K. (1986). Matthew effects in reading: Some consequences of individual differences in the acquisition of literacy. *Reading Research Quarterly, 21,* 360–407.

Tallal, P., Merzenich, M., Miller, S., & Jenkins, W. (1998). Language learning impairments: Integrating basic science, technology, and remediation. *Experimental Brain Research, 123,* 210–219.

Thomson, J., Abbott, R., Busse, J., Raskind, W., & Berninger, V. (1999). Self-regulation of cognitive and motoric processes and its relationship to language and academic skills in dyslexia. Submitted.

Thompson, G. B., & Johnston, R. (2000). Are nonword and other phonological deficits indicative of a failed reading process? *Reading and Writing: An Interdisciplinary Journal, 12,* 63–97.

Tønnessen, F. (1997). How can we best define 'dyslexia'? *Dyslexia: An International Journal of Research and Practice 3,* 78–92.

Torgesen, J., Rashotte, C., & Alexander, A. (2001). Principles of fluency instruction in reading: Relationships with established empirical outcomes. In M. Wolf (ed.), *Dyslexia, fluency and the brain* (pp. 333–355). Parkton, MD: York Press.

Torgesen, J., Alexander, A., Wagner, R., Rashotte, C., Voeller, K., & Conway, T. (2001). Intensive remedial instruction for children with severe reading disabilities: Immediate and long-term outcomes from two instructional approaches. *Journal of Learning Disabilities, 34,* 33–58.

Torgesen, J., Wagner, R., Rashotte, C., Rose, E., Lindamood, P., Conway, T., & Garvin, C. (1999). Preventing reading failure in young children with phonological processing disabilities: Group and individual responses to instruction. *Journal of Educational Psychology, 91,* 579–593.

Trauner, D., Wulfeck, B., Tallal, P., & Hesselink, J. (2000). Neurological and MRI profiles of children with developmental language impairment. *Developmental Medicine & Child Neurology, 42,* 470–475.

Vellutino, F. (1979). *Dyslexia, theory, and research.* Cambridge, MA: MIT Press.

Vellutino, F., Scanlon, D., & Lyon, G. R. (2000). Differentiating between difficult-to-remediate and readily remediated poor readers: More evidence against the IQ-achievement discrepancy definition of reading disability. *Journal of Learning Disability, 33,* 223–238.

Wadsworth, S., Olson, R., Pennington, B., & DeFries, J. (2000). Differential genetic etiology of reading disability as a function of IQ. *Journal of Learning Disabilities, 33,* 192–199.

Wagner, R., & Torgesen, J. (1987). The nature of phonological processing and its causal role in the acquisition of reading skills. *Psychological Bulletin, 101,* 192–212.

Wolf, M., Bally, H., & Morris, R. (1986). Automaticity, retrieval processes, and reading: A longitudinal study in average and impaired reading. *Child Development, 57,* 988–1000.

Wolf, M., & Bowers, P. (1999). The double-deficit hypothesis for the developmental dyslexias. *Journal of Educational Psychology, 91,* 415–438.

Wolff, P.H., Cohen, C., & Drake, C. (1984). Impaired motor timing control in specific reading retardation. *Neuropsychologia, 22,* 587–600.

Wolff, P., & Melngailis, I. (1994). Family patterns of developmental dyslexia. *American Journal of Medical Genetics (Neuropsychiatric Genetics), 54,* 122–131.

Wood, F., & Felton, R. (1994). Separate linguistic and attentional factors in the development of reading. *Topics in Language Disorders, 14,* 42–57.

Wood, F., & Flowers, D. (1999). Functional neuroanatomy in dyslexic subtypes. In D. D. Duane (ed.), *Reading and attention disorders: Neurobiological correlates* (pp. 129–159). Baltimore, MD: York Press.

Wood, F., & Grigorenko, E. (in press). Emerging issues in the genetics of dyslexia: A methodological preview. *Journal of Learning Disabilities.*

Yates, C., Berninger, V., & Abbott, R. (1995). Specific writing disabilities in intellectually gifted children. *Journal for the Education of the Gifted, 18,* 131–155.

# Does Third Grade Discrepancy Status Predict the Course of Reading Development?

*Lynn Flowers*

*Marianne Meyer*

*James Lovato*

*and Frank Wood*

Wake Forest University School of Medicine
Winston-Salem, North Carolina

*Rebecca Felton*

Simmons College
Boston, Massachusetts

*There is persisting debate concerning the use of an ability-achievement discrepancy formula to define and identify learning disabled—including reading disabled—students. This study employs mixed effects regression growth curve analysis to assess the developmental course of discrepant and nondiscrepant readers (within poor readers) who were identified in third grade and retested in fifth, eighth, and twelfth grades. The results showed that discrepancy status does not differentiate the developmental course of basic reading skills (word identification or decoding), reading comprehension, or underlying cognitive abilities (phonemic awareness and fluency) in poor readers. The*

Supported by National Institute of Child Health and Development (NICHD) PHS Grant No. P01 HD 21887

Annals of Dyslexia, Vol. 50, 2000
ISSN 0736-9387

*ability-achievement discrepancy model is not supported. Educational and legislative reasons for the persisting difficulties of poor readers are explored and recommendations for changes in public policy are made.*

Longitudinal outcome research has challenged the original assumption that reading difficulties were simply due to a maturational lag and that over time, these students catch up with their peers (Satz, Taylor, Friel, & Fletcher, 1978). Lyon (1996) cites findings from NICHD studies showing that poor readers, identified in elementary school, do not catch up; rather, their reading problems persist through eighth and ninth grades. That reading difficulties persist, and that there are concomitant underlying cognitive weaknesses, is taken as strong evidence for a deficit model; that is, specific congenital cognitive weaknesses are the basis for the deficit. Given a deficit model hypothesis, the next question is whether general ability as measured by IQ tests predicts a differential outcome for poor readers. This study addresses the question by examining the developmental course of several reading and reading-related skills in students originally identified as IQ discrepant or nondiscrepant poor readers in third grade and following them through twelfth grade.

In the 1970s, when concerns about reading disabilities increased, there was a prevailing view that children with average or above-average ability had the potential to learn and that their failure to learn was both unexpected and unexplained. In contrast, children with less ability, described variously as "slow learners" or as "garden variety" poor readers (Gough & Tunmer, 1986), could not be expected to learn as well because, in this view, their potential itself was compromised. Indeed, the 1977 U.S. Office of Education definition of learning disabilities that included "severe achievement-ability discrepancy" as a major component of learning disability criteria formalized that assumption.

Over the next three decades, research studies converged to reveal the underlying cognitive abilities needed to acquire reading skills. Well-replicated research has demonstrated that a core deficit for reading disabled individuals—both children and adults—is phonemic awareness, the ability to understand how sounds and sound patterns work in our language system (Felton, Naylor & Wood, 1990; Liberman, Shankweiler, & Liberman, 1989; Stanovich & Siegel, 1994). Although phonemic awareness and phonological decoding are necessary prerequisites to efficient reading, they are not considered to be sufficient (Adams, 1990; Juel, Griffith, & Gough, 1986). Indeed, subsequent research has highlighted the role of other factors such as orthographic processing (Badian, 1995), short-term auditory memory (Torgeson, 1994), and particularly fluency (Denckla & Rudel, 1976; Wolf, Bally, & Morris, 1986).

As these underlying cognitive abilities were identified, researchers considered whether IQ-achievement discrepant ("underachievers") and nondiscrepant ("garden variety") students exhibited the same deficits, a test of whether slow learners are different in meaningful ways from their counterparts of average ability. Rutter and Yule (1975) suggested that students with higher verbal ability have more severe nonword reading deficits. While Stanovich (1988) initially found evidence that students whose reading is poor in spite of average verbal intelligence show more severe and more focal deficits in nonword reading than children whose verbal skills are lower, in a later article (Stanovich & Siegel, 1994) he found no such difference when using a new statistical model of regression-based logic. Other researchers (Badian, 1996, 2000; Biddle, 1996; Wolf, 1997) also have reported consistently a higher proportion of multiple deficits in underlying abilities or cognitive subprocesses (phonemic awareness, naming speed, and orthographic skills) among discrepant poor readers.

However, the weight of the evidence is to the contrary, especially when more comprehensive longitudinal assessments have been used. Thus, using regression-based individual growth curve analysis, Stanovich and Siegel (1994), Fletcher, et al., (1994), Francis, Stuebing, Shaywitz, Shaywitz, and Fletcher (1996), and Foorman, Francis, Fletcher, and Lynn (1996) found no differences between IQ discrepant and nondiscrepant readers on a variety of underlying abilities such as word recognition, short-term verbal and nonverbal memory, vocabulary knowledge, and orthographic memory. Importantly, there has been general agreement across investigators that phonemic awareness is a core deficit for reading disabled individuals, whether discrepant or nondiscrepant.

Our longitudinal study results also have not shown a disproportionate deficit in discrepant readers. Felton & Wood (1992) found pervasive nonword reading deficits in poor readers at third and fifth grades in comparison to nondisabled first graders (matched for single word reading), and nondiscrepant poor readers were slightly *more* impaired than were discrepant readers. Felton (1998) presented data showing that discrepancy can increase over the period from third to eighth grades, since reading standard scores can often decline over this time. This suggests that discrepancy may sometimes be confounded with age. In this study, neither group showed significant gains over time.

An even more basic challenge to the ability-achievement discrepancy concept is raised by the assumptions about IQ tests themselves. Thorndike (1963) repeatedly cautioned that IQ scores are only appropriate as estimates of current levels of functioning, not as estimates of future potential. More recently, Siegel (1989, 1998) argued that many of the subtests on IQ assessments are heavily weighted toward acquired learning and, therefore, are not independent from achievement. Furthermore, because poor readers read less (Allington, 1980; Lyon, 1998) they acquire less knowledge. Consequently, there is the tendency for IQ scores of reading disabled students to decline over time, a fact that Stanovich (1986) referred to as the "Matthew effect" whereby differences in their access knowledge through print increases the gap between good and poor readers.

In summary, the existing evidence raises serious questions whether an ability-achievement discrepancy is a valid definition of reading disability, either for purposes of definition or allocation of remedial resources. To clarify these issues, we conducted this growth curve analysis of the outcome of discrepant and nondiscrepant students identified in third grade and followed to twelfth grade in order to assess their developmental course on tests of overall and specific reading skills. This is the first study to examine the developmental course of a broad spectrum of reading skill measures in a large epidemiological sample from early elementary grades through high school.

# METHOD

## SUBJECTS

Subjects for this analysis were drawn from two epidemiologically derived samples, one acquired during first grade and the other during third grade, studied intermittently through the twelfth grade. All subjects (initially a total $N$ of 515) were first acquired from the random selection of students in the city-county school system in a medium sized southern city. The first grade random sample was selected from the general school population and was normally distributed on reading and IQ scores. The third grade sample was obtained by first identifying students from all third grade classes who were more than one standard deviation below the school system-wide mean on the end of second grade administration of the California Achievement Test, or were 15 points lower on reading than on IQ. All who were followed had reading scores below the tenth percentile.

A battery of standardized reading tests and measures of underlying skills (i.e., phonemic awareness and rapid, sequential naming) were administered to these children in the third, fifth, eighth, and twelfth grades. *The Wechsler Intelligence Scale for Children-Revised* (Wechsler, 1974) was given to all children in the third grade. Parents were interviewed extensively to obtain information about emotional and attentional issues, medical history, school history including educational and other services, and the family's socioeconomic status. Children with a Full Scale IQ score of 76 or above were retained for longitudinal study. Children with symptoms of attention deficit hyperactivity disorder (ADHD) were not excluded if they were otherwise eligible.

For this analysis, poor readers were defined by a score below the 11.5 percentile on the *Woodcock-Johnson Psycho-Educational Battery* (1977) Letter/Word Identification subtest in the third grade. This cutoff was chosen because it corresponded to the raw score nearest the tenth percentile, the cutoff used previously in genetics studies from our laboratory (Grigorenko, et al., 1997; Grigorenko, Wood, Meyer, & Pauls, in press). All others were said to be "normal" readers, although it is acknowledged that this group includes non-impaired borderline readers. Within normal and poor readers, discrepancy was defined according to the guidelines of the Department of Public Instruction in the state where these children attended school throughout the study, having a standardized *Woodcock-Johnson Psycho-Educational Battery Reading Cluster* score 15 points or more (at least one standard deviation) below the concurrent WISC-R Full Scale IQ. This yielded the following initial groups: poor readers who were discrepant (D-PR; $n = 51$) and poor readers who were not discrepant (ND-PR; $n = 89$). These will be the focus of the study. However, this also allowed us to identify normal readers who were discrepant (D-NR; $n = 83$), and normal readers who were not discrepant (ND-NR; $n = 292$), and they will be shown for comparison.

## ASSESSMENT INSTRUMENTS

*Wechsler Intelligence Test for Children-Revised (WISC-R) (Wechsler, 1974).* This global measure of intelligence yields a Full Scale IQ (FSIQ); that is, a composite score obtained from five subtests in each of two domains, Verbal and Performance. The mean score is 100; the standard deviation is 15.

*Woodcock-Johnson Psycho-Educational Battery Reading Cluster (WJBP) (Woodcock & Johnson, 1977).* The reading cluster score is a composite measure of Word Identification (WID), Word Attack (WA), and Passage Comprehension (PC) subtests. It yields an age-referenced standard score with a mean of 100 and a standard deviation of 15. WID requires reading single words in isolation. WA requires reading a list of nonwords, defined as "letter combinations that are not actual words or are extremely low frequency words in the English language" (Woodcock, 1978, p. 35). PC uses a "cloze" procedure that requires reading sentences or passages and supplying the missing word that would make sense. Raw scores are reported for the three subtests as there are no corresponding standard scores. Concurrent validity coefficients between the reading cluster and a number of standardized reading measures, ranging from .75 to .92, are furnished by Woodcock (1978). No data are given for the subtests; however, Felton & Wood (1989) reported the concurrent validity coefficient between the WID subtest and the single word reading portion of the Decoding Skills Test (Richardson & DeBenedetto, 1985) to be .92.

*Lindamood Auditory Conceptualization Test (LAC) (Lindamood & Lindamood, 1979).* This test assesses several aspects of phonemic processing including the ability to discriminate sounds, hold strings of sounds in short-term memory, and sequence and manipulate sounds within word-like strings (e.g., changing "tif" to "tof" or "tofs" to "ofs"). Difficult items are weighted more heavily and the authors report that a maximum converted score of 100 is expected by the end of sixth grade. Converted scores are reported as there is no standard score conversion. Lindamood, Lindamood, and Calfee (1974) reported LAC correlations between .66 and .81 across the grade span with Wide Range Achievement Test (WRAT) (Jastak & Bijou, 1946) reading and spelling subtests.

*Test of Auditory Analysis Skills (TAAS) (Rosner, 1979).* The *TAAS* measures phonemic awareness by requiring subjects to segment syllables, delete initial and final consonants, and segment consonant blends. Students are expected to perform this task perfectly by the end of the third grade. Raw scores are reported on this 13-item test as there is no standard score conversion. Rosner reported validation of his original test using Scholastic Aptitude Tests (SAT) scores (1971).

*Rapid Automatized Naming Test (RAN) (Denckla & Rudel, 1976).* This naming test is a measure of fluency and automaticity in retrieving labels for highly practiced items (colors, numbers, objects, and lower-case letters) under strictly timed conditions. Stimuli are presented on individual cards containing five rows of randomly arranged items, ten to a row. Scores are reported as mean seconds with graphological symbols (letters/numbers) and nongraphological symbols (colors/objects) combined because there is no standard score conversion. (See Meyer, Wood, Hart, & Felton, 1998, for the rationale behind this scoring procedure.) Wolf , Bowers, & Biddle (2000) summarized the evidence that the *RAN* contributes significant independent variance to reading skills as compared to tests of phonological awareness.

*Diagnostic Interview for Children and Adolescents (DICA) (Herjanic & Reich, 1982).* This structured diagnostic interview is keyed to criteria described in the *Diagnostic and Statistic Manual of Mental Disorders, 3rd Edition.* Parents or guardians were interviewed on the scale assessing inattentive, impulsive, and hyperactive features of attention deficit disorder in their third-grade children.

*Four Factor Index of Social Position (Hollingshead, 1957).* Socioeconomic status (SES) is determined from parental occupation and educational level. Information was obtained by interviewing parents of third-grade students.

## STATISTICAL ANALYSIS

T-tests comparing discrepancy groups on subject demographics and reading skills measured in the third grade were conducted separately within poor readers and normal readers. Chi square tests were performed on the categorical variables of sex and race.

For each reading score of interest, we potentially had measurements on each child at third, fifth, eighth, and twelfth grades. We assumed that the measurements were independent from child to child but that they were correlated within each child. Developmental course was analyzed using a mixed effects regression growth curve model incorporating both fixed and random effects. We preformed separate analyses for poor readers and normal readers. Fixed effects—race, gender, SES level, and grade level—were associated with particular levels of variables used in the model and represent deviations from an overall mean. When modeling each of the reading measures, we allowed fixed effects to enter the model and also allowed for these effects to vary by grade by allowing interaction terms. We included an

individual child random effect to account for the correlation of
scores within each child, and because we were interested in making inferences about the population of children from which these
particular children are drawn. After a good explanatory and predictive model was built, developmental course was investigated
by adding to the model the effect of discrepant status and its interaction with grade level. The full model with discrepant status
and its interaction with grade level was tested against the model
without the interaction term using the likelihood ratio test.
Developmental course was said not to differ between discrepant
and nondiscrepant readers if this test was not significant.

# RESULTS

## COMPARISON OF DISCREPANCY GROUPS
## WITHIN READING CATEGORY

Table I summarizes third grade means across a range of variables by discrepancy status, within poor and normal reading
categories. As a function of the discrepancy definition, discrepant students were significantly higher than nondiscrepant
students ($p < .0001$) on all WISC-R IQ scores.

For poor readers, there were more nonwhites in the nondiscrepant group ($p = .006$). WJPB reading cluster standard scores
were not different as a function of discrepancy group; however,
nondiscrepant poor readers performed more poorly than the
discrepant poor readers in third grade on the LAC test ($p = .006$)
and TAAS ($p = .01$).

For normal readers, SES was higher ($p < .001$) and there
were more males ($p = .01$) in the discrepant group; but, as with
poor readers, there were more nonwhites in the nondiscrepant
group ($p < .001$). Discrepant students had significantly poorer
WJPB reading cluster scores ($p = .002$). Nondiscrepant normal
readers differed significantly from discrepant normal readers on
third grade WID ($p = .004$), WA ($p < .001$), LAC ($p < .001$) and
RAN Number/Letter tests ($p = .009$).

## DEVELOPMENTAL COURSE OF DISCREPANT
## AND NONDISCREPANT READERS ACROSS TASKS

Mixed effects regression results, described below by task, are
summarized in table II. The values in the "effect of being discrepant" column are the adjusted differences between discrepant and nondiscrepant readers. For example, for two poor
reading students in the same grade and of the same sex, race,

**Table I.** Grade 3 Variables within Reading Category by Discrepancy Group: Mean (SD).

| | ND-PR | D-PR | | ND-NR | D-NR | |
|---|---|---|---|---|---|---|
| | N=89 | N=51 | p-value | N=292 | N=83 | p-value |
| Age | 9.2 (0.5) | 9.3 (0.7) | NS | 9.0 (0.6) | 9.0 (0.5) | NS |
| Race (% white) | 28.1 | 52.9 | 0.006 | 62.3 | 83.1 | < 0.001 |
| Sex (% male) | 57.3 | 64.7 | NS | 54.5 | 71.1 | 0.01 |
| SES | 27.7 (11.8) | 31.6 (10.4) | NS | 37.7 (13.4) | 45.3 (11.3) | < 0.001 |
| VIQ | 89.3 (8.1) | 99.4 (9.8) | < 0.001 | 104.1 (15.2) | 117.3 (11.7) | < 0.001 |
| PIQ | 90.4 (8.7) | 103.8 (9.9) | < 0.001 | 100.1 (12.5) | 117.3 (13.0) | < 0.001 |
| FSIQ | 88.8 (6.9) | 101.4 (8.7) | < 0.001 | 102.4 (13.9) | 119.3 (12.5) | < 0.001 |
| WJPB Cluster | 80.9 (5.4) | 80.4 (7.0) | NS | 102.3 (13.9) | 97.3 (11.0) | 0.002 |
| WJPB-WI | 23.2 (2.6) | 23.5 (2.7) | NS | 32.5 (3.4) | 31.2 (3.3) | 0.004 |
| WJPB-WA | 4.2 (2.4) | 4.0 (2.5) | NS | 12.9 (6.2) | 9.1 (5.2) | < 0.001 |
| WJPB-PC | 9.8 (2.3) | 9.7 (2.3) | NS | 14.0 (2.6) | 13.7 (2.4) | NS |
| LAC | 41.3 (15.2) | 48.9 (16.0) | 0.006 | 57.5 (23.2) | 67.5 (19.0) | < 0.001 |
| TAAS | 7.1 (3.1) | 8.5 (3.1) | 0.01 | 10.4 (2.7) | 10.7 (2.2) | NS |
| RAN C/O | 59.1 (13.6) | 61.9 (13.7) | NS | 52.0 (10.6) | 52.0 (10.4) | NS |
| RAN N/L | 34.4 (7.3) | 37.0 (10.3) | 0.08 | 28.2 (6.1) | 30.3 (6.4) | 0.009 |

*Note:* ND = Nondiscrepant; D = Discrepant; PR = Poor Readers; NR = Normal Readers; NS = $p$-value > 0.2; RAN = Rapid Automatized Naming; C/O = Combined color and Object naming in seconds; N/L = combined Number and Letter naming in seconds; IQs and WJPB Cluster reported as Standard Scores (mean of 100); all other test scores are raw scores.

and SES level, the discrepant student is expected on average to score 7.02 points higher than the nondiscrepant student on the LAC test. Average raw scores are plotted in figures 1 through 7 for poor and normal readers by discrepancy group.

Among poor readers, WID and the WA scores did not differ significantly between the discrepant and nondiscrepant groups in development course from third to twelfth grade. Among normal readers, a discrepancy group by grade interaction ($p = .03$ for WID and $p < .001$ for WA) reflected lower initial scores on these tests in the D-NR group, with both group means approaching the test ceilings by twelfth grade.

### Table II. Mixed Effects Regression Results.

| | Poor Readers[*] | | Normal Readers | | | | | | |
|---|---|---|---|---|---|---|---|---|---|
| | Main Effects Model | | Main Effects Model | | Interaction Model | | | | |
| | | | | | | Effect of Being Discrepant | | | |
| | Effect of Being Discrepant | P-value | Effect of Being Discrepant | P-value | 3rd | 5th | 8th | 12th | P-value[**] |
| W-J Single Word | −0.11 | 0.83 | | | −2.6 | −2.7 | 1.8 | −1.4 | 0.03 |
| W-J Word Attack | −0.47 | 0.40 | | | −5.5 | −3.9 | −2.7 | −2.4 | <0.001 |
| W-J Comprehension | 0.03 | 0.92 | −0.93 | <0.001 | | | | | |
| LAC | 7.02 | <0.001 | | | 4.5 | −1.6 | −5.4 | −6.3 | <0.001 |
| TAAS | 0.63 | 0.09 | −0.42 | 0.05 | | | | | |
| RAN N/L | 1.75 | 0.14 | 2.22 | <0.001 | | | | | |
| RAN C/O | 1.77 | 0.36 | 0.63 | 0.58 | | | | | |

*Notes:* [*]None of the interaction models were significant in poor readers.
[**]A test of the interaction term.

RAN = Rapid Automatized Naming; N/L = combined Number and Letter naming in seconds; C/O = Combined color and Object naming in seconds.

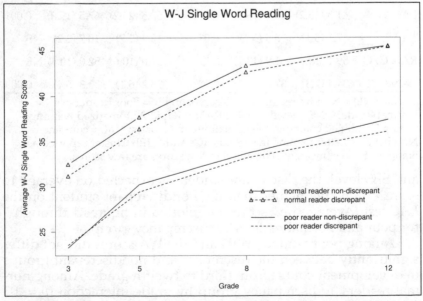

*Figure 1.*    Plot of average Woodcock-Johnson (W-J) *single Word Reading raw scores as a function of grade for poor and normal, discrepant and nondiscrepant readers.*

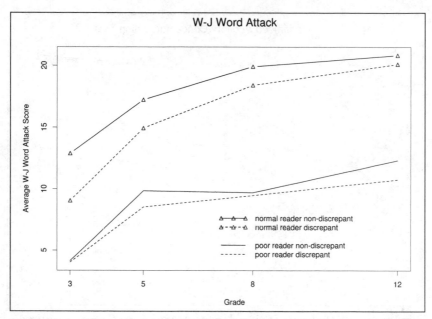

*Figure 2.* Plot of average Woodcock-Johnson (W-J) Word Attack raw scores as a function of grade for poor and normal, discrepant and nondiscrepant readers.

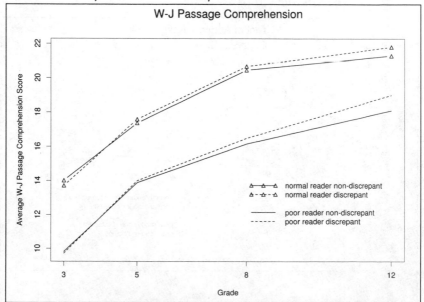

*Figure 3.* Plot of average Woodcock-Johnson (W-J) Passage Comprehension raw scores as a function of grade for poor and normal, discrepant and nondiscrepant readers.

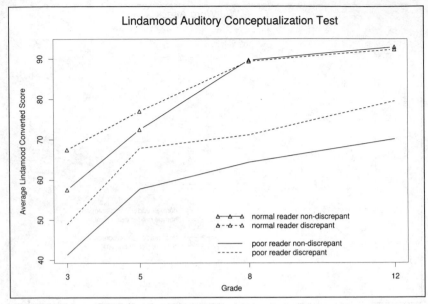

*Figure 4.* Plot of *average* Lindamood Auditory Conceptualiza-tion Converted (LAC) *scores as a function of grade for poor and normal, discrepant and nondiscrepant readers (maximum = 100).*

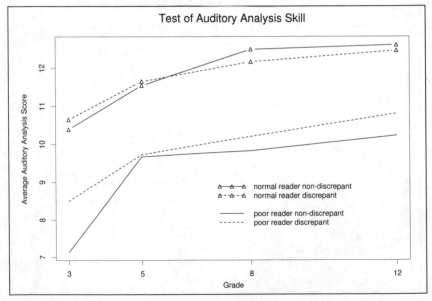

*Figure 5.* Plot of *average* Test of Auditory Analysis Skill (TAAS) *raw scores as a function of grade for poor and normal, discrepant and nondiscrepant readers.*

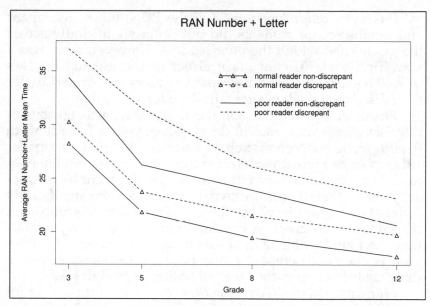

*Figure 6.* Plot *of average* Rapid Automatized Naming (RAN) *Number and Letter time in seconds as a function of grade for poor and normal, discrepant and nondiscrepant readers.*

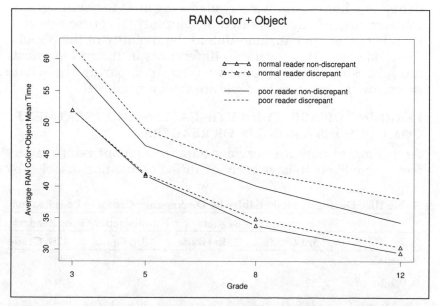

*Figure 7.* Plot *of average* Rapid Automatized Naming (RAN) *Color and Object time in seconds as a function of grade for poor and normal, discrepant and nondiscrepant readers.*

*Passage Comprehension.*   On the PC subtest, discrepant and nondiscrepant students did not differ significantly across the grade span within the poor readers. However, there was a statistically significant main effect in the normal readers ($p < .001$) such that nondiscrepant readers performed better than discrepant readers after adjusting for sex and race.

*Phonemic Awareness.*   On the *TAAS*, there was no statistically significant difference in development course from third to twelfth grade between discrepant and nondiscrepant groups for either poor or normal readers. On the *LAC* test, within the poor readers, there was a main effect but no development by discrepancy interaction; that is, discrepant students were significantly better at each grade level, but the difference between groups was the same at each grade. A development by discrepancy interaction was found within normal readers on the *LAC* test ($p < .001$). That is, the nondiscrepant group began with poorer scores in third grade but approached the test ceiling by twelfth grade.

*Fluency.*   On the RAN, either for letters and numbers or for colors and objects, the developmental course of naming fluency did not differ significantly between discrepancy groups either within the poor readers or within the normal readers.

All analyses were repeated with a truncated sample of students for whom scores were available for third to twelfth grades to determine whether reported developmental course was confounded by subject attrition due to the mobility of the population. However, there were no differences in the mixed effects models. Some demographic variables comparing the whole sample to the truncated sample are shown in table III.

## LEARNING DISABILITY IDENTIFICATION AND TREATMENT COMPARISONS AMONG POOR READERS

According to parent interview data, discrepant poor readers were more likely to have been identified as learning disabled by

Table III.   Demographic Variables by Discrepancy Group in Poor Readers.

|  | Discrepant Poor Readers | | Nondiscrepant Poor Readers | |
|---|---|---|---|---|
|  | 3rd Grade | 12th Grade | 3rd Grade | 12th Grade |
| % Female | 48 | 27 | 38 | 46 |
| % White | 52 | 53 | 33 | 24 |
| SES Mean (*SD*) | 33.5  (12.2) | 30.1   (8.3) | 30.9   (11.0) | 25.1  (12.0) |
| FSIQ Mean (*SD*) | 101.0   (9.2) | 101.7   (8.5) | 89.8   (7.5) | 88.0   (6.4) |

*Note:* SES=Socioeconomic Status; FSIQ=Wechsler Full Scale IQ

the school system by the fifth grade ($p < .005$), 76 percent and 10 percent for discrepant and nondiscrepant groups, respectively. However, of those discrepant students identified, only 57 percent were provided school LD services.

# DISCUSSION

There is a long-standing assumption that reading disability is properly defined by a discrepancy between ability and achievement and that in some essential way, the two are different. Since in most North American jurisdictions, discrepancy determines allocation of reading resources, the implication is that discrepant students have an advantage over nondiscrepant students by virtue of their higher intelligence. However, in this study, the developmental course of discrepant readers is not different from that of their nondiscrepant counterparts. This finding is true for word identification and nonword decoding, as well as for the underlying skills associated with reading acquisition, phoneme awareness, and rapid naming.

These results also confirm and extend to the end of the secondary school level what most other investigators (Francis, et al., 1996; Share & Silva, 1986; Vellutino, Scanlon, & Lyon, 2000) have suggested: reading disabilities as measured by decoding skill in early elementary school persist, not just into later elementary and middle schools but through the end of high school. On two reading skills considered the critical markers of dyslexia, real word identification and decoding of nonwords, all students in this sample made rapid gains between third and fifth grades. However, while all categories of students continued to make gains in word identification to grade twelve, neither discrepant nor nondiscrepant poor readers caught up to their normal reading peers. Furthermore, word attack skills appeared to level off for all poor readers by fifth grade.

These results are consistent with those reported by Francis, et al. (1996) who investigated the developmental lag versus deficit model of reading disability. Using third grade reading and IQ measures just as those employed here, they tracked discrepant and nondiscrepant poor readers through ninth grade and compared them to normal readers. Applying individual growth curve analysis similar to ours, they found that reading disabled and normal students both reached a plateau at about 15 years; but poor readers differed from normal readers in the level of reading skill they attained, a deficit as opposed to a developmental lag model. In the present study, although good readers continued to make notable improvement through eighth grade on measures of phoneme awareness, reaching levels at or close to the test ceilings, poor readers progressed slowly after fifth grade. As a group, normal readers attained the expected scores on phonemic measures and achieved fully average scores on both word identification and word attack. In contrast, poor readers—regardless of discrepancy status—remained impaired on measures of reading skills as well as on the cognitive correlates of dyslexia.

Note, however, that discrepant poor readers began with higher *LAC* and *TAAS* scores and maintained higher *LAC* scores across all grades. Because the discrepant poor readers had higher IQs, the high correlation between full scale IQ and the *LAC* ($r = .69$, $p < .0001$) and between full scale IQ and the TAAS ($r = .45$, $p < .0001$) likely explains these findings. It is interesting that the better phoneme awareness skills of the discrepant poor readers do not translate into an advantage in word attack or word identification. Perfetti, Beck, Bell, & Hughes (1987), Stanovich (1986), and Wagner, Torgesen, & Rashotte (1994) notice that, rather than a linear relationship between phoneme awareness or processing and early acquisition of reading and spelling, there is a reciprocal (Perfetti and colleagues) or a bidirectional (Wagner and colleagues) relationship. It is possible that for the discrepant poor readers this reciprocal/bidirectional relationship never became fully functional. That is, their phoneme awareness never achieved a level sufficient to positively affect decoding. Moreover, it is likely that repeated failure of poor readers to associate sounds and sound patterns with letters and orthographic patterns made them inattentive to the features necessary for decoding and more reliant on alternative techniques such as use of context or guessing based on word configuration.

Similar to the acquisition of phonemic awareness skills, fluency as measured by naming rate—whether of graphological (letters and numbers) or nongraphological (colors and objects) items—showed the greatest improvement between third and fifth grades. There was gradual, continued improvement through twelfth grade for all groups with normal readers approaching a ceiling effect (in this case, increasingly lower scores). Poor readers as a group, regardless of discrepancy status, had naming rates below the tenth percentile for graphological or nongraphological items up through the eighth grade when compared to norms from a large, nonaffected sample

(Meyer, et al., 1998). That same study indicated that rapid naming deficits assessed in third grade selectively predicted continued poor reading among reading disabled students, but not among their normal counterparts. Rapid naming in adults has also been shown to be statistically related to reading improvement across the lifespan (Flowers, 1994).

Discrepancy status was associated with greater likelihood that a student had received services. However, according to parental reports in the school system from which this sample was drawn, only 76 percent of discrepant poor readers in this study were actually identified as learning disabled by the school system. In other words, even though they should have qualified by state guidelines—15 points between IQ and reading achievement where this study was conducted—nearly a quarter of children failed to be identified. Assuming the parental reports were accurate, possible explanations are the students' use of compensatory strategies, the failure to attribute academic problems to poor reading, and the lack of parental consent for testing. However, only slightly over half of those identified received learning disability services in their schools through a resource model. Under the LD-resource model in the local school system at that time, students typically received 35 to 45 minutes a day of direct instruction by a certified LD teacher with a small group of peers in the resource room.

There are various explanations for the persistence of reading difficulties despite special education services. For example, Lyon (1996) noted that interventions begun after age nine may be less successful than those begun earlier, due to various factors including declining motivation and impaired self-concept. In addition, instruction may not match the child's needs, may be too short in duration, or may be inconsistently applied. Felton (1998) attributed the lack of progress during middle school to the fact that direct instruction in decoding and word identification was not available. She concluded that, rather than IQ/achievement discrepancy, the factors determining outcome for individual students may be the set of processing weaknesses (e.g., phonemic awareness, automaticity in naming, verbal short-term memory) interacting with instructional factors (e.g., onset and duration of instruction, type of reading methods used, and ways these are delivered).

Changes in federal and state education policy also may help account for the poor outcome of reading disabled students. One such policy is "mainstreaming," which promotes an inclusion model. In some states, inclusion occurs as early as elementary school, but as students reach middle school, it becomes even less likely that poor readers will receive direct, systematic reading instruction. In the inclusion model, the LD teacher helps pupils in their regular classrooms, rather than in a resource room. Assistance often focuses on completion of immediate classroom assignments and indirect (nonsystematic) teaching of reading skills within specific content areas. The inclusion model conflicts with recommendations from the *National Reading Panel Report* (2000) that supported direct, explicit, systematic instruction for poor readers, not just limited to elementary school instruction. In addition to "mainstreaming," compensatory accommodations (books on tape, test modifications, and the like) without appropriate remediation also may serve to mask the real extent of a child's underlying reading disability.

In a recent report, Vellutino et al. (2000) examined factors— including IQ—that differentiate difficult-to-remediate versus readily remediated students. A group of first graders with problems acquiring initial reading skills received daily one-to-one tutoring in first grade. In following these students through fourth grade, they found that IQ scores did not differentiate poor readers who readily remediated from poor readers who were difficult to remediate. Rather, deficits in underlying cognitive correlates such as phoneme awareness were the significant factors predicting ease of remediation. These findings made the case that early determination of underlying skills is an effective way to identify which students will need further intervention. This, in turn, would allow more efficient use of educational personnel and more economical allocation of financial resources.

Our results directly challenge the construct of an ability-achievement discrepancy in regard to the definition and identification criteria for reading disability. They add to a growing body of evidence that discrepancy, as the construct is currently defined and interpreted, is neither valid nor useful. If the discrepancy model does not differentiate the developmental course of basic reading skills or underlying cognitive correlates, then it serves little useful purpose.

Perhaps the most general public policy issue arising from the apparent invalidity of the discrepancy formula is the basic constitutional guarantee of the equal protection of the law. As a general principle, government may not afford unequal treatment to its citizens when there is no sound public purpose for doing so. If, as our data suggest, there is no long-term validity to the discrepancy formulation, then its application by schools could be considered to be arbitrarily discriminatory.

Not to be ignored are the practical issues regarding the application of the discrepancy criteria in placement decisions. MacMillan, Gresham, & Bocian (1998) report that school placement committees are inconsistent in their application of discrepancy criteria, sometimes certifying students for LD services based on their low absolute achievement, disregarding IQ tests. Furthermore, it is well known that IQ-achievement discrepancy criteria can vary from place to place. For example, in the United States, where federal guidelines never defined discrepancy numerically, each state sets its own definition. Thus, a student can be certified as LD in one geographic location but have services denied in another.

There is ongoing discussion about whether students with fully average or above average achievement should receive LD services (Fuchs, Fuchs, Mathes, Lipsey, & Eaton, 2000). Discrepancy guidelines technically allow for services, based on the underlying assumption that there is a strong correspondence between IQ and achievement. On the one hand, some argue that LD services should be given to any students whose achievement is below their "potential" while others argue the LD designation should be reserved only for students with below-average achievement. In the present study, some normal readers had unexpectedly low underlying skills (especially in third grade nonword decoding); and some twelfth grade normal readers had scores on tests of underlying skills (*LAC* and *TAAS*) that were equal to or less than the mean scores of the poor reading group. Although not addressed in this study, a better understanding of how similar students are able to achieve normal reading status would be worth future study. It is possible that the students we define here as "normal" were handicapped by other reading difficulties not measured such as speed when reading connected text. For example, Fuchs et al. (2000) reported that performance on timed tests differentiated older students with and without the label of learning disability.

In conclusion, these findings, converge with those of other investigators to indicate that the ability-achievement discrepancy construct as it is typically employed contributes little to our understanding of reading disabilities. In fact, employing the construct may be harmful. It promotes a "wait to fail" approach rather than one of early identification and early intervention using proven treatment protocols. Furthermore, employing a discrepancy rule may mask serious underlying problems in otherwise capable students.

Given our findings and those of other investigators (Spear-Swerling & Sternberg, 1994; Berninger & Abbot, 1994; Siegel, 1989, 1998; Lyon, 1995; Wolf & Bowers, 1999), it is our view that the following components should be considered when updating the definition and identification of reading disabilities.

1.  IQ-achievement discrepancy criteria should be replaced by criteria stressing age and grade discrepant weaknesses in underlying processing abilities and basic reading skills as the defining characteristics of reading disability.

2.  IQ measures should be used only to rule out mental handicap. Although IQ measures may be useful in assessing an individual's overall cognitive strengths and weaknesses, they should not be used to decide whether services are allocated.

3.  The "wait to fail" policy engendered by the application of the IQ-achievement discrepancy criteria prevents many children from being identified until third grade, whereas the emphasis should be placed on research-based identifiers in K through 2.

4.  Although emphasis should be on early identification, assessment for higher level problems (vocabulary knowledge, comprehension, reading fluency/speed, orthographic and morphological patterns) at various stages of reading development is also critical.

5.  Following a thorough evaluation identifying the nature and extent of the reading disability, a response to remediation criteria using research proven treatment protocols administered over a sufficient amount of time should be instituted. This, in turn, would allow more efficient use of educational personal and more economical allocation of financial resources.

Address correspondence to D. L. Flowers, Wake Forest University School of Medicine, Department of Neurology, Winston-Salem, NC 27157-1043. Telephone 336-716-2261, Fax 336-716-9810. e-mail: <lflowers@wfubmc.edu> <mmeyer @wfubmc.edu> <jlovato@wfubmc.edu> <felton@bcinet.net> <fwood@wfubmc.edu>

## References

Adams, M. J. (1990). *Beginning to read: Thinking and learning about print.* Cambridge, MA: The MIT Press.

Allington, R. L. (1980). Poor readers don't get to read much in reading groups. *Language Arts, 57,* 872–876.

Badian, N. A. (1995). Predicting reading ability over the long term: The changing roles of letter naming, phonological awareness and orthographic processing. *Annals of Dyslexia, 40,* 79–96.

Badian, N. A. (1996). Dyslexia: Does it exist: Dyslexia, garden-variety poor reading and the double deficit hypothesis. Poster presented at the Orton Dyslexia Society conference, Boston, MA.

Badian, N. A. (2000) Do pre-school orthographic skills contribute to prediction of reading? In N. A. Badian (ed.), *Prediction and prevention of reading failure* (pp. 31–56). Baltimore, MD: York Press.

Berninger, V. W., & Abbot, R. D. (1994). Redefining learning disabilities: Moving beyond aptitude-achievement discrepancies in failure to respond to validated treatment protocols. In G. R. Lyon, (ed.), *Frames of reference for the assessment of learning disabilities* (pp. 163–168). Baltimore, MD: Paul H. Brookes Publishing Co.

Biddle, K. R. (1996). Timing deficits in impaired readers: An investigation of visual naming speed and verbal fluency. Unpublished doctoral dissertation, Tufts University, Boston, MA.

Denckla, M. B., & Rudel, R. G. (1976). Rapid automatized naming (RAN): Dyslexia differentiated from other learning disabilities. *Neuropsychologia, 14,* 471–479.

Felton, R. H. (1998). The development of reading skills in poor readers: Educational implications. In C. Hulme & R. M. Joshi (eds.), *Reading and spelling: Development and disorders* (pp. 219–233). Hillside, NJ: Lawrence Erlbaum Associates.

Felton, R. H., Naylor, C. E., & Wood, F. B. (1990). Neuropsychological profile of adult dyslexics. *Brain and Language, 39,* 485–497.

Felton, R. H., & Wood, F. B. (1992). Cognitive deficits in reading disability and attention deficit disorder. A reading level match study of nonword reading. *Journal of Learning Disabilities, 22,* 3–13.

Felton, R. H., & Wood, F. B. (1992). A reading level match study of nonword reading skills in poor readers with varying IQ. *Journal of Learning Disabilities, 25,* 318–326.

Fletcher, J. M., Shaywitz, S. E., Shankweiler, D. P., Katz, L., Liberman, I. Y., Stuebing, K. K., Francis, D. J., Fowler, A. E., & Shaywitz, B. (1994). Cognitive profiles of reading disability: Comparisons of discrepancy and low achievement definitions. *Journal of Educational Psychology, 86,* 6–23.

Flowers, D. L. (1994). Neuropsychological profiles of persistent reading disability and reading improvement. In C. K. Leong, & R. M. Joshi (eds.), *Developmental and acquired dyslexia: Neuropsychological and neurolinguistic perspectives* (pp. 61–77). Netherlands: Kluwer Academic Publishers.

Foorman. B. R., Francis, D. J., Fletcher, J. M., & Lynn A. (1996). Relation of phonological and orthographic processing to early reading: Comparing two approaches to regression-based, reading-level match designs. *Journal of Educational Psychology, 33,* 639–652.

Francis, D. J., Stuebing, K. K., Shaywitz, S. E., Shaywitz, B. A., & Fletcher, J. M. (1996). Developmental lag versus deficit models of reading disability: A longitudinal, individual growth curves analysis. *Journal of Educational Psychology, 88,* 3–17

Fuchs, D., Fuchs, L. S., Mathes, P. G., Lipsey, M. E., & Eaton, S. (2000). A meta-analysis of reading differences between underachievers with and without the disabilities label: A brief report. *Learning Disabilities: A Multidisciplinary Journal, 10,* 1–3.

Gough, P. B., & Tunmer, W. E. (1986). Decoding, reading and reading disability. *Remedial and Special Education, 7,* 6–10.

Grigorenko, E., Wood, F. W., Meyer, M. S., Hart, L. A., Speed, W. C., Shuster, A., & Pauls, D. L. (1997). Susceptibility loci for distinct components of developmental dyslexia on chromosomes 6 and 15. *American Journal of Human Genetics, 60,* 27–39.

Grigorenko, E., Wood, F., Meyer, M., & Pauls, D. (In press). Linkage studies suggest a possible locus for developmental dyslexia on chromosome 1. *American Journal of Medical Genetics (Neuropsychiatric Genetics).*

Herjanic, B., & Reich, W. (1982). Development of a structured psychiatric interview for children: Agreement between child and parent on individual symptoms. *Journal of Abnormal Child Psychology, 10,* 307–24.

Hollingshead, A. B. (1957). Four factor index of social status. Unpublished manuscript. (Available from P.O. Box 1965, Yale Station, New Haven, CT 06520).

Jastak, J., & Bijou, S. (1946). *Wide range achievement test.* Wilmington: Jastak Associates.

Juel, C., Griffith, P. L., & Gough, P. B. (1986). Acquisition of literacy: A longitudinal study of children in first and second grade. *Journal of Educational Psychology, 78,* 243–255

Liberman, I. Y., Shankweiler, D., & Liberman, A. M. (1989). The alphabetic principal and learning to read. In D. Shankweiler, & I. Y. Liberman (eds.), *Phonology and reading disability* (pp. 1–33). Ann Arbor, MI: The University of Michigan Press.

Lindamood, C. H., & Lindamood, P. C. (1979). *Lindamood Auditory Conceptualization Test.* Allen, TX: DLM.

Lindamood, C. H., Lindamood, P. C., & Calfee, R. C. (1974). The LAC test: A new look at auditory conceptualization and literacy development K-12. Paper presented at the meeting of the International Reading Association Convention, Detroit, MI.

Lyon, G. R. (1995). Toward a definition of dyslexia. *Annals of Dyslexia, 45,* 3–27.

Lyon, G. R. (1996). Learning disabilities. *The Future of Children, 6,* 54–77.

Lyon, G. R. (1998). Critical advances in understanding reading acquisition and reading difficulty. Paper presented at the North Carolina Branch of the International Dyslexia Association, November 1998, Boone, NC.

MacMillan, D. L., Gresham, F. M., & Bocian, K. M. (1998). Discrepancy between definitions of learning disabilities and school practices: An empirical investigation. *Journal of Learning Disabilities, 31,* 314–326.

Meyer, M. S., Wood, F. B., Hart, L. A., & Felton, R. H. (1998). Selective predictive value of rapid automatized naming in poor readers. *Journal of Learning Disabilities, 31,* 106–117.

*National Reading Panel Report.* (2000). National Institute of Child Health and Human Development.

Perfetti, C. A., Beck, L., Bell, L., & Huges, C. (1987). Phonemic knowledge and learning to read are reciprocal: A longitudinal study of first grade children. *Merrill-Palmer Quarterly, 33,* 283–319.

Richardson, E., & DeBenedetto, G. (1985). *The decoding skills test.* Parkton, MD: York Press.

Rosner, J. (1979). *Helping children overcome learning difficulties.* New York, NY: Walker & Co.

Rosner, J., & Simon, D. P. (1971). The auditory analysis test: An initial report. *Journal of Learning Disabilities, 4,* 384–392.

Rutter, M., & Yule, W. (1975) The concept of specific reading retardation. *Journal of Child Psychology and Psychiatry, 16,* 181–197.

Satz, P., Taylor, H. G., Friel, J., & Fletcher, J. M. (1978). Some developmental and predictive precursors of reading disability: A six-year follow-up. In A. L. Benton & D. Pearl (eds.), *Dyslexia: An appraisal of current knowledge* (pp. 313–347). New York: Oxford University Press.

Siegel, L. S. (1989). IQ is irrelevant to the definition of learning disabilities. *Journal of Learning Disabilities, 22,* 469–478.

Siegel, L. S. (1998). The discrepancy formula: Its use and abuse. In B. K. Shapiro, P. J. Accardo, & A. J. Capute (eds.), *Specific reading disabilities: A view of the spectrum.* Timonium, MD: York Press.

Share, D. L., & Silva, P. A. (1986). The stability and classification of specific reading retardation: A longitudinal study from age 7 to 11. *British Journal of Educational Psychology, 56,* 32–39.

Spear-Swerling, L., & Sternberg, R. J. (1994). The road not taken: An integrative theoretical model of reading disability. *Journal of Learning Disabilities, 27,* 91–103, 122.

Stanovich, K. E. (1986). Matthew effects in reading: Some consequences of individual differences in the acquisition of literacy. *Reading Research Quarterly, 21,* 360–407.

Stanovich, K. E. (1988). Explaining the differences between the dyslexic and the garden-variety poor reader: The phonological-core variable-difference model. *Journal of Learning Disabilities, 21,* 590–612.

Stanovich, K. E., & Siegel, L. S. (1994). Phenotypic performance profile of children with reading disabilities: A regression-based test of the phonological-core variable-difference model of reading. *Journal of Educational Psychology, 86,* 24–53.

Thorndike, R. L. (1963). *The concepts of over- and underachievement.* New York: Columbia University Bureau of Publications.

Torgeson, J. K., Wagner, R. K., & Rashotte, C. A. (1994). Longitudinal studies of phonological processing and reading. *Journal of Learning Disabilities, 27,* 276–286.

Vellutino, F. R., Scanlon, D. M., & Lyon, G. R. (2000). Differentiating between difficult-to-remediate and readily remediated poor readers: More evidence against the IQ-achievement discrepancy definition of reading disability. *Journal of Learning Disabilities, 33,* 223–238.

Wagner, R. K., Torgesen, J. K., & Rashotte, C. A. (1994). Development of reading-related phonological processing abilities: New evidence of bi-directional causality from a latent variable longitudinal study. *Developmental Psychology, 30,* 73–87.

Wechsler, D. (1974). *Wechsler intelligence test for children-revised.* San Antonio, TX: Psychological Corporation.

Wolf, M. (1997). A provisional, integrative account of phonological and naming deficits in dyslexia. Implications for diagnosis and intervention. In B. L. Blachman (ed.), *Cognitive and linguistic foundations of reading acquisition: Implications for intervention research* (pp. 67–92). Hillsdale, NJ: Lawrence Erlbaum Associates.

Wolf, M., Bally, H., & Morris, R. (1986). Automaticity, retrieval processes, and reading: A longitudinal study in average and impaired readers. *Child Development, 57,* 988–1000.

Wolf, M., Bowers, P. G., & Biddle, K. (2000). Naming-speed processes, timing, and reading: A conceptual review. *Journal of Learning Disabilities, 33,* 387–407.

Woodcock, R. W. (1978). *Development and standardization of the Woodcock Johnson psycho-educational battery.* Hingham, MA: Teaching Resources.

Woodcock, R. W., & Johnson, M. B. (1977). *Woodcock-Johnson psycho-educational battery.* Allen, TX: DLM.

# PART III
## Research into Practice:
## Instruction and Intervention

One of the goals of *Annals of Dyslexia* is to provide well-documented reports of effective practice; another is to present significant reviews on an important aspect of dyslexia. In Part III the first three papers are research studies that have implications for instruction and teaching practice. The fourth paper is a review of research on teaching spelling.

Recently, there has been controversy over the efficacy of Tallal's FastForWord (FFW) training program for children with reading disabilities. It is important that educators familiarize themselves with the issues surrounding the debate and that there be empirical evidence to support its use. Here, Pamela Hook and her colleagues provide some new empirical evidence from a study examining the short- and long-term impact of FFW. Their preliminary findings, based on a small sample, suggest that FFW does not provide any added benefits among children who received multisensory structured language instruction over two years. The authors caution that additional studies are needed to substantiate their findings, and they suggest some directions for future research.

In the second paper Candace Bos and her colleagues extend and embellish a study by Louisa Moats in 1994 on inservice teachers' knowledge about the structure of language. Here they examine and compare the perceptions and knowledge of both preservice and inservice educators about early reading instruction. Their findings have important implications for the preparation of teachers.

*Annals* readers who are interested in what the research says about teaching spelling will find the next two articles useful. Yolanda Post and her colleagues compared two approaches to spelling instruction in the first grade. One approach emphasized a linguistically explicit method based on instruction of phoneme/grapheme patterns; the other was an implicit method based mainly on rime analogies. Readers will be interested in seeing what the authors found out when they compared the two groups. The authors then provide several implications of their findings for spelling instruction.

In the past, Robert Schlagel has written a number of articles about the history of spelling and its development. Here he reviews several approaches to spelling; in particular, he describes findings that support a developmental view of spelling. Dr. Schlagel presents practical, research-based instructional suggestions on how to diagnose and teach spelling for teachers and clinicians. His comprehensive bibliography provides an up-to-date resource for both educators and researchers.

# Efficacy of Fast ForWord Training on Facilitating Acquisition of Reading Skills by Children with Reading Difficulties—A Longitudinal Study

*Pamela E. Hook*

MGH Institute of Health Professions
Boston, Massachusetts

*Paul Macaruso*

Community College of Rhode Island
Providence, Rhode Island

*Sandra Jones*

Independent Educational Consultant
Boston, Massachusetts

*We explored the effects of Fast ForWord (FFW) training on reading and spoken language skills in children with difficulties in phonemic awareness and word identification. Gains were examined both immediately after treatment and over a period of two years. In the short term, children who received FFW training were compared to children who received Orton Gillingham (OG) training. The FFW group was also compared to a matched longitudinal control group (LC); all participants in the FFW and LC groups received similar multisensory structured language instruction over two academic years. The FFW and OG groups made similar gains in phonemic awareness. However, the children who received FFW training did not show significant*

Annals of Dyslexia, Vol. 51, 2001
ISSN 0736-9387

*gains in word identification or word attack whereas the children who received OG training made significant gains in word attack. Immediately after treatment, the FFW group showed significant gains in speaking and syntax, but these gains were not maintained over two years. The FFW group did not differ significantly from the LC group in any areas over the two years. Children in both groups made significant progress in phonemic awareness and reading.*

Difficulty in acquiring reading skills is a substantial problem for at least 80 percent of children diagnosed with specific learning disabilities (Lyon, 1995). While effective reading requires both adequate underlying oral language skills and the ability to identify words in print automatically, research has shown that difficulties in automatic word identification seriously interfere with reading fluency and comprehension (Perfetti & Hogaboam, 1975; Share & Stanovich, 1995). A "core phonological processing deficit" has been posited as the most salient problem associated with weaknesses in word identification (Share & Stanovich, 1995; Torgesen, Wagner, & Rashotte, 1997). Within the area of phonological processing, phonemic awareness (i.e., the ability to perceive, segment, and manipulate sounds) is considered critical for learning word decoding strategies (Adams, 1990; Foorman, Francis, Novy, & Liberman, 1991; Liberman & Shankweiler, 1985: Wagner, & Torgesen, 1987). Additional phonological processing difficulties associated with reading problems include rapid automatic naming (Bowers & Swanson, 1991; see also the double deficit hypothesis discussed by Wolf, 1997) and verbal short-term or working memory (Brady, 1986; Stone & Brady 1995).

Tallal and her colleagues have argued that the phonological processing difficulties of children with reading problems may reflect a broader auditory processing impairment that includes processing of nonverbal tones (e.g., Tallal, Miller, Jenkins, & Merzenich, 1997). Tallal (1980) found that children with reading impairments had significantly more difficulty than normal readers on both temporal order judgment and discrimination tasks involving nonverbal auditory perception. The distinction was evident, however, only when stimuli were presented rapidly. For example, when two computer-generated non-speech tones were presented with short interstimulus intervals (8–305 ms), children with reading disabilities had significantly more difficulty responding than normals, but not when the interstimulus interval was longer (428 ms). She found a high correlation between number of errors on reading nonsense words and number of errors on responses to rapidly presented auditory stimuli. Tallal suggested that children with reading disorders suffer from ". . . inefficiencies or deficiencies of the processing mechanisms essential for processing the rapidly changing acoustic spectra which characterize the ongoing speech stream . . ." (Tallal, 1984, p. 168). She argued that "difficulty in analyzing rapid information may lead to difficulty in analyzing speech at the phonemic level. This basic perceptual difficulty may account, at least in part, for some of the difficulties Liberman et al. [1976] have found poor readers to have segmenting and recoding phonemically" (Tallal, 1980, p. 196).

Reed (1989) also found that children with reading disabilities have significantly more difficulty than normal readers in processing auditory cues, particularly when dealing with very brief tones and stop consonants. In an extensive review of the literature, Farmer and Klein (1995) concluded that children with reading disabilities evidence difficulties in "temporal processing" for nonverbal, auditory, visual, and tactile information. They described difficulties in discriminating rapid acoustic changes as well as in motor sequencing abilities.

It should be noted, however, that some researchers have failed to find a relationship between temporal processing deficits and phonological processing problems in normal and poor readers (e.g., McAnally, Hansen, Cornelissen, & Stein, 1997; Nittrouer, 1999). In fact, Tallal and Stark (1982) did not find significant temporal processing deficits in children identified as having reading difficulties but without spoken language impairments. They concluded that reading impaired children with and without spoken language deficits may show different patterns of auditory perception abilities.[1]

---

[1] There is considerable debate in the literature regarding what constitutes a "temporal processing deficit." Studdert-Kennedy and Mody (1995) argue that "difficulties of some impaired readers with rapid temporal order judgments in speech and/or nonspeech seem to reflect independent deficits in discriminative capacity of unknown origin, not a general deficit in either 'temporal processing or rate of auditory perception'"(p. 513). They believe the problem in discriminating speech sounds is phonetic in origin and results from similarity in production rather than from speed of formant transitions. For example, in a group of reading disabled children, they found deficits in the ability to discriminate the syllable pair /ba/ and /da/, but adequate ability to discriminate /ba/ and /sa/. These stimuli contain equally rapidly changing consonant transitions but differ in phonetic similarity (/ba/ and /da/ differ only on place of articulation whereas /ba/ and /sa/ differ on place and voicing). It has been suggested that phonetic similarity makes /ba/ and /da/ difficult to discriminate; thus, the deficit is in the area of phonological coding rather than rate of auditory perception (Mody, Studdert-Kennedy & Brady, 1997; Nittrouer, 1999).

Prior to their work with children with reading problems, Tallal and her colleagues studied children with spoken language disorders and concluded that they have deficits in speed of auditory processing, particularly affecting the perception of rapidly occurring consonant transitions (e.g., as seen in the formants distinguishing /ba/ from /da/) (Tallal & Piercy, 1973). Given the assumption that these deficits in auditory processing significantly affect the child's ability to acquire spoken language skills, Tallal and her colleagues developed remedial activities using acoustically modified speech. The speech was altered by expanding the rapid consonant transitions from 40 to 80 milliseconds and intensifying that part of the stimulus by 20 db. Although the information processing effects of these modifications are not yet fully understood, the activities appear to improve processing of normal speech. Researchers have reported significant gains in language comprehension and expression through the use of this modified speech (Merzenich et al., 1996; Tallal et al., 1996; Tallal, Miller, & Fitch, 1993; Tallal et al., 1997). Based on this research, the Fast ForWord (FFW) computer programs (currrently called Fast ForWord Language) were developed to increase auditory processing skills in children with spoken language disability. Although the FFW programs were initially developed for children with spoken language disorders, Scientific Learning Corporation, publishers of FFW, proposed that FFW training also benefits children with reading disabilities (Fast ForWord, 1998). Their current website includes the following statement: "Developed by leaders in brain research, Fast ForWord Language helps students simultaneously cross-train multiple skills and adapts each exercise based on a student's progress to improve language and reading skills" (Scientific Learning Corporation, 2001).

There is, therefore, a need to carefully examine the efficacy of FFW in improving phonemic awareness and reading skills in children with reading disabilities. Although it is well recognized that difficulties in developing phonemic awareness may impede the acquisition of word identification skills, current methods of teaching phonic word attack strategies to children with reading disabilities are usually effective in developing these skills (Brady, Scarborough, & Shankweiler, 1996; Torgesen, Wagner, & Rashotte, 1994). Specifically, structured language techniques such as Orton Gillingham (Gillingham & Stillman, 1997) or the Lindamood Phoneme Sequencing Program (LiPS) (Lindamood & Lindamood, 1998) have been designed to develop an understanding of the phonological structure of language while also teaching alphabetic reading skills. Even if FFW is shown to contribute to increasing phonemic awareness, and thus word identification skills, it is important to determine whether more traditional methods on their own are equally effective, particularly considering the time-intensive nature and the relatively high cost of the FFW programs (Brady et al., 1996).

In this study, we investigated the benefits of FFW training on the development of reading/spelling skills in children with reading disabilities, as well as its effect on receptive and expressive spoken language skills including phonemic awareness, semantics, syntax, rapid naming, and verbal working memory. Previous research has not considered carefully the impact of FFW treatment on all of these skills in children with reading disabilities. We considered both short-term benefits and long-term gains over a period of two academic years. In the short term, we compared a group of children receiving FFW training (FFW group) to a group of children who participated in a relatively intensive Orton Gillingham program (OG group). In the long term, we compared the FFW group to a longitudinal control group (LC group); children in both groups had similar levels of reading difficulties and received multisensory structured language instruction over a period of two academic years.

This research study addressed the following questions:

1. Did children in the FFW group show immediate improvements in phonemic awareness, word identification accuracy, and word attack strategies relative to the OG group?

2. Did children in the FFW group show facilitated acquisition of phonemic awareness, reading, and spelling skills over a period of two years in comparison to the LC group?

3. Did children in the FFW group show immediate and long-term gains in receptive and expressive language, rapid naming, and verbal working memory?

4. Were gains over the two-year period greater than for the LC group?

5. Did certain FFW activities prove to be harder for children in the FFW group, and did performance on any of these activities correlate with changes in reading?

# METHOD

## PARTICIPANTS

Children in the FFW group were selected on the basis of a flyer distributed through a newspaper in the greater Boston, Massachusetts, area recruiting children with reading difficulties. Children whose parents responded to the flyer were screened for reading level with the Word Attack and Word Identification subtests from the *Woodcock Reading Mastery Test-Revised* (Woodcock, 1987). All respondents had previously been administered the *Wechsler Intelligence Scale for Children-Third Edition (WISC-III)* (Wechsler, 1991). To be considered for participation in the study, children were required to have a Full Scale IQ of 80 or above and a Verbal IQ of 90 or above. Children were included in the study if they scored below the 16th percentile on the Word Attack and/or Word Identification subtests, or had a Verbal IQ at least 1 standard deviation above their Word Attack and/or Word Identification scores. Subjects with a history of significant emotional disturbance were excluded from the study. Eleven children met the criteria for participation in the FFW group. They ranged from 7 to 12 years and demonstrated adequate vision (with correction if needed) and hearing as evidenced through screening across the frequencies (500 hz, 1000 hz, 2000 hz, and 4,000 hz) at 20 db. All children were Caucasian from middle- to upper middle-class backgrounds.

Members of the OG group were chosen from students enrolled in a summer school for children with reading difficulties. Children closely matched to the FFW group on the basis of age, Full Scale IQ, phonemic awareness ability as measured by the *Lindamood Auditory Conceptualization Test (LAC)* (Lindamood & Lindamood, 1979), and reading level were selected for this study. There were nine children in the OG group. Children in the LC group were matched to the FFW group on the basis of the same criteria as well as a similar educational program/curriculum. This group was comprised of 11 children.

Descriptive data for the three groups are shown in table I. There were no significant differences between the FFW and OG groups in age, IQ, *LAC*, Word Identification, or Word Attack. The only significant difference between the FFW and the LC groups occurred on the Performance IQ ($t(20) = 2.69$, $p < .014$). However, treatment gains in phonemic awareness, spoken language, and written language did not correlate significantly with Performance IQ.

Table I.    Basic Descriptive Information for Groups.

| | FFW Group N=11 (9 boys, 2 girls) | | OG Group N=9 (8 boys, 1 girl) | | LC Group N=11 (7 boys, 4 girls) | |
|---|---|---|---|---|---|---|
| | Mean | (SD) | Mean | (SD) | Mean | (SD) |
| Age (mos) | 116 | (20) | 117 | (10) | 116 | (17) |
| WISC-III (SS) | | | | | | |
| Verbal | 103 | (11) | 96 | (9) | 107 | (10) |
| Performance | 92 | (10) | 100 | (9) | 103 | (10) |
| Full Scale | 97 | (9) | 98 | (9) | 105 | (9) |
| LAC (WS) | 65 | (22) | 68 | (17) | 70 | (18) |
| WRMT-R (SS) | | | | | | |
| Word Identification | 77 | (10) | 74 | (11) | 73 | (15) |
| Word Attack | 83 | (10) | 82 | (6) | 82 | (8) |

*Note:* WISC-III = Wechsler Intelligence Scale for Children—III; LAC = Lindamood Auditory Conceptualization Test; WRMT-R = Woodcock Reading Mastery Test-Revised; SS = standard score; WS = weighted score.

## PROCEDURES

*FFW Treatment.*    The FFW treatment period lasted for two months, from late June to late August. Participants worked five days a week for approximately two hours a day. They completed five out of seven computer activities daily that took roughly 20 minutes each for a total of 100 minutes with two 10-minute breaks. Treatment continued until the child had reached the criterion set by Scientific Learning which was successful completion of five of the seven activities at a level of 90 percent or better, or until an obvious plateau had been reached. Children varied in completion time from 22 to 44 days, depending on individual performances (see table III.)

A group lab was set up with 8 to 10 children in each lab. There were 1 or 2 research assistants per lab with aides to monitor children during breaks. The researchers were available on-site during the treatment for consultation and analysis of data. Token reinforcement was used to motivate the children to remain engaged in the activities.

A description of the FFW activities can be found in figure 1. All speech-based activities began with acoustically modified speech (consonant transitions are stretched to 80 ms. and intensified by 20 db.) and systematically moved to normal speech based on the child's performance.

1.  Circus Sequence: child must identify the order of nonspeech tones with an increasingly short inter-stimulus interval (ISI) (from 80ms to 20ms) across the speech spectrum (from 500Hz to 2000Hz). Child indicates whether the first tone was higher, lower, or the same as the second.

2.  Old MacDonald's Flying Farm: requires child to distinguish phonemic sound changes in acoustically modified speech, such as /chu/ – /shu/ and /ge/ – /ke/.

3.  Phoneme Identification: child must discriminate between minimal pairs such as /va/ – /fa/ and /bi/ – /di/.

4.  Phonic Match: child must discriminate between and remember simple word structures differing by one or more consonants in words such as "train" – "plain."

5.  Phonic Word: child must recognize words that differ in one phoneme (e.g. "wash" – "watch") and chooses the appropriate picture.

6.  Block Commander: child must indicate comprehension of commands of increasingly complex syntax (e.g. "Touch the red circle." [Easy] to "Touch the squares except the yellow one." [Difficult]). Child uses the computer mouse to follow the given direction.

7.  Language Comprehension Builder: child must indicate comprehension of sentences containing increasingly complex morphology and syntax (e.g. "The clown has a balloon." [Easy] to "The clown that is holding the balloon that is blue is red." [Difficult]). Child chooses the appropriate picture.

Note:  All activities using speech stimuli begin with acoustically modified speech (consonant transitions are lengthened from 40 to 80 ms and intensified by 20 db) and systematically move to normal speech while keeping the child at 80 percent accuracy levels.

Figure 1.    Description of Fast ForWord Activities

*OG Treatment.* The Orton Gillingham (OG) treatment involved one hour a day of one-on-one remediation five days a week for five weeks from late June to early August. The OG teaching method is a multisensory structured language approach that incorporates the following principles of teaching: emphasis on the alphabetic code, systematic and explicit presentation of concepts, consistent review of previously presented material, and emphasis on rule acquisition and application. This type of explicit phonics approach has been found to be effective in increasing reading skills in children who have specific reading disabilities (Torgesen et al., 1997).

*Educational Programs: FFW and LC Groups.* Children in the FFW and LC groups participated in multisensory structured language programs through their school districts or after-school programs. Although the programs were not identical, all children received explicit instruction based on their individual needs throughout the two year follow up.

## ASSESSMENT TIME FRAME

There were four assessment periods. The first one occurred in early summer (T1) prior to the FFW and OG treatments. The FFW group received a full battery of tests while the OG group received a partial test battery. The test battery is described later in this study.

The second assessment period occurred at the end of summer/early fall (T2) immediately following FFW or OG treatment. The FFW group received the full test battery and the OG group was given the partial battery. At this time, the LC group received the full battery.

The last two assessment periods were at the end of Academic Year 1 (T3) and end of Academic Year 2 (T4). The FFW and LC groups both received the full battery.

## MATERIALS

The full test battery was administered to the FFW and LC groups and required approximately three hours to complete. The OG group received a partial test battery (*LAC*, Word Identification, and Word Attack) that took about 45 minutes.

*Phonemic Awareness.* The *Lindamood Auditory Conceptualization Test* (LAC) (Lindamood & Lindamood, 1979) was administered to assess phonemic awareness. This test required mapping a sound pattern onto a pattern of colored blocks, first with individual phonemes and then within nonsense syllables. Raw scores on this test were used to create a weighted score that reflects the increasing difficulty of items. The first section gives one point for each correct response, the second section gives three points for each correct response and the last section gives six points for each correct response.

*Spoken Language.*    As a tool to assess receptive and expressive spoken language skills, the appropriate level of the *Test of Language Development (TOLD)* was administered to children in the FFW and LC groups: *TOLD-P:3* [ages 4–8] (Hammill & Newcomer, 1997); *TOLD-I:2* [ages 8–12] (Hammill & Newcomer, 1988); and *Test of Adolescent and Adult Language Development (TOAL-3)* [ages 12–24]) (Hammill, Brown, Larsen, & Wiederholt, 1994). Publishers of the *TOLD* report highly significant intertest correlations between the *TOLD-I:2* and *TOAL-P:3* and suggest that these tests may be used interchangeably (Hammill & Newcomer, 1988). Subtests of the *TOLD* assess various aspects of spoken language comprehension and use of vocabulary and grammar. Standard scores (mean 100, *SD* 15) derived from the composite scores for Listening, Speaking, Semantics, and Syntax were used in the analyses. For ease of reporting, all of these tests are referred to as the TOLD/TOAL in Results and Discussion sections. Due to scheduling difficulties, data on the TOLD/TOAL for two LC participants were not collected.

*Reading.*    Reading skills were assessed with three subtests from the *Woodcock Reading Mastery Test-R* (Woodcock, 1987): Word Identification (WI) requires reading isolated words aloud; Word Attack (WA) requires reading nonsense words aloud; and Passage Comprehension (PC) requires silent reading of sentences and determination of a missing word through a cloze procedure. Alternate forms were used at each testing. Each subtest yields a standard score (mean 100, *SD* 15).

*Spelling.*    The ability to spell both regular and irregular words was measured by the *Test of Written Spelling-3 (TWS-3)* (Larsen & Hammill, 1994). Predictable Words have regular sound/symbol correspondences, whereas Unpredictable Words have some irregular sound/symbol correspondences. These subtests also provide standard scores (mean 100, *SD* 15).

*Rapid Naming.*    The test of *Rapid Automatic Naming and Rapid Alternating Stimulus (RAN-RAS)* (Denkla & Rudel, 1976) was used to assess rapid naming skills. Four tasks required the rapid naming of a series of five repeated objects (*RAN* Objects), numbers (*RAN* Numbers), or letters (*RAN* Letters), or four to six alternating letters and numbers (RAS). Results are reported as number of items named per second. Data from one FFW participant were deemed invalid and omitted from the analyses because he had very long pauses seemingly related to fluency issues.

*Working Memory.* The Numbers Reversed subtest from the *Woodcock-Johnson Test of Cognitive Abilities* (Woodcock & Johnson, 1989) was administered to assess working memory. This task required the repetition of increasingly complex strings of numbers in reverse order. Standard scores (mean 100, *SD* 15) were analyzed.

# RESULTS

A complete summary of results for each group (OG, FFW, LC) across the four time periods (T1–T4) is shown in table II. Below, we provide analyses to address the four research questions.

## FFW AND OG

Did children in the FFW group show immediate improvements (T1 versus T2) in phonemic awareness (LAC), word identification (WI), and word attack (WA) relative to the OG group?

For the LAC, a repeated measures ANOVA revealed a significant effect of Time ($F[1,18] = 9.07$, $p = .007$; effect size: $\eta^2 = .33$) but no significant Group by Time interaction. Thus both groups made similar gains on the LAC. For WI, there was no significant effect of Time or a significant interaction between Group and Time. For WA, the effect of Time was not significant; however, the Group by Time interaction reached significance ($F[1,18] = 5.55$, $p = .030$; effect size: $\eta^2 = .22$). Post hoc t tests revealed significant gains in WA for the OG group ($t[8] = 2.49$, $p = .038$) but not the FFW group. Note that there was no significant gain in passage comprehension (PC) for the FFW group from T1 to T2 (not tested in the OG group).

## FFW AND LC (PHONEMIC AWARENESS, READING, AND SPELLING)

Did children in the FFW group show facilitated acquisition of phonemic awareness (LAC), reading (WI, WA, PC), and spelling (TWS) over a period of two years (T2 versus T3 versus T4) in comparison to the LC group?

A significant effect of Time ($F[2,40] = 6.61$, $p = .003$; effect size: $\eta^2 = .24$) but no significant Group by Time interaction was found for the LAC. A test of Time main effects (collapsed across Group) revealed a significant gain from T2 to T4 ($F[1,21] = 13.46$, $p < .001$), but intermediate gains from T2 to T3 and T3 to

**Table II.   Mean Scores and Standard Deviations** *(in parentheses)* **for the OG, FFW, and LC Groups.**

| | T1: June before AY 1 | | T2: Sept begin AY 1 | | | T3: End of AY 1 | | T4: End of AY 2 | |
|---|---|---|---|---|---|---|---|---|---|
| | OG | FFW | OG | FFW | LC | FFW | LC | FFW | LC |
| LAC (WS) | 68.2 | 65.0 | 76.0 | 74.5 | 70.4 | 76.5 | 78.5 | 85.2 | 82.4 |
| | (17.0) | (22.0) | (13.1) | (13.5) | (17.8) | (16.2) | (11.6) | (17.0) | (15.1) |
| **WRMT (SS)** | | | | | | | | | |
| WI | 74.3 | 76.5 | 75.3 | 74.4 | 73.3 | 77.8 | 78.6 | 83.7 | 78.1 |
| | (10.9) | (9.9) | (12.0) | (12.5) | (15.0) | (13.4) | (11.2) | (12.0) | (13.5) |
| WA | 82.4 | 83.3 | 88.2 | 81.7 | 81.6 | 86.9 | 89.9 | 89.8 | 90.5 |
| | (5.9) | (9.8) | (6.3) | (9.8) | (8.0) | (8.6) | (7.1) | (8.3) | (12.7) |
| PC | | 74.9 | | 75.6 | 73.7 | 80.9 | 76.4 | 85.1 | 81.7 |
| | | (16.7) | | (10.8) | (14.6) | (15.8) | (14.2) | (11.3) | (15.8) |
| **TWS (SS)** | | | | | | | | | |
| PRE | | 82.5 | | 81.1 | 83.8 | 84.8 | 85.7 | 86.1 | 83.9 |
| | | (7.3) | | (6.5) | (8.1) | (7.8) | (5.9) | (8.7) | (5.4) |
| UNPRE | | 71.4 | | 73.3 | 72.7 | 72.5 | 72.5 | 74.2 | 72.8 |
| | | (6.3) | | (9.9) | (7.6) | (10.2) | (8.5) | (12.0) | (9.6) |
| **TOLD/ TOAL (SS)** | | | | | | | | | |
| LIS | | 100.1 | | 103.2 | 98.0 | 102.2 | 100.4 | 98.8 | 96.4 |
| | | (12.9) | | (13.0) | (12.7) | (12.3) | (13.8) | (14.3) | (14.1) |
| SP | | 90.2 | | 94.5 | 81.6 | 91.5 | 81.0 | 87.6 | 85.2 |
| | | (13.8) | | (12.3) | (12.2) | (11.3) | (14.0) | (14.3) | (17.0) |
| SEM | | 100.5 | | 102.5 | 95.7 | 103.4 | 99.3 | 96.5 | 97.9 |
| | | (13.2) | | (12.3) | (13.9) | (12.2) | (15.4) | (14.1) | (15.5) |
| SYN | | 86.5 | | 93.7 | 84.7 | 89.8 | 82.9 | 89.8 | 83.8 |
| | | (11.1) | | (10.8) | (11.8) | (11.5) | (13.2) | (13.4) | (16.1) |
| W/J-NR (SS) | | 88.5 | | 92.1 | 88.5 | 92.2 | 94.5 | 91.8 | 100.2 |
| | | (8.4) | | (11.1) | (13.0) | (7.7) | (17.4) | (12.6) | (18.3) |
| RAN-COM (I/S) | | 1.21 | | 1.22 | 1.27 | 1.57 | 1.36 | 1.62 | 1.57 |
| | | (.45) | | (.36) | (.41) | (.41) | (.33) | (.37) | (.39) |
| RAS (I/S) | | 1.03 | | 1.09 | 1.09 | 1.44 | 1.22 | 1.49 | 1.41 |
| | | (.40) | | (.42) | (.40) | (.40) | (.36) | (.39) | (.42) |

*Note:* OG = Orton Gillingham group; FFW = Fast ForWord group; LC = Longitudinal Control group; T = time of testing; AY = academic year; LAC = Lindamood Auditory Conceptualization Test; WRMT = Woodcock Reading Mastery Test-Revised; WI = Word Identification; WA = Word Attack; PC = Passage Comprehension; TWS = Test of Written Spelling; PRE = Predictable; UNPRE = Unpredictable; TOLD = Test of Language Development; TOAL = Test of Adolescent Language; LIS = Listening; SP = Speaking; SEM = Semantics; SYN = Syntax; W/J-NR = Woodcock/Johnson Numbers Reversed; RAN = Rapid Automatic Naming; COM = Composite; RAS = Rapid Alternating Stimulus; WS = weighted score; SS = standard score; I/S = items per second

T4 failed to reach significance. Significant effects of Time but no significant Group by Time interactions were obtained for all three reading tests: WI ($F[2,40]$ = 10.40, $p$ < .001; effect size: $\eta^2$ = .32), WA ($F[2,40]$ = 13.99, $p$ < .001; effect size: $\eta^2$ = .41), and PC ($F[2,40]$ = 10.00, $p$ < .001; effect size: $\eta^2$ = .33). Tests of main effects revealed significant gains from T2 to T3 for WI ($F[1,21]$ = 8.14, $p$ = .010), and from T2 to T3 for WA ($F[1,21]$ = 27.00, $p$ < .001). For PC, significant gains were found from T2 to T3 ($F[1,21]$ = 5.06, $p$ = .035) and T3 to T4 ($F[1,21]$ = 5.75, $p$ = .026). No significant Time or Group by Time effects were obtained on the TWS Predictable or Unpredictable subtests. Note that there were no significant gains for the FFW group on the TWS subtests from T1 to T2 (not tested in the LC group).

### FFW AND LC (SPOKEN LANGUAGE, RAPID NAMING, AND VERBAL WORKING MEMORY)

Did children in the FFW group show immediate and long-term gains in receptive and expressive language (TOLD/TOAL), rapid naming (RAN-RAS), and verbal working memory (Numbers Reversed)? Were gains over the two-year period greater than for the LC group?

The first set of analyses examined immediate gains (T1 versus T2) for the FFW group in receptive and expressive language, rapid naming, and working memory. The FFW group made significant gains on composite Speaking and Syntax scores from the TOLD/TOAL (Speaking: t(10) = 4.24, $p$ = .002; effect size: $r^2_{pb}$ = .64; Syntax: t(10) = 5.45, $p$ < .001; effect size: $r^2_{pb}$ = .75). No significant gains were found on the composite Listening and Semantics scores. To simplify analyses of RAN-RAS performance, we created a composite RAN score by averaging performance (mean items per second) across the three RAN tasks (Objects, Numbers, Letters). All pair-wise correlations among the three RAN tasks at each time period (for the FFW and LC groups analyzed separately and combined) were significant ($p$ < .05). The FFW group showed no significant gains from T1 to T2 on composite RAN, RAS, and Numbers Reversed.

The second set of analyses compared gains made by the FFW and LC groups from T2–T4 on TOLD/TOAL, RAN-RAS, and Numbers Reversed. There were no significant effects of Time or any Group by Time interactions for the four composite scores from TOLD/TOAL. Additional analyses for the FFW group showed that the initial gains from T1 to T2 on composite Speaking and Syntax scores from the TOLD/TOAL were not maintained when T1 was compared to T3 and T4.

For composite RAN, there was a significant effect of Time ($F[2,38] = 61.46$, $p < .001$; effect size: $\eta^2 = .69$) and a significant Group by Time interaction ($F[2,38] = 8.19$, $p = .001$; effect size: $\eta^2 = .09$). The Group effect was not significant. Posthoc t–tests revealed that the FFW group made a significant gain from T2 to T3 ($t[9] = 6.82$, $p < .001$), but the gain from T3 to T4 failed to reach significance. In contrast, the LC group did not show a significant gain from T2 to T3 but the gain from T3 to T4 was significant ($t[10] = 5.24$, $p < .001$). Analyses of RAS performance showed similar results as composite RAN scores. No significant Time or Group by Time effects were found for Numbers Reversed.

## FFW ACTIVITIES AND READING

Did certain FFW activities prove to be harder for children in the FFW group and did performance on any of these activities correlate with changes in reading?

The seven FFW activities required processing of different kinds of auditory information: nonverbal tones (Circus Sequence), isolated speech sounds (Phoneme Identification, Old MacDonald's Flying Farm), and meaningful words and sentences (Phonic Match, Language Comprehension Builder, Phonic Word, Block Commander). Successful completion of an activity was defined as at least 90 percent completion over three sessions. As shown in table III, four of the 11 children reached this level on five activities (defined as successful completion of the FFW Program) whereas four others achieved this level on four out of seven activities. There was a significant correlation between the total number of activities that were successfully completed (TAC) and age ($r = .66$, $p = .030$), but no significant correlations between TAC and gains from T1 to T4 on any measures of receptive or expressive language, phonemic awareness or reading.

As can be seen in table III, some of the activities were more difficult than others for the children to master. Only one of the 11 children reached criterion of >90 percent completion level (PCL) on Circus Sequence. Five children obtained a <10 percent PCL, indicating minimal mastery of the task. Only two children reached a >90 percent PCL on Phoneme Identification. On the other phoneme level tasks (Old MacDonald's Flying Farm, Phonic Match), some children experienced difficulty reaching criterion but the majority did not (9 and 7 children reached criterion, respectively).

All children scored >90 percent PCL on two of the meaning-based activities, Language Comprehension Builder and Phonic Word. On the third meaning based activity, Block Commander, only one child had difficulty (31 percent PCL) while the other five children who did not meet criterion reached asymptote around 74 percent PLC.

Table III.  Percent Completion of Fast ForWord Activities, Days in Program, and Total Number of Activities Successfully Completed.

| | | | | Activities | | | | | |
|---|---|---|---|---|---|---|---|---|---|
| | CS | FF | PI | PM | PW | CB | BC | DIP | TAC |
| Student | (PC) | (PC) | (PC) | (PC) | (PC) | (PC) | (PC) | | |
| 1. MV | 2 | 98 | 14 | 73 | 99 | 97 | 31 | 31 | 3 |
| 2. KB | 99 | 98 | 90 | 96 | 98 | 99 | 96 | 22 | 7 |
| 3. MR | 18 | 98 | 58 | 95 | 98 | 97 | 97 | 36 | 5 |
| 4. RP | 1 | 98 | 14 | 91 | 99 | 96 | 74 | 28 | 4 |
| 5. MS | 0 | 5 | 4 | 52 | 95 | 97 | 74 | 38 | 2 |
| 6. CD | 73 | 98 | 97 | 96 | 99 | 99 | 96 | 22 | 6 |
| 7. JB | 0 | 100 | 18 | 93 | 98 | 98 | 74 | 44 | 4 |
| 8. BR | 39 | 90 | 51 | 80 | 98 | 97 | 96 | 41 | 4 |
| 9. JK | 33 | 98 | 74 | 95 | 99 | 99 | 93 | 27 | 5 |
| 10. NC | 2 | 36 | 10 | 50 | 98 | 98 | 73 | 42 | 2 |
| 11. MJ | 11 | 93 | 41 | 92 | 97 | 96 | 75 | 40 | 4 |

Note: CS = Circus Sequence; FF = Old MacDonalds's Flying Farm; PI = Phoneme Identification; PM = Phoneme Match; PW = Phonic Word; CB = Comprehension Builder; BC = Block Commander; PC = Percent Completion; DIP = days in program; TAC = total number of activities successfully completed

Correlations were examined between the PCL for the five FFW activities in which criterion was not met by all children (i.e., Circus Sequence, Old MacDonald's Flying Farm, Phoneme Identification, Phonic Match, Block Commander) and gains in WI, WA, and PC from T1 to T2 and T1 to T4. The only significant correlations were between Circus Sequence and gains in WI ($r = .70$, $p = .020$) and between Phoneme Identification and gains in WI ($r = .73$, $p = .010$) from T1 to T2. Block Commander, Circus Sequence, and Phoneme Identification were also significantly correlated with age ($r = .68$, $p = .020$; $r = .82$, $p = .002$; $r = .77$, $p = .005$, respectively).

## DISCUSSION

In this study, we examined the efficacy of Fast ForWord (FFW) for increasing written and spoken language skills in children with reading difficulties. To assess immediate effects of treatment, a FFW treatment group was compared to a matched Orton Gillingham treatment group (OG). We also examined the long-term effects of FFW treatment; the FFW group was compared to a matched longitudinal control group (LC) of children with reading disabilities. Both of these groups received similar intensive multisensory structured language remediation over a period of two academic years.

Analysis of outcomes showed that both treatment groups (FFW and OG) made gains in phonemic awareness immediately after treatment, while only the OG group made gains in word attack. Neither group made gains in word identification. The gains in phonemic awareness were consistent with research indicating that phonemic awareness is trainable (Ball & Blachman, 1991; Share & Stanovich, 1995). In the area of word attack, the increased gains made by the children in the OG treatment group were consistent with evidence that combining phonemic awareness training with direct instruction in the alphabetic code (how letters map onto sounds) was more successful in increasing reading skills than training in phonemic awareness alone (Ehri, 1989; Hatcher, Hulme, & Ellis, 1994). The lack of gains by either group in word identification concurred with other short-term studies and almost certainly reflected the length of time (only 5–8 weeks) between T1 and T2 (e.g., Torgesen et al., 1997).

Over the course of two academic years, the FFW group and the LC group made gains in phonemic awareness and all areas of reading (word attack, word identification, and passage comprehension). The extent of gain in each area was similar for both groups. Although some of the gains in phonemic awareness could be attributed to increased age (given that this test does not have standard scores), the higher standard scores in all areas of reading indicated that the children made more than one year gain per year. It appears that the multisensory structured approaches used with these children resulted in significant advances but that FFW did not result in additional or faster improvement.

In the area of spoken language, results indicated that the FFW group made gains in speaking and syntax immediately after FFW treatment. These findings were consistent with those of Merzenich et al. (1996) and could be interpreted as evidence that FFW improved spoken language function. Another possible explanation for these immediate gains, however, is that they were due to enhanced auditory attention after listening intensively to stimuli for an extended period of time. These gains also could be attributed in part to practice effects in that there is only one form of the TOLD/TOAL, and T2 occurred just two to three months after T1. Regardless of why the FFW group showed gains from T1 to T2, the gains were not maintained after two years.

Neither group made gains in spelling or verbal working memory over the two-year period. There were no gains in rapid naming immediately after FFW treatment, but increases were apparent in the FFW and LC groups over the two year follow-up period. Results for rapid naming are consistent with normative evidence that children increase in their naming speed with age (Wagner, Torgesen, & Rashotte, 1999).

Many of the participants in the FFW group did not reach the criterion established by Scientific Learning of at least 90 percent completion on five of the seven programs. The total number of activities successfully completed (TAC) was significantly correlated with age. Our findings were similar to those in a study of six- to eight-year-olds where none of the participants reached the criterion level (Nulty, Throneburg, & Smitley, 1999). The criterion has since been changed by Scientific Learning to 20 days of participation in the program, in which case all of our participants would be considered to have successfully completed the program. Nevertheless, TAC did not correlate with gains in phonemic awareness, reading, or receptive or expressive language; thus, the percent completion rate did not seem to be relevant in determining the effectiveness of FFW.

All children except one in the FFW group had trouble completing some of the FFW activities, particularly those involving identification of rapidly changing auditory stimuli signaling high versus low tones (Circus Sequence), or discriminating phonemes in nonsense syllables (Phoneme Identification). Children had an inordinate amount of difficulty on Circus Sequence. It is not clear whether this was related to the speed of the auditory stimuli or the complexity of the task. The children not only had to determine if the tones were the same or different but also, in the case of different tones, whether the higher or lower tone had come first. Performance was also correlated with age in that younger subjects had more difficulty on this task (see similar results in Waber et al., 2001).

Performance on Circus Sequence and Phoneme Identification correlated significantly with gains in word identification. The outcome for Circus Sequence was consistent with results of Waber et al. (2001), indicating that difficulties in single-word reading were related to poorer processing of nonlinguistic auditory stimuli. However, Waber et al.'s findings were not consistent with Tallal's theory that children with reading disabilities would show deficits related to stimuli presented at rapid rates but not slower rates; the effects of timing were comparable in children with and without learning disabilities.

Although we found that the children's performance on Circus Sequence was related to gains in word identification, their performance was not related to gains in phonemic awareness or word attack. It is unclear, therefore, whether our findings provided support for Tallal's hypothesis that reading disabled children had a deficit in processing rapidly presented auditory stimuli that affected their ability to perceive speech and, in turn, to develop phonemic awareness and related reading skills. We did find that the FFW group showed improvement in phonemic awareness immediately after treatment, indicating that some benefit may have been gained from participating in the tone identification activity, even if they could not master it. On the other hand, perhaps the fact that the speech in all FFW activities was acoustically modified at the level of the phoneme helped heighten their sensitivity of individual phonemes, thereby increasing their general phonemic awareness.

In conclusion, FFW improved phonemic awareness immediately after treatment but not more than a less intensive OG program, and the OG group made greater improvement in word attack. Over a two-year period, FFW did not appear to provide benefits in the rate of acquisition of word identification, word attack, or passage comprehension skills in children with reading disabilities who were receiving appropriate multisensory structured language intervention. Therefore, the intensive amount of time needed to complete the FFW activities and the expense involved did not seem warranted.

## LIMITATIONS OF THE STUDY

In drawing conclusions from our study, it must be kept in mind that the number of children involved was small. Larger samples need to be studied to consider more fully the effectiveness of FFW for children with reading difficulties.

Additionally, in terms of the efficacy of the FFW program for children with language-based learning disabilities, the selection criteria employed in this study may have had some effect on the outcomes. All of our participants initially had difficulties in phonemic awareness but average (or above) Verbal IQ and receptive language skills. As a group, the children did show some difficulties in syntax. The spoken language characteristics of our participants were consistent, however, with those often seen in children with specific reading disability (see Smith, Macaruso, Shankweiler, & Crain, 1989; Stein, Cairns, & Zurif, 1984). For this reason, it was felt that this study appropriately addressed claims made by Scientific Learning regarding the benefits of FFW for children with reading disabilities. Results of this study, on the other hand, did not address the efficacy of FFW for children who have more extensive or different kinds of auditory processing and spoken language difficulties. It is, therefore, critical to consider the spoken language characteristics of children referred for FFW.

**IMPLICATIONS FOR FUTURE RESEARCH**

Scientific Learning has recently developed programs designed specifically to teach reading such as Fast ForWord Language to Reading. Currently, children are encouraged to go through Fast ForWord Language before completing Fast ForWord Language to Reading. Regardless of the effectiveness of the Fast ForWord Language to Reading program, results of our study indicate that it may not be necessary for some children with reading problems (e.g., those with average receptive language skills) to complete Fast ForWord Language prior to completing the Fast ForWord Language to Reading program. A current study is underway to examine the efficacy of the Fast ForWord Language to Reading program for children with specific reading problems who have had Fast ForWord Language compared to a matched control group of children who have not.

# ACKNOWLEDGEMENTS

Funding for this research was provided by the Stratford Foundation. We also would like to thank Cindy Patten for her invaluable help in completing this study as well as the children, parents, and teachers who were involved in the project. Additionally, we are grateful for the helpful suggestions of the anonymous reviewers.

Address correspondence to Pamela E. Hook, Graduate Program in Communication Sciences and Disorders, MGH Institute of Health Professions, 101 Merrimac Street, Boston, MA 02114; e-mail: phook@partners.org.

## References

Adams, J. J. (1990). *Beginning to read: Thinking and learning about print.* Cambridge, MA: The MIT Press.

Ball, E. W., & Blachman, B. A. (1991). Does phoneme awareness training in kindergarten make a difference in early word recognition and spelling development? *Reading Research Quarterly, 26,* 46–66.

Bowers, P. G., & Swanson, L. B. (1991). Naming speed deficits in reading disability: Multiple measures of a singular process. *Journal of Experimental Child Psychology, 51,* 195–219.

Brady, S. (1986). Short-term memory, phonological processing and reading ability. *Annals of Dyslexia, 36,* 138–153.

Brady, S., Scarborough, H., & Shankweiler, D. (1996). A perspective on two recent research reports. *Perspectives:* (The International Dyslexia Association), 5–8.

Denkla, M. B., & Rudel, R. G. (1976). Rapid automatized naming (R. A. N.): Dyslexia differentiated from other learning disabilities. *Neurpsychologia, 14,* 471–79.

Ehri, L. C. (1989). Development of spelling knowledge and its role in reading acquisition and reading disabilities. *Journal of Learning Disabilities, 22,* 356–365.

Farmer, M. E., & Klein, R. (1995). The evidence of a temporal processing deficit linked to dyslexia: A review. *Psychonomic Bulletin and Review, 2(4),* 460–493.

Fast ForWord: Language takes us everywhere. Your summer jump start kit. (1998). Berkeley, CA: Scientific Learning Corporation.

Foorman, B. R., Francis, D. J., Novy, D. M., & Liberman, D. (1991). How letter sound interaction mediated progress in first-grade reading and spelling. *Journal of Educational Psychology, 83,* 456–459.

Gillingham, A., & Stillman, B. W. (1997). *The Gillingham manual,* 8th edition. Cambridge, MA: Educators Publishing Service, Inc.

Hammill, D. D., Brown, V.A., Larsen, S. C., & Wiederholt, J. L. (1994). *Test of adolescent and adult language—intermediate,* 3rd edition. Austin: PRO-ED.

Hammill, D. D., & Newcomer, P. L. (1988). *Test of language development—intermediate:* 2nd edition. Austin: PRO-ED.

Hammill, D. D., & Newcomer, P. L. (1997). *Test of language development—primary,* 3rd edition. Austin: PRO-ED.

Hatcher, P., Hulme, C., & Ellis, A. W. (1994). Ameliorating early reading failure by integrating the teaching of reading and phonological skills: The phonological linkage hypothesis. *Child Development, 65,* 41–57.

Larsen, S. C., & Hammill, D. D. (1994). *Test of written spelling,* 3rd edition. Austin: PRO-ED.

Liberman, I. Y., & Shankweiler, D. (1985). Phonology and the problems of learning to read and write. *Remedial and Special Education, 6,* 8–17.

Liberman, I. Y., Shankweiler, D., Liberman, A. M., Fowler, D. C., & Fischer, F. W. (1976). Phonetic segmentation and recoding in the beginning reader. In A. S. Reber & D. Scarborough (eds.), *Reading: Theory and practice.* Hillsdale, NJ: Lawrence Erlbaum Associates.

Lindamood, C., & Lindamood, P. (1979). *Lindamood auditory conceptualization test.* Austin, PRO-ED.

Lindamood, C., & Lindamood, P. (1998). *Lindamood phoneme sequencing program (LiPS).* Austin, PRO-ED.

Lyon, F. R. (1995). Research initiatives in learning disabilities: Contributions from scientists supported by the National Institute of Child Health and Human Development. *Journal of Child Neurology, 10,* 120–126.

McAnally, K. I., Hansen, P. C., Cornelissen, P. L., & Stein, J. F. (1997). Effect of time and frequency manipulation on syllable perception in developmental dyslexics. *Journal of Speech, Language, and Hearing Research, 40*, 912–924.

Merzenich, M. M., Jenkins, W. M., Johnson, P., Scheiner, C., Miller, S. L., & Tallal, P. (1996). Temporal processing deficits of language-learning impaired children ameliorated by training. *Science, 271*, 77–81.

Mody, M., Studdert-Kennedy, M., & Brady, S. (1997). Speech perception deficits in poor readers: Auditory processing or phonological coding? *Journal of Experimental Child Psychology, 64*, 199–231.

Nittrouer, S. (1999). Do temporal processing deficits cause phonological processing problems? *Journal of Speech Language and Hearing Research, 42*, 925–942.

Nulty, M., Throneburg, R., & Smitley, J. (1999). Impact of Fast ForWord training on phonologic awareness, reading and other language skills, Poster session presented at the American Speech and Hearing Association Convention, November, 1999, San Francisco.

Perfetti, C., & Hogaboam, T. (1975). The relationship between single word decoding and reading comprehension. *Journal of Education Psychology, 67*, 461–469.

Reed, M. A. (1989). Speech perception and the discrimination of brief auditory cues in reading disabled children. *Journal of Experimental Child Psychology, 48*, 270–292.

Scientific Learning Corporation. Retrieved March 11, 2001, from the World Wide Web: http://www.scientificlearning.com

Share, D. L., & Stanovich, K. E. (1995). Cognitive processes in early reading development: A model of acquisition and individual differences. *Issues in Education: Contributions from Educational Psychology, 1*, 1–57.

Smith, S., Macaruso, P., Shankweiler, D., & Crain, S. (1989). Syntactic comprehension in young poor readers. *Applied Psycholinguists, 10*, 429–454.

Stein, C. L., Cairns, H. S., & Zurif, E. B. (1984). Sentence comprehension limitations related to syntactic deficits in reading-disabled children. *Applied Psycholinguistics, 5*, 305–322.

Stone, B., & Brady, S. D. (1995). Evidence for phonological processing deficits in less-skilled readers. *Annals of Dyslexia, 45*, 51–78.

Studdert-Kennedy, M., & Mody, M. (1995). Auditory temporal perception deficits in the reading-impaired: A critical review of the evidence. *Psychonomic Bulletin and Review, 2(4)*, 508–514.

Tallal, P. (1980). Auditory temporal perception, phonics, and reading disabilities in children. *Brain and Language, 9*, 182–198.

Tallal, P. (1984). Temporal or phonetic processing deficit in dyslexia? That is the question. *Applied Psycholinguistics, 5*, 167–169.

Tallal, P., Miller, S. L., Bedi, G., Byma, G., Wang, X., Nagarajan, S. S., Schreiner, C., Jenkins, W. M., & Merzenich, M. M. (1996). Language comprehension in language learning impaired children improved with acoustically modified speech. *Science, 271*, 81–84.

Tallal, P., Miller, S. L., & Fitch, R. H. (1993). Neurobiological basis of speech: A case for the preeminence of temporal processing. *Annals of the New York Academy of Sciences, 682*, 27–47.

Tallal, P., Miller, S. L., Jenkins, W. M., & Merzenich, M. M. (1997). The role of temporal processing in developmental language-based learning disorders: Research and clinical implications. In B. Blachman (ed.), *Foundations of reading acquisition and dyslexia: Implications for early intervention* (pp. 49–66). Hillsdale, NJ: Lawrence Erlbaum Associates.

Tallal, P., & Piercy, M. (1973). Defects of non-verbal auditory perception in children with developmental aphasia. *Nature, 241*, 468–469.

Tallal, P., & Stark, R. E. (1982). Perceptual/motor profiles of reading impaired children with or without concomitant oral language deficits. *Annals of Dyslexia, 32,* 163–176.

Torgesen, J. K., Wagner, R. D., & Rashotte, C. A. (1994). Longitudinal studies of phonological processing and reading. *Journal of Learning Disabilities, 27(10),* 276–286.

Torgesen, J. K., Wagner, R. D., & Rashotte, C. A. (1997). Approaches to the prevention and remediation of phonologically based reading disabilities. In B. Blachman (ed.), *Foundations of reading acquisition and dyslexia: Implications for early intervention* (pp. 287–304). Hillsdale, NJ: Lawrence Erlbaum Associates.

Waber, D. P., Weiler, M. D., Wolff, P. H., Bellinger, D., Marcus, D. J., Ariel, R., Forbes, P., & Wypij, D. (2001). Processing of rapid auditory stimuli in school-age children referred for evaluation of learning disorders. *Child Development, 72(1),* 37–49.

Wagner, R. D., & Torgesen, J. K. (1987). The nature of phonological processing and its causal role in the acquisition of reading skills. *Psychological Bulletin, 101(2),* 192–212.

Wagner, R. D., Torgesen, J. K., & Rashotte, C. A. (1999). *Comprehensive test of phonological processing.* Austin: PRO-ED.

Wechsler, D. (1991). *Wechsler intelligence scale for children—III.* San Antonio, TX: Harcourt Brace Jovanovich.

Wolf, M. (1997). A provisional, integrative account of phonological and naming-speed deficits in dyslexia: Implications for diagnosis and intervention. In B. Blachman (ed.), *Foundations of reading acquisition and dyslexia: Implications for early intervention* (pp. 67–92). Hillsdale, NJ: Lawrence Erlbaum Associates.

Woodcock, R. W. (1987). *Woodcock reading mastery tests-revised.* Circle Pines, MN: American Guidance Service.

Woodcock, R. W., & Johnson, M. B. (1989). *Woodcock-Johnson tests of cognitive ability-revised.* Circle Pines, MN: American Guidance Service.

# Perceptions and Knowledge of Preservice and Inservice Educators About Early Reading Instruction

*Candace Bos*[*]

University of Texas at Austin
Austin, Texas

*Nancy Mather*

University of Arizona
Tucson, Arizona

*Shirley Dickson*

Texas Education Agency
Austin, Texas

*Blanche Podhajski*

Stern Center for Language and Learning
Williston, Vermont

David Chard

University of Oregon
Eugene, Oregon

*A major conclusion from research regarding children with poor reading performance is that early, systematic instruction in phonological awareness and phonics improves early reading and spelling skills and*

[*] Just prior to publication, the editorial office was informed of the untimely death of the first author, Candace Bos, who died on August 13, 2001.

Annals of Dyslexia, Vol. 51, 2001

*results in a reduction of the number of students who read below grade level. The purpose of this study was to examine the perceptions and knowledge of presevice and inservice educators about early reading instruction. The results indicated that these educators expressed positive attitudes toward explicit and implicit code instruction, with inservice educators more positive about explicit code instruction than preservice educators and preservice educators more positive about implicit code instruction. Preservice and inservice educators demonstrated limited knowledge of phonological awareness or terminology related to language structure and phonics. Additionally, they perceived themselves as only somewhat prepared to teach early reading to struggling readers. These findings indicate a continuing mismatch between what educators believe and know and what convergent research supports as effective early reading instruction for children at risk for reading difficulties. Implications support continuing efforts to inform and reform teacher education.*

". . . lower level language mastery is as essential for the literacy teacher as anatomy is for the physician" (Moats, 1994, p. 99).

In the early elementary school years, general education teachers face the challenging task of teaching young children how to read. Although many children accomplish this task successfully, an increasing number fail to acquire basic reading skills in the early elementary years (Lyon, 1999). Unfortunately, children who read poorly in first and second grade tend to remain poor readers throughout school (Blachman, 2000; Snow, Burns, & Griffin, 1998). Approximately 75 percent of the children who struggle with reading in third grade will still be poor readers at the end of high school (Francis, Shaywitz, Stuebing, Shaywitz, & Fletcher, 1996; Lyon, 1998). Each subsequent year, these children face increasing obstacles to reading development (Adams & Bruck, 1995; Torgesen & Burgess, 1998) in that their difficulties with word recognition and fluency affect their abilities to comprehend and gain conceptual knowledge (Juel, 1988; Shaywitz et al., 1995; Torgesen et al., 2001; Torgesen, Wagner, & Rashotte, 1994).

National, state, and local administrators, politicians, and publishers increasingly attend to the importance of teaching phonemic awareness and phonics and integrating these skills into reading instruction for at-risk students as reflected in new teacher certification guidelines in reading (e.g., California Reading Initiative, 1997; No Child Left Behind, 2001; Texas Reading Initiative, 1996). Research findings of the last decade have demonstrated that early, systematic instruction in phono-

logical awareness and phonics provided in the general education classroom improves children's early reading skills (e.g.,
Blachman, Ball, Black, & Tangel, 1994; O'Connor, Jenkins, &
Slocum, 1995). This type of instruction results in a reduction of
the number of students who read below grade level and are
identified as having learning disabilities (Dickson & Bursuck, in
press; O'Connor, 1999).

Limited research evidence links educator knowledge of
what and how to teach reading to classroom practice and
long-lasting positive student outcomes (Anders, Hoffman, &
Duffy, 2000; Richardson, 1996). There is, however, a small but
growing body of evidence suggesting that educators who have
knowledge of phonological awareness, the alphabetic principle, the structure of language, and phonics instruction and
apply it in classrooms can affect student outcomes (Bos,
Mather, Friedman Narr, & Babur, 1999; McCutchen &
Berninger, 1999; O'Connor, 1999). This research implies that
educators need to know how to use effective teaching methodologies and instructional programs that have as core elements
explicit instruction in phonemic awareness, phonic skills, and
application of phonics to reading text (O'Connor, 1999;
Torgesen, 2000; Vellutino et al., 1996). They need an understanding of how poor phonological awareness and/or poor orthographic awareness (ability to recall letter strings) can
contribute to reading and spelling failure. They also need to
have knowledge of the skills associated with phonological
awareness, how the English language is constructed, and how
speech sounds relate to print (Brady & Moats, 1997). Furthermore, positive perceptions about the role of systematic explicit
instruction (Mather, Bos, & Babur, 2001) also may be important
given evidence of the relation between teacher beliefs and
practices (Duffy & Anderson, 1982; Guskey, 1986; Richardson,
1996).

The National Reading Panel (2000) noted that an analysis
of reading and reading instruction involves four interacting
factors: students, tasks, materials, and teachers. Although
teachers and teacher preparation are critical factors, studies
consistently find that teachers have limited knowledge about
the structure of language and how it interfaces with the teaching of early reading (Mather et al., 2001; Moats, 1994; Troyer &
Yopp, 1990).

While we have much to learn about what and how much
knowledge about reading to include in preservice and inservice professional development (Anders et al., 2000), one place

to start is with what preservice and inservice educators currently know and believe. The major purpose of this study was to examine perceptions and knowledge of elementary level educators about early reading instruction and to update and broaden the study conducted by Moats (1994) in which she investigated inservice teachers' knowledge about the structure of language. Moats found that many of these teachers, who had volunteered to take a course on the structure of language, lacked sufficient knowledge regarding systematic reading instruction. The present study extended the Moats study to focus on preservice and inservice educators. Like Moats, we wondered whether educators would be knowledgeable about language structure and able to apply this knowledge to tasks such as counting the number of syllables and phonemes within words. The present study also broadened the Moats study to ascertain educators' perceptions regarding the converging research findings from the National Institute of Child Health and Human Development (NICHD) (Lyon, 1999) and the National Reading Panel (2000) that underscore the importance of systematic and explicit reading instruction for at-risk learners. For example, would educators believe that phonemic awareness plays a foundational role in reading development, beginning readers need to be able to segment words into phonemes and blend phonemes into words, and the ability to recognize words accurately and easily is essential for rapid decoding? We also were interested in educators' perceptions regarding statements more reflective of a whole language or code implicit orientation to reading. For example, would they believe that learning to use context clues (syntax and semantics) is more important than learning to use phonological and orthographic knowledge (letters and sounds) when learning to read, and that children can learn to read using literature-based, authentic texts?

Because both preservice and inservice educators were included in the present study, their knowledge of the language elements and their perceptions about the role of explicit and implicit code instruction in early reading were compared. In addition, the preservice and inservice educators were grouped by their roles (special and general educators) to determine possible differences among the groups.

The present study was part of a federally funded project, Project RIME, Reading Instructional Methods of Efficacy (Bos, et al., 1999) that employed an interactive, collaborative professional development model (Anders & Bos, 1992; Bos, Nahmias,

& Urban, 1997) to increase teachers' knowledge and skills about using explicit instruction to improve reading outcomes for primary grade students. Project RIME was adapted, in part, from TIME for Teachers™ (Podhajski, 2000), a professional development program created in 1994 to address concerns regarding the inadequacy of teacher education and professional development for early reading instruction. Both TIME for Teachers and Project RIME's professional development programs included didactic instruction followed by ongoing, site-based support and collaboration. The programs emphasized knowledge about language structure (how the language works) and focused on teaching research-based practices in phonological awareness and phonics instruction, and their generalization to reading texts.

As part of Project RIME, we developed measures of teacher perception and knowledge. The purpose of the perception survey and knowledge assessment was to determine whether teachers' beliefs, perceptions, and knowledge changed after having participated in the professional development project (Bos et al., 1999). While not a direct measure of teacher practice, evidence suggests that perceptions can influence teacher practice (Guskey, 1986; Richardson, 1996). For the present study, shortened versions of the measures were developed to describe the perceptions and knowledge of preservice and inservice educators in multiple sites across the U.S.

# METHOD

## PARTICIPANTS

The study consisted of two groups of educators: preservice ($n = 252$) and inservice ($n = 286$). The preservice educators had completed the methods course for teaching reading and were either in their last semester before student teaching or engaged in student teaching in general or special education. They were from three major universities located in the midwest and southwest. Of the 252 preservice educators, 88 percent were female, 60 percent were under 30 years of age, and 84 percent were either Anglo or Hispanic (see table I). A number of the preservice educators noted some type of experience working with children: teaching (32 percent), working as an instructional aide (36 percent), and teaching reading in an instructional setting (e.g., tutoring) (47 percent).

Table I.    Demographics for the Preservice and Inservice Educators.

| Demographics | Preservice Educators | | Inservice Educators | |
|---|---|---|---|---|
| | *n* = 252 | % | *n* = 286 | % |
| Gender | | | | |
| Female | 222 | 88 | 261 | 92 |
| Male | 30 | 12 | 25 | 8 |
| Age | | | | |
| 24 or under | 152 | 60 | 14 | 5 |
| 25-30 | 50 | 20 | 43 | 15 |
| 31-40 | 27 | 11 | 70 | 24 |
| 41-50 | 22 | 9 | 125 | 44 |
| 51+ | 1 | 0 | 34 | 12 |
| Ethnicity | | | | |
| Anglo | 179 | 71 | 217 | 76 |
| Hispanic | 33 | 13 | 29 | 11 |
| African American | 2 | 0 | 4 | 1 |
| Asian/Pacific Islander | 10 | 4 | 6 | 2 |
| Native American | 4 | 2 | 6 | 2 |
| Other | 24 | 10 | 24 | 8 |
| Speak other language in addition to English | 61 | 24 | 55 | 19 |
| Certification[a] | | | | |
| Elementary education | 164 | 65 | 243 | 85 |
| Special education | 79 | 31 | 59 | 21 |
| Bilingual/ESL | 21 | 8 | 34 | 12 |
| Teaching experience (preservice only)[a] | | | | |
| Instructional aide | 90 | 36 | | |
| Teacher | 80 | 32 | | |
| Taught reading in instructional setting | 119 | 47 | | |
| Teaching experience (inservice only) | | | | |
| 1 to 2 years | | | 66 | 23 |
| 3 to 5 years | | | 49 | 17 |
| 6 to 10 years | | | 54 | 19 |
| 11 to 20 years | | | 71 | 25 |
| 20+ years | | | 46 | 16 |
| Primary role (inservice only)[a] | | | | |
| Elementary | | | 181 | 63 |
| Special education | | | 44 | 15 |
| Bilingual/ESL | | | 12 | 4 |
| Reading Specialist/Title I Reading | | | 24 | 9 |
| Speech/Language | | | 10 | 4 |
| Other | | | 15 | 5 |

[a] Categories are not mutually exclusive and may have a cumulative total of more than 100%.

The inservice educators were employed as elementary-level teachers in the midwest, southwest, and northeast. They were kindergarten through third-grade general and special educators from approximately 20 school districts who were participating in the professional development associated with Projects RIME or TIME for Teachers. Similar to the preservice educators, the majority were females (92 percent). Most participants were between 31 and 50 years of age (68 percent) and were general education teachers. Their teaching experience was distributed relatively evenly, ranging from 1 to more than 20 years (see table I).

As part of the descriptive information, the preservice and inservice educators were asked to rate their level of preparedness for teaching reading, teaching struggling readers, and using specific approaches to reading (phonological awareness/phonics, guided reading/reading recovery, and whole language). Overall, the preservice and inservice educators indicated that they felt somewhat prepared. Mean ratings by preservice and inservice educators ranged from 2.32 to 2.26, respectively, on a scale of 1 (not prepared) to 4 (well prepared) with all ratings reported in table II.

Table II. Perceived Level of Preparedness to Teach Reading.

| Area | Preservice[a] | | Inservice[a] | |
|---|---|---|---|---|
| | M | (SD) | M | (SD) |
| Teaching reading (generally) | 2.32 | (.77) | 2.6 | (.79) |
| Teaching struggling readers | 2.20 | (.84) | 2.3 | (.82) |
| Teaching approaches to reading | | | | |
| Phonological awareness & phonics | 2.12 | (.90) | 2.2 | (.83) |
| Guided reading/Reading recovery | 2.13 | (.90) | 1.9 | (.87) |
| Whole language | 2.08 | (.82) | 2.2 | (.84) |

[a] Ratings: 1 = not prepared, 2 = somewhat prepared, 3 = adequately prepared, 4 = well prepared

## MEASURES

Data were collected on two measures: a perception survey and a knowledge assessment. The Teacher Perceptions About Early Reading and Spelling was modeled after an instrument developed by DeFord (1985). DeFord developed a survey to differentiate among three theoretical orientations toward reading: phonics, skills, and whole language. In DeFord's study, only two theoretical orientations clearly emerged: phonics and whole language. For the current study, seven statements from

DeFord's survey were modified and additional statements developed to focus on two theoretical orientations: six items on explicit code instruction (EC) and six items on implicit code instruction (IC). Items related to both explicit and implicit code instruction were included so that information could be obtained about teachers' perceptions regarding both of these orientations. In addition to items representing each orientation, several statements were added as foils that were considered best practices in early literacy and not representative of any particular theoretical orientation (e.g., literacy experiences in the home contribute to early reading success). The order of the explicit code, implicit code, and best practices items were randomly assigned. Educators were asked to rate each of the 15 items on a six-point Likert scale ranging from strongly disagree (1) to strongly agree (6).

The technical properties of the current survey were determined using a longer survey (25 items) that was administered to 41 practicing educators in an initial field test (Mather et al., 2001). The factor analysis using principal components extraction and varimax rotation indicated that two factors emerged: explicit code instruction (EC) with an explained variance of 24 percent, and implicit code instruction (IC) with an explained variance of 16 percent. The internal consistency of the items on the longer survey was high (Cronbach's coefficient alpha = .74). For the current study, the longer measure was revised to clarify items and shorten the time of assessment. On the revised 15-item version used for this study, the same two factors emerged using the same factor analysis procedures on the sample of 286 inservice teachers: explicit code instruction ($r^2$ = 14 percent) and implicit code instruction ($r^2$ = 9 percent). Each item loaded in a positive direction onto its factor. The internal consistency (Cronbach's coefficient alpha) for each factor was EC = .70 and IC = .50. While not high (e.g. greater than .7), the lower reliability can be accounted for by the decreased number of items and hence decreased total variance (Pedhazur & Schmelkin, 1991). Given the purpose of this study, to describe and compare groups rather than make placement decisions, the researchers deemed the level of reliability as tolerable (Pedhazur & Schmelkin, 1991). Table III presents the items for each factor with the mean ratings for preservice and inservice educators.

The Teacher Knowledge Assessment: Structure of Language is a 20-item multiple-choice assessment that examined knowledge of the structure of the English language at both the word

Table III. Mean Ratings for the Items on the Perception Survey
for Preservice and Inservice Educators by Factors.

| Factors/Items | Preservice[a]<br>$n = 252$<br>M (SD) | Inservice[a]<br>$n = 286$<br>M (SD) |
|---|---|---|
| **Explicit Code Instruction** | | |
| K-2 teachers should know how to assess and teach phonological awareness (i.e., knowing that spoken language can be broken down to into smaller units: words, syllables, phonemes). | 5.74 (0.55) | 5.86 (0.37) |
| Controlling text through consistent spelling patterns (The fat cat sat on a hat.) is an effective method for children who struggle to learn to identify words. | 4.83 (1.06) | 4.90 (0.93) |
| Poor phonemic awareness (awareness of the individual sounds in words) contributes to early reading failure. | 4.72 (1.09) | 5.27 (0.79) |
| K-2 teachers should know how to teach phonics (letter/sound correspondences). | 5.59 (0.61) | 5.79 (.44) |
| It is important for teachers to demonstrate to struggling readers how to segment words into phonemes when reading and spelling. | 5.23 (0.76) | 5.33 (0.70) |
| Phonic instruction is beneficial for children who are struggling to learn to read. | 5.17 (0.86) | 5.38 (0.70) |
| **Implicit Code Instruction** | | |
| Time spent reading contributes directly to reading improvement. | 5.56 (0.73) | 5.63 (0.62) |
| Learning to use context clues (syntax and semantics) is more important than learning to use grapho-phonic cues (letters and sounds) when learning to read. | 3.40 (1.30) | 3.13 (1.16) |
| If a beginning reader reads "house" for the written word "home," the response should not be corrected. | 3.25 (1.56) | 3.49 (1.35) |
| Picture cues can help children identify words in the early stages of reading. | 5.52 (0.91) | 5.68 (0.60) |
| Adult-child shared book reading enhances language and literacy growth. | 5.77 (0.54) | 5.84 (0.40) |
| All children can learn to read using literature-based, authentic texts. | 3.75 (1.49) | 3.14 (1.45) |

[a] Ratings: 1 = strongly disagree, 2 = disagree, 3 = mildly disagree, 4 = mildly agree, 5 = agree, 6 = strongly agree

and sound levels. Items were developed or adapted from several sources (Lerner, 1997; Moats, 1994; Rath, 1994). Items were selected to represent content about phonological awareness and phonics. The original technical properties were determined on a longer assessment (25 items) with 55 inservice teachers. Overall internal consistency was .83 (Cronbach's coefficient alpha). The knowledge assessment used for this study was reduced to 20 items with an overall internal consistency of .60 (Cronbach's alpha) based on the 286 inservice teachers, with the reduced reliability related to the decreased variability and number of items (Pedhazur & Schmelkin, 1991). Table IV presents each item on the assessment with the percent of preservice and inservice educators correctly answering each item.

**Table IV.  Percentage of Correct Answers by Items on the Knowledge Assessment for the Preservice and Inservice Educators.**

| Item | Preservice[a] ($n = 252$) % | Inservice[a] ($n = 286$) % |
|---|---|---|
| Which word contains a short vowel sound? (a) treat (b) start **(c) slip** (d) cold (e) point | 81 | 93 |
| A phoneme refers to: (a) a single letter **(b) a single speech sound** (c) a single unit of meaning (d) a grapheme | 90 | 88 |
| A pronounceable group of letters containing a vowel sound is a: (a) phoneme (b) grapheme **(c) syllable** (d) morpheme | 53 | 64 |
| If *tife* were a word, the letter i would probably sound like the i in: (a) if (b) beautiful **(c) find** (d) ceiling (e) sing | 88 | 93 |
| A combination of two or three consonants pronounced so that each letter keeps its own identity is called a: (a) silent consonant (b) consonant digraph (c) diphthong **(d) consonant blend** | 43 | 61 |
| Example of a voiced and unvoiced consonant pair would be: (a) b-d **(b) p-b** (c) t-f (d) g-j (e) c-s | 19 | 22 |
| Two combined letters that represent one single speech sound are a: (a) schwa (b) consonant blend (c) phonetic **(d) digraph** (e) diphthong | 23 | 48 |
| How many speech sounds are in the word "eight"? **(a) two** (b) three (c) four (d) five | 76 | 81 |
| How many speech sounds are in the word "box"? (a) one (b) two (c) three **(d) four** | 8 | 15 |

*continued*

**Table IV.  Percentage of Correct Answers by Items on the Knowledge Assessment for the Preservice and Inservice Educators.** *(continued)*

| Item | Preservice[a] (n = 252) % | Inservice[a] (n = 286) % |
|---|---|---|
| How many speech sounds are in the word "grass"? (a) two (b) three **(c) four** (d) five | 46 | 43 |
| What type of task would this be? Say the word "cat." Now say cat without the /c/ sound. (a) blending (b) rhyming (c) segmentation **(d) deletion** | 42 | 59 |
| What type of task would this be? "I am going to say some sounds that will make one word when you put them together. What does /sh/ /oe/ say?" **(a) blending** (b) rhyming (c) segmentation (d)manipulation | 67 | 69 |
| Mark the statement that is false: (a) Phonological awareness is a precursor to phonics (b) Phonological awareness is a oral language activity **(c) Phonological awareness is a method of reading instruction that begins with individual letters and sounds** (d) Many children acquire phonological awareness from language activities and reading. | 30 | 33 |
| What is the **second sound** in the word "queen"? (a)u (b) long e (c) k **(d) w** | 41 | 32 |
| A reading method that focuses on teaching the application of speech sounds to letters is called: **(a) phonics** (b) phonemics (c) orthography (d) phonetics (e) either a or d | 45 | 30 |
| A soft **c** is in the word: (a) Chicago (b) cat (c) chair **(d) city** (e) none of the above | 71 | 91 |
| Identify the pair of words that begins with the same sound. joke - goat **(b) chef – shoe** (c) quiet – giant (d) chip = chemist | 90 | 94 |
| If you say the word, and then reverse the order of the sounds, "ice" would be: (a) easy (b) sea (c) size **(d) sigh** | 54 | 67 |
| If you say the word, and then reverse the order of the sounds, "enough" would be: (a) fun (b) phone **(c) funny** (d) one | 65 | 72 |
| All of the following nonsense words have silent letters, except: (a) bamb (b) wrin (c) shipe (d) knam **(e) phop** | 28 | 46 |

Adapted from: Lerner, 1997; Moats, 1994; Rath, 1994.

## DATA COLLECTION AND ANALYSIS

For the preservice educators, the perceptions and knowledge measures were collected after they completed their reading methods courses and during student teaching or prior to student teaching. The inservice educators completed the measures prior to participating in professional development.

We analyzed the data to address four questions. First, how can perceptions regarding explicit and implicit code instruction and knowledge of the structure of language be characterized for preservice and inservice educators? Second, within the group of inservice educators, how do perceptions and knowledge vary based on years of experience? Third, how do preservice and inservice general and special educators' perceptions and knowledge compare? And fourth, how do preservice and inservice educators' perceived level of preparedness to teach relate to their perceptions of explicit and implicit code instruction and their knowledge of the structure of language?

To address the first question, perceptions and knowledge of preservice and inservice educators, the means for each group were computed and the means of the individual item responses were visually examined. To address the second question regarding perceptions and knowledge of inservice educators with varying years of teaching experience, we grouped the inservice educators according to number of years of experience: 1 to 5 years ($n = 94$), 6 to 10 years ($n = 54$), and 11 or more years ($n = 117$), excluding educators with less than one year of experience. An omnibus F-test in an analysis of variance (ANOVA) for each measure was computed and, if significant, a Tukey (HSD) was used to determine the groups demonstrating significant differences.

For the third question, the preservice and inservice educators were grouped by special and general educators, and 2 × 2 ANOVAs (type of educator—preservice or inservice by educator role—general or special education) were conducted for each measure. These analyses compared preservice educators pursuing elementary certification only ($n = 130$); inservice educators with elementary education as a primary role ($n = 164$); preservice educators seeking special education certification ($n = 79$); and inservice educators with special education, reading specialist/Title I reading, or speech /language pathologist as primary roles ($n = 78$). To address the fourth question, the relationships between the level of preparedness and the perceptions and knowledge of preservice and inservice educators, Pearson Product-Moment Correlation coefficients were computed and significance was examined.

# RESULTS

## GENERAL PERCEPTIONS AND KNOWLEDGE OF EDUCATORS

The first question focused on preservice and inservice educators' perceptions of explicit and implicit code instruction and their knowledge of English language structure.

*Preservice Educators.* On the Teacher Perceptions About Early Reading and Spelling, the preservice educators agreed with the importance of explicit code instruction ($M$ = 5.2) (see table V) with the means for items ranging from 4.72 (phonemic awareness) to 5.74 (assess and teach phonological awareness) (see table III). Their agreement with implicit code instruction fell between mildly agree and agree ($M$ = 4.5) with the means for items ranging between 3 and 4 (3.25 for not correcting semantically related words; 3.40 for importance of context clues; 3.75 for literature-based text) to more than 5 (5.52 for importance of picture clues; 5.56 for time spent reading; 5.77 for adult-child shared reading).

Table V.  Mean Ratings for the Perception Survey and Mean Scores for the Knowledge Assessment by Preservice and Inservice Educators.

|  | Preservice Educators $n$ = 252 | | Inservice Educators $n$ = 286 | |
|---|---|---|---|---|
| Measures | M | SD | M | SD |
| Perceptions survey[a] | | | | |
|   Explicit code instruction | 5.2 | .5 | 5.4 | .4 |
|   Implicit code instruction | 4.5 | .6 | 4.5 | .5 |
| Knowledge assessment[b] | 10.6 | 2.8 | 12.0 | 2.8 |

[a] Ratings: 1 = strongly disagree, 2 = disagree, 3 = mildly disagree, 4 = mildly agree, 5 = agree, 6 = strongly agree

[b] Number of items is 20.

For Teacher Knowledge Assessment: Structure of Language, the preservice educators scored an average of 10.6 items correct out of 20 items (see table V). Fifty percent or more preservice educators answered incorrectly four of eight items related to phonics and seven of 12 items related to phonological awareness. (See table V for percent of perservice and inservice educators who answered each item correctly.) The four items related to phonics included silent letters, consonant blends, digraphs, and the definition of phonics. For the items related to phonological awareness, 50 percent or fewer failed to identify deletion, segmentation, or blending tasks; identify the second sound in the word "queen;" identify voiced and unvoiced consonants; and distinguish between teaching phonological awareness and teaching letter/sound correspondences. While 50 percent or more correctly segmented a word with two sounds, they incorrectly segmented words with four sounds.

*Inservice Educators.* On the Teacher Perceptions About Early Reading and Spelling, the inservice educators also expressed positive perceptions of explicit code instruction ($M$ = 5.4) (see table V) with a range from 4.9 (controlled text) to 5.86 (assess and teach phonological awareness) (see table III). For implicit code instruction, the inservice educators' mean rating fell within mildly agreed to agreed ($M$ = 4.5) with the means for items ranging from between 3 and 4 (3.13 for importance of context clues, 3.14 for literature-based text, and 3.49 for not correcting semantically related words) to more than 5 (5.63 for time spent reading; 5.68 for picture clues; 5.84 for adult-child shared reading).

The inservice educators scored an average of 12 out of 20 correct responses in Teacher Knowledge Assessment: Structure of Language. Fifty percent of the inservice educators missed three of the eight items related to phonics and five of the 12 items related to phonological awareness (see table IV). The missed phonics items included silent letters, digraphs, and the definition of phonics. Unlike the preservice educators, 50 percent or more of the inservice educators identified consonant blends. More than 50 percent of the inservice educators correctly segmented a word that had two sounds but incorrectly segmented words that had four sounds, could not identify the second sound in the word "queen;" could not identify voiced and unvoiced consonants, and confused teaching phonological awareness with teaching letter/sound correspondences. Unlike the preservice educators, more than 50 percent of the inservice educators identified deletion, segmentation, and blending tasks.

## COMPARISONS OF INSERVICE EDUCATORS
## BASED ON YEARS OF TEACHING EXPERIENCE

Based on the inservice educators' years of teaching experience, no significant differences existed among groups regarding their perceptions toward explicit and implicit code instruction on the Teacher Perceptions About Early Reading And Spelling measure (see table VI). A significant difference existed among groups for their knowledge on the Teacher Knowledge

Assessment: Structure of Language ($F[2, 262] = 5.51, p < .01$). The inservice educators with more than 11 years of experience demonstrated significantly higher knowledge scores than the inservice educators with 1 to 5 years experience ($p < .01$). No significant differences existed between inservice educators with 6 to 10 years experience and their peers with 1 to 5 years or more than 11 years experience.

Table VI. Means for Perceptions and Knowledge of Inservice Educators with Varying Years of Experience.

|  | Years of Teaching Experience | | | | | |
|---|---|---|---|---|---|---|
|  | 1-5 ($n$= 94) | | 6-10 ($n$ = 54) | | 11+ ($n$ = 117) | |
| Measures | Mean | SD | Mean | SD | Mean | SD |
| Perception survey[a] |  |  |  |  |  |  |
| Explicit code instruction | 5.4 | .4 | 5.4 | .4 | 5.4 | .4 |
| Implicit code instruction | 4.6 | .6 | 4.6 | .6 | 4.4 | .5 |
| Knowledge assessment[b] | 11.4* | 2.8 | 12.3 | 2.7 | 12.6* | 2.7 |

[a] Ratings: 1 = strongly disagree, 2 = disagree, 3 = mildly disagree, 4 = mildly agree, 5 = agree, 6 = strongly agree.

[b] Number of items is 20.

* $p < .01$

## COMPARISONS AMONG PRESERVICE AND INSERVICE GENERAL AND SPECIAL EDUCATORS

*Perceptions about Early Reading and Spelling.* For this question, the preservice and inservice educators were grouped by roles as general and special educators and 2 × 2 ANOVAs were computed. Analyses were completed for both explicit and implicit code instruction on the Teacher Perceptions About Early Reading and Spelling. The results for explicit code instruction indicated two main effects with no interaction effect. Means and standard deviations are presented in table VII. Inservice educators (general and special) expressed a more positive attitude toward explicit code instruction than did preservice educators ($F[3, 447] = 13.0, p < .01$). Special educators (preservice and inservice) expressed a more positive attitude toward explicit code instruction than general educators ($F[3, 447] = 16.3, p < .01$). For implicit code instruction, there was one main effect and no interaction. Results indicated that general educators, regardless of whether preservice or inservice, expressed a more positive attitude toward implicit code instruction than did special educators ($F[3, 447] = 19.0, p < .01$) (see table VII).

Table VII. Means for Perception Survey and Knowledge Assessment of Preservice and Inservice Educators by Roles as Elementary and Special Educators.

| | Preservice Educators | | | Inservice Educators | | | Total | | |
|---|---|---|---|---|---|---|---|---|---|
| | *n* | Mean | SD | *n* | Mean | SD | *n* | Mean | SD |
| **Explicit Code[a]** | | | | | | | | | |
| Elem. educators | 130 | 5.2 | .5 | 164 | 5.4 | .4 | 294 | 5.3 | .4 |
| Special educators | 79 | 5.4 | .5 | 78 | 5.5 | .4 | 157 | 5.4* | .4 |
| Total | 209 | 5.2 | .5 | 242 | 5.4* | .4 | | | |
| **Implicit Code[b]** | | | | | | | | | |
| Elem. educators | 130 | 4.7 | .5 | 164 | 4.6 | .5 | 294 | 4.6* | .5 |
| Special educators | 79 | 4.4 | .8 | 78 | 4.4 | .6 | 157 | 4.4 | .7 |
| Total | 209 | 4.6 | .6 | 242 | 4.5 | .5 | | | |
| **Knowledge[b]** | | | | | | | | | |
| Elem. educators | 130 | 10.3 | 2.5 | 164 | 12.0 | 2.6 | 294 | 11.3 | 2.7 |
| Special educators | 79 | 11.6 | 3.1 | 78 | 12.7 | 2.7 | 157 | 12.1* | 3.0 |
| Total | 209 | 10.8 | 2.8 | 242 | 12.2* | 2.7 | | | |

[a] Possible ratings: 1 = strongly disagree, 2 = disagree, 3 = mildly disagree, 4 = mildly agree, 5 = agree, 6 = strongly agree. Number of items is 10.

[b] Number of items is 20.

* $p < .01$

***Knowledge of Language Structure.*** Results from the 2 × 2 ANOVA on the Teacher Knowledge Assessment: Structure of Language indicated two main effects with no interaction effect for educators' scores on the knowledge assessment. Inservice educators demonstrated significantly more knowledge of the English language structure than did preservice educators ($F[3, 447] = 29.6, p < .01$), and special educators demonstrated significantly more knowledge than did general educators ($F[3, 447] = 13.4, p < .01$) (see table VII).

## PERCEPTIONS OF PREPARATION TO TEACH

In general, the preservice and inservice educators perceived themselves as somewhat prepared to teach early reading to children and struggling readers in particular (see table II). Preservice and inservice educators also generally perceived themselves as somewhat prepared to use phonological awareness/phonics, guided reading/Reading Recovery, and whole language for teaching early reading.

*Correlations between Perceptions of Preparedness and Explicit and Implicit Code Instruction.* For explicit code instruction as measured on the Teacher Perceptions About Early Reading and Spelling, a positive attitude toward explicit code instruction was significantly and positively correlated with perception of preparedness to teach children ($r = .14$) and struggling readers ($r = .24$) and to teach using phonological awareness/phonics ($r = .28$) for the preservice teachers (see table VIII). For inservice teachers, a positive attitude toward explicit code instruction was significantly and positively correlated with teaching using phonological awareness ($r = .17$). In the analyses, the correlations are significant, but low. Low correlations occur when the variance between groups is small (Glass & Hopkins, 1984), the case in this study.

**Table VIII.**  Correlations between Perceived Preparedness to Teach and Perceptions and Knowledge for Preservice and Inservice Educators.

| | Teach children to read | Teach struggling readers to read | Use phonological awareness/ phonics | Use guided reading/ Reading Recovery | Use whole language |
|---|---|---|---|---|---|
| **Preservice educators** | | | | | |
| Explicit code | .14* | .24* | .28* | .03 | −.07 |
| Implicit code | −.14* | −.27* | −.23* | .0 | .28* |
| Knowledge | .13* | .19* | .25* | .07 | .07 |
| **Inservice educators** | | | | | |
| Explicit code | .08 | .09 | .17* | −.1 | −.09 |
| Implicit code | .03 | -.02 | -.03 | .02 | .20* |
| Knowledge | .12* | .20* | .25* | .04 | -.05 |

* $p < .05$

For implicit code instruction, a positive attitude toward implicit code instruction was significantly and negatively correlated with perceptions of preparedness to teach children ($r = -.14$), struggling readers ($r = -. 27$), and using phonological awareness/phonics ($r = - .23$) for the preservice educators. A positive attitude toward implicit code instruction was significantly and positively correlated with preparedness to teach using whole language for preservice educators ($r = .28$). For inservice educators, a significant positive correlation between implicit code instruction and whole language was also evident ($r = .20$).

*Correlations between Perceptions of Preparedness and Knowledge Assessment.* For preservice and inservice educators, knowledge of the structure of the English language was significantly and positively correlated with perceptions of preparedness to teach children ($r = .13; r = .12$) and struggling readers ($r = .19, r = .20$) and to teach using phonological awareness/phonics ($r = .25; r = .25$) (see table VIII).

## DISCUSSION

This study examined educators' perceptions and knowledge about early literacy instruction at the preservice and inservice levels. Specifically, we examined whether educators were knowledgeable about recent research findings that identify critical components of instruction for teaching reading to a broad range of learners (National Reading Panel, 2000; Snow et al., 1998) and were favorably disposed to using an explicit, systematic approach for students who struggle to learn to read.

Both preservice (53 percent) and inservice (60 percent) educators' inability to answer nearly half of the Knowledge of Language Structure questions highlights a concern that recent research findings have not yet been communicated effectively to teachers. While educators with more years of teaching experience (>11) demonstrated greater knowledge of language structure than their colleagues who are relatively new to the profession (1 to 5 years), and while special educators demonstrated more knowledge than general educators, all groups had scores falling below two-thirds correct. These results suggest that educators who are directly responsible for teaching children how to read have relatively limited knowledge about the structure of the English language. Similar to Moats' (1994) findings, less than two-thirds of both the preservice and experienced teachers had mastered the meanings of structured language terminology such as "syllable," "consonant blend," and "digraph."

Whereas more than 50 percent of the preservice and inservice teachers were able to segment the phonemes in a two-phoneme word, they were unable to do this for more complex four-phoneme words. As noted by McCutchen et al. (in press), a teacher's knowledge of phonemic segmentation is integral to teaching children to segment the sounds in words and develop the phonemic awareness that is fundamental to learning to read. Although in general, preservice educators were less knowledgeable about concepts related to the English language structure than their inservice peers, a few items were answered correctly by nearly all of the preservice and inservice teachers. Most educators were able to define a phoneme, identify a short vowel sound, and identify the two words that began with the same sound. While this analysis provides some insights into educator knowledge of the structure of language, it does not address the important questions of what types and levels of knowledge are needed for teachers to be effective at promoting positive outcomes for students or that some types of knowledge may be inherently more difficult to acquire. For example, do teachers need to define a syllable, separate words by syllables, and list and apply key syllable rules, or is intuitive knowledge sufficient for teaching reading to students with dyslexia? Initial research in professional development would suggest that knowledge about the structure of language and its application in the classroom results in positive students outcomes (Bos et al., 1999; McCutchen & Berninger, 1999), but the interaction of type and level of knowledge and its application is an important area for study. Furthermore, it will be important to evaluate if the large-scale efforts in professional development and changes in certification requirements such as those initiated in California (California State Department of Education, 1996) and Texas (Texas Education Agency, 1996) will increase the knowledge of educators and impact student outcomes.

When comparing knowledge and perceptions, some paradoxes are evident. Whereas inservice teachers agreed ($M = 5.27$) that poor phonemic awareness contributes to early reading failure, two-thirds thought that phonological awareness was "a method of reading instruction that begins with individual letters and sounds." Whereas both preservice ($M = 5.59$) and inservice ($M = 5.79$) educators strongly agreed that K-2 teachers should know how to teach phonics, their scores on the phonics items on the knowledge assessment indicated they lacked basic knowledge.

The relationships between educators' perceptions of their preparedness to teach and their attitude ratings and knowledge scores indicate that in general, preservice educators' attitudes toward a particular instructional approach may have had a greater effect on their feelings of preparedness to teach than their inservice colleagues. Those who favored an explicit approach felt more prepared to teach all children, struggling readers, and phonological awareness and phonics. This finding was not repeated with the inservice respondents. With this group, the educators who had a more positive attitude toward explicit instruction perceived themselves as more prepared to teach phonological awareness/phonics, but not to teach all readers or struggling readers. For both preservice and inservice teachers, the connection between knowledge of language structure and preparedness to teach suggests that those who feel more comfortable with the knowledge of language structure also perceived themselves as more prepared to teach all children how to read. Educators in both groups who felt more positive about implicit code instruction seemed to feel more prepared to teach using whole language. These findings are particularly important because research on teachers' sense of efficacy suggests that educators who express a greater sense of preparedness are more willing to innovate in their approach to teaching (Smylie, 1988) and are more likely to perceive their instruction as integral to improving outcomes for struggling learners (Simmons, Kame'enui, & Chard, 1996).

The present study had several limitations that are important to consider in interpreting the findings. First, the results relied exclusively on self-report data. While evidence suggests that teachers' self-reports reflect their classroom instructional practices (Barr & Sadow, 1989; Sosniak & Stodolsky, 1993), the lack of field-based observations is a limitation. A second limitation is that the data were collected in a face-to-face context. These data then may be prone to social desirability bias (Dillman, 1978). Furthermore, the manner in which the survey was worded might be a contributing factor that resulted in more "highly agree" ratings. The resulting limited amount of variance that is accounted for by the educators' perceptions calls into importance the need to consider alternative factors that account for teachers' beliefs. Third, the factor loadings did not match completely our coding of items as being representative of primarily implicit instruction. Finally, the survey and assessment tools require further refinement to determine if the tools can be brought to a higher level of internal consistency.

Several specific implications can be drawn from the research findings. First, advances in knowledge about reading instruction appear to have not yet had a substantial impact on educator knowledge, despite increased emphasis in the literature as well as national and state initiatives. Our results support the conclusions drawn by Moats (1994) over seven years ago: many teachers are confused about the differences between phonological awareness and phonics and would be limited in their skills to teach reading explicitly to children who struggle.

Teachers need to understand the salient differences and similarities between spoken and written language. They need to possess sufficient knowledge about the structure of English words so that they can systematically address the instructional needs of children struggling to learn to read. Our findings would suggest that general education teachers may not be adequately prepared to instruct students with dyslexia and related reading problems. Furthermore, even when these children receive special education, special educators also appear to have somewhat limited knowledge about language structure and how to implement systematic, explicit reading instruction.

Second, an encouraging finding from this study is that both preservice and inservice teachers expressed positive attitudes toward explicit and implicit instruction, indicating that they do not fully embrace one theoretical orientation or approach to reading instruction. As observed by Pressley et al. (2001), well-informed teachers combine practices that work well for them and do not worry about theoretical purity when teaching. The most effective teachers were able to integrate substantial instruction in basic skills within the context of reading and writing activities and literature-rich environments.

Finally, important implications exist for teacher education. Teacher preparation does not apparently include sufficient or in-depth content training (Hill, 2000) and may seriously impact implementation of recommendations such as those offered by the National Reading Panel (2000) for the use of systematic phonics instruction. We concur with Lyon (1999) that teacher preparation and professional development programs within colleges of education must "develop preparation programs to foster the necessary content and pedagogical expertise at both preservice and inservice levels" (p. 8). Initial research suggests that with preparation, both general and special educators can increase their knowledge and provide systematic instruction that will assist at risk children with reading development (Bos et al., 1999; McCutchen & Berninger, 1999; O'Connor, 1999). Given the accumulated knowledge with regard to the importance of teaching phonological awareness, and providing phonics instruction to children with dyslexia and struggling readers, teacher preparation programs should ensure that teachers possess the foundational knowledge necessary for providing early systematic reading instruction. Continued efforts to focus and evaluate teacher preparation programs in the area of reading are critical if we are to provide balanced instruction for struggling readers (Brady & Moats, 1997; Chard & Osborn, 1999; Moats, 2000), and more research is needed to establish a better understanding of the influence of teacher education on teacher performance and subsequent student achievement in reading.

## ACKNOWLEDGMENTS

This study was conducted with support from the United States Department of Education, Office of Special Education Programs Grant H029K960081-98. We would like to give special thanks to Kamiar Kouzekanani at the University of Texas at Austin who provided the data analysis for this study. We would also like to thank Janice Sammons, Deborah Rhein, Judith Kroese, Nalan Babur, and Patricia Foreman for their continued contributions to this project.

Address correspondence to Nancy Mather, University of Arizona, Department of Special Education, Rehabilitation and School Psychology, Education 409, Tucson, AZ 85721. e-mail: nmather@u.arizona.edu

*References*

Adams, M. J., & Bruck, M. (1995). Resolving the great debate. *American Educator, 19(2)*, 7–20.

Anders, P. L., & Bos, C. S. (1992). Dimensions of professional development: Weaving teaching beliefs and strategic content. In M. Pressley, K. R. Harris, & J. T. Guthrie (eds.), *Promoting academic competence and literacy in schools* (pp. 457–476). San Diego: Academic Press.

Anders, P. L., Hoffman, J. V., & Duffy, G. G. (2000). Teaching teachers to teach reading: Paradigm shifts, persistent problems, and challenges. In M. L. Kamil, P. B. Mosenthal, P. D. Pearson, & R. Barr (eds.), *Handbook of reading research* (Vol. 3, pp. 719–742). Mahwah, NJ: Lawrence Erlbaum Associates.

Barr, R., & Sadow, M. W. (1989). Influence of basal programs on fourth-grade reading instruction. *Reading Research Quarterly, 24*, 44–71.

Blachman, B. A. (2000). Phonological awareness. In M. L. Kamil, P. B. Mosenthal, P. D. Pearson, & R. Barr (eds.), *Handbook of reading research* (Vol. 3, pp. 251–284). Mahwah, NJ: Lawrence Erlbaum Associates.

Blachman, B. A., Ball, E. W., Black, R. S., & Tangel, D. M. (1994). Kindergarten teachers develop phoneme awareness in low-income, inner-city classrooms. *Reading and Writing: An Interdisciplinary Journal, 6*, 1–18.

Bos, C. S., Mather, N., Friedman Narr, R., & Babur, N. (1999). Interactive, collaborative professional development in early literacy instruction: Supporting the balancing act. *Learning Disabilities Research & Practice, 14*, 215–226.

Bos, C. S., Nahmias, M., & Urban, M. (1997). Implementing interactive professional development in a workshop course on educating students with AD/HD. *Teacher Education and Special Education, 20*, 132–145.

Brady, S., & Moats, L. C. (1997). Informed instruction for reading success: Foundations for teacher preparation. A position paper of the International Dyslexia Association. Baltimore, MD: International Dyslexia Association.

California State Department of Education. (1996). *The California reading initiative.* Sacramento, CA: Author.

Chard, D. J., & Osborn, J. (1999). Phonics and word recognition instruction in early reading programs: Guidelines for accessibility. *Learning Disabilities Research & Practice, 14,* 107–117.

DeFord, D. E. (1985). Validating the construct of theoretical orientation in reading instruction. *Reading Research Quarterly, 20,* 361–367.

Dickson, S. V., & Bursuck, W. (in press). Early intervention for at-risk readers: A 3-year teacher change model. In D. Wiseman (ed.), *Research strategies for education.*

Dillman, D. A. (1978). *Mail and telephone surveys: The total design method.* New York: Wiley.

Duffy, G. G., & Anderson, L. (1982). Conceptions of reading project: Final report. East Lansing, MI: Michigan State University, Institute for Research on Teaching. (ERIC Document Reproduction Service No. ED218583).

Francis, D. J., Shaywitz, S. E., Stuebing, K. K., Shaywitz, B. A., & Fletcher, J. M. (1996). Developmental lag versus deficit models of reading disability: A longitudinal, individual growth curves study. *Journal of Educational Psychology, 88,* 3–17.

Glass, G. V., & Hopkins, K. D. (1984). *Statistical methods in education and psychology* (2nd ed., p. 92). Boston: Allyn & Bacon.

Guskey, T. (1986). Staff development and the process of teacher change. *Educational Researcher, 15,* 5–12.

Hill, H. B. (2000). Literacy instruction in teacher education: A comparison of teacher education in Australia, New Zealand, and the United States of America. Unpublished doctoral dissertation, Columbia University, Teachers College, New York.

Juel, C. (1988). Learning to read and write: A longitudinal study of 54 children from first through fourth grades. *Journal of Educational Psychology, 80,* 437–447.

Lerner, J. (1997). *Learning disabilities: Theories, diagnosis, and teaching strategies.* Boston, MA: Houghton Mifflin Company.

Lyon, G. R. (1998). Why reading is not natural. *Educational Leadership, 3,* 14–18.

Lyon, G. R. (1999). The NICHD research program in reading development, reading disorders and reading instruction. Washington, DC: National Center for Learning Disabilities.

Mather, N., Bos, C., & Babur, N. (2001). Perceptions and knowledge of preservice and inservice teachers about early literacy instruction. *Journal of Learning Disabilities, 4,* 471–482.

McCutchen, D., Abbott, R. D., Green, L. B., Beretvas, S. N., Cox, S., Potter, N. S., Quiroga, T., & Gray, A. L. (in press). Beginning literacy: Links among teacher knowledge, teacher practice, and student learning. *Journal of Learning Disabilities.*

McCutchen, D., & Berninger, V. W. (1999). Those who know, teach well: Helping teachers master literacy-related subject-matter knowledge. *Learning Disabilities Research & Practice, 14,* 215–226.

Moats, L. C. (1994). The missing foundation in teacher education: Knowledge of the structure of spoken and written language. *Annals of Dyslexia, 44,* 81–102.

Moats, L.C. (2000). *Whole language lives on: The illusion of "balanced" reading instruction,* New York: Thomas B. Fordham Foundation.

National Reading Panel. (2000). *Teaching children to read: An evidence based assessment of the scientific research literature on reading and its implications for reading instruction.* Bethesda, MD: National Reading Panel, National Institute of Child Health and Human Development.

O'Connor, R. (1999). Teachers learning Ladders to Literacy. *Learning Disabilities Research & Practice, 14,* 203–214.

O'Connor, R. E., Jenkins, J. R., & Slocum, T. A. (1995). Transfer among phonological tasks in kindergarten: Essential instructional content. *Journal of Educational Psychology, 87,* 202–217.

Pedhazur, E. J, & Schmelkin, L. P. (1991). *Measurement, design, and analysis: An integrated approach.* Hillsdale, NJ: Lawrence Erlbaum Associates.

Podhajski, B. (2000). TIME for Teachers: A model professional development program to increase early literacy. *Their World,* 35–37.

Pressley, M., Wharton-McDonald, R., Allington, R., Block, C. C., Morrow, L., Tracey, D., Baker, K., Brooks, G., Cronin, J., Nelson, E., & Woo, D. (2001). A study of effective first-grade literacy instruction. *Scientific Studies of Reading, 5,* 35–58.

Rath, L. K. (1994). The phonemic awareness of reading teachers: Examining aspects of knowledge. Unpublished doctoral dissertation, Harvard University, Cambridge, MA.

Richardson, V. (1996). The role of attitudes and beliefs in learning to teach. In J. Sikula (ed.), *Handbook of research on teacher education* (2nd ed., pp. 109–112). New York: Macmillan.

Shaywitz, B. A., Holford, T. R., Holahan, J. M., Fletcher, J. M., Stuebing, K. K., Francis, D. J., & Shaywitz, S. E. (1995). A Matthew effect for IQ but not for reading: Results from a longitudinal study. *Reading Research Quarterly, 30,* 894–906.

Simmons, D. C., Kame'enui, E. J., & Chard, D. J. (1996). General education teachers' assumptions about learning and students with learning disabilities: Design-of-instruction analysis. *Learning Disability Quarterly, 21,* 6–21.

Smylie, M. A. (1988). The enhancement function of staff development: Organizational and psychological antecedents to individual teacher change. *American Educational Research Journal, 25(1),* 1–30.

Snow, C. E., Burns, M. S., & Griffin, P. (1998). *Preventing reading difficulties in young children.* Washington, DC: National Academy Press.

Sosniak, L. A., & Stodolsky, S. S. (1993). Teachers and textbooks: Materials used in four fourth-grade classrooms. *The Elementary School Journal, 93,* 249–275.

Texas Education Agency. (1996). *The Texas reading initiative.* Austin, TX: Author.

Torgesen, J. K. (2000). Individual differences in response to early interventions in reading: The lingering problem of treatment resisters. *Learning Disabilities Research & Practice, 15,* 55–64.

Torgesen, J. K., Alexander, A. W., Wagner, R. K., Rashotte, C. A., Voeller, K. K. S., & Conway, T. (2001). Intensive remedial instruction for children with severe reading disabilities: Immediate and long-term outcomes from two instructional approaches. *Journal of Learning Disabilities, 34,* 33–58, 78.

Torgesen, J. K., & Burgess, S. R. (1998). Consistency of reading-related phonological processes throughout early childhood: Evidence from longitudinal-correlational and instructional studies. In J. C. Metsala & L. C. Ehri (eds.), *Word recognition in beginning reading* (pp. 161–188). Hillsdale, NJ: Lawrence Erlbaum Associates.

Torgesen, J. K., Wagner, R., & Rashotte, C. A. (1994). Longitudinal studies of phonological processing and reading. *Journal of Learning Disabilities, 27,* 276–286.

Troyer, S. J., & Yopp, H. K. (1990). Kindergarten teachers' knowledge of emergent literacy concepts. *Reading Improvement, 27,* 34–40.

Vellutino, F. R., Scanlon, D. M., Sipay, E. R., Small, S. G., Pratt, A., Chen, R., & Denckla, M. B. (1996). Cognitive profiles of difficult-to-remediate and readily remediated poor readers: Early intervention as a vehicle for distinguishing between cognitive and experiential deficits as basic causes of specific reading disability. *Journal of Educational Psychology, 88,* 601–638.

White House. (2001). *No child left behind.* Washington, DC: Author.

# The Spelling of Final Letter Patterns:
# A Comparison of Instruction at the Level of the
# Phoneme and the Rime

*Yolanda V. Post*

*Suzanne Carreker*

*Ginger Holland*

Neuhaus Education Center
Bellaire, Texas

*Two groups of first graders (n = 63) participated in a brief 10-day intervention study in which they were instructed in the spelling of five final letter patterns in monosyllabic words. Apart from the final letter pattern sh, the other four patterns (nk, ke, sk, and ck) incorporated the phoneme /k/. One group received phoneme-based instruction that emphasized the direct relation between final speech sounds and their spelling patterns, whereas the second group received linguistically implicit instruction that focused solely on the spelling of the rime. The group receiving phoneme instruction (PI) improved accuracy of final pattern spelling as well as speed of word reading over the group receiving rime instruction (RI). The representation of one sound with the digraphs sh or ck did not confuse first graders as much as the discrimination and representation of two sounds with the blends sk and nk, or spelling of /k/ with ke when preceded by a long or tense vowel. The results suggest that the difficulty for beginning spelling does not*

Annals of Dyslexia, Vol. 51, 2001
Copyright ©2001 by The International Dyslexia Association®
ISSN 0736-9387

*necessarily lie in the letter pattern but in the sound sequence that is represented by letters. The results seem to support phoneme-based spelling instruction.*

# INTRODUCTION

It is difficult for beginning readers and spellers to remember the spelling of "regular" words (Reitsma, 1983). How spelling is initially taught in the early grades might make a difference in learning efficiency, as well as for speed of access to and accuracy of retained spelling representation of words. In the current study, spelling instruction that emphasized the phonemic structure of a word was compared with instruction in the spelling of rimes. The question was posed whether students more readily learn how letter patterns represent individual speech sounds (Adams, 1990) through linguistically explicit, phoneme-based instruction, or whether exposure to a group of uniformly spelled words with similar rimes (so called "word families") is sufficient. This last type of spelling approach is linguistically implicit because pronunciation of individual phonemes is not systematically taught to be connected with a spelling pattern. Although onset-rime provides stability within the rime, it does not highlight separate speech segments and their interactions with spelling (Hulme, Muter, & Snowling, 1998; Nation & Hulme, 1997). Nevertheless, currently it is a common method by which introductory spelling is taught in schools.

In contrast to the rime approach with "word families," in the phonemic approach, spelling words are first presented in pairs that differ in one phoneme (cf., *pat* and *mat; pat* and *pet*) and each letter is presented in different word positions (cf., *pat* and *tap*). In this way, children learn that phonologically contrasting segments are represented by different letters and that each letter unites systematic allophonic variations of phonemes under a single visual label (Olson, 1996). We will refer to these two basic prerequisites for literacy acquisition as establishing the letter-allophone association, a cognitively and linguistically more demanding association to learn for beginning spellers than is commonly assumed (Post, Swank, Hiscock, & Fowler, 1999).

Systematic allophonic variation of a segment is defined as the regularly occurring phonetic variation depending on the position of a segment in a word and on the neighboring segments. For instance, immediately before a vowel, an initial stop consonant such as the first /p/ in *pop* is pronounced with aspiration, in contrast to the stop consonant in final position, which can be pronounced with or without release, but is never aspirated (Lisker, 1999). In general, the final consonant (the coda) is perceptually less distinct than the initial consonant (the onset) in monosyllabic words (Helfer & Huntley, 1991; Miller & Nicely, 1955; Raphael & Dorman, 1980; Redford & Diehl, 1999; Wolf, 1978). Greenberg (1999, p. 163–166) vividly describes the onset of a word in speech production as a "survivor" because it maintains the clearest pronunciation over speaking conditions; in contrast, the vowel nucleus acts as a "chameleon," whereas the coda is an entirely "disposable" sound. Apart from positional variation, a segment such as /k/ in final position varies in its pronunciation depending not only on whether the /k/ is preceded by a vowel or consonant, but also on the type of preceding vowel (cf. *tack, take,* and *tuck*) or consonant (cf. *task* or *tank*, see Denes & Pinson, 1963). Since part of the process of segment identification entails recognition of positional and context-determined variation in speech (Samuel, 1989), it might be difficult for a child to establish the identity of a speech sound unless regular speech variation between initial and final consonants (e.g., the two [p]s in *pop*) or context determined variation (e.g., pronunciation differences between the two final [k]s in *tack* and *take*) is recognized.

Difficulty accurately perceiving all the phonemes in spoken words has been documented for children having limited success at learning to read (see reviews by Brady, 1997, and McBride-Chang, 1995). In an identification task with two-syllable words in which allophonic variation was manipulated, all second and third graders could easily identify the initial consonant, but identification of the vowel immediately following the consonant varied, depending on level of reading skill (Post, Foorman, & Hiscock, 1997). The ease with which the initial consonant was identified in the perception studies by Post, Foorman, and Hiscock (1997) and Redford and Diehl (1999) is compatible with studies in which unimpaired readers made fewer reading errors on initial than final consonants when reading CVC words (e.g., Fowler, Liberman, & Shankweiler 1977; Weber, 1970) and with studies with similar results in spelling (e.g., Treiman, Berch, & Weatherston, 1993). Fox (1994) confirmed differences in reading initial and final segments in words with less skilled readers. In her study, she measured the response speed to a same-different task in four different conditions in which visual (V) and auditory (A) presentation conditions matched or did not match. The following conditions were studied: V-V, A-A, V-A, or A-V. Apart from taking more time for reading in the nonmatching condition, dyslexic readers were specifically error-prone if words differed on their end-sound rather than their beginning sound in mixed visual-auditory conditions in the same-different task.

A strategy that beginning readers often exhibit is that they decode initial consonant(s) phonetically and guess the rest of the word (Marchbanks & Levin, 1965), an indication that they have not achieved awareness of the internal structure of words. In Treiman (1985), the positional consonant effect was explained by positing that the vowel and final consonant in the "rime" part of a CVC word are not perceived as separate segments by children at this stage in reading acquisition. Goswami (1988) showed that beginning spellers made use of orthographic analogies of shared sounds for spelling, independent of whether the corresponding sounds were located at the beginning or end of a word (see also Goswami & Bryant, 1990). In her experiment 1, beginning spellers ($n$ = 16) were able to make analogies from a clue word (*beak*) that was read to them by the experimenter and then placed in front of them, to a new word that shared the rime (*peak*). The children also improved in the spelling of the word that shared the onset (*bean*) with the clue word but not by as much, perhaps because spelling the onset already was relatively accurate. As expected, they did not improve on the control words (*rain*) or on words that had letters in common (*lake*). It should be noted that the words with common letters almost never shared the vowel pronunciation with the clue word or with the onset or rime comparison words. Therefore, her experimental words were not controlled for phonetic (i.e., allophonic) or phonological variation except in one sequence (i.e., *rail* [clue] and *raid/hail/lain*). Also, the children participating in her study were checked on number of whole words spelled correctly, not on the correct spelling of separate segments. Further information may have been gained from the Goswami study if she had identified which segments the children were able to spell in the incorrectly spelled words. Subsequent research on the role of the rime in instruction showed accelerated acquisition in the initial stage, but no lasting benefits (Bruck & Treiman, 1992; see also the review by Hiebert & Martin, 2001). Bruck and Treiman attributed this effect to the ease with which rime-based analogies are made, thereby encouraging a child to bypass the intricate process of learning to grasp the interactions between the separate phonological segments of a word and their often complicated relation to spelling.

One factor in considering the relative difficulty of spelling monosyllabic words is the consistency of spelling patterns for different positions within the word. According to Kessler and Treiman (2001), the consistency with which letters in monosyllabic words spell the vowel is .529; for the onset it is .910 and for the coda .821. Given the vowel, spelling consistency of the coda improves by almost 9 percent. Given the coda, spelling consistency of the vowel improves by almost 17 percent. With such large improvements, it makes sense to pay attention in spelling instruction to the internal structure of a spelled word. A second common difficulty that beginning spellers display occurs with specific sound sequences in words such as nasal or liquid consonants in final clusters (the coda). Beginning spellers often treat the nasal (e.g., the /n/ in *went*) or liquid (the /l/ in *silk*) as part of the vowel and tend not to represent these segments (e.g., spelling *went* as *wet* and *silk* as *sik*) (Read, 1971; Treiman, Zukowski, & Richmond-Welty, 1995). A further challenge for spelling the coda occurs for final clusters, such as the /sk/ in *task*. Errors in /sk/ spelling might point to difficulty becoming aware of the individual phonemes in clusters.

It seems that a number of skills are involved in reading and spelling monosyllabic words such as *pop, tank,* or *task*. One is the recognition of allophonic variation depending on word position. A consonantal segment is assigned a letter regardless of the subtle allophonic variation of the consonant with respect to position in the word. Although initial /p/ and final /p/ in a CVC word are pronounced slightly differently, they carry the same phonological identity and are also spelled the same. A second skill is the challenge of becoming aware of each of the consonants in a final cluster. A third is the ability to isolate the vowel from its surrounding consonants. A spoken vowel in English is variable in pronunciation (Chen, 1970), carrying its own identity plus the identity of the preceding and following consonants (Jenkins, Strange, & Trent, 1999; Liberman, Cooper, Shankweiler, & Studdert-Kennedy, 1967; Strange & Gottfried, 1980; Strange, Verbrugge, Shankweiler, & Edman, 1976). As we saw, nasals and liquids that follow the vowel, in particular, are often heavily co-articulated with the preceding vowel (Olive, Greenwood, & Coleman, 1993; Treiman, Zukowski, & Richmond-Welty, 1995). This may suggest that accuracy in vowel identification may have an impact on identification of the subsequent consonant(s). In onset-rime studies of speech or literacy acquisition, the vowel and subsequent consonant(s) within the rime are generally not manipulated systematically as separate segments because the vowel and consonantal segments in the rime are considered to constitute a unit. Spelling errors are also counted per whole word and not per segment, as we saw in the Goswami (1988) study. Analyzing a phoneme or phoneme cluster within the rime, while holding the remaining rime part steady (Kessler & Treiman, 2001), makes it possible to describe the influence that one segment holds over the other within the rime. When words whose subrime units are analyzed in this way are also phonologically similar, allophonic variation is controlled. Furthermore, spelling consistency is controlled when such phonologically similar words are orthographically transparent. In short, the choice of such a set of spelling words creates for English the situation that commonly exists in consistently spelled languages; that is, that almost no phonological neighbors have deviant spellings.

For children learning to read and write English, it would seem that a systematic explanation of the interaction between the phonological and orthographic characteristics of a word would have a greater impact on the accuracy of the spelling image, speed of retrieval, and learning efficiency than a mere spelling presentation of the same set of phonologically and orthographically controlled words. The current study focused on how to teach the spelling of the final patterns (coda) in monosyllabic words with the assumption that by mid-year (i.e., the time of testing), the first grade children in the intervention were already familiar with the spelling of initial patterns (onset). The question also was posed whether the difficulty for beginning spellers is located in the letter pattern or in the sound sequence that is represented by the letters in the coda. The representation of one sound with two letters (i.e., digraphs) should not be as difficult to learn than the representation of two sounds with two letters (i.e., clusters). Unlike digraphs, codas containing a cluster require the linguistic flexibility to abstract across the allophonic variations of two interacting speech sounds. We predicted that the ease of mastering the spelling of the more complex cluster patterns and subsequent speedy access to the spelling representation for reading depends on the extent to which instruction clarifies the internal structure of words. Accordingly, we expected that explicit instruction at the level of the phonemic structure would be more effective than less analytic teaching of word patterns, and that this could be shown in an intensive intervention of relatively short duration. Earlier studies have shown that brief, linguistically informed interventions can have an impact that is felt years later (e.g., Byrne, Fielding-Barnsley, & Ashley, 2000).

To test this prediction, two different approaches to the teaching of final spelling patterns in monosyllabic words were compared—explicit phoneme instruction (PI) and nonsegmental rime instruction (RI)—each taught in a two-week intervention period. The instruction in both interventions targeted the same group of monosyllabic words. The words ended in the digraphs *ck* or *sh* and the blends *nk* or *sk*, which are always preceded by a short vowel, and the pattern *ke* after a long vowel. In the first approach (PI), spelling instruction was phonemically explicit. In PI-instruction, the choice of the four final spelling patterns for spelling of final /k/ was completely determined by the interaction of the final /k/ with the preceding vowel or consonant. In the second approach (RI), final /k/ spellings were taught through rime families such as *ank, ink, unk, ake, ike, uke*, and instruction was entirely based on orthographic similarity of the words (cf., word walls).[1]

## GOALS

The study explored whether a brief spelling intervention, drawing either explicit or implicit attention to phonemes in spelling instruction, would improve spelling accuracy and speed of reading. A second question was whether learning to spell two-letter patterns that represent information about two sounds in the coda (i.e., blends) or that require noting the presence of a long or tense vowel (as in *take*) would be more demanding to acquire than two letters representing a single phoneme (i.e, digraphs).

# METHOD

## PARTICIPANTS

First grade students from four classes in two different schools participated in the intervention: 28 children received linguistically explicit instruction based on the phoneme (PI), and 35 children linguistically implicit instruction based on the rime (RI). Each school contributed one class to each group. Children with language and/or severe emotional problems, or acquired

---

[1] The orthographic rime or word wall approach is commonly used in the classroom (i.e., words with similar orthographic rimes are listed on the blackboard or on a classroom wall). This approach should not be confused with the onset-rime approach, as proposed by Goswami (1988), since she emphasized the phonological aspects of the onset-rime division in spelling.

neurological disorders were excluded from the study. The two schools were located in the same neighborhood and both served a lower middle-class population that was over 90 percent Hispanic. In the PI group, 24 children were Hispanic, 2 Asian, and 2 black; in the RI group, 30 children were Hispanic, 2 Asian, and 3 black. Slightly fewer females than males were present in both groups: In the PI group, 13 participants were female and 15 male; in the RI group, 16 were female and 19 male. The age in months for the PI group was 79.8 months (SD = 5.3) and for the RI group 81.3 months (SD = 5.8), and did not differ significantly. Although all children were taught in English because they had passed a test of English fluency, most children came from homes in which Spanish was spoken.

## INSTRUCTIONAL METHOD

In both interventions, the same five letter patterns were targeted and the daily lesson plan was kept the same where possible. Both groups engaged in visual discovery, visual sort, auditory sort, and spelling activities, but the visual exercises always were combined with auditory activities in PI. For instance, in visual discovery, the students in RI were limited to the discovery of word families in written words, whereas in PI they combined the detection of auditory similarities in dictated words with visual similarities in written words. In visual sort, the students in RI identified the letter patterns and sorted them in word families (*ick, ike, ink, isk*), whereas in PI they sorted words by the spelling pattern for final /k/ (*ck, ke* or *k*). In the auditory sort, the RI students sorted dictated words by letter patterns in word families. In contrast, the PI students sorted words either by the consonant or the vowel sound they heard immediately before the /k/. Thus, they discriminated the /s/ in *sk* and the /n/ in *nk*, or the lax (short) vowel before *ck* and the tense (long) vowel before *ke*. In spelling, the RI students spelled dictated words by analogy (e.g., if this word says *pick*, spell *sick*), whereas the PI students first analyzed the words segment-by-segment and then spelled them.

## INSTRUMENTS AND PROCEDURE

*Instruments Measuring Group Comparability.* Measures of reading, receptive vocabulary, phonemic awareness, and alphabet knowledge determined comparability of the two groups at the outset. Two reading subtests of the *Woodcock-Johnson Psycho-Educational Test Battery* (Woodcock & Johnson, 1989), the Word Attack and Letter-Word Identification subtests, were given to assess word reading skill. The combination of scores (the Basic Reading Cluster) provided standard scores for each of the participants. The Basic Reading Cluster reliability for six-year olds is .98 and for nine-year olds is .96. The *Peabody Picture Vocabulary Test* (*PPVT-lll*, Dunn & Dunn, 1997) was administered to measure receptive verbal knowledge in standard scores. The *PPVT-lll* has a coefficient-a of .95 for eight-year-old children. The children were also administered the early elementary version of the *Test of Phonological Awareness* (*TOPA*: Torgesen & Bryant, 1994). The raw correct scores were used to evaluate recognition of shared final consonants for 20 illustrations of objects. The TOPA has a coefficient-a of .89 for eight-year-old children. In an alphabet knowledge test, children were scored on knowledge of the correct names and speech sounds for 10 letters (*i, t, p, n, s, a, l, d, f, h*) and on the ability to generate a word with each speech sound (30 responses).

*Growth and Control Measures.* The growth and control measures consisted of 30 words that were the same for the reading and the two spelling tasks. In one spelling task, "addition," the student was provided with the initial cluster (onset) and following vowel (nucleus) of a word and was asked to add the final letters (the coda). In the second spelling task, the student wrote the entire word. Each reading and spelling word (e.g., *brush*) was scored separately for errors in onset (*br*), vowel nucleus (*u*), and coda (*sh*). The addition task (e.g., *bru*----) was used to check on the spelling accuracy of the coda in the entire word spelling.

Measures of word reading speed, as well as spelling accuracy of the final letter pattern in the "addition" and the "entire word" spelling tasks, determined possible differential growth between the two groups. Spelling of the middle vowel and the initial consonant pattern, as well as entire word reading, scored separately for onset, vowel nucleus, and coda errors, were used as control measures of improvement because neither the spelling of the middle vowel and initial consonant(s) nor reading were targeted in the intervention.

The orthographic similarity of the 30 experimental words was reflected in their high internal reliability. The coefficient-alpha for the final pattern of the 30 words over 63 children for reading, spelling, and addition was .94, .87, and .89, respectively. The *sh* pattern (six words) had the highest reliability (.93 for reading, .93 for spelling, and .94 for addition, respectively), and the *ke* pattern (six words) the lowest (.72 for reading, .69 for spelling, and .78 for addition).

*Description of Stimuli.* The stimuli used in the two interventions consisted of 30 monosyllabic words selected on the basis of middle vowel and final letter pattern. The experimental words started with one or two consonant letters, followed by the vowel letter *a*, *i*, or *u*, and the five final letter patterns *ck*, *ke*, *nk*, *sk*, or *sh*. Due to gaps in the phonological word structure in English, the initial consonant letter pattern could not be matched completely, except for fl in *flack, flake, flank, flask, flash*. Each final letter pattern occurred in six words (i.e., two words for each vowel letter), giving the total of 30 stimuli (see table I).

The spelling of the final /k/ follows specific spelling rules in monosyllabic words: final /k/ is spelled *ck* (*duck*) immediately after a short or lax vowel, *ke* (*duke*) after a long or tense vowel, and *k* (*dunk* and *dusk*) after a consonant. Thus, spelling of the /k/ is conditioned on the preceding vowel or consonant. Both the *sk* and the *nk* present the specific spelling difficulty of the representation of two segments. The combination of /s/ and /k/ occurs infrequently at the end of a word in English. With respect to *nk*, the /n/ between a vowel and a consonant manifests itself as nasalization of the vowel (Olive, Greenwood, & Coleman, 1993) and is pronounced as [ŋ] before the /k/.

The /sk/ and /nk/ clusters preclude preceding tense vowels and diphthongs (Giegerich, 1992). The vowel before /ʃ/ is also usually short or lax, except in words such as *bush, leash, sheesh*, and *whoosh*. In a few French loan words, usually not familiar to children, the /ʃ/ preceded by the tense vowel is spelled with *ch* (*quiche, niche*). By orthographic definition, the vowel before *ck* is "short" as it is in complementary distribution with the "long" vowel followed by *ke*. The pattern *ke* was treated as one unit in order to prevent a confound of orthographic complexity (all patterns contained two letters) with phonological complexity (one sound for *sh, ck, ke* or two sounds for *nk* and *sk*). At the same time, the *ke* pattern completed the description of final /k/ spelling (Cox, 1977, p. 129). Other researchers also have pondered over how best to describe the function of the silent *e*. In Kessler and Treiman (2001), the silent *e* was considered a marker for the pronunciation of the preceding consonant in words such as *badge, beige, house, wreathe*, and *have*, a marker for the vowel in words such as *hate, haste*, or *toe*, and a marker for both in *cage*. Initial treatment of the silent *e* and the preceding consonant letter as one unit (*ke*) also could be considered a good transition for the introduction of the spelling of tense vowels and diphthongs later in the curriculum. Through the contrasting spelling pattern of *ck* and *ke*, the quality of the preceding vowel could be explained without orthographic interference of single and digraph spelling of the vowel (cf., *stack* and *steak*). Furthermore, the phonological disambiguation of the preceding vowel before /nk/, /sk/, and /ʃ/ to a short or lax vowel could bring into focus the spelling consistency of the phonological contrast between the lax and tense vowel before the /k/ (cf., *tack* versus *take*). Thus, aside from control of phonetic variation, the set of experimental words was unique because the single vowel letter preceding the five letter patterns denoted either a tense vowel according to orthographic convention or a lax vowel in all other cases, either because of a phonological limitation (/ʃ/, /sk/ and /nk/) or an orthographic one (*ck*).[2]

The experimental words were not controlled for neighborhood density or frequency in written language. The frequencies of the words ranged from 1 for *flack, frisk,* and *stash* to 1,513 for *fish* (Carroll, Davies, & Richman, 1971). The mean frequency of the six words ending in the letter pattern *ck* (see the first column

Table I. Experimental Word Set and Their
Reliability on Reading, Addition, and Spelling Tasks.

**A. Experimental Word Set**

| Letter | (Sound) | *ck* (/k/) | *ke* (/k/) | *nk* (/nk/) | *sk* (/sk/) | *sh* (/ʃ/) |
|---|---|---|---|---|---|---|
| *a*[*1] | ([æ] or [Eʲ]) | stack | stake | tank | task | stash |
| | | flack | flake | flank | flask | flash |
| *i* | ([I] or [Aʲ]) | brick | bike | brink | brisk | wish |
| | | flick | spike | slink | frisk | fish |
| *u* | ([Λ] or [Uʷ]) | duck | duke | dunk | dusk | brush |
| | | luck | luke | clunk | tusk | lush |

**B. Coefficient-alpha Reliability (Pretest, *n* = 63)**

| | 30 words | Final Patterns Each Containing 6 Words | | | | |
|---|---|---|---|---|---|---|
| Reading | .94 | .73 | .72 | .87 | .82 | .93 |
| Addition[*2] | .89 | .90 | .78 | .80 | .82 | .94 |
| Spelling | .87 | .84 | .69 | .71 | .86 | .93 |

*Note 1:* A vowel letter (*a, i,* or *e*) represents either a lax ("short") or a tense ("long") vowel.

*Note 2:* Tested insertion of letter(s) in a partly spelled, dictated word.

[2] The spelling of /k/ with letter *c* was not addressed in the intervention because it occurs only in the unstressed syllable of multisyllabic words (*cognac, prolific*) and in *tic, tac,* or *toc.* The occurrence of the spelling *que* in words of French origin (e.g. as in *pique*) was considered too infrequent to be included.

in table I from *stack* to *luck*) was 16.4 (15.6), in *sh* was 76.6
(110.9), in *ke* was 4.9 (5.2), in *nk* was 5.5 (11.5), and in *sk* was 8.1
(12.5). Thus, words ending in *sh* and *ck* had much higher frequencies than those ending in *ke*, *nk*, and *sk*. The 10 words that
contained the letter *i* had the highest frequency of occurrence
(45.6, SD 91.5), whereas the frequencies of the words containing
the letter *u* (11.34, SD 15.0) or letter *a* (10.0, SD 12.3) were much
lower. Independent of location in the word, frequency of the *sk*
pattern was much lower than for the *sh* pattern: a frequency of 2
for *sk* versus 16 for *sh* (Carroll, Davies, & Richman, 1971). The
frequencies of the vowel letters *i*, *u*, and *a* also differed. The letters *a* and *i* are much more frequently used than the letter *u*,
7.88 percent, 7.07 percent, and 2.89 percent, respectively, according to Dewey (1970).

**Procedure.**   The five tests measuring comparability between the groups were part of a battery of tests in a nine-
month study and were administered to individual children
three months earlier.  The two-week intervention study with
first grade students took place at the end of January in the
middle of the school year. The same teacher instructed each
participating class for 20 minutes a day, five days a week for
two weeks. Her southern dialect was similar to the Texan dialect of the children. This teacher had extensive experience as
a regular teacher in the classroom. Before her training in
Alphabetic Phonics, a method of explicit phonics instruction,
she used linguistically implicit spelling instruction similar to
the instruction in the intervention. Each intervention lesson
was carefully scripted and followed guidelines for each specific teaching strategy. The intervention teacher dictated the
words in the "entire word" spelling and the addition test on
two consecutive schooldays immediately before and after the
intervention in the classroom. She pronounced each test word
two times.

The reading test was administered individually by test assistants in a separate room, both immediately before and after
the intervention. The 30 words were presented in a different
order for each assessment. Each student was told that accuracy
as well as speed was important in the reading task. The test as-
sistant wrote down reading errors and measured word reading
speed in seconds with a stopwatch per row of six words.
Before a row was shown to a student, it was covered with a
piece of paper. Because the entire word reading task was
taped, reading accuracy and speed of reading was later directly scored from the tape. The measurements and written

comments by the test assistants provided an extra check on the reliability of the measurement of accuracy and speed directly from the taped record. For instance, hesitancy in reading was included in the speed score, coughing spells were not.

# RESULTS

## INSTRUMENTS MEASURING
## COMPARABILITY BETWEEN THE TWO GROUPS

A MANOVA on the four variables tested three months before the intervention showed that the two groups did not differ significantly on the Basic Reading Cluster, PPVT, TOPA, or on Knowledge of Letters/Sounds, $F[4, 58] = .26, p = .90, \eta^2 = .02$.

## INSTRUMENTS MEASURING
## CHANGE BETWEEN THE TWO GROUPS

*Final Spelling Pattern.* The multivariate test on the difference between pre/post scores for reading, spelling, and addition of the final pattern was significant, $F[3, 59] = 15.7, p = .001$, h2=.44. Separately, reading was not significantly different, $F[1,61]=2.1, p = .15, \eta^2 = .03$, whereas addition $F[1,61]=17.0, p = .001, \eta^2 = .22$, and spelling $F[1,61]=43.4, p = .001, \eta^2 = .42$, were. In order to establish whether the two spelling tests were comparable in their interaction with group, they were subjected to a repeated measures analysis. As expected, the three-way interaction of addition, spelling, and group was not significant. In contrast, when each spelling test was separately compared with reading, the three-way interaction in each analysis was significant, $F[1,61]=32.8, p = .001, \eta^2 = .35$ for group $\times$ reading $\times$ spelling and $F[1,61]=23.4, p = .001, \eta^2 = .28$ for group $\times$ reading $\times$ addition. The similar results for the two spelling tests signify that an addition test can be substituted for whole word spelling when the spelling words are within the spelling range of the participants. The fact that both spelling tests differed from the reading test show that spelling is a more sensitive metric than reading.

To determine the relative difficulty of the five final letter patterns *sh*, *ck*, *sk*, *ke*, and *nk* (Pat5) over time (PP), the five letter patterns were separately analyzed for reading, addition, and spelling. Subsequently, four planned orthogonal contrasts were placed on the letter pattern variable. The two "orthographic" patterns, the digraphs *sh* and *ck*, were compared with the three "linguistic" patterns, the blends *sk/nk* and the unit *ke* (C1). Within the "orthographic" component, the two digraphs *sh* and *ck* were compared (C2) and within the "linguistic" component, the *ke* unit was compared with the mean of the blends *nk* and *sk* (C3), and *nk* was compared with *sk* (C4). The means and standard deviations of the final letter patterns for reading, addition, and spelling are described in table II.

Table II.  Descriptive Statistics for Reading, Addition, and Spelling of the Final Letter Pattern.

| | | Phoneme Instruction | | Rime Instruction | |
| | | Pretest | Posttest | Pretest | Posttest |
| Task | Type | M (SD) | M (SD) | M (SD) | M (SD) |
|---|---|---|---|---|---|
| Reading | nk | 2.4 (2.1) | 0.8 (1.2) | 3.4 (2.4) | 1.9 (2.0) |
| | ke | 0.8 (1.0) | 0.7 (1.1) | 2.2 (1.9) | 1.7 (1.7) |
| | sk | 2.9 (2.2) | 1.6 (1.5) | 3.7 (2.1) | 2.3 (2.3) |
| | ck | 0.9 (1.0) | 1.1 (1.2) | 1.6 (1.9) | 1.7 (1.7) |
| | sh | 1.4 (2.0) | 0.6 (0.8) | 3.5 (2.6) | 1.4 (1.9) |
| Addition | nk | 5.2 (1.6) | 3.6 (2.6) | 5.3 (1.2) | 4.9 (1.6) |
| | ke | 5.0 (1.6) | 2.9 (3.2) | 5.0 (1.4) | 4.7 (1.6) |
| | sk | 3.6 (2.3) | 1.1 (1.6) | 3.1 (2.0) | 2.8 (2.4) |
| | ck | 1.7 (2.3) | 0.9 (1.6) | 2.9 (2.4) | 2.5 (2.6) |
| | sh | 1.0 (2.0) | 0.2 (0.6) | 1.8 (2.4) | 1.0 (2.0) |
| Spelling | nk | 5.5 (1.2) | 3.5 (2.5) | 5.4 (1.0) | 4.6 (1.8) |
| | ke | 5.0 (1.3) | 2.1 (1.8) | 5.0 (1.4) | 5.1 (1.2) |
| | sk | 4.2 (2.0) | 1.2 (1.6) | 3.8 (2.3) | 3.5 (2.4) |
| | ck | 3.1 (2.2) | 2.1 (2.1) | 3.4 (2.2) | 3.2 (2.3) |
| | sh | 1.4 (2.1) | 0.1 (0.4) | 1.9 (2.5) | 1.1 (2.0) |

Note: Each letter pattern included six words. The data are error scores.

*Reading.*    Whereas the two main factors of the five patterns (Pat5: $F[4, 58] = 13.4$, $p = .001$, $\eta^2 = .48$) and pre-post testing (PP: $F[1, 61] = 49.2$, $p = .001$, $\eta^2 = .45$) and their interaction (Pat5 × PP: $F[4, 58] = $ , $p = .001$, $\eta^2 = .43$) were significant, the three-way interaction with group was not (Pat5 × PP × G: $F[4, 58] = 1.9$, $p = .12$, $\eta^2 = .12$). Thus, the spelling intervention brought advances in accuracy of reading for both groups depending on pattern, but no significant reading improvement of one group over the other. Subsequently, three of the contrasts were significant (C1, C3, and C4) but no interaction of contrast and group, which confirmed corresponding improvement of both groups on reading accuracy (see table III). The two digraphs, *ck* and *sh*, were easier to read than *sk*, *nk*, and *ke* (C1). Slightly more errors were made on the *sk* than on the *nk* blend (C4). The *ke* unit was much easier to read than the two blends *nk* and *sk* (C3) and showed, therefore, not much improvement over time. Furthermore, *ck* was easier to read than *sh* depending on pre/post (C2). In sum, few errors were made in reading of *ke* and *ck* in pre- or posttest, whereas reading of the letter patterns *sh*, *nk*, *sk* improved.

In contrast to reading accuracy, on which the two groups did not differ, speed of reading of the 30 intervention words became more than half a minute faster in the PI group but barely changed for the RI group (see table IV). Thus, advancement in reading speed ($F[1, 61] = 7.0$, $p = .01$, $\eta^2 = .10$) could be attributed entirely to advances in the PI group (Reading Speed × Group: $F[1, 61] = 5.5$, $p = .02$, $\eta^2 = .08$). Apparently, type of spelling intervention has consequences for the development of efficient access to stored word spelling in reading.

*Spelling Addition.* The two main factors of five spelling patterns (Pat5: $F[4, 58] = 52. 9$, $p = .001$, $\eta^2 = .78$) and pre/post testing (PP: $F[1, 61] = 95.5$, $p = .001$, $\eta^2 = .49$) were significant, as was the two-way interaction between group and pre/post testing (GxPP: $F[1, 61] = 17.0$, $p = .001$, $\eta^2 = .22$) and the three-way interaction of group, pre/post testing, and five spelling patterns (G × PP × Pat5: ($F[4, 58] = 3.2$, $p = .02$, $\eta^2 = .18$). Further analysis of the three-way interaction of G × PP × Pat5 with planned contrasts on pattern showed that for both groups the *nk*, *ke*, and *sk* patterns were more difficult than the two digraphs *ck* and *sh*, but that only the PI group improved more on the "linguistic" than the "orthographic" patterns (C1). Furthermore, the *nk* pattern (unlike reading) was more difficult than the *sk* pattern (C4) and the *ck* than the *sh* pattern (C2).

*Spelling.* The two main factors of five spelling patterns (Pat5: $F[4, 58] = 62. 2$, $p = .001$, $\eta^2 = .81$) and pre/post testing (PP: $F[1, 61] = 89.4$, $p = .001$, $\eta^2 = .59$) were significant, as was the two-way interaction between group and pre/post testing (G × PP: $F[1, 61] = 42.7$, $p = .001$, $\eta^2 = .41$) and the three-way interaction of group, pre/post testing, and five spelling patterns (GxPPxPat5: $F[4, 58] = 6. 5$, $p = .001$, $\eta^2 = .31$). Further analysis of the three-way interaction of G × PP × Pat5 with planned contrasts on pattern showed that for both groups the *nk*, *ke*, and *sk* patterns were more difficult to spell than the two digraphs *ck* and *sh*, but that only the PI group improved more on the "linguistic" (the two blends and the *ke*-unit) than on the "orthographic" (the two digraphs) pattern (C1). Furthermore, the *nk* pattern was more difficult to spell than the *sk* pattern (C4) and the *ck* more difficult than the *sh* pattern (C2).

Thus, independent of type of testing (addition or spelling), the PI group made fewer errors after the intervention than did the RI group. These results were, however, dependent on type of letter pattern. Both groups made few errors on the *sh* pattern and they improved on the two "orthographic" letter patterns (*ck* and *sh*) equally, whereas the PI group improved on spelling or addition of the "linguistic" patterns (*nk*, *sk*, and *ke*), in contrast to the RI group. Furthermore, at the start of the intervention, both groups of students were more advanced in reading than in spelling of the final pattern, with exception of the *sh* pattern. Not surprisingly, spelling and reading of the five spelling patterns did not develop in complete tandem: Recognition (reading) is easier than recall (spelling).

Table III.    Planned Contrasts for Reading, Addition, and Spelling of the Final Letter Pattern.

| Contrast | | Reading | | | Addition | | | Spelling | | |
|---|---|---|---|---|---|---|---|---|---|---|
| | | *F* | *p* | $\eta^2$ | *F* | *p* | $\eta^2$ | *F* | *p* | $\eta^2$ |
| C1 | G | 8.9 | 0.004 | 0.13 | 9.0 | 0.004 | 0.13 | 8.8 | 0.004 | 0.13 |
| *nk/ke/sk* | PP | 45.5 | 0.001 | 0.43 | 56.8 | 0.001 | 0.48 | 91.1 | 0.001 | 0.60 |
| vs. | C | 21.5 | 0.001 | 0.26 | 119.4 | 0.001 | 0.66 | 99.9 | 0.001 | 0.62 |
| *ck/sh* | PP*G | | | | 13.4 | 0.001 | 0.18 | 39.1 | 0.001 | 0.39 |
| | PP*C*G | | | | 10.8 | 0.002 | 0.15 | 10.2 | 0.002 | 0.14 |
| C2 | G | 8.8 | 0.004 | 0.13 | 7.0 | 0.010 | 0.10 | | | |
| *ck* vs. *sh* | PP | 19.5 | 0.001 | 0.24 | 18.0 | 0.001 | 0.23 | 24.7 | 0.001 | 0.29 |
| | C | | | | 18.7 | 0.001 | 0.24 | 40.1 | 0.001 | 0.40 |
| | PP*C | 27.1 | 0.001 | 0.31 | | | | | | |
| C3 | G | 9.2 | 0.003 | 0.13 | | | | 14.3 | 0.001 | 0.19 |
| *nk/sk* | PP | 35.2 | 0.001 | 0.37 | 39.6 | 0.001 | 0.39 | 62.5 | 0.001 | 0.51 |
| vs. | C | 44.3 | 0.001 | 0.42 | 10.0 | 0.002 | 0.14 | | | |
| *ke* | PP*C | 21.9 | 0.001 | 0.26 | | | | | | |
| | PP*G | | | | 19.4 | 0.001 | 0.24 | 48.8 | 0.001 | 0.44 |
| C4 | PP | 61.6 | 0.001 | 0.50 | 45.0 | 0.001 | 0.42 | 40.0 | 0.001 | 0.40 |
| *nk* vs. *sk* | C | 9.4 | 0.003 | 0.13 | 82.6 | 0.001 | 0.58 | 68.0 | 0.001 | 0.53 |
| | PP*G | | | | 20.9 | 0.001 | 0.26 | 17.6 | 0.001 | 0.22 |

*Note:* G = group; PP = pre vs post; C = contrast; the alpha was .05 divided by 4.

Table IV.   Descriptive Statistics of Reading and Spelling Errors for the Initial Consonant Pattern and Middle Vowel, and Speed of Reading in Seconds of the Whole Word.

| Task | | Phoneme Instruction | | Rime Instruction | |
|---|---|---|---|---|---|
| | | Pretest M (SD) | Posttest M (SD) | Pretest M (SD) | Posttest M (SD) |
| Initial C | Reading | 8.2 (6.4) | 4.1 (3.0) | 11.1 (9.0) | 7.2 (8.3) |
| | Spelling | 5.4 (4.1) | 3.1 (2.5) | 6.0 (5.2) | 5.0 (5.4) |
| Vowel | Reading | | | | |
| | i | 3.5 (2.9) | 2.0 (2.2) | 4.8 (2.8) | 3.2 (2.6) |
| | u | 3.3 (2.6) | 1.8 (2.1) | 5.2 (3.2) | 4.1 (2.8) |
| | a | 3.0 (2.5) | 1.8 (2.3) | 4.9 (3.2) | 3.2 (2.6) |
| | Spelling | | | | |
| | i | 2.7 (2.3) | 1.9 (1.7) | 3.6 (3.2) | 2.8 (3.0) |
| | u | 3.3 (2.0) | 2.0 (2.1) | 3.9 (3.2) | 3.5 (3.2) |
| | a | 1.1 (1.4) | 0.6 (1.1) | 1.3 (1.5) | 1.7 (1.8) |
| Speed | Reading | | | | |
| | | 181.1 (77.5) | 141.9 (68.0) | 174.2 (86.2) | 171.9 (117.8) |

Note: The initial consonant variable contained 30 words. The middle vowel contained 10 words per letter. The initial consonant and vowel were tested on reading and spelling only.

*Vowel.*   A Manova was used on the difference score of pre- and posttest on vowel reading and spelling by group. The multivariate test indicated that there was significant change over time ($F[2, 60] = 38.7, p = .001, \eta^2 = .56$) but the fact that the group effect was not significant ($F[2, 60] = 2.3, p = .10, \eta^2 = .07$) meant that the change did not depend on group. This result is to be expected since spelling of final letter patterns was the main focus of the intervention.

*Initial Consonant Pattern.*   A Manova was used on the difference score of pre- and posttest on reading and spelling of initial consonant by group. The multivariate test indicated that there was significant improvement in reading and spelling over time ($F[2, 60] = 20.9, p = .001, \eta^2 = .41$), independent of group ($F[2, 60] = 1.3, p = .27, \eta^2 = .04$).

*Comparison of Pretest Scores of Intervention Words.*   The two groups were also compared on the scores they received on the different pretests of the intervention words. At the beginning of the intervention, the two groups did not differ on addition of the final consonant pattern, $F[1,61]=1.2, p = .29, \eta^2 = .02$. The MANOVA for spelling of the vowel, initial, and final consonant pattern was also not significant, $F[3, 59] = .75$, $p = .53$, $\eta^2 = .04$. However, the group receiving phoneme instruction performed significantly better on reading of the vowel and the final consonant pattern at the outset of the intervention: The MANOVA for reading of the vowel, initial and final consonant pattern was significant, $F[3, 59] = 5.7$, $p = .002$, $\eta^2 = .22$. Separately, reading of the vowel, $F[1,61] = 6.6$, $p = .01$, $\eta^2 = .10$, and the final consonant pattern, $F[1,61] = 9.5$, $p = .003$, $\eta^2 = .13$, were both significant, reading of the initial consonant pattern was not, $F[1,61] = 1.9$, $p = .17$, $\eta^2 = .03$. Speed of reading of the intervention words did also not differ at the outset of the intervention, $F[1,61] = .11$, $p = .74$, $\eta^2 = .002$ .

## DISCUSSION

A brief intervention with two groups of first graders explored how to teach spelling of final /k/ in monosyllabic words. Each group consisted of two classes, one class from each of the two participating schools and both groups were taught by the same teacher. The explanation and practice of the spelling pattern took 20 minutes of daily instruction during 10 consecutive school days. The spelling program in which the mediating nature of the speech sound was emphasized (phoneme instruction), was more effective than rime instruction. Phoneme instruction of the final spelling pattern did not only boost spelling accuracy, specifically of the two blends and the *ke* unit, it also improved reading speed by more than half a minute. The participants in the two programs did not differ in components that were not directly targeted such as spelling of initial consonants (the onset) and following vowel (the nucleus). The study, therefore, showed the consequences of drawing implicit versus explicit attention to the internal phonological structure of a word in spelling instruction. In light of the vanishing effect of rime instruction (Bruck & Treiman, 1992; Hiebert & Martin, 2001) and apparent lasting effects of phonemic awareness activities in kindergarten (Byrne, Fielding-Barnsley, & Ashley, 2000), long-term follow up could establish whether the results of phoneme-based instruction in the PI condition would hold up over time.

Apart from speed of word reading, the two groups did not differ in rate of improvement in reading accuracy. The results of the reading accuracy test contrasted with those of the two spelling tests (spelling of the final letter pattern as part of whole word spelling or letter addition in a partly spelled word) of the same words, which had very similar outcomes. Thus, a focus on phonological representation in combination with a complete description of the orthographic representation improves spelling, but not necessarily reading accuracy in the same time frame. Furthermore, at the start of the intervention, both groups of children were more advanced in reading than in spelling of the final pattern, with exception of spelling of the *sh*. This observation supports findings in other studies that although reading and spelling are built on the same foundation, they do not develop simultaneously (e.g., Bosman & Van Orden, 1997; Gough, Juel, & Griffith, 1992). This is understandable since different skills are involved in the two activities. Reading involves recognition while spelling requires reconstruction of a word's pronunciation with the 26 graphemes of our alphabet. In our study, we equated the reading and spelling requirements of the words, and still spelling was more difficult than reading.

In the experimental words, five final letter patterns followed the vowel letters *i*, *u*, or *a*. Four letter patterns (*nk*, *sk*, *ck*, sh) were always preceded by a vowel letter representing a lax ("short") vowel and the fifth (*ke*) a tense ("long") vowel. Because of the way the experimental words were selected, the rime condition (e.g., *ank* or *ake*) was actually subsumed in the vowel and coda condition (e.g., a combination of *a* and *nk* or *a* and *ke*). By choosing a consistently spelled group of words with phonologically transparent relations, we simulated a one-on-one or bidirectional relation as exists in transparent orthographies. Instead of "phonological" manipulation of a spelling pattern such as the *ough* in *bough, bought, cough, dough, through* with its five different pronunciations or "orthographic" manipulation such as the phonological /ik/ pattern in *peek, peak*, or *pique*, we avoided "orthographic interference." At the same time, "phonological interference" was limited to controlled allophonic variation in similar sounding words. Therefore, we brought the spelling requirements for the English experimental words in accordance with those that exist in languages that show orthographic consistency and transparency. In addition, the explanation of the spelling pattern in phoneme instruction was entirely founded in phonology, again as is common in transparent orthographies. It is known that children acquire literacy much faster and at younger ages in languages that show orthographic consistency and transparency such as Finnish, Dutch, German, Spanish, and Italian than in languages with less transparent orthographies such as English and French (e.g., Landerl, Wimmer, & Frith, 1997; Paulesu et al., 2001). For that reason, progress in literacy acquisition in transparent orthographies is routinely measured in reading speed, not accuracy (Van der Leij & van Daal, 1999), as we did in the current study.

## DISTRIBUTION OF THE FIVE SPELLING PATTERNS

Also noteworthy was the distribution of the final spelling pattern for both groups: *nk* and *ke* were the most difficult to spell, immediately followed by *sk*, whereas *ck* and *sh* were the easiest to spell. The *sh*-pattern was as easy for reading as for spelling. Apparently, the fact that *sh* and *ck* represented one sound with a letter pattern did not confuse the first graders as much as having to discriminate and represent in writing the two sounds in *sk* and *nk*. In discussing children's spelling of final consonant clusters (Treiman, Zukowski, & Richmond-Welty, 1995), the authors also noted that the "n" in *sink* was seldom represented in the children's spelling. Such results suggest that the difficulty for beginning spellers does not lie in the letter pattern they have to remember (*sh* and *ck* were easy), but in the sound sequence that is represented by letters (*sh* and *ck* represent one sound, *sk* and *nk* two sounds). Adding to the importance of phonology in literacy development is the observation that the phoneme /ʃ/ as in *fish* is not only easy to spell, as was shown in this study, but also is easy to perceive. In a phoneme confusion study, the fricative /ʃ/ was confused least often of any phoneme (Redford & Diehl, 1999).

The instruction of *–ke* as a unit (see Cox, 1977) did not conflict with the way the silent *e* is usually taught in the classroom, namely as a combination of vowel, consonant, and silent *e* (VC*e*), since the children had not reached that stage yet. How linguistically and cognitively demanding the concept of the silent *e* actually is, was expressed in the fact that the *ke*-pattern showed the lowest reliability of the five spelling patterns.

A possible confound in the study was that the words ending in *sh* and *ck* had a higher frequency of occurrence than those ending in *ke*, *nk*, and *sk*. A replication of this study might attempt to choose stimuli that reduce the differences in frequencies for the different spelling patterns. The use of more recent databases for frequency estimates would support such an endeavor (e.g., Zeno, Ivenz, Millard, & Duvvuri, 1995). One approach to reduce the frequency difference of the word set for digraphs could be to include words that undergo, for instance, doubling of the final letter (e.g., *fuss*), resulting in a comparison of words such as *luck*, *lush*, and *fuss*. An alternative would be to create pseudoword stimuli, although this does not entirely avoid the same confound, since the letter pattern *sk* is also less common than *sh*. Furthermore, the use of pseudowords has its own problems. Pseudowords containing high-probability constituents are more easily recognized than pseudowords with low-probability constituents (Frisch, Large, & Pisoni, 2000). Thus, pseudowords are, apparently, processed according to stored knowledge about the sound patterns of existing words in the lexicon. Spelling instruction with words ending in one phoneme (here /k/) and containing minimally contrasting phonemes might always encounter words that differ in frequency of occurrence, neighborhood density, or whose constituents differ in phonotactic probability. It would be interesting to experimentally evaluate whether low-word frequency or low-neighborhood density is an advantage or a hindrance to application of spelling patterns for "regularly spelled" words when initial spelling instruction is explicitly founded on understanding and application of the alphabetic principle (Carreker, 1999).

A second concern regarding the superior performance for words ending in *sh* and *ck* is whether deliberate or accidental exposure to these spelling patterns had occurred in class before the intervention took place. It seems that the reading or spelling of these digraphs had not received particular attention in the curricula at the two schools because the "one-on-one relation between letter and phonological segment" was still being emphasized in the classroom (e.g., *bin, ben, bit, bet*). The students also had practiced the blending of initial consonant clusters. Whether the students were accidentally introduced to digraphs before the intervention began is not possible to determine. Because it was an important finding of this study that some digraphs apparently are easy to apply in reading and spelling, in a future spelling study, evaluation of this phenomenon could be shifted to the beginning of first grade to minimize possible interference with prior learning.

A third concern was that the students receiving phoneme instruction were somewhat further along in their reading of the intervention words at the beginning of the intervention, although they did not manifest this advantage in their speed of reading or on the standardized test of reading. It is possible that students who are further along in reading might acquire spelling faster. Future spelling interventions might pay special attention to what the impact of a reading advantage is on spelling acquisition by always testing spelling as well as reading achievement simultaneously.

## CONSEQUENCES FOR TEACHING

Orton (1937) assumed that the auditory competence and the kinesthetic functions in persons with dyslexia were intact and could be capitalized on to teach reading and spelling. Earlier, we discussed the possibility that in less-skilled spellers access to the phoneme is weak. We proposed that explicit teaching of spelling patterns combined with phonological patterns might aid spellers in two ways. Explicit instruction with a carefully chosen set of phonologically similar words unites allophonic variations of the phoneme with a letter pattern, thereby strengthening the constancy in the representation of a phonological pattern and simultaneously providing an orthographic anchor for potentially weak phonemes. Additionally, heightened sensitivity to all of the speech segments in a word clarifies the choice of spelling patterns. The success of the linguistically explicit phoneme instruction may have depended on the careful description of the interaction of spelling pattern and phonological word structure.

The results of the current study are in agreement with the new within-rime emphasis of Kessler and Treiman (2001). The occurrence of positional allophonic variation in a word also suggests that sound-spelling associations should be taught for various positions in a word (i.e., initial, medial, final) separately. Without awareness of positional sound variation, beginning spellers might not recognize that the letter *p* has the same association with the aspirated [p] in initial, the flap in middle and the released [p] in final position. The results are also compatible with the Alphabetic Phonics method (Cox, 1984), and many other approaches that target direct instruction of word structure and are accredited by the International Multisensory Structured Language Education Council (Birsh, 1999).

From the current study, we can conclude that it seems advantageous in initial instruction to focus on words grouped on phonological similarity that have a consistent spelling (see also Post & Carreker, in press). A second successful component seems to be to present a limited initial phoneme set in various positions in a word so that minimal phonological contrasts can be more easily detected and, at the same time, phonetic variation is controlled. Last, it appears to be advantageous to indicate the precise relation between phonological and orthographic patterns. Since reading and spelling inform each other, simultaneous instruction and assessment of corresponding concepts in both aspects of literacy could provide a rich source of information for student and teacher alike (Juel & Roper-Schneider, 1985). We do not suggest that each and every spelling pattern should be taught in the same exhaustive detail. As long as the precise relation with pronunciation is emphasized in consistently spelled words, the explanation of less common spelling patterns can be postponed or treated cursorily. The extent of attention to more complex spelling patterns is likely to vary for children depending on their aptitude for phonological tasks (Byrne, Fielding-Barnsley, & Ashley, 2000). At the same time, beginning readers and spellers also should be exposed to irregularly spelled, high-frequency words. If carefully selected, these spelling exceptions may highlight the regularity of systematically spelled words (Cox, 1984) and develop flexibility with respect to the English orthography. In short, the results of the current study suggest that early spelling be taught by exposing children to a group of similarly spelled and phonologically transparent words with a method that is systematic and linguistically informed.

## ACKNOWLEDGEMENT

The research was supported by Neuhaus Education Center. The results were presented at the IDA conference in Washington, D.C., on November 9, 2000. We thank the first graders who participated in the study. We also thank the teachers and the staff in the two participating schools for their cooperation. The comments of the two reviewers and the editor of the *Annals of Dyslexia* were stimulating. One reviewer was especially helpful.

Address correspondence to Yolanda V. Post, 117 NW 15th Street, #16, Oklahoma City, OK 73103. Telephone: 405/232-1460; e-mail: yolandapost@hotmail.com

## References

Adams, M. (1990). *Beginning to read: Thinking and learning about print.* Cambridge, MA: MIT Press.

Birsh, J. R. (1999). *Multisensory teaching of basic language skills.* Baltimore: Brookes.

Bosman, A. M. T., & Van Orden, G. C. (1997). Why spelling is more difficult than reading. In C. A. Perfetti, L. Rieben, and M. Fayol (eds), *Learning to spell. Research, theory, and practice across languages* (pp. 173–194). Mahwah, NJ: Lawrence Erlbaum Associates.

Brady, S. A. (1997). Ability to encode phonological representations: An underlying difficulty of poor readers. In B. Blachman (ed.), *Foundations of reading acquisition and dyslexia: Implications for early interventions* (pp. 21–47). Mahwah, NJ: Lawrence Erlbaum Associates.

Bruck, M., & Treiman, R. (1992). Learning to pronounce words: The limitations of analogies. *Reading Research Quarterly, 27,* 375–388.

Byrne, B., Fielding-Barnsley, R., & Ashley, L. (2000). Effects of preschool phoneme identity training after six years: Outcome level distinguished from rate of response. *Journal of Educational Psychology, 92,* 659–667.

Carreker, S. (1999). Teaching spelling. In J. R. Birsh (ed.), *Multisensory teaching of basic language skills* (pp. 217–256). Baltimore: Brookes.

Carroll, J. B., Davies, P., & Richman, B. (1971). *The American heritage word frequency book.* Boston: Houghton Mifflin Co.

Chen, M. (1970). Vowel length variation as a function of the voicing of the consonant environment. *Phonetica, 22,*129–59.

Cox, A. R. (1977). *Situation spelling. Formulas and equations for spelling the sounds of spoken English* (rev. ed.). Cambridge, MA: Educators Publishing Service.

Cox, A. R. (1984). *Structures and techniques. Multisensory teaching of basic language skills.* Cambridge, MA: Educators Publishing Service.

Denes, P. B., & Pinson, E. N. (1963). *The speech chain. The physics and biology of spoken language.* Baltimore, MD: Waverly Press, Inc.

Dewey, G. (1970). *Relative frequency of English spellings.* New York: Teachers College Press.

Dunn, L. M., & Dunn, L. M. (1997). *Peabody picture vocabulary test* (3rd ed.). Circle Pines, MN: AGS.

Fowler, C. A., Liberman, I. Y., & Shankweiler, D. (1977). On interpreting the error pattern in beginning reading. *Language and Speech, 20,* 162–173.

Fox, E. (1994). Grapheme-phoneme correspondence in dyslexic and matched control readers. *British Journal of Psychology, 85,* 41–53.

Frisch, S. A., Large, N. R., & Pisoni, D. B. (2000). Perception of word likeness: Effects of segment probability and length on the processing of nonwords. *Journal of Memory and Language, 42,* 481–496.

Giegerich, H. J. (1992). *English phonology: An introduction.* Cambridge: CUP.

Goswami, U. (1988). Children's use of analogy in learning to spell. *British Journal of Developmental Psychology, 6,* 21–33.

Goswami, U., & Bryant, P. (1990). *Phonological skills and learning to read.* Hove, UK: Lawrence Erlbaum Associates.

Gough, P. B., Juel, C., & Griffith, P. L. (1992). Reading, spelling, and the orthographic cipher. In P. B. Gough, L. C. Ehri, & R. Treiman (eds.), *Reading acquisition* (pp. 35–48). Hillsdale, NJ: Lawrence Erlbaum Associates.

Greenberg, S. (1999). Speaking in shorthand—A syllable-centric perspective for understanding pronunciation variation. *Speech Communication, 29,* 159–176.

Helfer, K. S., & Huntley, R. A. (1991). Aging and consonant errors in reverberation and noise. *Journal of the Acoustical Society of America, 90,* 1786–1795.

Hiebert, E. H., & Martin, L. A. (2001). The texts of beginning reading instruction. In S. B. Neuman & D. K. Dickinson, (eds.), *Handbook of early literacy research.* New York: The Guilford Press.

Hulme, C., Muter, V., & Snowling, M. (1998). Segmentation does predict early progress in learning to read better than rhyme: A reply to Bryant. *Journal of Experimental Child Psychology, 71,* 39–44.

Jenkins, J. J., Strange, W., & Trent, S. A. (1999). Context-independent dynamic information for the perception of coarticulated vowels. *Journal of the Acoustical Society of America, 106,* 438–448.

Juel, C., & Roper-Schneider, D. (1985). The influence of basal readers on first grade reading. *Reading Research Quarterly, 20,* 134–152.

Kessler, B., & Treiman, R. (2001). Relationships between sounds and letters in English monosyllables. *Journal of Memory and Language, 44,* 592–617.

Landerl, K., Wimmer, H., & Frith, U. (1997). The impact of orthographic consistency on dyslexia: A German-English comparison. *Cognition, 63,* 315–334.

Liberman, A. M., Cooper, F. S., Shankweiler, D. P., & Studdert-Kennedy, M. (1967). Perception of the speech code. *Psychological Review, 74,* 431–461.

Lisker, L. (1999). Perceiving final voiceless stops without release: Effects of preceding monophthongs versus nonmonophthongs. *Phonetica, 56,* 44–55.

Marchbanks, G., & Levin, H. (1965). Cues by which children recognize words. *Journal of Educational Psychology, 56,* 57–61.

McBride-Chang, C. (1995). Phonological processing, speech perception, and reading disability: An integrative review. *Educational Psychologist, 30,* 109–121.

Miller, G. A., & Nicely, P. E. (1955). An analysis of perceptual confusions among some English consonants. *Journal of the Acoustical Society of America, 27,* 338–352.

Nation, K., & Hulme, C. (1997). Phonemic segmentation, not onset-rime segmentation, predicts early reading and spelling skills. *Reading Research Quarterly, 32,* 154–167.

Olive, J. P., Greenwood, A., & Coleman, J. (1993). *Acoustics of American English speech. A dynamic approach.* New York: Springer Verlag.

Olson, D. R. (1996). Towards a psychology of literacy: On the relations between speech and writing. *Cognition, 60,* 83–104.

Orton, S. T. (1937). *Reading, writing and speech problems in children.* New York: W. W. Norton and Company.

Paulesu, E., Demonet, J.-F., Fazio, F., McCrory, E., Chanoine, V., Brunswick, N., Cappa, S. F., Cossu, G., Habib, M., Frith, C. D., & Frith, U. (2001). Dyslexia: Cultural diversity and biological unity. *Science, 291,* 2165–2167.

Post, Y. V., & Carreker, S. (in press). Orthographic similarity and phonological transparency in spelling. *Reading and Writing: An Interdisciplinary Journal.*

Post, Y. V., Foorman, B. R., & Hiscock, M. (1997). Speech perception and speech production as indicators of reading disability. *Annals of Dyslexia, 47,* 3–27.

Post, Y. V., Swank, P. R., Hiscock, M., & Fowler, A. E. (1999). Identification of vowel speech sounds by skilled and less skilled readers and the relation with vowel spelling. *Annals of Dyslexia, 49,* 161–194.

Raphael, L. J., & Dorman, M. F. (1980). Silence as a cue to the perception of syllable-initial and syllable-final stop consonants. *Journal of Phonetics, 8,* 269–275.

Read, C. (1971). Pre-school children's knowledge of English phonology. *Harvard Educational Review, 41,* 1–34.

Redford, M. A., & Diehl, R. L. (1999). The relative perceptual distinctiveness of initial and final consonants in CVC syllables. *Journal of the Acoustical Society of America, 106,* Pt. 1, 1555–1565.

Reitsma, P. (1983). Printed word learning in beginning readers. *Journal of Experimental Child Psychology, 36,* 321–339.

Samuel, A. G. (1989). Insights from a failure of selective adaptation: Syllable-initial and syllable-final consonants are different. *Perception & Psychophysics, 45,* 485–493.

Strange, W., & Gottfried, T.L. (1980). Task variables in the study of vowel perception. *Journal of the Acoustical Society of America, 68,* 1622–1625.

Strange, W., Verbrugge, R. R., Shankweiler, D. P., & Edman, T. R. (1976). Consonant environment specifies vowel identity. *Journal of the Acoustical Society of America, 60,* 213–224.

Torgesen, J. K., & Bryant, B. R. (1994). *Test of phonological awareness.* Austin, TX: PRO-ED.

Treiman, R. (1985). Onsets and rimes as units of spoken syllables: Evidence from children. *Journal of Experimental Child Psychology, 39,* 161–181.

Treiman, R., Berch, D., & Weatherston, S. (1993). Children's use of phoneme-grapheme correspondences in spelling: Roles of position and stress. *Journal of Educational Psychology, 85,* 466–477.

Treiman, R., Zukowski, A., & Richmond-Welty, E. D. (1995). What happened to the "n" of *sink?* Children's spellings of final consonant clusters. *Cognition, 55,* 1–38.

Van der Leij, A., & van Daal, V. H. P. (1999). Automatization aspects of dyslexia: Speed limitations in word identification, sensitivity to increasing task demands, and orthographic compensation. *Journal of Learning Disabilities, 32,* 417–428.

Weber, R. M. (1970). A linguistic analysis of first-grade reading errors. *Reading Research Quarterly, 5,* 427–451.

Wolf, C. G. (1978). Perceptual invariance for stop consonants in different positions. *Perception & Psychophysics, 24,* 315–326.

Woodcock, R. W., & Johnson, M. B. (1989). *Woodcock-Johnson psycho-educational battery-revised.* Allen, TX: DLM.

Zeno, S. M., Ivenz, S. H., Millard, R. T., & Duvvuri, R. (1995). *The educator's word frequency guide.* Brewster, NY: Touchstone Applied Science Associates.

# Traditional, Developmental, and Structured Language Approaches to Spelling: Review and Recommendations

*Bob Schlagal*

Department of Language, Reading, and Exceptionalities
Appalachian State University
Boone, North Carolina

*Current research does not support the notion that spelling is a simple rote-memory task. Learning to spell is better understood as a complex developmental process that is interconnected with phonological awareness and reading ability. In this review, three perspectives on spelling theory, research, and instruction are examined. Traditional classroom-based, developmental, and structured language approaches are outlined and their implications for assisting poor spellers explored. Instructional recommendations are made by drawing from and combining some of the strengths of each method.*

There is a robust body of clinical insight, research, and theory that ties phonological awareness to reading *and* spelling ability (Ehri, 1989,1994; Henderson, 1981; Morris & Perney, 1984; Orton, 1931/1999; Perfetti, 1985, 1992; Zutell & Rasinsky, 1989). This evidence has lent great weight to the argument for code instruction in reading, an argument that has captured public attention and effected changes in teacher preparation and practice, as well as in basal reading materials. This evidence,

Annals of Dyslexia, Vol. 51, 2001

however, has had far less impact on the general discussion and teaching of spelling. Despite some recent upsurge of interest in spelling instruction—an outgrowth largely of the standards movement and a retreat from whole language positions generally—spelling continues to be viewed by many teachers, and in many schools and school districts, as a minor area of study disconnected from the core issues of basic literacy. Samuel Orton (1931/1999) observed many years ago that "an inability to spell is treated as of more or less minor importance" (p. 247) despite the fact that it is often associated with difficulties in reading. Unfortunately, schools' lukewarm concern about spelling instruction deprives students, particularly those in the upper grades, of potentially important information about the orthographic system, information important both to reading and writing (Henderson, 1981; Perfetti, 1985).

The purpose of this paper is to consider three approaches to spelling instruction and the implications within each for instruction in spelling. An additional purpose is to suggest ways that each approach may strengthen the others in meeting the needs of poor spellers. Because these bodies of information come from different areas of inquiry and practice, practitioners within one tradition may not always be aware of useful techniques, information, or insights derived from the others.

At present, there are at least four positions taken on spelling instruction among professional educators. Some argue for systematic spelling instruction along traditional classroom lines using a basal speller (Templeton & Morris, 2000). Others argue for systematic instruction keyed to students' developmental spelling levels (Bear, Invernizzi, Templeton, & Johnston, 2000). Still others argue for spelling instruction keyed to progress through a structured language approach (Gillingham & Stillman, 1965/1997; Moats, 1995). A last group argues for incidental spelling instruction integrated with other subject areas (Wilde, 1990). Each of these positions has its adherents in educational circles, although in fact, only the first three positions have either a research base or productive clinical tradition to support them.

Despite a general indifference to and confusion about spelling instruction in school settings, there are bodies of research, clinical theory and practice that lend weight to the first three positions outlined above. The whole language position, the last, tends to be neither a systematic nor a uniform approach to spelling. As such, it does not submit well to general evaluation; therefore, I will confine my discussion to the first three positions.

# THE TRADITIONAL APPROACH TO SPELLING INSTRUCTION

Research on traditional classroom spelling instruction has been concerned chiefly with such things as word frequency, word selection, memory techniques, generalizability, and the organization of spelling lists and plans for the instructional week. Historically, two competing views of the English spelling system have dominated the study of instruction and consequently the preparation of instructional materials: the rote memory position and the generalization position (Nelson, 1989; Yee, 1966).

## MEMORIZATION

The belief that English spelling is underprincipled and unpredictable has had much influence on the history of spelling instruction (Hanna, Hodges, & Hanna, 1971). This inherited assumption tended to dominate the first half of the 20th century as researchers began seeking answers to questions about spelling materials and methods. The idea that spelling could be taught by generalizing letter-sound rules was raised repeatedly during this period, but studies investigating its effectiveness were contradictory (Yee, 1966). Due to the dominance of the memory position, basal spellers generally offered words to be learned without attention to orthographic principles to guide their selection and presentation. In essence, words were presented as separate units to be memorized one by one.

It was not until the 1930s that educators began to use word frequency as a way to improve spelling instruction (Horn, 1967). More commonly used words tend to be more easily learned and remembered than less commonly used words. Therefore, lists became graded for difficulty by their frequency—the more commonly used words being taught first—and by word length. Attention to frequency also offered some guarantee that the words children were taught would be useful in their writing.

Memory research was combined with the new frequency controlled word lists, and in the 1930s and 1940s, there evolved new strategies for dealing with word learning (Hanna, et al., 1971), including the study method. In the simplified version of the study method, students (1) look at a word, (2) say the word, (3) close their eyes and visualize the word, (4) write the word, and (5) check their spelling against the original, repeating all the steps if necessary. The practice of copying words repeatedly at one's desk until they were supposedly committed to memory gave way to the practice method wherein missed spelling words were rewritten correctly three times. In the context of ordinary spelling instruction, copying a word over more than three times was demonstrated to have mimimal additional effect.

During this time as well, investigators found support for the test-study-test approach. The pretest can be a particularly helpful component when combined with self-correction, thus calling attention to the words and parts of words to which children need to attend (Horn, 1947). Attention to the results of pretests also led investigators to an increasing awareness of individual differences among students. This increased awareness led authorities to exhort teachers that "The varying needs of individuals be considered. The learning of the gifted child," said Fitzgerald (1951, p. 8), "should not be limited to that of the average, nor should the very slow child be *overwhelmed in the hopeless undertaking of studying the normal allotment of words for the average child*" (emphasis added). In addition to the weekly plan of instruction, the practices of periodic review and of distributing small amounts of study across the week (as opposed to a massed period of instruction) found continued support and were adopted into the instructional scheme (Horn, 1969). And last, experts argued that there should be a balance between known and unknown spellings prior to the study of a list of words, a balance that is crucial in predicting the likelihood of the student mastering and retaining correct spellings from the exercise (Henderson, 1990).

## GENERALIZATION

Most basal spellers continued to present lists of disconnected words into the 1950s. At this time, Hanna and Moore (1953) at Stanford University reported a study of the orthography from a more complex and informed point of view than any taken hitherto. Hanna and Moore examined a corpus of 3,000 words that comprised the bulk of an elementary school student's spelling vocabulary. Rather than analyzing simple letter-sound correspondences in a linear way as had been done previously (Yee, 1966), they examined predictable correspondences in relation to stress and position in words; that is, they examined orthographic regularities in the environment of syllables, the organizational units into which words are bound for spelling and decoding. Based on this analysis, Hanna and Moore found that the orthography held a much higher degree of predictability than had been understood to this point. Indeed, they found that "four fifths of the phonemes contained in the words comprising the traditional spelling vocabulary of the elementary school child approximate the alphabetic principle in their letter representations" (Hanna, et al., 1971, p. 76).

To strengthen these claims, the Stanford team undertook the first major computerized investigation of the orthography (Hanna, Hanna, Hodges, & Rudorf, 1966). Due to the power of the newly available technology, they were able to study a far larger corpus of words: over 17,000. The results of the computer study demonstrated more powerfully than before the surprising degree of consistency in the system, a consistency that extended well beyond the basic high-frequency vocabulary taught in spellers. In fact, Hanna, Hodges, and Hanna (1971) observed that the more words the computer had to deal with, the more principled the orthography seemed. Hanna concluded that only 3 percent of English words are true "spelling demons" and require strict memorization (Hanna, et al., 1966).

Further studies have substantiated and extended these results, going beyond basic syllable constraints to take into account the morphological character of English spelling, a highly regular principle in the system (Venezky, 1967). Following on the publication of these studies, it became more difficult to claim that the orthography was neither systematic nor linguistically based. Soon, basal spellers were revised and word lists were designed to illustrate the orderly functioning of the spelling system based both on frequency of use and frequency of pattern. As a result of these changes, many basal spelling series have come to offer students a progressive overview of the spelling system, moving from simple to complex in terms of familiarity, word length, and orthographic structure. In fact, some basals have further tried to bring their programs in line with insights derived form developmental research (described below). The goal of list learning from this point of view, then, is no longer just the words themselves. Instead, words are learned to help build systematic knowledge that will generalize to other words of similar form.

# THE DEVELOPMENTAL POSITION

## LEARNING ENGLISH ORTHOGRAPHY

In the last three decades of the twentieth century, spelling researchers turned their attention away from issues that had concerned them previously. Specifically, they turned away from long-standing inquiries into instructional formats and the appropriate choice of words for spelling lists. Instead, they began to focus attention on learners—and in particular on learners' errors—in an effort to understand the development of spelling ability (Nelson, 1989). As a result of this shift in attention, there now exist numerous studies that document the predictable ways that children's emerging phonemic awareness connects with the increasing demands of the orthography (Chomsky, 1970, 1979; Henderson & Beers, 1980; Luelsdorff, 1991; Morris, Nelson, & Perney, 1986; Templeton & Bear, 1992).

Researchers have observed a progression of error-types as children move from concrete phonemic analysis to increasingly abstract linguistic representation in the orthography. There is no uniform agreement about how precisely to describe this development. Yet the study of this changing array of error-types has led a number of researchers to describe development in terms of either stages or of evolving problem solving strategies (Ehri, 1994; Henderson & Beers, 1980; Moats, 1995; Read, 1986). Moreover, these descriptive schemes document a hierarchy of difficulties for the learner. These difficulties are posed both by the learner's emerging phonological awareness and by the system itself (Luelsdorff, 1991; Schlagal, 1992).

Despite variations in descriptive systems, it is generally accepted that English orthography is at root alphabetic but that it also moves beyond this principle in order to represent other kinds of information (Chomsky, 1970; Venezky, 1967). In part, this abstraction is the consequence of expressing the 40-some phonemes in the language with the 26 letters of the alphabet; in part it reflects the diverse historical sources for the English lexicon and the broad adoption of nonnative spellings. All of these sources have contributed to a complex and broadly organized whole. The late Edmund Henderson (1990), his colleagues (Henderson & Beers, 1980; Templeton & Bear, 1992), and others (Henry, 1993; Veltman, 1992), argue that the spelling system is organized in three dimensions. English spelling represents words (1) through direct phoneme-grapheme mapping. This can be seen in the concrete representation of sound in most CVC words (closed syllables) and their variants (*bed, split, blend, contract*). On top of this alphabetic base (2) are imposed patterns representing phonemic elements. This can be seen in the common expressions of the CVCe and CVVC words (e.g., *came* and *keep*) but also in the joining of syllables as seen in the VCCV (*rab-bit* and *hit-ting*) and VCV (na-tive and pi-lot) patterns, and in stress sensitive doubling (*omitted* versus. *limited*). Finally, English (3) represents derivational meaning in its spelling. This can be seen in the common orthographic base of words with sometimes significant sound variation (e.g., *sign-signal, compose-composition, tragedy-tragedian*). In order to be complete, developmental descriptions must make sense of these core elements of the orthography.

Henderson became convinced during the mid 1960s that "understanding how children *spell* words can provide insight into how they *read* words" (Templeton & Morris, 2000, p. 531). Charles Read (1975) and Carol Chomsky's (1979) breakthrough work into children's grasp of phonology as reflected in invented spelling gave Henderson and his colleagues at the University of Virginia the analytic tools to undertake a series of studies to document the range of students' orthographic development from its earliest beginnings to its full maturity. Henderson's sense that developing word knowledge (including phonological and orthographic information) was key to the reading process has been supported by a number of studies (Ehri, 1994; Invernizzi, 1992; Perfetti, 1992), as has the notion that reading and spelling skills are deeply interrelated (Bruck, 1988; Morris & Perney, 1984). The results of studies at the University of Virginia produced a detailed descriptive system that labels the orthographic features students explore at each stage of their development. While developmental schemes often vary from one set of scholars to another, they consistently document a movement from concrete phonetic approximations through conventional phonemic choices to increasingly abstract, orthographically driven representations. In my discussion, I will rely on the stages outlined in the Virginia studies, in part because it is a descriptive system that is tied to analytic, observational, and instructional hierarchies. (For stage descriptions that highlight somewhat different analytic emphases, see Ehri, 1989; and Moats, 1995.) These stages describe common developmental themes seen across many children. They should not be taken as rigid, airtight, and invariant categories.

*Nonphonetic Stage.*  Many young children play with letters in an effort to represent language. Their earliest efforts, however, are not informed by insights into the phonological character of alphabetic language. Their experiments are nonphonetic (Read, 1986) and involve random arrays of letters. For example, one little girl wrote THHZ3TE. When asked what she had written, she replied "Sad stories and happy stories," revealing the fact she had not yet discovered that letters encode speech sounds (Henderson, 1981).

*Semiphonetic Stage.* The first significant step forward into literacy is a stage of partial alphabetic discovery often termed semiphonetic or prephonetic. At this stage, children begin to use the names (or principal sounds embedded within the names) of letters to represent words or syllables, or word or syllable boundaries (e.g., WE LKRNHS: We like our new house MI KT HS KTS: My cat has kittens). These spellings reveal the beginnings of phonemic awareness and also its developmental limits (Morris, 1999). Initial consonant phonemes are typically grasped first and appear to stabilize before other speech sounds, particularly medial vowels. While consonant phonemes are somewhat easier to isolate, not all consonant letter names provide an apt clue to their identity. In particular, *w, h, g,* and *y,* do not hold phonemic clues in their names. Nor does knowledge of letter names address the problems posed by the phonemes represented by digraphs. In these instances, children make do as best they can, borrowing phonetic properties from letters that contain some hint of the target phoneme. For example, /*w*/is often represented by *y* and /ch/ by *h*. In addition, minimally contrastive consonant phonemes (*b-p* and *d-t,* for example) are readily confusable.

At this stage, phonemic analysis remains incomplete. The difficulty that young children have in segmenting phonemes in spoken words due to their coarticulation was well understood by Samuel Orton (1937/1999) in relation to dyslexic students: "The spoken word has been acquired in both the auditory memory and in the speech mechanism as a unit and not a blend of its parts, and often the child is completely at sea at first as to how to approach the dissection. Occasionally, even the breaking up of long words into syllables is difficult or impossible although this seems more readily learned than the further step of analyzing the syllables themselves into sounds" (pp. 99–100). Children at the semiphonetic stage cannot tease out all of the constituent phonemes within a word or syllable, but they are exploring those that reside on the boundaries of the syllable. This common and early expression of phonemic awareness reveals that it is not an all-or-nothing proposition but, in fact, demonstrates that phonemic awareness emerges over time based on experience and influenced by instruction (Perfetti, Beck, Bell, & Hughes, 1987). Commonly, children are able to hear phonemes first in the initial, then in the final, and last in the medial position.

Generally, students at the semiphonetic level are regarded as "emergent readers" (Morris, 1999). As readers, they make use of initial consonants as clues to word recognition (Ehri, 1994).

Instruction that supports and extends knowledge of simple consonants in beginning positions is important at this juncture. Once beginning consonants are under control, teaching simple short vowel word families is especially useful (Morris, 1999). Because they do not require complete phonemic segmentation, practicing reading and spelling a series of words that contrast simple CVC patterns across a single vowel (*mad* versus *sat* versus *rag*) reinforces awareness of beginning consonants, forces attention to final consonants, and sensitizes children to vowel coloration when family patterns are contrasted (*mat* versus *pig*) (Morris, 1999).

*Phonetic Stage.* As children's experience in supported reading activities and word analysis grows, they begin segmenting and representing phonemes in increasingly complex ways. The errors (or inventions) they create have been variously termed phonetic, phonemic, lettername or alphabetic, and this stage correlates strongly with beginning reading (Morris & Perney, 1984). Phonetic stage spellings are often strikingly unconventional in appearance but reveal a high degree of attention both to articulatory detail and to the phonetic makeup of letter names (Read, 1975). Two examples are WE WET ONA NACHR CHRAL (We went on a nature trail) and I AUM NOT FOLON THE RULS ET SKUL, PLEZ TOK TO ME (I am not following the rules at school, please talk to me).

Perhaps most significant at this stage is that children are able to access basic vowel phonemes in their analyses. Of particular note is their treatment of long versus short vowels. Long vowels tend to be classified correctly "because they say their own names." Long vowel inventions, however, are spelled by their letter names alone, omitting the diacritical graphemes used to mark vowels long (e.g., *make, feet*). Short vowels follow a pattern of letter-name substitutions based on articulatory analysis. That is, children represent a short vowel by choosing the name of a vowel letter that fits most closely with the target short vowel in point of articulation. For example, *bed* may be spelled as BAD, *sick* as SEK, and *cut* as KOT.)

Vowels are not the only challenge at this level. Children may continue having difficulty with some of the consonant phonemes in the semiphonetic stage (e.g., letter name and minimal pair confusions), although these confusions often are worked out quickly as sight vocabulary increases and as letter-sounds are taught. In addition, phonetic stage learners experience problems with consonant blends in both initial and final positions. Even though consonants frequently retain their individual identity in blends, children experience difficulty in segmenting them, particularly preconsonantal nasals (e.g., BOP for *bump*). Until they are able to fully analyze the phonemic segments, their spellings tend to honor only the most salient element of a blend. Thus, early on, *slap* might be spelled as SAP and *bend* as BAD. Children also experience difficulty with the incidental affrication in the *dr-* and *tr-* blends; these may be rendered as J or H, or in a more advanced student, as JR- and CHR-, respectively. Thus, *drain* might be spelled JAN or JRAN, and *trip* HEP, CHEP, or CHREP. Further, students at this stage give phonetic spellings for past tense *-ed* endings (e.g., LEKT for *licked*, ROLD for *rolled*, BATID for *batted*) and for plural forms (RUNZ for *runs* and BONCHIZ for *bunches*). They also tend to omit vowels from unaccented syllables, especially those with vocalic or nasal consonants (e.g., BADL for *battle*, SESTR for *sister*, SODN for *sudden*), and to represent the reduced /t/ as /d/ in words like *butter* (BODR).

This stage represents an extended exploration of the alphabetic principle. Children's errors reveal a high degree of attention to phonetic detail, a level of detail that conventional spelling does not always represent. It is during this stage that most children learn phonemic segmentation in increasingly complete ways. While children begin this stage with naive intuitions about phoneme-grapheme mappings, with experience, their spellings grow not only more complete but also more conventional. Speech sounds that are initially difficult for beginners to tease out (like consonant blends) gradually submit to analysis, though more complex blends (e.g., *scr-*, *spl-*, *tr*) can cause more protracted difficulty.

Perhaps the most challenging facet of work at this stage is learning the conventional classifications of short vowels, an effort that takes a number of months for most children and still longer for others. This stage is a particularly ripe time for the kind of phonics instruction that helps students clarify and extend the features their analysis makes available to them. In particular, attention needs to be paid to single consonant accuracy, to basic consonant digraphs, and to consonant clusters in initial, then final position. Special care needs to be taken with short-vowel spellings.

***Within Word Pattern Stage.*** As students gain competence in phonemic analysis and learn the basics of conventional alphabetic spelling, and as they acquire a larger store of sight vocabulary, they become increasingly attentive to more abstract features of the spelling system. They begin to attend to the role that silent letters or relational elements (e.g., CVCe and CVVC) play in signaling specific vowel phonemes. It is as if by fully grasping the alphabetic principle that children can then begin to make sense of elements of spelling that their preoccupation with speech sounds had earlier excluded (Invernizzi, 1992). Those elements are largely the patterns by which we mark long vowels. This stage has been referred to as the within word pattern or transitional stage of word knowledge. At the earlier phonetic stage, some select individual long-vowel words may be spelled correctly. When a long-vowel spelling is not known, however, phonetic stage children will represent only what can be heard (BOT for *boat*). At the within word pattern stage, however, their errors generally reflect a growing attention to orthographic structures (BOTE for *boat*). Although they continue to build accuracy, completenesss, and automaticity in phonemic segmentation and phoneme representation at this stage, the shift in student error-types demonstrates that they understand that spelling involves more than phonological analysis. In struggling to control basic long-vowel spellings, students are beginning to treat selected phonemes in terms of more complex graphemic patternings.

During the within word pattern stage, students tend to "use but confuse" common long-vowel patterns in the following ways:  BOTE: *boat*; RAIT: *rate*; KEEPE: *keep*; BRANE: *brain*; and GAYME: *game*. Although not as frequently, they may also overgeneralize vowel markers to words that do not need them (FRUME: *from*; SHOTE: *shot*), demonstrating the kinds of inaccuracies that commonly attend rule learning and generalization (Beers, 1980; Zutell, 1980). At this stage, student errors suggest a sensitivity to syllabic form in English. That is, they tend to represent a vowel for every syllable, whether those vowels are phonemically apparent or not. While phonetic stage errors in unaccented syllables look like SODN for *sudden* and HADL for *handle*, within word pattern errors look like SUDAN and HANDIL. By the end of this stage, students have typically stabilized spellings for inflected endings (*-ed*, *-ing*, and *-s/-es*).

Developmental spelling instruction seeks to help students stabilize the patterns they have begun to use but use inaccurately (Henderson, 1981). Therefore, word study at this level generally introduces basic marking patterns for long vowels in contrast to short vowels. Instruction generally moves vowel by vowel, teaching the most stable and common pattern. Multiple versions of a long vowel (*take, rain, say*) are not introduced together. Instead, the most common pattern must be well understood before introducing a variant pattern. It is at the within word pattern level as well that common vowel diphthongs (e.g., *ow, oi, aw*) are introduced for study after basic long-vowel patterns are under control.

*Syllable Juncture Stage.* Once students have mastered basic long- and short-vowel patterns in single syllable words, they face an issue that draws on and extends from this base of knowledge. It is an issue that forces them to think not only at the level of syllable patterns but also across syllables (Luelsdorff, 1991; Zutell & Rasinsky, 1989) This stage is called syllable juncture, although in some developmental schemes it may fall under the rubrics morphemic (Ehri, 1994) or morphophonemic (Moats, 1995). When adding suffixes, particularly inflected endings, the structure of the CVC or CVCe base is manipulated. When adding *-ed* or *-ing* to a CVC stem, the consonant is doubled in order to maintain the closed syllable structure and preserve or mark the short vowel (*tap/tap-ping*). Failure to double inadvertently creates a new word: *taping*. When adding *-ed* or *-ing* to a CVCe base, the silent *-e* is dropped and the stem, in effect, becomes an open syllable (*tape/ta-ping*) (Henderson, 1990). This preserves the integrity of the long vowel and makes the e-marker redundant. Common juncture errors at this stage involve failing to double consonants when appropriate (HUMING for *humming*) or overgeneralizing doublets to words which do not need them (KEEPPING for *keeping*). Similarly, students may fail to drop silent *-e's* when necessary or may (more rarely) overgeneralize a silent *-e* to a word which does not have one (RUNEING for *running*), even when the correct spelling of the stem is well understood.

These junctural principles provide a basic understanding of closed and open syllables in bi-syllabic words where those features are part of a single morpheme, as in *puddle* and *butane*, respectively. While there are a fair number of exceptions to the doubling principle in bi-syllabic, single morpheme words (*never, habit*), these can be taken into account once the principle is understood in its more common and rule-governed form. These junctural principles are challenging, and while mastering them in one condition does not guarantee that they will extend to more complex versions (as in the doubling of stressed CVC syllables like *omitted* versus *edited*), it is a prerequisite. These junctural operations require students to add another layer of abstraction onto the basic patterning distinctions that they learned in the within word pattern stage.

At its most complex level, consonant doubling occurs in the assimilation of prefixes to root words. In both pronunciation and spelling, some prefixes (e.g, *cum-*, *in-*, *ad-*) have been absorbed with the root. This creates another type of juncture problem. Words like c̲o̲mmunity, c̲o̲rrect, i̲r̲regular, i̲n̲nate, and a̲d̲dition and a̲n̲nounce reveal the assimilation of the Latin prefixes; *cum-*, *in-* and *ad-* have been joined to a root, creating a consonant doublet in the process.

At this stage, developmental instruction takes into account simple consonant doubling and *e-* drop operations for inflected words, as well as closed and open syllables in two syllable words (*pillow* versus *pilot*). It also begins to direct students to focus on stress in multisyllabic words and to syllable segmentation for reading and spelling. Spelling with basic prefixes and suffixes and more advanced doubling issues come later.

***Derivational Constancy Stage.*** Once students have moved beyond the simple linear, one-phoneme-at-a-time assumptions about spelling, and once they have developed a working knowledge of how patterns encode sound both within and across syllables, they are in a position to see that orthographic patterning is also used to represent meaning. The ground work for learning about lexical consistency in English is laid in the earlier stages as children learn correct spellings for past tense and plural endings, as they absorb homophones into their sight and spelling vocabularies, and as they learn simple prefixes. As achieving spellers move into the later elementary years and into the middle grades, they confront a growing vocabulary of polysyllabic words. These words are chiefly composed of Greek and Latin borrowings that constitute much of the vocabulary of educated discourse. The spelling of this new vocabulary is deeply informed by meaning. This stage has been termed derivational constancy, derivational relations, and morphemic or morphophonemic.

A central theme of this advanced stage of word knowledge includes discovering how derivationally connected words share spelling patterns despite variations in pronunciation. The power of this derivational economy can be seen in low-frequency words such as tragedian and telephony which, though strange to the ear, declare themselves to the eye. That is to say, the semantic core of these words is more clearly articulated in their orthographic than in their spoken form. For informed readers and spellers, this dimension of the orthography is a powerful one.

Learners in the derivational constancy stage struggle with difficulties created by sound variations across common roots

and stems. In particular, students are troubled by vowel alternation (*insane/insanity*) and vowel reduction (*normal/normality;
compete/competition*), by consonant alternation (*medicine/medi-
cal*), and by silent/sounded consonants (*column/columnist*).
Thus, students may write INSANNITY, NORMEL, COMPUTI-
TION, MEDICKAL, and COLUM because they do not know or
do not make the lexical connection with the derivational mate.
In addition, at this stage students may work out the appropriate
applications of the *-able/-ible* and *-ant/-ent, -ance/-ence* suffixes.

Work at this level largely entails learning to attend to the
meaning/spelling connection in upper-level vocabulary (Henry,
1993; Nagy, Diakidoy, & Anderson, 1993). At this time, a gradual introduction to the role of Greek and Latin roots can be
helpful. It is interesting to note that when words are organized
by frequency, they offer a picture of the orthography which, on
the whole, matches the descriptions of its structure and historical development (Henderson, 1990).

**MEETING INDIVIDUAL NEEDS**

One of the instructional consequences of the developmental
perspective is the implication that teaching students at their developmental level will help them make better sense of instruction. Morris, Nelson, and Perney (1986) have found that
spelling instructional level was a strong predictor of developmental level in spelling; and Morris, Blanton, Blanton, and
Perney (1995) have shown evidence that spelling instructional
level is a strong predictor of learning and retention in conventional spelling instruction. Teaching students beyond their developmental level invites rote memorization of words, an
inefficient and often impermanent form of learning. In contrast,
teaching students at their developmental level involves clarify-
ing emerging concepts through the careful study of words that
illustrate those concepts. The developmental position does not
imply, as some have mistakenly concluded, that development
should be left to take care of itself. In fact, just the opposite is
true; developmental stages inform instructional intervention
(Schlagal & Trathen, 1998).

*Assessment for Instruction.*   To teach at an appropriate developmental level entails careful assessment. This is most efficiently and reliably accomplished by administering a graded
spelling inventory that samples a broad variety of features common at each level of difficulty (Henderson, 1990; Morris,
Nelson, & Perney, 1986). Errors at students' instructional level
are then examined for stage and particular error-types. In order

to complete a qualitative analysis of a student's errors, the teacher must have basic knowledge of the featural problems posed at each stage and, more particularly, must pay careful attention to the student's individual confusions. Detailed discussions of developmental assessment can be found in Bear et. al. (2000), Schlagal (1996), and Moats (1995).

*Word Study.* Henderson's conviction was that word knowledge, however perfectly or imperfectly conceived, provides the common base from which word identification and spelling emerge. He recommended that clinical instruction involve the systematic study of words ("word study" referred to above) in a concept building format. This entails categorization tasks in which preselected words (written on cards) are named and sorted into a set of contrastive groups established by the teacher. This sorting activity serves to highlight similarities and differences among the target phonemes and structures of the words (Bear, et. al., 2000; Morris, 1999; Schlagal, 1996). A particular word sort will be used until the student can (1) name and sort the words quickly and accurately, (2) recognize them in and out of context, (3) isolate and articulate the target features, and (4) spell the target words and generalize their patterns to similar words. As an example, here is a completed sort highlighting contrastive short vowels in CVC words.

| cat | sit | hot |
|-----|-----|-----|
| bad | lip | mop |
| nap | rid | rob |
| rag | hid | nod |

Except for semiphonetic stage students who commonly work with contrastive word families (e.g. -*at* words versus -*ap* and -*ag* words), the majority of words used in word study must be sight words so that students are working from an established knowledge base and are not being taught features from words they have not yet stabilized, at least at the level of recognition. The focal features of a word sort are targeted in an inductive manner through teacher questioning (e.g. "Read down this list. Good. How are all these words alike? Yes, and what sound does "i" make in these words? If I said the word "neck," in which column would it have to go?). There is a degree of recursiveness built into a developmental sequence of instruction: for instance, as a new pattern is introduced, it is studied in relation to those recently taught.

This method of word study follows a scope and sequence suggested by the developmental stages described above, but it is also shaped by specific difficulties students are having with features at their particular level. Although this system of word study is being discussed in the light of spelling development, it serves a broader purpose than spelling instruction alone. Word recognition, word analysis, and word representation are thought of as complementary processes, and each of these is actively incorporated toward the improvement of word knowledge (Henderson, 1981; Perfetti, 1992). As a program of phonics instruction, it is analytic rather than synthetic.

## THE STRUCTURED LANGUAGE APPROACH

The long tradition of systematic, language-based instruction has grown chiefly from Samuel Orton's work with dyslexic readers and was extended and formalized by Gillingham and Stillman (1965/1997). Orton conceived of reading disability along a continuum of developmental impairment that included both genetic and environmental factors (Miles & Miles, 1994), and he contended that "adequate special methods should correct it"(1929/1999, p. 201). Orton also observed that spelling and reading disabilities were interconnected, and that improvements in one domain could have effects in the other domain, and that neither domain should be neglected. Although he stated that the popular "look-say" (whole word) memory-based methods of his day were adequate for the average child, he contended that these were inimical to the success of disabled readers. Along with his use of instruction that appealed to multiple sense modalities simultaneously, Orton developed methods for "retraining" students in the specifically linguistic character of reading.

Central to Samuel Orton's "special methods" was the development of word recognition and spelling skill by thorough grounding in the alphabetic principle. Although for Orton the etiology of dyslexia rested in the visual-perceptual problems of mixed dominance he called strephosymbolia, he also wrote of reading disability (or "developmental alexia") as a language difficulty. Interestingly, Orton felt that the spoken language of his dyslexic students was both a source of strength and weakness. In his view, the spoken language of his students, though not always ideal, was basically intact. His intent was to capitalize on that language competence by tying instruction directly to it.

Orton began retraining with the basic units of speech and spelling (sounds and letters) and taught these to mastery before proceeding to larger units. Great pains were taken to develop accurate links between letters and sounds, and these were continually reviewed to ensure that they remained "secure." Strict attention was paid to the clear articulation of individual sounds (purged of extraneous vowel components, e.g., /b/ instead of "buh") and to the use of visual and kinesthetic methods to fix the "mnemonic linkage" between elements. From a firm grapheme-phoneme and phoneme-grapheme base followed the dynamic application of this alphabet knowledge in the "blending" of letter-sounds into words (decoding) and the "dissecting of sounds" (phonemic analysis) for spelling. In addition, Orton employed nonsense words to further extend skill with decoding and encoding and to eliminate his students' tendency to guess at words.

Orton also took great interest in dyslexic spelling errors. In these he observed great difficulty with letter reversals—a difficulty not currently supported by contemporary research—and he also discovered a pronounced difficulty in the accurate spelling of vowels, short vowels in particular. This latter is a prominent finding among developmental researchers who have documented it extensively in phonetic and within word pattern stage spellers (Read, 1975; Schlagal, 1992). Other researchers also confirm that short-vowel errors are extremely common among poor readers and spellers (Post, Swank, Hiscock, & Fowler, 1999; Sawyer, Wade, & Kim, 1999). To help with this difficulty, Orton employed "a campaign of speech therapy" to create "a more accurate spoken reproduction" of words so that their sounds might be more clearly recognized. He also employed the practice of taking apart the "constituent phonetic units" of a spoken word to "name and write each unit as it is isolated" (1999, p. 100). The practice of "tapping out phonemes"was further added to assist with "dissection" and "blending" of words and sounds.

The most important development in the early core of Orton's practices, however, is the systematic teaching of spelling and decoding in the context of a detailed analysis of regularities of English spelling. Because the syllable is the organizational unit for both spelling and decoding, students are taught to apply the alphabetic principle in the context of a distinctive analysis of syllable types. There are six of these: the closed syllable (VC: *slap*), the silent -*e* syllable (VCe: *time*), the open syllable (CV: *no*), the r-controlled syllable (Vr: *park*), the consonant -*le* syllable (Cle: *little*), and the diphthong or double vowel syllable (VV: *beet*, *brown*).

In the main, how written words may be pronounced is determined by their syllable structure, and, in polysyllabic words, by the presence or absence of stress within the syllables. In Orton-based methods, reading, spelling, and word analysis exercises are carried out under careful control of the syllable types and phoneme options. Initially, students are given limited exposure to irregular words and to word structures that have not been taught directly. Phoneme-grapheme relations are introduced in the context of the closed syllable. This core syllable type is the organizational unit in which the alphabetic principle has its richest and most concrete expression. In structured language methods, students do not pass beyond it until they can encode and decode this syllable type in all of its predictable variants. The pace, then, of instruction is determined by the progress of the student.

The direct teaching and exercise of syllable segmentation of polysyllabic words is also important. If individuals are not able to distinguish syllable boundaries in polysyllabic words, their syllable-specific decoding and encoding skills cannot be used reliably. Like most things in the study of English orthography, this is a complex area. There are inconsistencies between the segmentation of syllables in speech and those in writing, and some doubt the value of teaching students to divide words into syllables for spelling (Venezky, 2000). However, even when their phonemic segmentation skills have been remediated, dyslexics often struggle to read or spell polysyllabic words, addressing them as overlong strings of phonemes rather than as relational units (Miles, 1993; Moats, 1995). As Hanna et al. (1971) observe, "some form of syllabication is necessary for an understanding of phoneme-grapheme relationships. . . ." (p. 228). Cummings (1988) also notes that "the syllable plays an immediate and concrete role in spoken language" (p. 60) and demonstrates that in American English spelling, there is a powerful tendency for boundaries of "written elements" (the orthographic equivalent of morphemes in phonology) to coincide with spoken syllables. Further, several developmental studies of normally developing reader/spellers have documented the growing salience of the syllable as a perceptual unit in reading as it emerges as an organizational unit in spelling (Invernizzi, 1992). Evidently, this sensitivity to the relational "chunks" in spelling and decoding is hard for disabled readers to establish. Although specific training in syllable types and syllable division may not be necessary for normally developing children, the direct teaching of these concepts can be valuable for most children and is essential for those experiencing difficulty in learning to read.

Currently, there is no strong empirical support for any specific method of remedial instruction. There is, however, an abundance of evidence pointing to the value of systematic and direct phonics instruction for beginning and disabled readers (Snow, Burns, & Griffin, 1998). It stands to reason that the deeper the level of difficulty, the more explicit, direct, systematic, and memorable such instruction would need to be. While research into language-based learning disabilities appears to explain the success of a direct, systematic instructional program like Orton-Gillingham, it is less clear what contributions its multisensory components make (Moats & Ferrell, 1999). Be that as it may, practitioners have long felt that multisensory techniques are an important part of the approach, almost jumpstarting linguistic connections in students with severe phonological deficits. For reasons that are not entirely clear, it appears to work, perhaps for no other reason than "the effect of various sensory and motor experiences on attention and recall" (Moats & Ferrell, 1999, p. 15).

## CONFRONTING SPELLING DIFFICULTIES

### MEETING POOR SPELLERS' NEEDS WITH TRADITIONAL MATERIALS

Despite the improvement over time in the organization and presentation of English spelling in basals (described above), failure to meet the needs of poor spellers has long been an issue (Fitzgerald, 1951; Henderson, 1990; Horn, 1969; Wilde, 1990). In practice, few classroom teachers seriously modify their instruction to address individual instructional needs, and many doubt the efficacy of doing so. In an effort to answer questions about the efficacy of simple classroom modifications, Morris and several colleagues investigated the idea of instructional level in spelling.

In order to determine whether or not there was empirical validity in the idea of an instructional level for spelling, Morris, Nelson, and Perney (1986) explored the concept of "spelling instructional level" through an analysis of error-types among students on the Qualitative Inventory of Word Knowledge (Schlagal, 1992) graded lists of words. (For discussions of this diagnostic instrument, see Henderson, 1990; Moats, 1995;

Morris, et al., 1986; and Schlagal, 1992.) Morris et al. (1986) found that there was a strong correlation between the *quantity* and the *quality* of students' errors. More particularly, they found that there was a marked deterioration of the quality of students' errors when they were scoring less than 40 percent accuracy on a grade level spelling test. Above this score, the quality of errors remained high; that is, the target spelling was missed by just one or two features and was readily interpretable (e.g., MESURE or MEASHURE for measure; PREPAREING or PER-PAIRING for preparing). Below the list score of 40 percent accuracy, there were more errors per word and the errors often rendered the word difficult to read (e.g., MIZER for measure; PRPING for preparing). Morris and his colleagues concluded that students within their instructional level appear to have established sufficient conceptual knowledge to make sense of instruction dealing with that level of the orthography. Students working above their instructional level (at their frustration level) on the other hand, have not developed sufficient conceptual foundations to make sense of and retain words studied at that level.

In order to track the gains of high- and low-achieving spellers in classrooms using several different basal spellers, Morris, Blanton, Blanton, and Perney (1995) followed third- and fifth-grade students across a year of instruction. The investigators found that students working at their instructional level across the year learned and retained approximately 85 percent of the words they were taught. On the other hand, students working at their frustration level experienced small gains and retained only about 45 percent of the words they had been taught during the year. Interestingly, the authors found that low-achieving students did quite well on end of week tests (an average score of 86 percent accuracy). These apparent gains had washed out in six weeks' time, however. Orton (1931/1999) observed this phenomenon many years ago, noting that when students have not established a foundation for word learning they will rely on "rote memory." While such efforts may give an impression of learning, "these implants . . . are evanescent. . . ."(p. 245).

Morris and his colleagues concluded that for students taught at their instructional level, basal spellers such as the ones used in their study provide an effective, developmentally appropriate instructional tool. Such teaching enables students to develop concepts which they can extend to other words of similar kind. Students taught at their frustration level, however, are unlikely to retain many of the words they have been taught or internalize the patterns that underlie the words they do learn. In addition, the authors observed that the achieving spellers who had been taught at their instructional level now had a solid base for addressing the challenges of the next year's spelling work. Low-achieving spellers who had been given spelling lessons above their instructional level failed to establish a solid base of orthographic knowledge at their current grade level and, moreover, were at still greater risk for the next year's work.

In a follow-up study, Morris, Blanton, Blanton, Nowacek, and Perney (1995) tracked low-achieving third-grade spellers for a year, half of whom participated in an intervention in which they were taught at their instructional level (second grade) and half of whom were taught in grade-level (i.e., frustration level) spelling books. The results revealed significant year-end gains for the intervention group who were taught at their instructional level. Gains made by the comparison group who were taught with grade-level words were poor, mirroring the findings of the previous study. Interestingly, students taught at their instructional level not only made greater gains than the comparison group at their second-grade posttest but also scored no worse than the comparison group on the grade-level (third-grade) posttest. What is more, the intervention group scored significantly better than the comparison group on a transfer test of third-grade words they had not studied. How the intervention group made gains on third-grade words was not a question asked in the study, but the authors suggest that by solidifying their knowledge of the spelling system at a lower level of complexity, students were better able to make sense of grade-level patterns through incidental reading and writing. Morris and his group concluded that spelling achievement can be improved by using traditional materials flexibly. That is, if teachers provide instructionally appropriate spelling lists for their weakest students, significant gains can be made by many poor spellers.

## A DEVELOPMENTAL EXPLANATION FOR SPELLING INSTRUCTIONAL LEVELS

Learning to spell involves years of schooling and occurs at varying rates. From the developmental perspective outlined below, Henderson (1990) has argued that these differences in rate of learning are determined by children's word knowledge. In its simplest sense, word knowledge is taken to be a person's tacit grasp of the relationship between the orthography and the phonological character of words. In other words, the correspondence between a child's word knowledge and the complexity of the orthographic structures being taught will predict what can be learned, retained, and generalized. There are substantive dimensions of English spelling that are hierarchically organized (Cummings, 1988; Luelsdorff, 1991). Therefore, a learner who stabilizes orthographic principles at a basic level can more effectively learn to control principles at a more complex level. For example, a speller who understands and controls the rule governing long- versus short-vowel distinctions (*bat* versus *bake*) can better understand and control (when taught) the related rule governing the doubling of consonants when adding common inflected endings (*batting, baking*).

Well-organized basal spelling series embody a progressive representation of words in terms of their difficulty, broadly controlled by pattern and frequency. Students who have an adequate level of prior knowledge will be able to make sense of instruction because they can extend what they already know to words of similar kind and difficulty. When the general quality of errors is high (GRAVLE for *gravel* or DOCTER for *doctor*), concepts may be confirmed and refined and word specific spellings retained. When the general quality of errors is low (GAVL for *gravel* or DOTR for *doctor*), neither concepts nor specific spellings are likely to be learned (Morris, Nelson, & Perney, 1986; Miles, 1993). Instruction at the right level of difficulty will tend to match students with words that coincide with their current stage or strategy, whereas instruction at the wrong level of difficulty will not.

Specific issues in instructional and developmental spelling levels have not been of historic concern for Orton-based practitioners whose methods create their own "instructional levels" as they move along. Appropriate level difficulty is maintained in structured language approaches through a strict instructional sequence and the phonetic control of materials.

## SPELLING DIFFICULTIES AMONG DYSLEXIC STUDENTS

In light of current descriptions of spelling development, some researchers have examined spelling errors among disabled readers and writers. Since the time of Orton, spelling difficulty has been observed and documented among dyslexics and even among remediated dyslexics (Bruck, 1987; Orton, 1937/1999; Moats, 1995). In fact, the distinctive character of dyslexics' spelling errors has long been supposed to be a hallmark of the disability. However, spelling errors have not proven to be a distinguishing characteristic, at least in any obvious way. Careful examination of dyslexic students' misspellings suggests that their errors are not qualitatively different from those of normally developing children when compared by developmental level (Carlisle, 1987; Worthy & Invernizzi, 1990). Virtually all of the error-types committed by disabled spellers can be accounted for by the developmental scheme described above (or one of its variants). Because pronounced spelling difficulties go hand in hand with severe reading disability, and because these difficulties may be understood in developmental terms, one might conclude that dyslexia represents a developmental delay rather than a specific disability. As Bailet observes, however, "this does not mean . . . that poor spellers will become competent spellers if simply given additional time" (1991, p. 12) or a typical course of instruction.

While it appears that the spelling errors of dyslexics can be accounted for in normal developmental terms, it also appears that their development tends to remain incomplete (Moats, 1995). Disabled readers and poor spellers (1) tend to persist in making phonetically driven as opposed to phonemically accurate errors (like beginning phonetic stage children above) (Moats, 1995; Sawyer et. al., 1999), and (2) they experience difficulty perceiving and establishing orthographic invariances and so create errors of patterning (like students at the within word pattern and syllable juncture stages) (Bailet, 1991; Carlisle, 1987). Because dyslexics experience deficits in phonological awareness, specific phonemic environments that pose difficulties for normally developing students (e.g., preconsonantal nasals: *stamp*) can be shown to pose protracted and even insuperable difficulties for disabled spellers (Bailet, 1991; Moats, 1995). Compounding these problems are the additional levels of linguistic information beyond basic phoneme-grapheme mapping that are encoded in the orthography. Phonemic awareness—the most commonly documented weakness among dyslexics— appears to provide a critical foundation onto which are framed the increasingly abstract pattern-to-phoneme and pattern-to-meaning requirements of written English. Dyslexics have been shown to improve their skills with phonemic analysis through direct training (Lundberg, 1985); however, they may never acquire the "phonological immediacy" that normally developing readers and spellers do (Post, et al., 1999). In that case, dyslexics continue to struggle with the added problem of trying to join the various kinds of relational patterning they encounter in the orthography to their incomplete and/or inexact phonological representations of words. The result, then, may be an overreliance on visual memorization, precisely the kind of strategy that Orton observed among his students (1929/1999).

Further, Moats has found (1995) that even among older, carefully remediated dyslexics, spontaneous misspellings—at least among the poorest spellers—reveal continuing difficulties with phonologically demanding aspects of phoneme-grapheme representation in their spontaneous writing. In particular, she documented "a much higher rate of omissions, insertions, and substitutions of sonorants (/l/, /r/, /m/, /n/, /ng/)" (p. 63) among the poorest of these spellers. She also found that these same individuals expressed difficulty with consonant clusters, vowel substitutions, vowels in unaccented syllables, correct choice among minimal consonant pairs, and correct spelling of consonant digraphs. In addition, these students showed a continued tendency to spell inflected endings by their phonemic variants and not their single morphemic pattern. All of these error types are typical of the trouble spots learners face as they move into the early phases of the phonetic stage (described above), most often in the early part of first grade. This finding further underscores dyslexics' remarkable difficulties with typical instruction in moving past phonetic surface analyses to the accurate phoneme-grapheme representations on which more mature word knowledge is built.

# IMPLICATIONS FOR CLASSROOM AND CLINIC

## CLASSROOM INSTRUCTION

Moats (1994) has documented the fact that most teachers lack accurate and detailed knowledge about the structure of spoken and written English. Clearly, specific knowledge of this kind could play an important role in helping teachers better understand their work and better shape reading and spelling instruction for their students. For a variety of reasons, few teacher preparation programs at present provide that kind of information. What, then, can be done to improve classroom spelling instruction when teachers do not know how to tailor instruction for their least able students?

One place to begin is by placing students in basal spellers at their instructional level. Although it requires careful planning, this can be accomplished in the classroom by creating multiple instructional groups (Morris, Blanton, Blanton, & Perney, 1995). Teachers also should make use of traditional instructional strategies that have been shown to make some difference. These include use of a pretest with guided self-correction and practice, the study method ("look, say, cover, write, check"), and 15- to 20-minute instructional periods distributed across the days of the week.

Teachers can conduct word sorts with the patterns in spelling lists. Word sorts can be adapted to a variety of game formats such as Memory or Bingo in which words are compared and contrasted. If spelling lists are reduced as an accommodation for learning disabled students, the number of patterns illustrated should also be reduced; if there are too many patterns and too few exemplars, then there will still be a higher degree of difficulty and the contrastive patterns themselves may not be sufficiently illustrated.

Teachers also may be able to incorporate a few basic multisensory techniques for their low spellers. Simultaneous Oral Spelling can be used when writing list words. Phonemes can be "tapped out," (i.e., phonemes are segmented while tapping the fingers on the desktop from little finger toward thumb) to create a simultaneous, left-to-right kinesthetic analogue of the phonemes. This can be used not only to help identify speech sounds but also to call attention to patterns in relation to them: "Tap out the word *tape*. How many sounds are there? How many letters? What does that extra letter do?"

None of the suggested modifications here is likely to make much difference to poor spellers, however, if the words are not at the right level of difficulty. When resource teachers lack specific training in methods for addressing disabilities in reading and spelling, teachers or parents may wish to request as a minimal remedial step that the resource help their students receive be conducted at a carefully assessed individual instructional level.

## CLINICAL INSTRUCTION

*Using Developmental Word Study.* When working with highly disabled readers and/or spellers, a variety of techniques drawn from Orton-based approaches can be added to the basic sorts. Among these are phoneme segmentation activities to enhance the links between phonemes and graphemes. Once sorted, words can be "tapped." Words also can be tapped prior to writing them during spell-checks. When a set of contrastive patterns has been established, sound card drills also can be used. That is, using letter cards (sometimes called "sound cards"), a student "taps out" a word presented orally, then spells the word with the letter cards. Errors made during this exercise can be addressed by displaying exemplars from each of the patterns being studied; the student must then choose the correct pattern from among them and use it to correct the error. Or, the student may "tap" the word again more carefully or be prompted to self-correct by being asked to recall the letter or pattern that represents a particular phoneme.

In addition to these activities, letter cards can be used to review grapheme-phoneme and phoneme-grapheme connections to ensure that fundamental knowledge remains immediate. For phonemes that are not fully automatic, key words (with "sound clues" embedded in them: *"o-octopus-*/ah/") can be used as well as kinesthetic accompaniments (writing the letter with fingertips while naming it and saying the phoneme). Such activities as these can assist in developing and maintaining a detailed level of orthographic processing among children who may at times be better at figuring out the "rules of the sort" than assimilating the underlying concept.

*Using Structured Language Approaches.*   Tutors using a structured language approach may wish to consider incorporating word sorts into the word card reviews. These can provide another context for reviewing and manipulating spelling/reading concepts and perceiving orthographic regularities. Words can be sorted to target contrasting vowel sounds, syllable types, or even syllable division patterns. As students gain strength in reading regular words, a sort can provide a way of highlighting irregular words or exception words. A student can be told that one or two "trick words" have been introduced to a sort and that they must catch them. An *-ind* or *-old* pattern word or an exception like *was* could be hidden in a sort that sets up short *-a*, short *-i*, and short *-o* contrasts, for example.

Some dyslexic students are noted for having fairly large sight vocabularies. Although it may cause a tutor to reach beyond a typical Orton-style scope and sequence, words can be drawn from their sight vocabularies for a sort to illustrate a set of sounds or patterns which might prove helpful in the student's extratutorial work or which might set the stage for the more traditional introduction of those skills.

## CONCLUSION

A great deal of research has been conducted over the past twenty years on connections between phonological awareness and reading. This connection has been made so powerfully that in some cases it is taken to be the whole story. However, in discussing training studies that develop the phonological skills of at-risk readers in the context of spelling, Goulandris (1994) makes the following observation: "Teaching a child how spelling patterns represent sound patterns improves eventual reading and spelling ability more than teaching phonological skills in isolation" (413). This conclusion is echoed by other researchers. At least for school-aged children, phonological skills seem most efficiently developed in the context of basic reading and writing instruction, although for less able students, that instruction needs to be explicit, systematically implemented, and developmentally appropriate. As Orton understood many years ago, instruction in spelling is as critical a component in developing literacy as is instruction in decoding. This lexical amalgam of basic phonological and orthographic information appears to create the foundation on which subsequent pattern regularities are built. Despite all this, spelling instruction remains a topic which excites only occasional interest among educators. Failing to see the role that spelling instruction plays in developing word knowledge, schools tend to underplay a subject area with far-reaching consequences for less able students. Without the requisite knowledge to understand the importance of spelling, it is not taught well. As a result, schools fall victim to occasional public outcries about children's spelling. Then, spurred on by pressure from principals, parents, or legislators, students are schooled once again in the old rote-memory approach to word learning.

Traditional, developmental, and structured language approaches to teaching spelling each have something to offer the others, and each may be strengthened in turn by taking seriously the knowledge-base and methods of the others. Given the evidence reviewed here, it is possible to envision significant improvements in the type of instruction offered poor spellers. Clearly, teachers should know more about their students' levels, more about their instructional materials, and more about the kinds of teaching needed to move every child in significant ways. Some familiarity with the approaches to spelling instruction outlined here would enable teachers to work more effectively with the resources they have, and it would allow them to understand the significance of their efforts.

Address correspondence to: Bob Schlagal, Department of Language, Reading and Exceptionalities, Duncan Hall, Appalachian State University, Boone, NC 28608. Telephone (828)262-6038 (office); Fax (828262-6767. e-mail: Schlagal rc@appstate.edu

## References

Bailet, L. L. (1991). Development and disorders of spelling in the beginning school years. In A. M. Bains, L. L. Bailet, & L. C. Moats (eds.), *Written language disorders: Theory into practice* (pp. 2–21). Austin, TX: PRO-ED.

Bear, D. R., Invernizzi, M., Templeton, S., & Johnston, F. (2000). *Words their way: Word study for phonics, vocabulary, and spelling instruction.* Columbus, OH: Merrill.

Beers, J. (1980). Developmental strategies of spelling competence in primary school children. In E. Henderson & J. Beers (eds.), *Developmental and cognitive aspects of learning to spell: A reflection of word knowledge* (pp. 36–45). Newark, NJ: International Reading Association.

Bruck, M. (1987). The adult outcomes of children with learning disabilities. *Annals of Dyslexia, 37,* 252–263.

Bruck, M. (1988). The word recognition and spelling of dyslexic children. *Reading Research Quarterly, 23,* 51–69.

Carlisle, J. F. (1987). The use of morphological knowledge in spelling derived forms by learning-disabled and normal students. *Annals of Dyslexia, 37,* 90–108.

Chomsky, C. (1970). Reading, writing, and phonology. *Harvard Educational Review, 40,* 287–309.

Chomsky, C. (1979). Approaching reading through invented spelling. In L. B. Resnick, & P. A. Weaver (eds.), *Theory and practice of early reading* (Vol. 2, pp. 43–65). Hillsdale, NJ: Lawrence Erlbaum Associates.

Cummings, D. W. (1988). *American English spelling.* Baltimore: Johns Hopkins.

Ehri, L. (1989). The development of spelling knowledge and its role in reading acquisition and reading disability. *Journal of Learning Disabilities, 22,* 349–364.

Ehri, L. (1994). Development of the ability to read words. In R. Ruddell, M. Ruddell, & H. Singer (eds.), *Theoretical models and processes of reading* (4th ed., pp. 323–358). Newark, DE: International Reading Association.

Fitzgerald, J. A. (1951). *The teaching of spelling.* Milwaukee: Bruce.

Gillingham, A., & Stillman, B. W. (1997). *The Gillingham manual: Remedial training for students with specific disability in reading, spelling, and penmanship* (8th ed.), Cambridge, MA: Educators Publishing.

Goulandris, N. K. (1994). Teaching spelling: Bridging theory and practice. In G. D. A. Brown, & N. C. Ellis (eds.), *Handbook of spelling* (pp. 407–423). New York: Wiley.

Hanna, P. R., Hanna, J. S., Hodges, R. E., & Rudorf, H. (1966). *Phoneme-grapheme correspondences as clues to spelling improvement.* Washington, DC: U.S. Office of Education.

Hanna, P. R., Hodges, R. E., & Hanna, J. S. (1971). *Spelling: Structure and strategies.* Boston: Houghton Mifflin.

Hanna, P. R., & Moore, J. T. (1953). Spelling: From spoken word to written symbol. *Elementary School Journal, 53,* 329–337.

Henderson, E. H. (1981). *Learning to read and spell: The child's knowledge of words.* Dekalb, IL: Northern Illinois University Press.

Henderson, E. H. (1990). *Teaching spelling* (2nd ed.). Boston, MA: Houghton Mifflin.

Henderson, E. H., & Beers, J. W. (Eds.). (1980). *Developmental and cognitive aspects of learning to spell: A reflection of word knowledge.* Newark, DE: International Reading Association.

Henry, M. K. (1993). Morphological structure: Latin and Greek roots and affixes as upper grade code strategies. *Reading and Writing: An Interdisciplinary Journal, 5,* 227–241.

Horn, E. (1967). Teaching spelling. *What research says to the teacher.* Washington, DC: National Education Association.

Horn, T. D. (1947). The effect of the corrected test on learning to spell. *Elementary School Journal, 47, 277–285.*

Horn, T. D. (1969). Spelling. In R. L. Ebel (ed.), *Encyclopedia of educational research* (4th ed.) (pp. 1282–1299). New York: Macmillan.

Invernizzi, M. (1992). The vowel and what follows: A phonological frame of orthographic reference. In S. Templeton & D. Bear (eds.) *Development of orthographic knowledge and the foundations of literacy: A memorial festschrift for Edmund H. Henderson* (pp. 105–136). Hillsdale, NJ: Lawrence Erlbaum Associates.

Luelsdorff, P. A. (1991). *Developmental orthography.* Philadelphia, PA: Benjamins.

Lundberg, I. (1985). Phonemic awareness can be developed without reading instruction. In S. A. Brady & D. Shankweiler (eds.), *Phonological processes in literacy* (pp. 47–54). Hillsdale, NJ: Lawrence Erlbaum Associates.

Miles, T. R. (1993). *Dyslexia: The pattern of difficulties* (2nd ed.). London: Whurr.

Miles, E., & Miles, T. R. (1994). The interface between research and remediation. In G. D. A. Brown & N. Ellis (eds.), *Handbook of spelling: Theory, process, and intervention* (pp. 441–458). New York: Wiley.

Moats, L. C. (1994). The missing foundation in teacher education: Knowledge of the structure of spoken and written language. *Annals of Dyslexia, 44, 81–102.*

Moats, L. C. (1995). *Spelling: Development, disability, and instruction.* Baltimore, MD: York Press.

Moats, L. C., & Ferrell, M. (1999). Multisensory instruction. In J. R. Birsh (ed.), *Multisensory teaching of basic language skills* (pp. 1–17). Baltimore, MD: Brookes.

Morris, D. (1999). *Case studies in teaching beginning readers: The Howard Street tutoring manual.* New York: Guilford.

Morris, D., Blanton, L., Blanton, W. E., Nowacek, J., & Perney, J. (1995). Teaching low-achieving spellers at their "instructional level." *Elementary School Journal, 96, 163–177.*

Morris, D., Blanton, L., Blanton, W. E., & Perney, J. (1995). Spelling instruction and achievement in six classrooms. *Elementary School Journal, 92, 145–162.*

Morris, D., Nelson, L., & Perney, J. (1986). Exploring the concept of "spelling instructional level" through the analysis of error-types. *Elementary School Journal, 87, 181–200.*

Morris, D., & Perney, J. (1984). Developmental spelling as a predictor of first grade reading achievement. *Elementary School Journal, 84, 441–457.*

Nagy, W., Diakidoy, I., & Anderson, R. C. (1993). The acquisition of morphology: Learning the contribution of suffixes to the meanings of derivatives. *Journal of Reading Behavior, 25, 155–170.*

Nelson, L. (1989). Something borrowed, something new: Teaching implications of developmental spelling research. *Reading Psychology, 10, 255–274.*

Orton, S. T. (1999). *Reading, writing, and speech problems in children, and selected papers.* Baltimore, MD: International Dyslexia Association.

Perfetti, C. A. (1985). *Reading ability.* New York: Oxford University.

Perfetti, C. A. (1992). The representation problem in reading acquisition. In P. B. Gough, L. C. Ehri, & R. Treiman (eds.), *Reading acquisition* (pp. 145–174). Hillsdale, NJ: Lawrence Erlbaum Associates.

Perfetti, C. A., Beck, I., Bell, L., & Hughes, C. (1987). Phonemic knowledge and learning to read are reciprocal: A longitudinal study of first grade children. In K. Stanovich (ed.), *Children's reading and the development of phonological awareness* (pp. 39–75). Detroit, MI: Wayne State University.

Post, Y. V., Swank, P. R., Hiscock, M., & Fowler, A. F. (1999). Identification of vowel speech sounds by skilled and less skilled readers and the relation with vowel spelling. *Annals of Dyslexia, 49, 137–194.*

Read, C. (1975). *Children's categorizations of speech sounds in English.* Urbana, IL: National Council of Teachers of English.

Read, C. (1986). *Children's creative spelling.* London: Routledge and Kegan Paul.

Sawyer, D. J., Wade, S., & Kim, J. W. (1999). Spelling errors as a window on variations in phonological deficits among students with dyslexia. *Annals of Dyslexia, 49,* 137–159.

Schlagal, R. (1992). Patterns of orthographic development into the intermediate grades. In S. Templeton & D. Bear (eds.), *Development of orthographic knowledge and the foundations of literacy: A memorial festschrift for Edmund H. Henderson* (pp. 32–52). Hillsdale, NJ: Lawrence Erlbaum Associates.

Schlagal, R. (1996). Teaching disabled spellers. In L. R. Putnam (ed.), *How to become a better reading teacher: Strategies for assessment and intervention* (pp. 307–329). Englewood Cliffs, NJ: Merrill.

Schlagal, R., & Trathen, W. (1998). American spelling instruction: What history tells us. *Yearbook of the American Reading Forum, 18,* 25–41.

Snow, C. E., Burns, M. S., & Griffin, P. (1998). *Preventing reading difficulties in children.* Washington, DC: National Academy.

Templeton, S., & Bear, D. (Eds.). (1992). *Development of orthographic knowledge and the foundations of literacy: A memorial festschrift for Edmund H. Henderson.* Hillsdale, NJ: Lawrence Erlbaum Associates.

Templeton, S., & Morris, D. (2000). Spelling. In M. L. Kamil, P. B. Mosenthal, P. D. Pearson, & R. Barr (eds.), *Handbook of reading research* (Vol. 3, pp. 525–543). Mahwah, NJ: Lawrence Erlbaum Associates.

Veltman, R. (1992). An orthography as a theory of language. In C. M. Sterling & C. Robson (eds.), *Psychology, spelling, and education* (pp. 30–42), Philadelphia, PA: Multilingual Matters.

Venezky, R. L. (1967). English orthography: Its graphical structure and its relation to sound. *Reading Research Quarterly, 2,* 75–105.

Venezky, R. L. (2000). *The American way of spelling: The structure and origins of American English orthography.* New York: Guilford.

Wilde, S. (1990). A proposal for a new spelling curriculum. *Elementary School Journal, 90,* 275–289.

Worthy, M. J., & Invernizzi, M. (1990). Spelling errors of normal and disabled students on achievement levels one through four: Instructional implications. *Annals of Dyslexia, 40,* 138–151.

Yee, A. H. (1966). The generalization controversy on spelling instruction. *Elementary English, 43,* 154–161.

Zutell J. (1980). Children's spelling strategies and their cognitive development. In E. H. Henderson & J. W. Beers (eds.), *Developmental and cognitive aspects of learning to spell: A reflection of word knowledge* (pp. 52–73). Newark, DE: International Reading Association.

Zutell, J., & Rasinski, T. (1989). Reading and spelling connections in third and fifth grade students. *Reading Psychology, 10,* 137–155.

# PART IV
## Relating Oral Language Abilities to Reading

In 1925 Dr. Samuel T. Orton began his studies of children with specific language disabilities. Now, 75 years later, researchers are still exploring the intricate relationships between language and reading. The articles in Part IV are studies on aspects of speech/language processing difficulties that are likely to affect reading performance. The first two papers examine predictors of reading strength and weakness. The third article provides support for programs of instruction in "higher level" skills, in particular, an understanding and teaching of morphologically complex words. The fourth paper enhances our understanding of possible heritable components of language and the relationship of rapid naming speed to reading in good and poor readers.

Nathlie Badian examines the roles of phonological and orthographic processing in a study of students from kindergarten through seventh grade. She describes best predictors of reading at three stages of reading development (grades 1, 3, and 7) and compares early poor readers with late poor readers. Her findings suggest that for some children, early weaknesses in orthographic skills may result in later reading comprehension difficulties. For others, comprehension difficulties may be due to a phonological and/or more general verbal deficit. Her findings contribute to a growing body of literature on distinguishing children who may be at risk for earlier vs. later reading difficulties.

In three complementary studies, Ralph Wesseling and Pieter Reitsma examine relationships among language abilities of Dutch kindergartners and the extent to which various phonemic measures predict grade one reading skills. They focus on three prediction measures. One is "gating," a task of spoken word recognition that gauges the amount of auditory stimuli a listener requires for spoken word identification. The other two predictors are nonword repetition and cued word recall. Their findings indicate that there is considerable instability in these measures, with no measure strongly predicting first grade word decoding, though nonword repetition had some predictive power. The studies have implications for understanding how phonemic awareness develops.

Though much research attention has been given to phonological awareness and reading development, there are few studies on children's appreciation of the morphological structure of oral and written words. From a practical standpoint, teachers recognize that students with reading disabilities have particular difficulty reading morphologically complex words, especially as these words become more prominent in reading beyond the elementary years. Joanne Carlisle and her colleagues examine the speed and accuracy of naming a series of derived word forms, with and without phonological/orthographic shifts (such as occur between "nature" and "natural," for instance, but not between "culture" and "cultural"). Even more difficult are words that undergo more complex transformations (e.g., from "strong" to "strength"). Not surprisingly, the authors found that poor readers have particular difficulty with derived words with complex phonological representations. They suggest the need for instruction that involves a "deliberate analysis of the word form" and they refer the reader to several programs of study that focus on strategies for learning and practicing word derivations.

Chayna Davis and her colleagues examine the genetic and environmental etiology of the relationship between rapid naming and reading in a study of good/poor reader twin pairs. Their findings suggest that rapid naming differences may have a genetic basis and that the etiology of the relationships between reading and rapid naming may differ between good and poor readers. These results add support to a growing body of knowledge on the importance of rapid naming as a diagnostic indicator and provide further evidence for the heritability of reading-related oral language abilities.

# Phonological and Orthographic Processing: Their Roles in Reading Prediction

*Nathlie A. Badian*

Consultant, Holbrook Public Schools
and
Research Fellow in Neurology
Harvard Medical School
Boston, Massachusetts

*Ninety-six children were administered an orthographic test as preschoolers and two measures of nonphonemic phonological aware-ness (syllable segmentation, rhyme detection) in midkindergarten. The power of the three measures to predict reading at grades 1, 3, and 7 was examined. With earlier reading level, preschool verbal IQ and age, and verbal memory controlled, both phonological measures added sig-nificant variance to grade 1 word reading, and syllable segmentation also contributed to reading comprehension, but neither measure ac-counted for variance in reading at grades 3 and 7. The orthographic measure contributed significant variance to grade 1 word reading, and also to reading vocabulary and reading comprehension at grades 3 and 7, with the proportion of variance in reading comprehension increas-ing with grade level. When early (grade 1) and late (grade 7) poor readers were compared, late poor readers were significantly higher than early poor readers on a first grade phonological test, but signifi-cantly lower on a seventh grade orthographic measure. Evidence sug-gested that a late reading comprehension deficit may be due to poor orthographic processing skills in some children, but to a phonological and general verbal deficit in others.*

Annals of Dyslexia, Vol. 51, 2001
ISSN 0736-9387

For educators and researchers concerned with the early identification of children who are at risk for reading difficulties, a compelling problem continues to be how we can perfect the identification process. In a recent review of predictive studies, Scarborough (1998) pointed out that as many as 22 percent of children who developed reading disability were not classified as at risk as kindergartners, and an even larger proportion (45 percent) of children meeting risk criteria did not become disabled readers.

There is massive evidence that awareness of phonemes, which are the smallest sound units within words, has a strong association with reading and that poor readers have a deficit in phoneme awareness compared to normal readers of the same age and even to younger children who match them in reading level (Goswami & Bryant, 1990; Manis, Seidenberg, & Doi, 1999; Rack & Olson, 1993; Stanovich, 1988; Wagner & Torgesen, 1987). There is, however, debate about the direction of the relationship between phoneme awareness and reading. Many researchers are convinced that, rather than having a causal relationship with reading, awareness of phonemes develops primarily as a result of reading instruction (e.g., Bowey & Francis, 1991; Fowler, 1991; Goswami & Bryant, 1990) or that the relationship is reciprocal (Perfetti, Beck, Bell, & Hughes, 1987).

The term "phonological" refers to sounds within words and includes not only phonemes but also larger sound units. Phonological measures are on a continuum of difficulty, ranging from simple or emerging to complex or deep (Ball, 1993; Stanovich, 1992). Tasks at the simple end of the continuum include those involving word units larger than the phoneme whereas complex tasks involve phoneme manipulation (e.g., deletion, substitution). Awareness of larger word units such as syllables, onsets (initial consonant or consonant cluster), and rimes (vowel and final consonant or consonant cluster) can develop without knowledge of a writing system that represents speech at these levels (Treiman & Zukowski, 1991). Awareness of rhyme and alliteration also emerges quite early in childhood (Bradley & Bryant, 1983). Recent research with four- and five-year-old preschoolers indicates that the developmental progression of phonological awareness is rhymes, syllables, and rimes (Gipstein, Brady, & Fowler, 2000). Treiman and Zukowski (1991) argue that analysis of words into onsets and rimes is an intermediate step between analysis into syllables and into phonemes.

## PHONEME AWARENESS IN READING PREDICTION

The pivotal research of Liberman, Shankweiler, Fischer, and Carter (1974) demonstrated that no preschool child and only 17 percent of kindergarten children could segment words into phonemes. Thus, phonemic measures administered to prereaders may be ineffective predictors of later reading because the tasks are too difficult for them (de Jong & van de Leij, 1999; Muter & Snowling, 1998). Muter and Snowling, who followed a group of children from age four to age nine, found that a phoneme deletion task at age four did not contribute to prediction of reading at age nine, although phoneme deletion at ages five and six, following reading instruction, did contribute significantly. Ehri (1989) also stressed that five-year-old prereaders are generally poor at performing phoneme awareness tasks and that the majority of prereaders who lack phoneme awareness do not become poor readers. In their thoughtful and provocative book, Goswami and Bryant (1990) remark on the near impossibility of finding a good measure of phoneme detection in children who are too young to go to school. Thus, a crucial issue related to the development of phonological awareness in young children is the chronological age at which phonological tasks are both within the capabilities of prereaders and reliable enough to be useful predictors of reading.

Some researchers have included phonemic measures when testing kindergarten children and have found them useful predictors of reading in spite of the evidence that most children who are prereaders have not acquired awareness of phonemes (e.g., Elbro, Borstrøm, & Petersen, 1998; Mann, 1993; Share, Jorm, MacLean, & Matthews, 1984; Vellutino & Scanlon, 1987; Wagner et al., 1997). Most phonemic measures included in these studies have been relatively simple and have included such tasks as sound categorization and identifying the initial sound or onset of words. Half of the task referred to as "phoneme segmentation" by Share and his colleagues (1984) involved segmentation of the onset from the rime. Also, some studies do not control for differences in reading ability among kindergarten children, and those who do well on phonemic measures may be those who already have some reading skills.

## NONPHONEMIC PHONOLOGICAL MEASURES AS PREDICTORS OF READING

If, as at least some evidence suggests, tasks of phoneme awareness are beyond the capabilities of the majority of prereaders, which nonphonemic phonological tasks are both appropriate for children prior to formal reading instruction and also are strong predictors of reading? This is an urgent question to which we do not have a definitive answer. Measures involving rhyme and alliteration, syllables, and onset and rime have been used to predict the later reading of prereaders, but evidence for a predictive relationship between these nonphonemic phonological measures and reading is less strong than the relationship between phonemic awareness and reading for somewhat older children. One of the main aims of the study reported here was to investigate whether nonphonemic phonological measures (rhyme detection, syllable segmentation) are of value as predictors of the later reading of kindergarten children.

Numerous studies have included rhyming tasks as predictors of reading (Bradley & Bryant, 1983; Christensen, 1997; Lonigan, Burgess, Anthony, & Barker, 1998; Muter & Snowling, 1998; Muter, Hulme, Snowling, & Taylor, 1997; Stanovich, Cunningham, & Cramer, 1984; Vellutino & Scanlon, 1987). Bradley and Bryant (1983) demonstrated that rhyme awareness in four- and five-year-old prereaders was predictive of reading at eight to nine years, even with IQ, vocabulary, and memory controlled. However, as stressed by Ehri (1989), only a minority of the prereaders predicted to have difficulty learning to read actually became poor readers. In a recent review, drawing on her own research and that of others, Christensen (2000) concluded that preschool rhyme was a relatively poor predictor of reading. Similar conclusions were drawn by Duncan and Seymour (2000), who gave rhyme tasks to four-year-olds, and by Sawyer, Kim, and Lipa-Wade (2000), who administered rhyming tasks to kindergarten children. In their longitudinal studies, Muter et al. (1997) found that rhyming tasks at age four did not predict early reading skills, although they began to have an effect on spelling by the second year of reading instruction. In a follow-up at age nine, rhyming tests given at four, five, and six years were poor long-term predictors of reading accuracy and were not able to predict good and poor reading (Muter & Snowling, 1998). Bradley and Bryant (1991) argue, however, that preschool rhyme scores are reliable predictors of later reading ability and that studies that failed to relate rhyme to reading were with much older children and the rhyming tasks were generally too easy.

Fewer predictive studies have included measures based on syllables. Mann and Liberman (1984) gave a syllable segmentation task to kindergarten children and found that it correlated .4 with reading one year later. Other researchers who gave similar syllabic tasks to preschool or kindergarten children concluded that syllable segmentation was a relatively weak predictor of reading (Badian, 1994, 1998, 2000; Felton, 1992). It is possible that other types of measures based on syllables may be more effective. For example, in a study of children learning to read French, kindergarten syllable segmentation and syllable deletion correlated .47 with first grade decoding, compared with .36 for phoneme deletion and .40 for a rhyme choice measure (Casalis & Louis-Alexandre, 2000). By second grade, the correlations of the syllable and rhyme tasks with decoding decreased, but syllable deletion and rhyme choice correlated higher with reading comprehension than phoneme deletion.

## ORTHOGRAPHIC PROCESSING AS A PREDICTOR OF READING

Another aim of the present study was to reexamine the predictive validity of preschool orthographic processing with a new sample of children. As pointed out by Stanovich, phonological awareness or sensitivity is a necessary, but not sufficient, condition for efficient reading acquisition (Stanovich, 1992; Stanovich, West, & Cunningham, 1991). There must be at least one other "sticking point" where reading acquisition can flounder. Stanovich suggested that for some problem readers, differences in the ability to form accurate orthographic representations might be a "sticking point." If the ability to form orthographic representations does play a role in reading success, this ability also may add to prediction of reading. There is, however, a minimal amount of research on the role early orthographic skills play in the prediction of reading.

As an orthography is the system of marks that make up a printed language (Wagner & Barker, 1994), a problem when testing prereaders is that stimuli for orthographic measures must be letters and numerals. The usual orthographic measures such as distinguishing which one of a pair of homophones is correctly spelled (e.g., *bote, boat*) or recognizing the correct homophone (Which is a number: *ate, eight*?) (Olson, Forsberg, Wise, & Rack, 1994), are unsuitable for children with no reading experience. Such tasks also have been criticized as measuring word identification or spelling (Vellutino, Scanlon, & Chen, 1995).

On the theory that insufficient attention to letters or groups of letters may lead to incomplete or inaccurate orthographic representations (Foorman, 1994; Stanovich, 1992), Badian (1994, 1995, 1998, 2000) used a visual matching task based on letters and numerals to test the incipient orthographic processing skills of preschool children. This preschool orthographic measure, which requires attention to alphanumeric symbols, accounts for significant independent variance in reading at least through grade 7, and its predictive validity tends to increase over time. By contrast, the proportion of independent variance in reading predicted by early phonological awareness tends to decrease after about grade 3 (Badian, 1995, 2000). Preschoolers who are accurate at distinguishing among visually similar sequences of letters and numerals generally do well in later reading, when automatic recognition of words is crucial for reading fluency and comprehension. The importance of establishing automatic orthographic-phonological connections has been stressed by several researchers (Adams & Bruck, 1993; Ehri, 1992). Because of the evidence that early word recognition is associated with phonological skills, while orthographic skills become increasingly important in later reading and in reading comprehension, in particular, another aim of this study was to compare the phonological and orthographic skills of early (grade 1) and late (grade 7) poor readers.

## PURPOSE OF THE STUDY

In summary, this study attempts to answer three questions:

1. Are kindergarten nonphonemic phonological measures useful predictors of reading?
2. Will preschool orthographic skills predict later reading comprehension?
3. Do early and late poor readers differ in phonological and orthographic skills?

# METHOD

## PARTICIPANTS

The participants were the 96 children who entered kindergarten in a small school district in 1990 and who continued in the school district at least to the end of grade 3. There were 50 boys and 46 girls. English was the primary language of all children in the study. Ethnicity was 95 percent white and 5 percent African American. On a 5-point scale, in which 1 = professional, 2 = managerial and sales, 3 = skilled manual workers, 4 = unskilled manual and service workers, and 5 = laborers, mean parental occupation was 2.4 (*SD* 1.0).

All participants were initially tested as preschoolers six months before kindergarten entry. Mean age was 5.0 years (*SD* 0.3; range 4.6 to 5.6 years). At the final follow-up in the spring of grade 7, the mean age of the 79 participants remaining in the school district was 13.1 years (*SD* 0.3, range 12.6 to 13.7). The 17 participants who moved away did not differ significantly on any study variable from the 79 who remained.

## PRESCHOOL PREDICTIVE MEASURES

*Preschool Reading Achievement (PRA).*   When the children were tested as preschoolers, parents were asked whether their child could read not at all, a few words, many words, or books. Ratings ranged from 1 (not at all) to 4 (books).

*Verbal IQ.*   A short form verbal IQ was calculated from the Wechsler Preschool and Primary Scale of Intelligence (WPPSI) (Wechsler, 1967) Information, Arithmetic, and Similarities subtests, using norms provided in the WPPSI manual.

*Verbal Memory.*   The child repeats sentences gradually increasing in length (WPPSI Sentences: Wechsler, 1967). Raw scores were converted to scaled scores (*M* 10, *SD* 3), using the WPPSI norms.

*Orthographic Processing.*   The child points to the one of four stimuli that exactly matches the item at the left of the row (Badian, 1994). The 10 test items are: u, d. j, ((, 38, bo, NAZ, 369, saw, drop. The response stimuli deviate from the target items mainly in sequencing or spatial orientation (e.g., droq, drop, borq, brop).

## KINDERGARTEN PREDICTIVE MEASURES

*Rhyme Detection.*   The child listens to three words and is asked which one of the three does not rhyme with the other two (Bradley & Bryant, 1983). There were 10 test items.

*Syllable Segmentation.*   The child taps the number of syllables in 10 words containing one to three syllables (adapted from Mann & Liberman, 1984).

## GRADE 1 OUTCOME READING MEASURES

*Word Reading and Reading Comprehension.*   In Word Reading, the child reads several words and decides which word tells about a picture. Reading Comprehension measures understanding of simple written sentences and short passages.

*Word Study Skills.*   This subtest measures phonological awareness and knowledge of grapheme-phoneme relationships.

## GRADES 3 AND 7 OUTCOME MEASURES

*Reading Vocabulary and Reading Comprehension.* In Reading Vocabulary, the child reads a list of words and decides which one of them means the same as an underlined word. Reading Comprehension measures the ability to read passages and to answer multiple-choice questions about them.

*Spelling (Grade 7 Only).* Spelling tests ability to recognize whether words are correctly or incorrectly spelled, and is similar to standard orthographic tests (e.g., Olson et al., 1994).

Outcome reading measures (grades 1, 3, 7) are subtests of the Stanford Achievement Test (SAT), 8th Edition (Psychological Corporation, 1992). National percentile ranks on the reading measures were converted to standard scores (*M* 100, *SD* 15).

## PROCEDURE

Children were brought into school by parents for preschool testing in March before kindergarten entry. Each child was individually tested by each member of a team of specialists. Preschool tests described here are only a subset of the tests given.

Most of the children (*n* = 83) were individually tested in school in February of their kindergarten year by the same examiner. Mean age was 5.9 years (*SD* 0.3; range 5.5 to 6.5).

A limitation of the study was that the two sets of predictive measures (preschool and kindergarten) were given approximately 11 months apart. If they had been given at the same time, more accurate results might have been possible.

The Stanford Achievement Test was administered in the classroom in late March of each grade. Grades 1, 3, and 7 were selected to represent beginning, established, and automatic reading levels.

## CRITERIA FOR EARLY AND LATE POOR READING

To test the hypothesis based on previous findings (e.g., Badian, 1995) that early poor reading would be predicted by phonological deficits, while later poor reading would be predicted by orthographic deficits, early poor reading was defined by a first grade word reading score <25th percentile on the grounds that word recognition is the most important skill to be acquired in first grade. Late poor reading was defined by a seventh grade reading comprehension score <25th percentile because reading comprehension is the most important reading skill at that stage. Children meeting the poor reading criteria for both grades 1 and 7 were classified as persistent poor readers.

A score of more than one standard deviation below the group mean defined poor orthographic matching, syllable segmentation, and rhyme detection.

## DATA ANALYSIS

Intercorrelations among the predictor variables were computed, and also correlation coefficients between the predictors and reading at grades 1, 3, and 7. To determine the independent contributions of the predictors to reading, stepwise and hierarchical regression analyses were computed with earlier reading level, verbal IQ, chronological age, and in some analyses, verbal memory entered prior to the prereading variables.

Differences between groups of readers were assessed by means of a nonparametric statistic (Mann-Whitney Two Sample Test). Accuracy in prediction of individual good and poor readers was determined by classifying participants as valid positives (poor readers correctly predicted) and valid negatives (good readers correctly predicted).

# RESULTS

## PREREADING MEASURES

The means and standard deviations of the preschool and kindergarten measures are given for the sample in table I and the intercorrelations between the predictor variables are given in table II.

Table I.   Preschool and Kindergarten Characteristics
of the Sample ($n$ = 96).

|  | Mean | SD | Range |
|---|---|---|---|
| Variable |  |  |  |
| Preschool Age (Yrs) | 5.0 | 0.3 | 4.6–5.6 |
| Kindergarten Age (Yrs) | 5.9 | 0.3 | 5.5–6.5 |
| Verbal IQ | 107.1 | 11.4 | 82–132 |
| Preschool Reading Ability | 1.5 | 0.7 | 1–4 |
| Verbal Memory | 9.9 | 2.8 | 5–16 |
| Orthographic Matching | 4.7 | 2.0 | 1–10 |
| Syllable Segmentation | 7.3 | 2.4 | 1–10 |
| Rhyme Detection | 6.6 | 2.4 | 0–10 |

Note: Verbal memory is a scaled score. Scores for the orthographic and phonological measures are raw scores.

Table II.  Intercorrelations of Preschool and Kindergarten Variables.

| Variable | 1 | 2 | 3 | 4 | 5 | 6 |
|---|---|---|---|---|---|---|
| 1. Preschool Reading Ability | | | | | | |
| 2. Verbal IQ | .14 | | | | | |
| 3. Verbal Memory | .12 | .65*** | | | | |
| 4. Orthographic Matching | .20 | .24* | .19 | | | |
| 5. Syllable Segmentation | .23* | .31** | .27* | .19 | | |
| 6. Rhyme Detection | .12 | .53*** | .47*** | .41*** | .40*** | |

Note: * $p < .05$, ** $p < .01$, *** $p < .001$.

Preschool reading achievement (PRA) correlated significantly only with syllable segmentation. Orthographic matching correlated significantly with rhyme detection but not with syllable segmentation. Verbal memory and rhyme detection had moderate to high correlations with verbal IQ ($p < .001$). The correlation between the two phonological measures was .40 ($p < .001$).

## PRESCHOOL AND KINDERGARTEN PREDICTION OF READING SKILLS: CORRELATION COEFFICIENTS

To determine the predictive relationship of preschool and kindergarten skills with reading achievement at grades 1, 3, and 7, correlations between the predictors and reading were computed, and also partial correlations with verbal IQ controlled. These sets of correlations are shown in table III.

With the exception of first grade word reading, verbal IQ had correlations of .50 to to .60 with reading at each grade level. The correlations of verbal memory and rhyme detection with reading were considerably reduced when verbal IQ was partialled out, but orthographic matching was relatively unaffected by controlling for differences in verbal IQ. With verbal IQ controlled, syllable segmentation correlated significantly with both first grade reading variables, but not with grade 3 reading, although it had a significant correlation with grade 7 reading comprehension. Orthographic matching and rhyme detection were very consistent in the size of their correlations with reading at each grade level.

## PREDICTION OF READING: REGRESSION ANALYSES

Stepwise and hierarchical regression analyses were carried out to determine the independent contributions of the early predictors to reading. Earlier reading level (autoregressor) was entered first as recommended by Torgesen, Wagner, Rashotte,

Table III.   Simple and Partial Correlations of Prereading Variables with Reading in Grades 1, 3, and 7.

| | Grade Level | | | | | | | | | | | |
| | 1 | | | | 3 | | | | 7 | | | |
| | Reading Measures | | | | | | | | | | | |
| | WR | | RC | | RV | | RC | | RV | | RC | |
| Variables | r | partial r | r | partial r | r | partial r | r | partial r | r | partial r | r | partial r |
| PRA | .21* | .17 | .28** | .25* | .18 | .13 | .19 | .14 | .31** | .28* | .26* | .23* |
| Verbal IQ | .35*** | | .50*** | | .57*** | | .50*** | | .55*** | | .60*** | |
| Verbal Memory | .37*** | .20 | .54*** | .32* | .57*** | .32* | .48*** | .24* | .51*** | .24* | .45*** | .10 |
| Orth. Matching | .47*** | .43*** | .40*** | .34*** | .49*** | .45*** | .47*** | .42*** | .46*** | .41*** | .44*** | .39*** |
| Syllable Segm. | .45*** | .38*** | .47*** | .38*** | .33** | .19 | .25* | .12 | .33* | .20 | .46*** | .36** |
| Rhyme Detection | .44** | .33* | .47*** | .28* | .53*** | .32* | .49*** | .30** | .52*** | .32* | .51*** | .29* |

Note: WR = Word Reading; RV = Reading Vocabulary; RC = Reading Comprehension; PRA = Preschool Reading Ability.
* $p < .05$, ** $p < .01$, *** $p < .001$.

Burgess, and Hecht (1997). These researchers stress that, unless the autoregressive effects of prior reading level are included in predictive analyses, it is impossible to know whether a variable independently influences reading growth or whether the relationship with later reading is due to its correlations with earlier reading.

In the first grade analyses, PRA was entered as the autoregressor. The autoregressor for third and seventh grade reading vocabulary was grade 1 word reading; for later reading comprehension, it was grade 1 reading comprehension .

In the set of regression analyses in table IV, the autoregressor, verbal IQ, and preschool age were entered first, second, and third, respectively; then orthographic matching and the kindergarten phonological measures were entered in a stepwise procedure.

Table IV shows that the autoregressor and verbal IQ together accounted for nearly half of the variance in each reading subtest at grades 3 and 7. Syllable segmentation entered the re-

**Table IV.  Multiple Regression Analyses: Prediction of Reading at Grades 1, 3, and 7 by Prereading Variables.**

| | Word Reading/Reading Vocabulary | | |
|---|---|---|---|
| | Grade Level | | |
| | **1** | **3** | **7** |
| **Fixed Order Predictors** | % Variance | % Variance | % Variance |
| 1. Autoregressor | .06* | .27*** | .28*** |
| 2. Verbal IQ | .07* | .18*** | .16*** |
| 3. Preschool Age | .11** | .05** | .02 |
| | Additional Variance Accounted For | | |
| Syllable Segment. | .07** | Orth Matching .03* | Orth Matching .05* |
| Orth. Matching | .06** | | |
| | Reading Comprehension | | |
| | % Variance | % Variance | % Variance |
| **Fixed Order Predictors** | | | |
| 1. Autoregressor | .09** | .46*** | .40*** |
| 2. Verbal IQ | .18*** | .03* | .06* |
| 3. Preschool Age | .14*** | .01 | .02 |
| | Additional Variance Accounted For | | |
| Syllable Segment. | .05* | Orth Matching .03* | Orth Matching .06** |

*Note:* $^*p < .05$, $^{**}p < .01$, $^{***}p < .001$.

gression first after the three fixed order variables for both first grade reading variables. Orthographic matching contributed significant additional variance to first grade word reading, and was the only variable to contribute significant variance to the third and seventh grade reading measures, after the three fixed variables had been entered into the regression analyses. Rhyme detection added no significant variance to any reading measure.

Hierarchical regression analyses to predict first grade word reading and third and seventh grade reading vocabulary are shown in table V. Table VI gives similar analyses for reading comprehension. In each analysis, the autogressor, preschool age, verbal IQ, and verbal memory were entered first, followed by syllable segmentation, rhyme detection, and orthographic matching, each entered at steps 5 to 7. Verbal memory was included as one of the fixed order variables because memory may play a role in the rhyme detection task. The correlation between the two was .47 ($p < .001$).

Kindergarten syllable segmentation added significant variance to first grade word reading and reading comprehension, whether entered at step 5, 6, or 7. It added no variance to either

Table V.   **Hierarchical Regression Analyses: Prediction of Word Reading/Reading Vocabulary by Prereading Variables.**

| | Word Reading/Reading Vocabulary | | |
| --- | --- | --- | --- |
| | Grade Level | | |
| | 1 | 3 | 7 |
| Fixed Order Predictors | % Variance | % Variance | % Variance |
| 1. Autoregressor | .06* | .27*** | .28*** |
| 2. Preschool Age | .06* | .00 | .00 |
| 3. Verbal IQ | .12*** | .23*** | .18*** |
| 4. Verbal Memory | .02 | .03 | .01 |
| 5. Syllable Segment. | .07** | .00 | .01 |
| 5. Rhyme Detection | .06* | .01 | .01 |
| 5. Orth. Matching | .06* | .03* | .05* |
| 6. Syllable Segment | .07** | .00 | .00 |
| 6. Rhyme Detection | .03* | .01 | .01 |
| 6. Orth. Matching | .03* | .03* | .04* |
| 7. Syllable Segment | .05* | .00 | .01 |
| 7. Rhyme Detection | .01 | .01 | .01 |
| 7. Orth. Matching | .04* | .03* | .04* |

Note: *$p < .05$, **$p < .01$, ***$p < .001$.

Table VI.   Hierarchical Regression Analyses: Prediction of Reading
Comprehension by Prereading Variables.

| | Reading Comprehension | | |
| | Grade Level | | |
| | 1 | 3 | 7 |
| Fixed Order Predictors | % Variance | % Variance | % Variance |
| 1. Autoregressor | .09** | .46*** | .40*** |
| 2. Preschool Age | .05* | .00 | .00 |
| 3. Verbal IQ | .27*** | .03* | .08** |
| 4. Verbal Memory | .024* | .01 | .00 |
| 5. Syllable Segment. | .04* | .01 | .01 |
| 5. Rhyme Detection | .02 | .02 | .01 |
| 5. Orth. Matching | .01 | .04* | .06** |
| 6. Syllable Segment | .04* | .01 | .01 |
| 6. Rhyme Detection | .01 | .02 | .01 |
| 6. Orth. Matching | .01 | .03* | .05* |
| 7. Syllable Segment | .03* | .01 | .01 |
| 7. Rhyme Detection | .01 | .01 | .00 |
| 7. Orth. Matching | .01 | .03* | .05* |

Note: $^*p < .05$, $^{**}p < .01$, $^{***}p < .001$.

reading variable at grades 3 and 7, however, at any step. Rhyme
detection accounted for significant variance in grade 1 word reading, when entered at step 5 or 6, but not at step 7. It contributed
no significant variance to first grade reading comprehension, or
to either reading variable at grades 3 and 7. Orthographic matching contributed significant variance to word reading/reading vocabulary at each grade level, whether entered at step 5, 6, or 7,
and to third and seventh grade reading comprehension at each
entry step, though it added no significant variance to first grade
reading comprehension. The proportion of variance it added to
reading comprehension increased in the higher grades, with more
at grade 3 than at grade 1, and more at grade 7 than at grade 3.

## COMPARISON OF EARLY AND LATE POOR READERS ON
## ORTHOGRAPHIC AND PHONOLOGICAL MEASURES

Ten children (10/94 = 10.6 percent) met criteria for poor first
grade word reading and 10 (10/79 = 12.7 percent) for poor seventh grade reading. These figures do not include four children
who were poor readers at both grades 1 and 7 (persistent poor
readers) and one child not continuing to grade 7 who could not

be classified reliably as he was a poor reader at both grades 1 and 3. With the persistent poor readers included, the percentage of children who were poor readers was 14.9 percent at grade 1 and 17.7 percent at grade 7.

Reading skills of the two groups were compared at grades 1, 3, and 7, using a nonparametric statistic (Mann-Whitney). As first graders late poor readers were significantly higher than early poor readers on reading comprehension, as well as on word reading (word reading: $z = -3.78$, $p = .0002$; reading comprehension: $z = -2.23$, $p = .0257$). No late poor reader was low (< 25 percentile) on either grade 1 reading measure. Late poor readers were also significantly higher than early poor readers on the first grade phonological measure (word study skills): Early: $M = 92.8$ ($SD$ 5.0); Late: $M = 103.5$ (SD 10.7); $z = -2.27$, $p = .0233$.

By third grade, there were no differences between groups on either reading vocabulary or reading comprehension, and the mean of each group was in the average range. At seventh grade level, the two groups did not differ in reading vocabulary but late poor readers were significantly lower on reading comprehension ($z = 3.25$, $p = .0011$). On the seventh grade spelling test, which taps orthographic processing, early poor readers were significantly higher: Early: $M = 106.0$ (SD 7.0); Late: $M = 90.7$ ($SD$ 12.0); $z = 2.66$, $p = .0079$. Mean reading scores of the two groups of poor readers are shown in table VII. Table VII also includes mean scores on the prereading measures.

Table VII. Mean Scores of Early and Late Poor Readers on Prereading and Reading Measures.

| | Groups | | | |
| | Early | | Late | |
| Variable | M | SD | M | SD |
| --- | --- | --- | --- | --- |
| **Prereading** | | | | |
| Orth. Matching | 3.5 | 1.4 | 3.0 | 1.8 |
| Syllable Segment | 6.1 | 2.5 | 4.4 | 1.4 |
| Rhyme Detection | 3.9 | 2.8 | 5.1 | 1.7 |
| **Reading** | | | | |
| G.1 Word Reading | 86.7 | 3.4 | 99.2 | 6.3 |
| G.1 Reading Compreh. | 89.2 | 8.5 | 96.8 | 1.8 |
| G.3 Reading Vocab. | 103.9 | 9.9 | 96.6 | 7.2 |
| G.3 Reading Compreh. | 101.5 | 9.9 | 96.6 | 7.8 |
| G.7 Reading Vocab. | 97.5 | 5.9 | 94.0 | 9.6 |
| G.7 Reading Compreh. | 101.8 | 8.6 | 80.3 | 9.6 |

Mann-Whitney tests did not show significant differences between the groups on the prereading measures, although the difference on syllable segmentation approached significance ($p$ = .056). However, twice as many seventh grade as first grade poor readers were very low (raw score <2) on orthographic matching (40 percent versus 20 percent), and 3.5 times as many seventh grade poor readers were low (raw score <4) on syllable segmentation (50 percent versus 14.3 percent). On rhyme detection 4.6 times more first grade than seventh grade poor readers were very low (raw score <3) (57.1 percent versus 12.5 percent). Both early and late poor readers were average in mean preschool verbal IQ (Early: 101.4; Late: 99.0).

## PREDICTION OF INDIVIDUAL GOOD AND POOR READING AT GRADES 1 AND 7

Accuracy in predicting individual good and poor first and seventh grade reading was also examined. Persistent poor readers were not included in the analyses. A cutoff raw score of <4 on rhyme detection was the best classifier of individual first grade good and poor readers, with correct identification of 71 percent of poor readers and 85 percent of good readers. Syllable segmentation and orthographic matching classified most good readers correctly, but only a small percentage of poor readers (14 percent, 20 percent). For seventh grade reading comprehension, a cutoff raw score of <3 on orthographic matching classified 60 percent of poor and 80 percent of good readers correctly. Syllable segmentation (raw score <4) classified 50 percent of poor and 91 percent of good readers, and rhyme detection (raw score <4) classified 50 percent of poor and 83 percent of good readers.

The six seventh grade poor readers who scored <3 on orthographic matching ($M$ = 1.8, $SD$ 1.0) were compared with the four who scored >4 ($M$ = 4.8, $SD$ 1.0). The group lower on orthographic matching was higher in preschool verbal IQ: <3, $M$ = 104.2 ($SD$ 10.6); >4, $M$ = 91.3 ($SD$ = 9.8); $z$ = 1.92, $p$ = .055. This group was significantly higher on the first grade test of phonological skills: <3, $M$ = 108.7 ($SD$ 11.1); >4, $M$ = 95.8 ($SD$ 1.5); $z$ = 2.24, $p$ = .025. The groups did not differ on seventh grade spelling, or on the kindergarten phonological measures. A raw score total <14 for the three measures classified 71 percent of first grade poor readers and 74 percent of good readers, while a total cutoff <15 correctly identified 87.5 percent of seventh grade poor readers and 80 percent of good readers.

# DISCUSSION

This study followed a cohort of children who entered school together for eight years, from six months before kindergarten entry to spring of grade 7. Prekindergarten testing included a measure of orthographic processing. In midkindergarten, nonphonemic phonological tests of syllable segmentation and rhyme detection were administered. The main aims of the study were to examine the power of the preschool orthographic measure and the kindergarten phonological measures to predict reading at three stages of reading development (grades 1, 3, and 7). A further aim was to investigate whether early and late poor readers differed in orthographic and phonological skills.

Earlier research findings in longitudinal follow ups of other cohorts of children in the same school district indicated that preschool orthographic skills would be more predictive of reading in the later, than in the early, elementary grades, and of reading comprehension, in particular (Badian, 1995, 2000). In a cohort followed through grade 6, the preschool orthographic measure had a nonsignificant correlation with first grade reading comprehension, but by grade 6, the correlation was .49 ($p < .001$) (Badian, 1995). In another cohort, orthographic skills were a significant predictor of reading comprehension, even at first grade level, but the correlation was higher at grade 7 (Badian, 2000). In the present study, based on a new cohort of children, the correlations with reading comprehension were higher at grade 7 than at grade 1, though slightly less high than at grade 3. However, in hierarchical regression analyses, the trend for preschool orthographic skills to be more predictive of later reading comprehension was observed. The percentage of independent variance in reading comprehension, after the contributions of earlier reading level, preschool age, verbal IQ, and verbal memory had been controlled, increased from a nonsignificant amount at grade 1 to 4 percent ($p < .05$) at grade 3 and 6 percent ($p < .01$) at grade 7. The same trend was observed when the orthographic measure was entered after the kindergarten phonological measures. By contrast, preschool orthographic skills accounted for significant independent variance in word reading at first grade level, as well as in reading vocabulary at grades 3 and 7. Both word reading and reading vocabulary require ability to read words in isolation and to understand the meaning of the words.

As stressed earlier, preschool accuracy in distinguishing among visually similar sequences of letters and numerals tends to be associated with later accuracy and speed in reading. By the time children reach seventh grade, automatic and rapid recognition of words is essential for comprehension of passages read. At first grade level, when the text to be read is relatively simple and children are just acquiring a sight vocabulary, phonological skills play an important role in decoding new words. The trend for the preschool orthographic measure used in this and in previous studies (Badian, 1995, 2000) to be more predictive of later, than of earlier, reading comprehension suggests that there are some children whose weakness in orthographic skills observed at the preschool stage continues, with more serious effects in the later grades.

Based on previous studies of cohorts in the same population (Badian, 1995, 2000), it also was expected that phonological measures would be more predictive of early reading, than of later, and of word recognition, in particular, and this expectation was fulfilled. In regression analyses, earlier reading level, verbal IQ, and preschool age were entered first, and then the orthographic and phonological variables were allowed to enter in a stepwise procedure. For first grade word reading and reading comprehension syllable segmentation entered first, after the three fixed variables, accounting for a significant proportion of the variance. Rhyme detection did not contribute, and neither phonological measure contributed to third or seventh grade reading. The same pattern was observed in hierarchical regression analyses in which verbal memory also was included as one of the fixed variables entered at steps 1 to 4. Both syllable segmentation and rhyme detection accounted for a significant proportion of variance in first grade word reading when entered at step 5 or 6 into the regression analyses. Syllable segmentation also accounted for significant variance in grade 1 reading comprehension, but neither phonological measure added variance to either reading variable at grade 3 or 7.

Without controls for previous reading level, verbal IQ, verbal memory, and age, rhyme detection had moderately high correlations with reading at each grade level (.49 to .53 at grades 3 and 7), but it also had correlations of .53 and .47 with verbal IQ and verbal memory. Even controlling only for verbal IQ, the correlations of rhyme detection with reading decreased by approximately .20. Thus, rhyme detection appears to depend on general verbal abilities to a considerable degree.

This study provides evidence that nonphonemic phonological measures of syllable segmentation and rhyme detection administered to kindergarten children add to prediction of first grade reading, but are not useful long-term predictors. It can be assumed that their significant correlations with later reading are due to their correlations with first grade reading (Torgesen et al., 1997). Although preschool reading ability was used as the autoregressor in regression analyses of first grade reading, it was a very imprecise measure of differences in reading ability and accounted for only 6 percent to 9 percent of the variance. When the autoregressor was an actual reading measure, as at grades 3 and 7, the kindergarten phonological measures accounted for no independent variance in reading.

## EARLY AND LATE POOR READERS

Of interest was the possibility of differences in phonological and orthographic skills between early (grade 1) and late (grade 7) poor readers, with early poor reading defined by a cutoff score on the first grade word reading test and late poor reading by a cutoff on seventh grade reading comprehension. The small group of children who were average readers at grades 1 and 3, but who had a serious deficit in reading comprehension by grade 7, were twice as likely to be very low on the preschool orthographic measure as children who were poor readers only in first grade. They were also 3.5 times more likely to be low on syllable segmentation in kindergarten. Early poor readers were 4.6 times more likely to be very low on rhyme detection.

By the spring of first grade, late poor readers were significantly higher than early poor readers on a group test tapping phonological awareness and knowledge of grapheme-phoneme relationships. This finding of early poor readers' lower performance on this phonological test is consistent with findings in an epidemiological study of approximately 1,000 children that included a comparison of early and late poor readers (Badian, 1999). When early and late poor readers in the current study were compared on a seventh grade group test of recognition of correctly and incorrectly spelled words that measures orthographic skills, the late poor readers were significantly lower. Although it could be argued that such tests measure only spelling (Vellutino et al., 1995), they do assess "memory for specific visual/spelling patterns that identify individual words and word parts", as orthographic processing is defined by Barker, Torgesen, & Wagner (1992).

Many studies do not attempt to assess predictive accuracy by examining the number of individual children for whom prediction was successful. As stated earlier, prediction for individuals is generally very imperfect (Scarborough, 1998). Yet, for the practitioner, individual prediction provides more tangible and useful information than such statistical techniques as correlation coefficients and regression analyses.

Rhyme detection proved to be the best predictor of individual first grade good and poor reading, with correct classification of 71 percent of poor readers and 85 percent of good readers. Contrary to expectation, the orthographic and phonological measures each classified similar percentages of good and poor seventh grade readers, and each measure was more successful in classifying good readers than poor. Better results usually can be obtained by combining several variables, as is done in a screening battery. A cutoff score on the total of the three preschool and kindergarten measures identified 87.5 percent of seventh grade poor readers and 80 percent of good readers, but a cutoff on the total score was less successful than rhyme detection alone in classifying first grade readers.

Seventh grade poor readers who were low on the preschool orthographic measure were compared with those who were average on this test. The low scorers were 13 points higher in preschool verbal IQ and were significantly higher on the first grade test measuring phonological awareness and knowledge of grapheme-phoneme relationships. These findings suggest that while an early orthographic deficit contributed to prediction of reading comprehension in one small group of late poor readers with average to above average verbal IQ, the later poor reading comprehension of the other group may be attributed to a phonological deficit and to lower verbal ability.

## CONCLUSIONS

In conclusion, the questions whether the preschool orthographic test and the two kindergarten phonological measures are useful predictors of reading must be considered. One kindergarten phonological measure—syllable segmentation— added significant independent variance to the statistical prediction of first grade, though not later, reading, but was not successful in predicting which individual children would be good or poor readers. Rhyme detection did less well than syllable segmentation in regression analyses, mainly because of its moderately high correlations with verbal intelligence and verbal memory. It was relatively successful in predicting which children would be good or poor first grade readers, and could be useful as a quick screening test in early to middle kindergarten.

It was predicted that the preschool orthographic measure would be more predictive of later reading and of reading comprehension, in particular. In regression analyses, it accounted for an increasing percentage of independent variance in reading comprehension, even when earlier reading level was controlled. At the individual level, it was less successful, although it was more predictive of seventh grade than first grade reading, as was expected. In an earlier study (Badian, 2000), when the preschool orthographic measure was entered into predictive analyses as part of a battery of tests, it added significant variance to individual prediction, together with letter naming and verbal memory. In the current study, it was successful in predicting a subset of late poor readers, while phonological skills and general verbal ability predicted the other subset.

Address correspondence to Nathlie A. Badian, 101 Monroe Road, Quincy, MA 02169. Telephone and fax (617) 471-0986.

## References

Adams, M. J., & Bruck, M. (1993). Word recognition: The interface of educational policies and scientific research. *Reading and Writing: An interdisciplinary Journal, 5,* 113–139.

Badian, N. A. (1994). Preschool prediction: Orthographic and phonological skills, and reading. *Annals of Dyslexia, 44:* 3–25.

Badian, N. A. (1995). Predicting reading ability over the long term: The changing roles of letter-naming, phonological awareness and orthographic processing. *Annals of Dyslexia, 45:* 79–96.

Badian, N. A. (1998). A validation of the role of preschool phonological and orthographic skills in the prediction of reading. *Journal of Learning Disabilities, 31,* 472–481.

Badian, N. A. (1999). Reading disability defined as a discrepancy between listening and reading comprehension: A longitudinal study of stability, gender differences, and prevalence. *Journal of Learning Disabilities, 32,* 138–148.

Badian, N. A. (2000). Do preschool orthographic skills contribute to prediction of reading? In N. A. Badian (ed.), *Prediction and prevention of reading failure* (pp. 31–56). Baltimore, MD: York Press.

Ball, E. W. (1993). Phonological awareness: What's important and to whom? *Reading and Writing: An Interdisciplinary Journal, 5,* 141–159.

Barker, T. A., Torgesen, J. K., & Wagner, R. K. (1992). The role of orthographic processing skills on five different reading tasks. *Reading Research Quarterly, 27,* 335–345.

Bowey, J. A., & Francis, J. (1991). Phonological analysis as a function of age and exposure to reading instruction. *Applied Psycholinguistics, 12,* 91–121.

Bradley, L., & Bryant, P. E. (1983). Categorizing sounds and learning to read: A causal connection. *Nature, 301,* 419–421.

Bradley, L., & Bryant, P. (1991). Phonological skills before and after learning to read. In S. A. Brady & D. P. Shankweiler (eds.), *Phonological processes in literacy: A tribute to Isabelle Y. Liberman* (pp. 37–53). Hillsdale, NJ: Lawrence Erlbaum Associates.

Casalis, S., & Louis-Alexandre, M.-F. (2000). Morphological analysis, phonological analysis and learning to read French: A longitudinal study. *Reading and Writing: An Interdisciplinary Journal, 12,* 303–335.

Christensen, C. A. (1997). Onset, rhymes, and phonemes in learning to read. *Scientific Studies of Reading, 1,* 341–358.

Christensen, C. A. (2000). Preschool phonological awareness and success in reading. In N. A. Badian (ed.), *Prediction and prevention of reading failure* (pp. 153–178). Baltimore, MD: York Press.

de Jong, P. F., & van der Leij, A. (1999). Specific contributions of phonological abilities to early reading acquisition: Results from a Dutch latent variable longitudinal study. *Journal of Educational Psychology, 91,* 450–476.

Duncan, L. G., & Seymour, P. H. K. (2000). Phonemes and rhyme in the development of reading and metaphonology: The Dundee longitudinal study. In N. A. Badian (ed.), *Prediction and prevention of reading failure* (pp. 275–297). Baltimore, MD: York Press.

Ehri, L. C. (1989). The development of spelling knowledge and its role in reading acquisition and reading disability. *Journal of Learning Disabilities, 22,* 356–365.

Ehri, L. C. (1992). Reconceptualizing the development of sight word reading and its relationship to decoding. In P. B. Gough, L. C. Ehri, & R. Treiman (eds.), *Reading acquisition* (pp. 107–143). Hillsdale, NJ: Lawrence Erlbaum Associates.

Elbro, C., Borstrøm, I., & Petersen, D. K. (1998). Predicting dyslexia from kindergarten: The importance of distinctiveness of phonological representations of lexical items. *Reading Research Quarterly, 33,* 36–60.

Felton, R. H. (1992). Early identification of children at risk for reading disabilities. *Topics in Early Childhood Special Education, 12,* 212–229.

Foorman, B. R. (1994). Phonological and orthographic processing: Separate but equal? In V. W. Berninger (ed.), *The varieties of orthographic knowledge,* Vol.1 (pp. 321–357). Dordrecht, Netherlands: Kluwer Academic Publishers.

Fowler, A. E. (1991). How early phonological development might set the stage for phoneme awareness. In S. A. Brady & D. P. Shankweiler (eds.), *Phonological processes in literacy: A tribute to Isabelle Y. Liberman* (pp. 97–117). Hillsdale, NJ: Lawrence Erlbaum Associates.

Gipstein, M., Brady, S. A., & Fowler, A. (2000). Questioning the role of syllables and rimes in early phonological awareness. In N. A. Badian (ed.), *Prediction and prevention of reading failure* (pp. 179–216). Baltimore, MD: York Press.

Goswami, U., & Bryant, P. (1990). *Phonological skills and learning to read.* Hove, U. K.: Lawrence Erlbaum Associates.

Liberman, I. Y., Shankweiler, D., Fischer, F. W., & Carter, B. (1974). Explicit syllable and phoneme segmentation in the young child. *Journal of Experimental Child Psychology, 18,* 201–212.

Lonigan, C. J., Burgess, S., Anthony, J. L., & Barker, T. A. (1998). Development of phonological sensitivity in 2- to 5-year-old children. *Journal of Educational Psychology, 90,* 294–311.

Manis, F. R., Seidenberg, M. S., & Doi, L. M. (1999). See Dick RAN: Rapid naming and the  longitudinal prediction of reading subskills in first and second graders. *Scientific Studies of Reading, 3,* 129–157.

Mann, V. A. (1993). Phoneme awareness and future reading ability. *Journal of Learning Disabilities, 26,* 259–269.

Mann, V. A., & Liberman, I. Y. (1984). Phonological awareness and verbal short-term memory. *Journal of Learning Disabilities, 17,* 592–599.

Muter, V., Hulme, C., Snowling, M., & Taylor, S. (1997). Segmentation, not rhyming, predicts early progress in learning to read. *Journal of Experimental Child Psychology, 65,* 370–396.

Muter, V., & Snowling, M. (1998). Concurrent and longitudinal predictors of reading: The role of metalinguistic and short-term memory skills. *Reading Research Quarterly, 33,* 320–337.

Olson, R., Forsberg, H., Wise, B., & Rack, J. (1994). Measurement of word recognition, orthographic, and phonological skills. In G. R. Lyon (ed.), *Frames of reference for the assessment of learning disabilities: New views on measurement issues* (pp. 243–277). Baltimore, MD: Brookes Publishing Company.

Perfetti, C. A., Beck, L., Bell, L., & Hughes, C. (1987). Phonemic knowledge and learning to read are reciprocal: A longitudinal study of first grade children. *Merrill-Palmer Quarterly, 33,* 283–319.

Psychological Corporation (1992). *Stanford achievement test,* 8th edition. San Antonio, TX: Harcourt Brace.

Rack, J. P., & Olson, R. K. (1993). Phonological deficits, IQ, and individual differences in reading disability: Genetic and environmental influences. *Developmental Review, 13,* 269–278.

Sawyer, D. J., Kim, J. K., & Lipa-Wade, S. (2000). Application of Frith's developmental phase model to the process of identifying at-risk beginning readers. In N. A. Badian (ed.), *Prediction and prevention of reading failure* (pp. 87–103). Baltimore, MD: York Press.

Scarborough, H. S. (1998). Early identification of children at risk for reading disabilities: Phonological awareness and some other promising predictors. In B. K. Shapiro, P. J. Accardo, & A. J. Capute (eds.), *Specific reading disability: A view of the spectrum* (pp. 75–119). Timonium, MD: York Press.

Share, D. L., Jorm, A. F., MacLean, R., & Matthews, R. (1984). Sources of individual differences in reading acquisition. *Journal of Educational Psychology, 76,* 1309–1324.

Stanovich, K. E. (1988). Explaining the differences between the dyslexic and the garden-variety poor reader: The phonological-core variable-difference model. *Journal of Learning Disabilities, 21,* 590–604, 612.

Stanovich, K. E. (1992). Speculations on the causes and consequences of individual differences in early reading acquisition. In P. B. Gough, L. C. Ehri, & R. Treiman (eds.), *Reading acquisition* (pp. 307–342). Hillsdale, NJ: Lawrence Erlbaum Associates.

Stanovich, K. E., Cunningham, A. E., & Cramer, B. B. (1984). Assessing phonological processes in kindergarten children: Issues of task compatibility. *Journal of Experimental Child Psychology, 38,* 175–190.

Stanovich, K. E., West, R. F., & Cunningham, A. E. (1991). Beyond phonological processes: Print exposure and orthographic processing. In S. A. Brady & D. P. Shankweiler (eds), *Phonological processes in literacy: A tribute to Isabelle Y. Liberman* (pp. 219–235). Hillsdale, NJ: Lawrence Erlbaum Associates.

Torgesen, J. K., Wagner, R. K., Rashotte, C. A., Burgess, S., & Hecht, S. (1997). Contributions of phonological awareness and rapid automatic naming ability to the growth of word-reading skills in second-to-fifth-grade children. *Scientific Studies of Reading, 1,* 161-185.

Treiman, R., & Zukowski, A. (1991). Levels of phonological awareness. In S. A. Brady & D. P. Shankweiler (eds.), *Phonological processes in literacy: A tribute to Isabelle Y. Liberman* (pp. 67–83). Hillsdale, NJ: Lawrence Erlbaum Associates.

Vellutino, F. R., & Scanlon, D. M. (1987). Phonological coding, phonological awareness, and reading ability: Evidence from a longitudinal and experimental study. *Merrill-Palmer Quarterly, 33,* 321–363.

Vellutino, F. R., Scanlon, D. M., & Chen, R. S. (1995). The increasingly inextricable relationship between orthographic and phonological coding in learning to read: Some reservations about current methods of operationalizing orthographic coding. In V. W. Berninger (ed.), *The varieties of orthographic knowledge*, Vol. II (pp. 47–111). Dordrecht, Netherlands: Kluwer Academic Publishers.

Wagner, R. K., & Barker, T. A. (1994). The development of orthographic processing ability. In V. W. Berninger (ed.), *The varieties of orthographic knowledge*, Vol. I (pp. 243–276). Dordrecht, Netherlands: Kluwer Academic Publishers.

Wagner, R. K., & Torgesen, J. K. (1987). The nature of phonological processing and its causal role in the acquisition of reading skills. *Psychological Bulletin, 101*, 192–212.

Wagner, R. K., Torgesen, J. K., Rashotte, C. A., Hecht, S. A., Barker, T. A., Burgess, S. R., Donahue, J., & Garon, T. (1997). Changing relations between phonological processing abilities and word-level reading as children develop from beginning to skilled readers: A 5-year longitudinal study. *Developmental Psychology, 33*, 468–479.

Wechsler, D. (1967). *Preschool and primary scale of intelligence*. New York: Psychological Corporation.

# Preschool Phonological Representations and Development of Reading Skills

*Ralph Wesseling*

*Pieter Reitsma*

PI Research Amsterdam
Duivendrecht, The Netherlands

*Individual differences in the quality of phonological representations of kindergarten children may be predictive of Grade 1 phonological awareness and reading development. Three longitudinal studies are presented that attempt to measure variance in the quality of the phonological structures within lexical items using three tasks: nonword repetition, cued word fluency, and a gated auditory word recognition task. Nonword repetition was a consistent predictor of later phonological awareness, even after current phonological awareness and vocabulary knowledge were taken into account. The results of the three studies provide inconclusive support for the theory that individual differences in the quality of phonological representations play an important role in the development of explicit phonological awareness and reading acquisition. An important finding of the third study is that caution needs to be maintained in measuring skills in preschoolers as stability of results can be an issue when interpreting the relations between variables. However, the present studies do confirm that individual differences in vocabulary, nonword repetition, and phonological awareness are important factors in predicting the development of reading related skills.*

Annals of Dyslexia, Vol. 51, 2001
ISSN 0736-9387

One underlying deficit found in the majority of children with dyslexia is an impairment in phonemic awareness (Oakhill & Kyle, 1999; Stahl & Murray, 1994). There is much evidence to show that phonological awareness (PA) is causally related to the acquisition of reading skill (see Stanovich, 1992). However, there is also research to show that learning to read is the most effective way to become phonemically aware (Johnston, Anderson, & Holligan, 1996). Preschool children generally have no awareness of the phonemic nature of spoken language, and their first contact with formal reading instruction acts as a powerful trigger for development of phonemic awareness (Hatcher, Hulme, & Ellis, 1994; Wesseling & Reitsma, 1998).

The reciprocal relationship between phonemic awareness and reading makes it difficult to utilize phonemic awareness tasks in kindergarten as a means of predicting potential reading difficulties in grade school. Therefore, the question arises: Is it possible, in the absence of reading ability and letter knowledge, to measure the potential to become phonemically aware? It has been hypothesized that an important prerequisite for phonemic awareness is the quality of phonological representations within the lexicon; that is, the amount and extent of phonological information used to define lexical items (vocabulary) (Elbro, Nielsen, & Petersen, 1994; Fowler, 1991). The theoretical role of the quality of phonological representations for PA and reading acquisition is still largely untested but has in very recent years gained popularity amongst reading researchers (Elbro, Nielsen, & Petersen, 1994; Fowler, 1991). The central issue in the current article is the relationship of the quality of phonological representations measured in kindergarten to individual differences of Grade 1 PA and reading acquisition.

The quality of phonological representations pertains to differences in the amount of phonological information used to represent items in the lexicon. Fowler (1991) suggests that infants' words are initially represented as unanalyzable wholes; as new words are learned, existing lexical items must be refined into a more segmented form in order to ensure that sufficient distinguishing features are available for the purposes of accurate aural recognition. Fowler (1991) argues that individual differences in lexical segmentation can readily account for a number of reported deficiencies in poor readers, including verbal short-term memory, nonword repetition, and perceptual deficits of verbal stimuli.

Although the segmentation theory of Fowler (1991) accounts quite well for the development of PA, one difficulty is that differentiation of the lexicon is driven by vocabulary expansion. If the purpose of differentiation is to accommodate similar sounding words, then one could ask the question: "Why do lexically unique words also need to be refined to a phonological level?" Lexically unique words could remain represented as indivisible gestalts without hampering spoken word recognition. The distinctness theory (Elbro, Nielsen, & Petersen, 1994) avoids this difficulty by removing the requirement of vocabulary as the motor that drives the process of building an efficient lexicon. Instead, individuals "pack" vocabulary items with differing levels of (phonological) information to aid spoken word recognition. For a person listening to a sentence, a major difficulty in recognition is the variability of speech input due to environmental noise and differences in pronunciation. For example, the /d/ in the word *hand* seems to disappear if *hand* is followed by the word *me*, as in "hand me a hammer" (Lahiri & Marslen-Wilson, 1991). The skilled listener must be able to abstract away from the surface details but ensure that lexical representations remain distinct enough to keep them separate from other lexical items.

Elbro (1996) suggests that children who develop reading problems have less access to the most distinct variants of lexical representations. Distinctness of a lexical representation is the degree to which lexical items differentiate themselves from lexical neighbors. A lexical representation is distinct when it has many features that serve to distinguish it from other lexical items. The distinctness theory differs from the segmentation hypothesis because the highest level of distinction does not necessarily need to be at the phoneme level but also could incorporate allophones; for example *tomato* may be pronounced /təuma . . . təu/ or /təumeitəu/.

Elbro (1996) hypothesizes that less distinct words are harder to segment and manipulate. Furthermore, the extraction of grapheme to phoneme correspondences may directly relate to the distinctness or quality of the lexical representations. A recent Danish longitudinal study (Elbro, Borstrøm, & Petersen, 1998) supports this hypothesis using a task in which a child is asked to identify and correct mispronunciations of complex words made by a puppet (the experimenter acted as a ventriloquist). Three measures in kindergarten appeared to contribute independently to the prediction of dyslexia: letter naming, phoneme identification, and distinctness of phonological representations.

The distinctness of phonological representations does not appear to be related to the size of the vocabulary store. The results reported by Elbro, Borstrøm, and Petersen (1998) indicate that neither receptive nor productive vocabulary contributed independently to the prediction of PA in second grade. Rather, the quality of the phonological structure of lexical representations is crucial both for PA and learning to read. From this point on, when referring to individual differences in the phonological structure of lexical items, the term Quality of Phonological Representations (QPR) will be used.

## MEASURING THE QUALITY OF PHONOLOGICAL REPRESENTATIONS

Generally, preschoolers are not literate and have little or no awareness of phonemes; therefore, PA tasks are not appropriate to predict the potential of prereaders to develop reading difficulties in grade school. However, there may be tasks less dependent on literacy knowledge that measure the potential to become phonemically aware. One method may be to determine the extent of lexical differentiation. There are some empirical findings showing that it is possible to measure the process of lexical differentiation. Metsala (1997) presented evidence, using the gating paradigm, to argue that the lexicon of young children and poor readers is more holistic than the lexicon of older children and adults. The gating paradigm is a task of spoken word recognition that gauges the amount of auditory stimuli a listener requires for spoken word identification. Young children have a smaller vocabulary (lexicon) than older children and adults, so one could predict that younger children would find it easier to recognize words in a gating task due to fact that they have less items in their lexicon to search. However, the consistent finding is that older children and adults require less aural input for correct identification of words than young children. This finding provides evidence that gating tasks indicate the level of lexical differentiation (Metsala, 1997).

In the gating paradigm, the point where the partially presented word has no alternative word candidates is termed the *point of uniqueness*. The differences in lexical differentiation are more discernible when using words from sparse neighborhoods because point of uniqueness is arrived at sooner. For example, a listener is auditorily presented with the onset and the vowel of the two words "tulp" and "bord." In Dutch, the word "tulp" (*tulip*) has few lexical neighbors, whereas "bord" (*plate*) has many. The point of uniqueness in "tulp" is arrived after hearing /tu/; the point of uniqueness in "bord" is at the very end.

A study by Metsala (1997) showed that the gating performance of a seven-year-old child could predict concurrent reading ability. Words from sparse lexical neighborhoods were good predictors of reading ability (increase in $R^2$ = 0.11), even after the variance attributable to age, vocabulary, and phonological awareness were accounted for (total $R^2$ = 0.67).

There may be a number of other tasks, relatively unconfounded by current letter-sound knowledge, for measuring differentiation of the lexicon. One task of QPR could be *cued word fluency* in which the subject is provided with the onset of a word and asked to produce as many words in a short span of time that begin with the onset. The ease with which items are extracted from the lexicon indicates if lexical items can be accessed using partial phonological information.

Another task that may be suitable is *nonword repetition* (Fowler, 1991). Nonwords are, in essence, just like real words that have not yet been learned. One characteristic of a well-specified and distinct lexical system is the ability to assimilate new and novel words. In order to do this, the listener must have the required skills: accurate encoding, retention, and articulation ability. The nonword repetition task was first used by Snowling (1981), who found that children with poor reading ability were worse at repeating nonwords than reading matched younger children. Performance differences on a nonword repetition test are probably related to individual differences in the quality of speech encoding, storage, and articulation, and, therefore, also to the construction of stable phonological specifications in long-term memory during vocabulary acquisition (Gathercole, 1995). Nonword repetition should be related to vocabulary and this has been confirmed in empirical research. For example, Gathercole and Baddeley (1997) reported a mean correlation coefficient of 0.49 between nonword repetition and scores on standardized vocabulary tests for nine studies using this nonword repetition technique with children aged 4 and 6 years.

In total, three studies are presented. First, an initial small-scale study is reported that tests the suitability of measures of QPR. The second study is a larger scale replication of the initial study. Finally, in a third study, we examine the stability of various linguistic measures and the QPR measures over a period of two and a half years from early kindergarten until Grade 1. It is hypothesized that kindergarten children are likely to exhibit greater variation in cognitive skills than children attending grade school. This variation could manifest itself in less representative and stable measures of QPR, and other language related abilities in kindergarten children.

# STUDY 1

In the first study, we tested the suitability of three measures of the quality of phonological representations with a group of second year kindergarten children. There are three main aims for this study. The first is to examine the independence of the three chosen measures from both PA and letter-sound knowledge. The second aim is to examine if the three QPR task administered in kindergarten are unique predictors of PA and reading development in Grade 1; and the third is to ascertain the extent to which variance in Grade 1 reading ability can be predicted from kindergarten measures in general.

## METHOD

*Participants.*   Twenty-nine kindergarten children (17 boys and 12 girls)  with a mean age of 6 years and 1 months (SD = 4 months) participated. The study was conducted three months before the end of the second kindergarten year. The children came from four different kindergarten classes in one school. Each class had a mixture of first year and second year kindergarten children; however, only second year kindergarten children participated. In the Netherlands, no instruction in reading related skills is given during kindergarten. Thirty two percent of the children came from Dutch families; the remainder came from Turkish, Moroccan, or Surinam families (68 percent). Only those children that spoke Dutch as their first language participated.

## MATERIALS AND PROCEDURE

*Tests in Kindergarten.*   Eight tests were first administered to the children in kindergarten. The tests were administered in two sessions that took approximately 25 minutes each to complete. In the first session, the letter sound correspondences, visual word identification, phonemic awareness, nonword repetition, and cued word fluency tests were done. In the second session, the gating and vocabulary were administered.

*Letter Sound Correspondences.*   Twenty-seven different lower case graphemes used in Dutch were presented on a single page. The children were asked to provide the letter sounds without a time limit.

*Visual Word Identification.*   Ten common words used in children's books were arranged on a single sheet of paper. The children were asked to read the words and the number identified was recorded.

*Receptive Vocabulary.*   A standardized 98-item receptive vocabulary test was used (Verhoeven, Vermeer & Van de Guchte, 1986). Each item had four picture alternatives and the child was asked to point to the picture that best represented a word spoken by the experimenter. The test ended when the child failed to select two items or more correct out of eight consecutive items. The score was the number of correctly identified items.

**Phonemic Awareness.**   Phonemic awareness was measured using two tasks: phoneme blending and phoneme segmentation. The sum of the two tasks was used for analysis.

*Phoneme Blending.*   Ten digitally recorded (16 bit at 22Khz) segmented words were presented aurally by means of a computer. Each segment of the word was presented at one second intervals. The stimuli contained two items in each of the following word structures, VC, CVC, CCVC, CVCC, CCVCC (note: C = consonant, V = vowel). The words used were single syllable, high-frequency words that were known by more than 95 percent of children at this age level (Kohnstamm, Schaerlaekens, de Vries, Akkerhuis, & Froonincksx, 1981). The reliability score (Cronbach's alpha) for this test was 0.88.

*Phoneme Segmentation.*   Ten digitally recorded whole words were presented using a computer; the children were asked to verbally respond with the phoneme segments. The Cronbach's alpha test of reliability was 0.87.

*Gating Task.*   The children were asked to identify words from partial acoustic signals presented through headphones (Metsala, 1997). In this test there were five different, high-frequency, single syllable (C)CVC(C) words known unanimously by all five- and six-year olds. These words have few or no lexical neighbors. The average length of a word was 433 ms which took 10 gates to present. The stimulus array was started at 133 ms and after each round the gate was increased by 33 ms. The test took 8 to 11 minutes to complete. The score for the test was the number of gates required to name a word correctly given that the subsequent trial was also correctly answered. In further analyses, the mean number of gates required to identify the words is used. A lower score indicates better performance, but for correlational analyses, the scores were multiplied by −1 so that high scores indicate better performance.

*Cued Word Fluency.* Children were asked to say, within 20 seconds, as many words as they could think of that began with a certain consonant phoneme. For example, "Say as many words that you can think of that begin with /b/." The total number of words produced was noted. The first six questions in the test were cued with single stop or continuant consonants. The final four questions in the test were cued by consonant clusters (e.g., /br/, or /sp/). The split half test of reliability was 0.80. For further analyses, the sum of correctly named words was used.

*Nonword Repetition Task (NWR).* In this test the children were asked to repeat as accurately as possible 15 pseudowords. The words were either two or three syllables in length. A response was considered correct if all phonemes were articulated. The absence of phonemes, syllables, or the substitution of phonemes was considered incorrect. The score for this test was the total number of correctly repeated words. The test reliability (Cronbach's alpha) was 0.62.

**Tests in Grade 1.**   In Grade 1, the word decoding test and phonemic awareness tests were administered in a session that took about 15 minutes. The phoneme blending and phoneme segmentation tests were the same as administered in kindergarten (see above for descriptions).

*Word Decoding.* To measure the word decoding ability of children in Grade 1, the One-Minute-Test (OMT) of word decoding, a Dutch-normed test (Brus & Voeten, 1973) was administered. The difficulty of words ranged from single syllable words to multisyllabic words. Each word was scored correct if the child was able to read the word aloud. The score for this test was the number of correctly identified words within one minute.

## ANALYSIS OF DATA

To replicate the regression analysis from Metsala's (1997) study, the following procedure was used. For the first regression, the kindergarten variables PA, written language knowledge (letter-sound knowledge and visual word identification), and vocabulary were entered in a single step. These variables represent often used predictors of language and reading problems. Any predictor that significantly accounted for variance of the dependent variable in this first step remained in the equation. Next, the three QPR tests of NWR, cued word fluency, and gating were entered in a second step, and significant predictors were noted. The resulting predictive variables were used in a separate fixed order hierarchical regression analysis. Finally, the order of entry of variables in the latter analysis was reversed to determine the unique contribution of the variables.

## RESULTS

In table I, the results of tests in kindergarten and Grade 1 are shown. Twenty eight percent of the children were unable to identify a single letter, and in total, 70 percent of the entire group identified four or fewer letters. The majority of the children were not phonemically aware (PA). The average on the vocabulary test was within the expected average based on national norms for this age group.

On the gating task, the average number of gates required for identification was 3.28 which corresponds roughly to the first 220 ms of the entire word. Some children were able to successfully identify the item with only 133 to 150 ms of acoustic information, but others needed to hear almost the entire word. The cued word fluency task was difficult; many children were unable to produce a single item. The average correct on the NWR task was high. Even so, there were a number of children who had difficulty articulating what they had just heard.

Table II shows the Pearson correlations between kindergarten variables (below the diagonal). Children with good letter sound knowledge and visual word recognition tended to have better PA, and do better on the cued word fluency. PA was significantly correlated with the nonword repetition and the cued word fluency task. Gating and nonword repetition correlated with each other. Gating correlated with the vocabulary test but nonword repetition did not.

Table I.   Descriptive Statistics of Tests in Kindergarten and Grade 1.

|  | Test | M | SD | Range | |
|---|---|---|---|---|---|
| **Kindergarten** | Letter Sound Knowledge (27)* | 5.24 | 6.78 | 0.0 | 24.0 |
| | Visual Word Recognition (10) | 0.34 | 1.52 | 0.0 | 8.0 |
| | Phonemic Awareness (20) | 4.45 | 5.74 | 0.0 | 17.0 |
| | Nonword Repetition (15) | 11.97 | 2.40 | 7.0 | 15.0 |
| | Cued Word Fluency | 5.76 | 7.65 | 0.0 | 25.0 |
| | Gating (10) | 3.28 | 1.38 | 1.4 | 7.8 |
| | Vocabulary (98) | 50.03 | 14.20 | 28.0 | 81.0 |
| **Grade 1** | Phonemic Awareness (20) | 17.48 | 3.26 | 8.0 | 20.0 |
| | Word Decoding (116) | 13.79 | 6.21 | 4.0 | 27.0 |

* Number in parentheses refers to number of items in test.

Table II.   Kindergarten and Grade 1 Correlations.

| Variables | 1 | 2 | 3 | 4 | 5 | 6 | 7 | 8 | 9 |
|---|---|---|---|---|---|---|---|---|---|
| **Kindergarten (1-7)** | | | | | | | | | |
| 1. Letter Sound Knowledge | – | | | | | | | | |
| 2. Visual Word Identification | .57** | – | | | | | | | |
| 3. Phonemic Awareness | .65** | .35* | – | .38* | .82** | .16 | .13 | .27 | .23 |
| 4. Nonword Repetition | .42* | .27 | .54** | – | .25 | .39* | .07 | .52** | .14 |
| 5. Cued Word Fluency | .65** | .48** | .88** | .45* | – | .13 | .27 | .33 | .29 |
| 6. Gating | .17 | .05 | .24 | .41* | .20 | – | .44* | .51** | .47* |
| 7. Vocabulary | .06 | -.09 | .14 | .08 | .22 | .44* | – | .23 | .07 |
| **Grade 1 (8-9)** | | | | | | | | | |
| 8. Phonemic Awareness | .35 | .18 | .42* | .59** | .46* | .53** | .24 | – | .20 |
| 9. Decoding | .38* | .19 | .44* | .34 | .50** | .54** | .17 | .46* | – |

$^*p < 0.05$, $^{**}p < 0.01$

*Note:* Pearson's correlation coefficients are below the diagonal and partial correlations above the diagonal with variance attributable to letter knowledge partialed out.

Table III.   Hierarchical Regression Analyses
Predicting Decoding Scores in Grade 1.

| Predicted variable | Step | Variable | Change in $R^2$ | Total $R^2$ | F |
|---|---|---|---|---|---|
| **First Regression Analysis:** | | | | | |
| Grade 1 Word Decoding | I | 1. PA (Kindergarten) | .20 | .20 | 6.75 |
| | | 2. Gating | .20 | .40 | 8.57 |
| | II | 1. Gating | .29 | .29 | 10.96 |
| | | 2. PA (kindergarten) | .11 | .40 | 8.57 |
| **Second Regression Analysis:** | | | | | |
| Grade 1 Word Decoding | | 1. Age | .05 | .05 | 1.41 |
| | | 2. Vocabulary | .04 | .09 | 1.22 |
| | | 3. Phonological Awareness | .16 | .24 | 2.58 |
| | | 4. Gating | .21 | .45 | 4.96 |

As stated earlier, reading and letter-sound knowledge have profound effects on the development of PA. To examine the variables in the absence of literacy knowledge, we calculated partial correlations and controlled for the shared variance of kindergarten visual word recognition and letter-sound knowledge. The results are presented above the diagonal in table II in italics. PA continued to be significantly correlated to cued word fluency and to nonword repetition. The gating task correlated both with nonword repetition (0.39) and with vocabulary (0.44).

In Grade 1, the average on PA tasks approached ceiling level (table I). The mean score on the standardized word decoding test was almost 14, slightly above the average expected for this age group. In table II, correlations between kindergarten and Grade 1 variables are presented (see variables 8 & 9). Knowledge of letter sounds in kindergarten correlated significantly with decoding ability in Grade 1. PA in kindergarten correlated significantly with PA and word decoding in Grade 1. Nonword repetition, cued word fluency, and gating all correlated significantly with Grade 1 PA; the strongest coefficient was between nonword repetition and PA, $r = .59$. Of the three QPR tasks, only cued word fluency, and gating correlated with Grade 1 word decoding. The partial correlations between kindergarten variables and decoding show that nonword repetition and gating were the only kindergarten variables that correlated significantly with Grade 1 PA. For word decoding, only the gating task was significantly correlated after removing the shared variance with early literacy skills.

The results of the first regression analysis (see table III) revealed that kindergarten phonemic awareness accounted for 20 percent with gating accounting for an extra 20 percent. In the reverse order analysis, the gating task predicted 29 percent of variance in Grade 1 word decoding with an extra 11 percent taken up by phonemic awareness.

In the second regression analysis (see table 3), we replicated the analysis reported in Metsala (1997). Metsala found, in a crosssectional design, that gating of words from sparse neighborhoods was a significant predictor of reading ability after accounting for the contributions of age, vocabulary, and PA. In the present analysis, we replicated this by using similar variables to predict variance in Grade 1 word decoding. Age, kindergarten vocabulary knowledge, and kindergarten PA scores accounted for a total $R^2 = 0.24$ with PA accounting for 16 percent after entering age and vocabulary. The results also show that performance on the gating task in kindergarten accounted for an extra 21 percent of the variance in word decoding scores in Grade 1. Gating uniquely accounted for a considerable amount of variance, even when PA had been entered.

## DISCUSSION

The first study examined if nonword repetition, gated auditory word recognition, and cued word fluency could be used to measure differences in QPR in preschoolers. The results suggest that gating and NWR measure differences in QPR. The second goal was to examine if individual differences in the various tasks administered in kindergarten predicted variance in Grade 1 PA and reading skill. The results show that a sizeable amount of the variance in reading ability can be attributed to individual differences in kindergarten PA, and a unique proportion of the variance is accounted for by individual differences on the gating task in kindergarten.

Cued word fluency correlated with concurrent PA and with Grade 1 PA, which suggests that cued word fluency may be considered as a measure of PA in kindergarten. However, due to the strong correlation found with kindergarten literacy skills, the cued word fluency does not adhere to our requirements for a test of QPR.

Interestingly, in the current study, we found no relationship between nonword repetition and vocabulary ($r = 0.08$). This finding is inconsistent with Gathercole and Baddeley (1997). Perhaps the test in our study is not sufficiently reliable and could perhaps be improved by presenting the stimulus items in a prerecorded fashion, reducing variability in presentation as suggested by Gathercole and Baddeley (1997).

In the present study, we replicated part of Metsala's (1997) study in which she found that the scores on a gating task accounted for a significant amount of unique variance in word reading scores in 30 normal achieving eight-year-old readers. We used the gating task in the present study to predict Grade 1 PA and reading skill development based on measures gathered during kindergarten. The individual differences in scores on the gating task correlated both with nonword repetition and with vocabulary in kindergarten, and the gating task also appeared as a predictor of PA and word decoding skill in Grade 1. Grade 1 word decoding was predicted to a greater extent by variance on the gating task than by kindergarten PA, the only other significant variable.

The results with the gating task clearly confirm the previous findings of Metsala (1997). The current study, however, adds to Metsala's (1997) study in that a longitudinal design was used to evaluate the predictive power of the gating paradigm. Of course, the sample is relatively small ($n = 29$), and it is known that multiple regression analyses may be unstable in small samples.

The present study provides evidence that QPR plays a significant role in the development of PA and reading acquisition. The findings also suggest that tests can be created to measure reliably individual differences in QPR of kindergarten children. However, due to the small sample size, a larger replication is required to confirm findings. A replication study also would provide data regarding the reliability and stability of QPR in kindergarten.

# STUDY 2

The first study presented positive evidence that individual differences in the quality of phonological representations measured in kindergarten are predictive of Grade 1 PA and reading ability. The purpose of the second study was to replicate the previous findings.

The two specific questions remain the same as in the original study. Is it possible to measure differences reliably in the quality of phonological representations? Second, are individual differences in the quality of phonological representations related to the development of Grade 1 PA and reading skills?

## METHOD

*Participants.* Sixty-two second year kindergarten children participated. Their mean age was 6 years and 1 months (SD = 4 months). The first moment of testing was three months before the end of the school year and the posttest, five months into the new school year. The children came from six different classes spread over two schools. Each class had a mixture of first year and second year kindergarten children; only the second year kindergarten children participated. Approximately 45 percent of the children came from Dutch families. The remainder came from Turkish, Moroccan, or Surinam families. Only those children that spoke Dutch as their first language participated.

## TASKS AND PROCEDURE

*Pretests in Kindergarten*  Eight different tests were first administered to the children in kindergarten in one session taking approximately 35 minutes. The following tasks remained unchanged from those used in the first study: letter and word identification, passive vocabulary knowledge, cued word fluency, phoneme blending, and phoneme segmentation. The phoneme blending, and segmentation were combined into a single PA variable for analysis purposes.

*Gating Task.*   For the gating task, the number of items was increased from five to six. In order to keep the amount of time required for testing down, the first presentation was set at 150ms and the rest of the word was divided into even sections so that on the eighth trial, the entire word would be heard. The average step size was 40ms. Instead of using the isolation point, we scored the number of times a word was correctly identified. This provides a maximum score of 8, so that if a child identified the word at 230ms, and continued to identify it correctly for the rest of the trials, the score for that item would be six. The result of a Cronbach's alpha for reliability was 0.68.

*Nonword Repetition (NWR).*   The number of items in this test was increased to 25. The items included two one-syllable words, 7 two-syllable, 13 three-syllable, and 3 four-syllable words. The final score was the total number of correctly repeated words. The test reliability (Cronbach's alpha) was 0.70.

*Posttest in Grade 1.*   The phoneme blending and segmentation tests from the pretest were readministered. The first test of word decoding was the One-Minute-Test (OMT) of word decoding also used in the first study. The second test of decoding was a one-minute test of decoding that only contained CVC words. For analysis, word decoding was the average of the two tests of reading.

## RESULTS

In table IV, the pre- and posttest results for the children are presented. On average, the children recognized nine letters in the pretest, but 50 percent of the group recognized less than five letters. The two phoneme awareness tasks show that many children were insensitive to the phonological structure of language; 23 percent scored zero. The average on the nonword repetition test was 20, but some children scored as low as 14. The average on the gating task was 4.5 responses correct, approximately 280 milliseconds. The vocabulary test indicated that the average and the spread of scores were within expected norms.

The kindergarten group was retested in Grade 1. The correlations between the various tests are presented table V. Noticeable is that letter knowledge was related to almost all other kindergarten tests. Children with letter skills tended to be phonologically aware and had greater vocabulary knowledge. However, after literacy knowledge was partialled out, many of the correlations disappeared.

Table IV.  Descriptive Statistics of Tests in Kindergarten and Grade 1.

| N = 62 | Test | M | SD | Range | |
|---|---|---|---|---|---|
| Pretest | Letter Sound Knowledge (27)* | 9.05 | 8.09 | 0.0 | 24.0 |
| Kindergarten | Visual Word Recognition (10) | 0.94 | 1.92 | 0.0 | 7.0 |
| | Phoneme Awareness (20) | 3.94 | 4.91 | 0.0 | 18.0 |
| | Nonword Repetition (25) | 19.98 | 2.80 | 14.0 | 25.0 |
| | Cued Word Fluency | 2.34 | 3.13 | 0.0 | 12.0 |
| | Gating (8) | 4.57 | 0.76 | 2.5 | 6.0 |
| | Vocabulary (98) | 54.24 | 16.88 | 21.0 | 90.0 |
| Posttest | Phoneme Awareness (20) | 16.73 | 3.79 | 2.0 | 20.0 |
| Grade 1 | Word Decoding | 17.54 | 10.80 | 0.0 | 60.0 |

* Number in parentheses indicates number of items in test.

Table V.    Pre- and Postest Correlations.

| Variables | 1 | 2 | 3 | 4 | 5 | 6 | 7 | 8 | 9 |
|---|---|---|---|---|---|---|---|---|---|
| **Pretest Kindergarten (1-7)** | | | | | | | | | |
| 1. Letter Sound Knowledge | – | | | | | | | | |
| 2. Visual Word Identification | .65*** | – | | | | | | | |
| 3. Phonemic Awareness | .48*** | .70*** | – | .35*** | .46*** | .29** | .36*** | .25** | –.21 |
| 4. Nonword Repetition | .06 | .25** | .41*** | – | .13 | .03 | .12 | .35** | .00 |
| 5. Cued Word Fluency | .52*** | .48*** | .61*** | .17 | – | –.04 | .16 | .03 | –.23 |
| 6. Gating | .23* | .21 | .35** | .06 | .10 | – | .25* | -.01 | –.15 |
| 7. Vocabulary | .27** | .31** | .46*** | .17 | .30* | .31* | – | .22 | –.11 |
| **Posttest Grade 1 (8–9)** | | | | | | | | | |
| 8. Phonemic Awareness | .39*** | .23 | .34** | .32** | .22 | .07 | .29** | – | .30** |
| 9. Word Decoding | .64*** | .46*** | .23 | .06 | .19 | .04 | .10 | .46*** | – |

* p < 0.1, ** p < 0.05, *** p < 0.01

*Note:* Pearson's correlation coefficients appear below the diagonal. Partial correlations, with variance from letter and word knowledge removed, are printed above the diagonal.

In Grade 1, PA and word decoding showed relatively high correlation coefficients. However, PA scores in kindergarten were only weakly correlated with Grade 1 word decoding scores ($r = .23$, $p < 0.10$). The strongest correlation between kindergarten variables and Grade 1 word decoding was with kindergarten letter knowledge ($r = 0.64$, $p < 0.01$).

In the first study, kindergarten NWR ability correlated with Grade 1 PA, and in the current study, a similar correlation was found between NWR and grade 1 PA. In the first study, gating and cued word fluency were both correlated with Grade 1 PA ($r = .53$ and $r = .46$, respectively ). In the present study, these relations were absent. Neither gating nor cued word fluency were correlated with Grade 1 word decoding.

A hierarchical regression analysis was performed to determine the predictability of Grade 1 word decoding from kindergarten variables. Only kindergarten letter knowledge accounted for significant variance in Grade 1 word decoding ($R^2 = .41$). Replicating Metsala's (1997) regression analysis (see table III) produced no significant predictors of Grade 1 word decoding.

## DISCUSSION

Findings from Study 2 did not confirm the conclusions from the first study. The QPR measure did not have a direct relationship to Grade 1 PA or word decoding. Although NWR was related to Grade 1 PA, no relationship was found between Grade 1 PA and either gating or the cued word fluency task. Unlike the first study, in the second study, gating was not a predictor of either Grade 1 PA or word decoding. It is possible that the relatively higher letter-sound knowledge of the kindergarten children confounded performance on the gating task. However, recalculating the correlations by only including children who had no letter-sound knowledge did not significantly alter the correlational patterns.

Taken together, the results of the first two studies to predict PA and word decoding based on individual differences in the quality of phonological representations present some interesting problems. Although in both studies cued word fluency, nonword repetition, and gating were related to phonological skills in kindergarten children and Grade 1 children, the pattern of correlations reported in the two studies was not stable. Correlations found in the first study were not replicated in the present study. Although the internal stability of the tests was found to be reasonable, it is possible that the differences may have been due to the reliability of the measures over time. The variability in children's ability and experiences prior to Grade 1 appears to be greater than after formal schooling begins. It is possible that some of the differences found between Studies 1 and 2 were attributable to the scale of variability in kindergarten childrens' ability.

## STUDY 3

The first two studies revealed somewhat contradictory results. The findings suggest that measures of the quality of phonological representations can predict and account for individual differences in Grade 1 PA and reading acquisition. However, relationships between QPR, PA, and reading acquisition varied. We propose that these discrepancies may be due in part to individual differences in growth curves in preschool development of language and phonological representations (Vihman, 1993).

To gain some insight into the stability of the QPR tasks, we conducted a third study in which predictors from both the first and second year of kindergarten were used. The goals of this study were to replicate and expand the procedure of the previous two studies by examining if QPR in first and second year kindergarten can predict Grade 1 reading acquisition and phoneme awareness. A second aim was to examine the stability of reading skills, including word identification and letter knowledge, and the development of phonological awareness from the first year of kindergarten until Grade 1.

### METHOD

*Participants.*  Forty-two first year kindergarten children participated with a mean chronological age of 5 years and 1 months (SD = 5 months). The first moment of testing (T1) was 3 months before the end of the children's first school year; the second test moment (T2) was 4 months before their second kindergarten year, and the posttest, 6 months into Grade 1 (T3). Approximately 55 percent of the children were from Dutch descent while the other 45 percent were mainly Turkish, Moroccan, or from Surinam. Only those children that spoke Dutch as their first language participated.

### MATERIALS AND PROCEDURE

*Pretests in Kindergarten (T1 and T2).*  Eight different tests were first administered to the children in kindergarten in two sessions, taking a total of about 35 minutes for both. The tasks remained unchanged from those used in Study 2.

*Posttest in Grade 1 (T3).*  The PA, NWR, cued word fluency, and vocabulary test from the pretest (T1 & T2) were readministered. Two word decoding tests were administered: the OMT and a CVC word decoding task  (see Study 2). For analysis, letter and word reading scores were combined as a literacy variable.

## RESULTS

In table VI, the descriptive statistics for all three test moments are presented. At T1, the kindergarten children had little or no effective knowledge of reading or letters, and 52 percent had no knowledge of letters and words. The PA tasks were difficult. Fifty-seven percent of the children were unable to complete a single item. Of the three QPR tasks, cued word fluency suffered from floor effects. Nonword repetition and the gating task appeared to be attempted adequately by all children at T1.

At T2, more children were able to name or sound out at least one letter; only 16 percent still scored zero. Tasks requiring phonemic awareness continued to present great difficulty. On the phonological awareness tasks, 26 percent scored zero. The average scores on cued word fluency, NWR, and the gating tasks increased over those a year earlier. The vocabulary score also increased and was within the expected norms (Verhoeven, Vermeer, & Van de Guchte, 1986).

In Grade 1, the children were reading 22 words per minute on average and had mastered most of the letters. In table VII, correlations are presented for the various tests for all three test

**Table VI.   Descriptive Statistics of Three Testing Periods (T1, T2 & T3).**

| N = 42 | Test | M | SD | Range | |
|---|---|---|---|---|---|
| **T1** | Literacy | 2.14 | 2.91 | 0.0 | 10.0 |
| Kindergarten | PA | 0.98 | 1.57 | 0.0 | 7.0 |
| | Nonword Repetition (25) | 17.60 | 2.87 | 10.0 | 22.0 |
| | Cued Word Fluency | 0.40 | 0.80 | 0.0 | 3.0 |
| | Gating (8) | 3.94 | 0.83 | 2.3 | 5.3 |
| | Vocabulary (98) | 40.60 | 17.15 | 12.0 | 80.0 |
| **T2** | Literacy | 5.32 | 4.31 | 0.0 | 16.0 |
| Kindergarten | PA | 3.05 | 4.38 | 0.0 | 20.0 |
| | Nonword Repetition (25) | 20.73 | 3.47 | 12.0 | 25.0 |
| | Cued Word Fluency | 3.53 | 3.96 | 0.0 | 17.0 |
| | Gating (8) | 4.15 | 0.97 | 1.5 | 5.8 |
| | Vocabulary (98) | 51.73 | 16.78 | 25.0 | 84.0 |
| **T3** | Literacy | 34.08 | 20.24 | 1.0 | 85.0 |
| Grade 1 | PA | 15.38 | 3.33 | 6.0 | 20.0 |
| | Nonword Repetition (25) | 17.52 | 3.13 | 12.0 | 24.0 |
| | Cued Word Fluency | 13.45 | 6.11 | 3.0 | 31.0 |
| | Vocabulary (98) | 69.48 | 16.21 | 39.0 | 92.0 |

*Number in parentheses indicates number of items in test.

Table VII.  Pearson's Correlations for all Variables at T1, T2 and T3.

| Variables | 1 | 2 | 3 | 4 | 5 | 6 | 7 | 8 | 9 | 10 | 11 | 12 | 13 | 14 | 15 | 16 |
|---|---|---|---|---|---|---|---|---|---|---|---|---|---|---|---|---|
| **Kindergarten T1 (1-6)** | | | | | | | | | | | | | | | | |
| 1. Literacy | | | | | | | | | | | | | | | | |
| 2. PA | .17 | | | | | | | | | | | | | | | |
| 3. Nonword Repetition | .08 | .18 | | | | | | | | | | | | | | |
| 4. Cued Word Fluency | .08 | .14 | .12 | | | | | | | | | | | | | |
| 5. Gating | -.15 | .07 | .44** | .17 | | | | | | | | | | | | |
| 6. Vocabulary | .18 | -.01 | .36* | .45** | .02 | | | | | | | | | | | |
| **Kindergarten T2 (7-12)** | 1 | 2 | 3 | 4 | 5 | 6 | 7 | 8 | 9 | 10 | 11 | | | | | |
| 7. Literacy | .60** | -.30 | -.29 | -.17 | -.22 | -.05 | | | | | | | | | | |
| 8. PA | .01 | .17 | .30 | .12 | .02 | .15 | -.03 | | | | | | | | | |
| 9. Nonword Repetition | .28 | .20 | .39* | .15 | .13 | .29 | .01 | .20 | | | | | | | | |
| 10. Cued Word Fluency | .26 | .41* | .08 | .05 | .06 | .03 | .23 | .21 | .39* | | | | | | | |
| 11. Gating | .11 | .08 | .12 | -.06 | .10 | .25 | .07 | .06 | -.12 | -.06 | | | | | | |
| 12. Vocabulary | .36* | -.03 | .45** | .20 | .02 | .78** | .00 | .22 | .24 | .11 | .29 | | | | | |
| **Grade 1 T3 (13-17)** | 1 | 2 | 3 | 4 | 5 | 6 | 7 | 8 | 9 | 10 | 11 | 12 | 13 | 14 | 15 | 16 |
| 13. Literacy | .03 | -.02 | .05 | -.16 | -.05 | -.01 | .27 | .24 | .34 | .30 | -.32 | .07 | | | | |
| 14. PA | .11 | .11 | .38* | -.08 | .21 | .34* | .08 | .30 | .61** | .21 | -.03 | .48** | .54** | | | |
| 15. Nonword Repetition | .05 | .09 | .27 | .00 | .03 | .29 | -.07 | .15 | .38* | .06 | -.17 | .33* | .18 | .43** | | |
| 16. Cued Word Fluency | -.06 | .15 | .21 | .22 | .22 | .35* | .01 | .24 | .39* | .45** | -.12 | .33* | .61** | .61** | .45** | |
| 17. Vocabulary | .26 | -.03 | .20 | .17 | -.01 | .76** | .12 | .09 | .39* | -.04 | .32 | .77** | .01 | .51** | .35* | .25 |

* $p < 0.05$, ** $p < 0.01$

periods. At T1, nonword repetition was correlated to the gating task and vocabulary knowledge. The relationship between NWR and vocabulary was not found in either of the previous two studies even though the tasks were the same.

Some tasks at T1 correlated to tasks at T2. Literacy knowledge correlated to the same variables at T2. Phonemic awareness at T1 correlated to cued word fluency a year later. Nonword repetition correlated to the same task a year later and also at T3. The vocabulary scores at T1 had strong correlations to vocabulary T2 and T3.

There were a number of significant correlations between tasks at T2 and T3. Nonword repetition at T2 had strong correlations to a number of tasks at T3. The strong correlation between nonword repetition in preschool and Grade 1 phonemic awareness also was reported in the first two studies. Vocabulary at T2 correlated with PA, nonword repetition, cued word fluency, and vocabulary at T3.

The correlation analysis provided some information about the predictability of Grade 1 scores. Tasks administered at T1 had very little predictive ability for Grade 1 test scores. Only Grade 1 PA was predictable to some extent in the first year of kindergarten T1 measures of NWR and vocabulary. A regression analysis with all first year variables, including age, revealed that NWR was the single most significant predictor of grade 1 PA ($R^2 = .14$, F = 6.71, $p < 0.05$).

Measures taken at T2 were more predictive of T3 scores than ability at T1. Phoneme awareness in Grade 1 was accounted for by T2 NWR and vocabulary ($R^2 = .49$, F = 16.12, $p < 0.01$). NWR predicted an extra 26 percent of the variance in T3 PA after vocabulary at T2 had been entered, $\Delta R^2 = .26$. Entering T2 NWR first ($R^2 = .37$) and then T2 vocabulary knowledge resulted in $\Delta R^2 = .12$. Forcing T2 PA into the regression accounted for 11 percent of variance of PA at T3.

Reading ability in Grade 1 was difficult to predict from kindergarten measures. From all T2 variables, NWR was the single most significant predictor of literacy ($R^2 = .11$, $F_{(40)} = 4.22$, $p < 0.01$). To examine if reading ability could be partially accounted for by early QPR, we conducted a multivariate regression analysis with Grade 1 literacy as the dependent variable. First, we entered T2 literacy ($R^2 = 0.07$). In step 2, T2 NWR was entered ($\Delta R^2 = 0.12$). In step 3, PA from T3 was entered into the regression ($\Delta R^2 = 0.24$). We then reversed the order of steps 2 and 3, putting PA ($\Delta R^2 = 0.36$) before NWR ($\Delta R^2 = 0.00$). The variance shared between NWR and Literacy at T3 was entirely taken up by PA at T3.

## DISCUSSION

In the final study, results of a two-year longitudinal study were presented in which the development of reading skills, phoneme awareness, vocabulary, and QPR were followed from the first kindergarten year until Grade 1. One goal was to examine if measures of QPR predict Grade 1 reading acquisition and PA development. A second aim was to ascertain if preschool abilities are stable from the first to the second year of kindergarten.

The results of the final study confirmed that Grade 1 ability in reading and phonological awareness could be predicted in kindergarten children on the basis of measures of nonword repetition, PA, and vocabulary knowledge. Prediction of Grade 1 PA was successful and accounted for 49 percent of the variance in phonemic awareness. Reading ability was harder to predict: NWR accounted for 11 percent of variance. However, the variance shared between NWR and literacy was a subset of the variance share between Grade 1 PA and literacy. This finding illustrates how QPR is important for development of PA that, in turn, is crucial for literacy development.

In the discussion of Study 2, the possibility was raised that individual differences in the developmental experiences of preschoolers would cause an uneven and discontinuous advancement in cognitive abilities that would manifest itself in lower test-retest correlations between measures taken in kindergarten. From the first to the second year of kindergarten, only the literacy and vocabulary scores showed a reasonably high correlation. PA in kindergarten did not correlate with PA in the second year of kindergarten. Of the QPR tests, only NWR correlated between the first and second year of kindergarten. The auditory gated word recognition task was an inconsistent predictor of Grade 1 PA and reading acquisition. The gating task was also unreliable in the test-retest situation, as no correlation was found between gating at T1 and T2. At the time of writing, no information regarding test-retest reliability of the gating task was available in the literature for kindergarten children and so this finding presents an interesting topic for further investigation. The results suggest that abilities like PA and QPR may not develop in a continuous gradual slope and, instead, may be subject to spurts of rapid advancement. If this is the case, then caution must be taken when conducting prediction studies using kindergarten children. One possibility to reduce the effect of this variability would be to use multiple measures of cognitive constructs within a few weeks of each other.

## GENERAL DISCUSSION

As stated earlier, the reciprocal relationship of PA and reading development makes it difficult to use tests of explicit PA in kindergarten to predict Grade 1 reading difficulties. The findings of our three studies show that there are alternatives to the traditional phoneme blending and segmentations tasks that can be used to provide reasonable predictive potency. The nonword repetition task proved to be a consistent predictor of both concurrent and later phonemic awareness. Cued word fluency was effective as a measure of early phonemic awareness development as it was found to be a consistent correlate of concurrent PA. In the third study, cued word fluency correlated with Grade 1 cued word fluency, and in the same study, Grade 1 cued word fluency was strongly correlated with concurrent reading ability, PA, and NWR. The results of the cued word fluency task suggest that it warrants further investigation as a reasonably intuitive PA test for use with kindergarten children.

The results of Study 3 revealed that some tasks had low test-retest reliability. However, tasks such as vocabulary knowledge showed high test-retest correlations. Phonological awareness, word reading, and letter knowledge were very difficult for kindergarten children and exhibited floor effects at T1. The restriction of range was undoubtedly a big contributor to the low correlations. One explanation for the low QPR test-retest correlations between first and second kindergarten year could be that auditory word perception increases in qualitative spurts rather than gradually. The variation in development between subjects would then result in low correlations between test moments. Nevertheless, the gating task used in the current study was inconsistent and therefore possibly not suitable to use as a measure of QPR. Unlike the other QPR tasks, the nonword repetition task did have good test-retest correlation from T1 to T2. Kindergarten scores on the nonword repetition task consistently correlated to development of PA, better than kindergarten measures of PA.

The QPR tests, NWR, and gating resulted in a very different pattern of correlations. It is possible that the difference between the NWR task and the gating was due to the procedure. Repeating nonwords is a more "natural" task for preschoolers than listening to barely identifiable sounds played through headphones attached to a computer. Also, repeating nonwords requires not just perceptual ability but also retention (working memory) and articulation, all characteristics of a good lexical system. It would be interesting to narrow down what factor(s) in the nonword repetition task accounted for the variance in PA development. Recent work by Oakhill and Kyle (1999) suggests that working memory does not account for significant independent variance in performance on measures of phonological awareness(see also Dufva, Niemi, & Voeten, 2001). This leaves auditory perception and articulation as possible contributors to PA development. There is some evidence for both perception and pronunciation. In a study by Post, Foorman, and Hiscock (1997), skilled Grade 2 and 3 readers were compared to less-skilled readers on a speech perception and production task. No significant differences were found on the production of two-syllable words, but the less-skilled readers were significantly less accurate on a vowel identification task. Their conclusion was that vowel phonemes are less securely represented in the perceptual system of less-skilled readers and that selective perceptual impairment underlies some of the phonological awareness problems associated with poor reading ability.

Impairment in articulation has also been found in a study by Das, Mishra, and Kirby (1994) who reported on two cognitive tasks that differentiated between dyslexics and nondyslexics. These tasks required perception of phonological information and also rapid articulation, that is, arguably requirements of a nonword repetition task. Elbro, Borstrøm, and Petersen (1998) found that individual differences in preschool children's ability to accurately pronounce words uniquely predicted PA in Grade 2. The findings of our three studies confirm the potential of nonword repetition as a good predictor of PA development and support the findings reported above.

In Studies 1 and 2, no relationship was found between passive vocabulary knowledge and nonword repetition which is typically reported in the research literature. The finding of no relationship between nonword repetition and vocabulary is not without precedent. Edwards and Lahey (1998) reported that nonword repetition was only related to expressive and not to passive measures of vocabulary (as used in our studies). In our studies, nonword repetition was the most potent predictor of Grade 1 PA. Thus, it could be argued that an important component of the current nonword repetition test is related to the ability to form transient phonological representations in verbal short-term memory and to assemble articulatory instructions. Although no relationship with vocabulary was obtained, the results suggest that a nonword repetition test may be a sensitive measure of a latent phonological processing factor (Bowey, 1996) involved in processing segments of speech.

Typically, reading skills can be predicted, in part, by preschool phonemic awareness. The correlation coefficient between kindergarten PA with Grade 1 reading skills was lower than that found in a similar, well-known, study by Wagner, Torgesen, and Rashotte (1994). In their study with 288 American school children, correlations between kindergarten phoneme awareness, phoneme synthesis, and Grade 1 word decoding were $r = 0.82$ and $r = 0.59$, respectively. The magnitude of correlation coefficient differences between their study and the present study may lie in a number of areas. Wagner et al. (1994) used a latent variable design to predict Grade 1 reading. The latent variable was composed of tasks that may have tapped a greater amount of variance in kindergarten phonological skills. Alternatively, it has been argued that early phonological skills are more important for reading acquisition in English than in Dutch. English has a deep orthography, whereas Dutch has a more regular correspondence between graphemes and phonemes.

The teaching of reading in American schools and schools in the Netherlands also may have an effect on the relative importance of phonological skills for reading acquisition. Bast and Reitsma (1998) and De Jong and Van der Leij (1999) reported that the effect of PA on early reading acquisition in Dutch children was limited, possibly due to extensive use of phonics teaching methods employed in the Netherlands. Wesseling and Reitsma (1998) reported that children not phonologically aware at the end of kindergarten did not lag behind peers on tests of phonological skills five months after starting Grade 1. We suggest that differences in the scale of the correlations in the present study and that of Wagner, Torgesen, and Rashotte (1994) may be attributable to differences in language and/or teaching methods.

Measuring and testing the parameters of the theoretical quality of phonological representations have proved to be reasonably complex. The literature on phonological representations and reading development uses terms such as diffuse, incomplete, impoverished, and indistinct to describe how representations differ between normal and dyslexic children (Elbro, Nielsen, & Petersen, 1994; Fowler, 1991; Metsala, 1997). The manner in which phonological representations are related to lexical items is often referred to in a global manner and the exact relationship between the two is mostly left unspecified.

The results of our three studies provide inconclusive support for the theory that individual differences in the quality of phonological representations play an important role in the development of PA and, at least indirectly, to reading acquisition. The results of the present studies do confirm that individual differences in language skills, nonword repetition, and PA are important factors in predicting the development of reading related skills, but how the underlying quality of phonological representations is causally related to the development of phonemic awareness and reading problems has remained elusive. One important outcome has been to demonstrate that caution needs to be maintained in measuring skills in preschoolers as stability of results can be an issue when interpreting the relations between variables.

## ACKNOWLEDGEMENTS

The study was conducted as part of the doctoral thesis of the first author. We thank the children, parents, and teachers of the participating schools, who made this study possible.

Address correspondence to R. Wesseling, P. O. Box 38633, Howick, Auckland, New Zealand. e-mail: rfjqwesseling@hotmail.com or to Pieter Reitsma, PI Research Amsterdam, PO Box 366, 1115 ZH Duivendrecht, The Netherlands. e-mail: p.reitsma@psy.vu.nl

*References*

Bast, J., & Reitsma, P. (1998). Analyzing the development of individual differences in terms of Matthew effects in reading: Results from a Dutch longitudinal study. *Developmental Psychology, 34*, 1373–1399.

Bowey, J. A. (1996). On the association between phonological memory and receptive vocabulary in five-year-olds. *Journal of Experimental Child Psychology, 63*, 44–78.

Brus, B. T., & Voeten, M. J. M. (1973). *Een minuut test: Verantwoording en handleiding (One minute test: Manual)*. Nijmegen: Berkhout.

Das, J. P., Mishra, R. K., & Kirby, J. R. (1994). Cognitive patterns of children with dyslexia: A comparison between groups with high and average nonverbal intelligence, *Journal of Learning Disabilities, 27*, 235–242.

de Jong, P. & Van der Leij, A. (1999). Specific contributions of phonological abilities to early reading acquisition: Results from a Dutch latent variable longitudinal study. *Journal of Educational Psychology, 91*, 450–476.

Dufva, M., Niemi, P., & Voeten, M. J. M. (2001). The role of phonological memory, word recognition, and comprehension skills in reading development: From preschool to grade 2. *Reading and Writing: An Interdisciplinary Journal, 14*, 91–117.

Edwards, J., & Lahey, M. (1998). Nonword repetitions of children with specific language impairment: Exploration of some explanations for their inaccuracies. *Applied Psycholinguistics, 19,* 279–309.

Elbro, C. (1996). Early linguistic abilities and reading development: A review and a hypothesis, Reading and *Writing: An Interdisciplinary Journal, 8,* 453–485.

Elbro, C., Nielsen, I. & Petersen, D. K. (1994). Dyslexia in adults: Evidence for deficits in non-word reading and in the phonological representations of lexical items, *Annals of Dyslexia, 44,* 205–226.

Elbro, C., Borstrøm, I., & Petersen, D. K. (1998). Predicting dyslexia from kindergarten: The importance of distinctness of phonological representations of lexical items. *Reading Research Quarterly, 33,* 36–60.

Fowler, A. E. (1991). How early phonological development might set the stage for phoneme awareness. In S. Brady & D. Shankweiler (eds.), *Phonological processes in literacy. A tribute to Isabelle Y. Liberman* (pp. 97–118). Hillsdale, NJ: Lawrence Erlbaum Associates.

Gathercole, S. E. (1995). Nonword repetition: More than just a phonological output task. *Cognitive Neuropsychology, 72,* 857–861.

Gathercole, S. E., & Baddeley, A. D. (1997). Sense and sensitivity in phonological memory and vocabulary development: A reply to Bowey (1996). *Journal of Experimental Child Psychology, 67,* 290–294.

Hatcher, P., Hulme, C., & Ellis, A. W. (1994). Ameliorating early reading failure by integrating the teaching of reading and phonological skills: The phonological linkage hypothesis. *Child Development, 65,* 41–57.

Johnston, R., Anderson, M., & Holligan, C. (1996). Knowledge of the alphabet and explicit awareness of phonemes in pre-readers: The nature of the relationship. *Reading and Writing: An Interdisciplinary Journal, 8,* 217–234.

Kohnstamm, G. A., Schaerlaekens, A. M., de Vries, A. K., Akkerhuis, G. W., & Froonincksx, M. (1981). *Nieuwe Streeflijst Woordenschat voor 6-jarigen* (New word vocabulary list for six year olds). Lisse: Swets & Zeitlinger.

Lahiri, A., & Marslen-Wilson, W. D. (1991). The mental representation of lexical form: A phonological approach to the recognition lexicon. *Cognition, 38,* 245–294.

Metsala, J. L. (1997). Spoken word recognition in reading disabled children. *Journal of Educational Psychology, 89,* 159–169.

Oakhill, J., & Kyle, F. (1999). The relation between phonological awareness and working memory. *Journal of Experimental Child Psychology, 72,* 152–166.

Post, Y. V., Foorman, B. R. & Hiscock, M. (1997). Speech perception and speech production as indicators of reading difficulty. *Annals of Dyslexia, 47,* 3–27.

Snowling, M. J. (1981). Phonemic deficits in developmental dyslexia. *Psychological Research, 43,* 219–234.

Stahl, S. A., & Murray, B. A. (1994). Defining phonological awareness and its relationship to early reading. *Journal of Educational Psychology, 86,* 221–234.

Stanovich, K. E. (1992). Speculations on the causes and consequences of individual differences in early reading acquisition. In P. B. Gough, L. C. Ehri, & R. Treiman (eds.), *Reading acquisition* (pp. 307–342). Hillsdale, NJ: Lawrence Erlbaum Associates.

Verhoeven, L., Vermeer, A., & Van de Guchte, C. (1986). *Taaltoets allochtone kinderen* (Language test for Children).Tilburg: Zwijsen.

Vihman, M. (1993). Variable paths to early word production. *Journal of Phonetics, 21,* 61–82.

Wagner, R. K., Torgesen, J. K., & Rashotte, C. A. (1994). Development of reading-related phonological processing abilities: New evidence of bidirectional causality from a latent variable longitudinal study. *Developmental Psychology, 30,* 73–87.

Wesseling, R. F., & Reitsma, P. (1998). Phonemically aware in a hop, skip, and a jump. In P. Reitsma & L. Verhoeven (eds.) *Problems and interventions in literacy development* (pp. 81–94). Dordrecht: Kluwer.

# Genetic and Environmental Influences on Rapid Naming and Reading Ability: A Twin Study

Chayna J. Davis

Valerie S. Knopik

Richard K. Olson

Sally J. Wadsworth

and John C. DeFries

Institute for Behavioral Genetics
University of Colorado
Boulder, Colorado

*The present study assesses the genetic and environmental etiologies of reading, rapid naming (RN), and their covariation by fitting multi variate structural equation models to data from 587 twin pairs in which at least one member of the pair exhibited reading difficulties (low-range) and from 360 control (normal-range) twin pairs who were tested in the Colorado Learning Disabilities Research Center. Results from a bivariate phenotypic analysis with two hypothesized latent factors, READ and RN, indicated that the correlation between reading and rapid naming performance for the low-range sample was significantly higher than that of the normal-range sample. When this model was partitioned to include estimates of genetic, shared environmental, and nonshared environmental influences, resulting heritability estimates did not differ significantly for the low-range and normal-range samples for either READ or RN. However, similar to the phenotypic correlation, the genetic correlation between the READ and RN latent*

Annals of Dyslexia, Vol. 51, 2001
ISSN 0736-9387

*factors could not be equated for the two groups. Thus, the etiology of the relationship between reading performance and rapid naming may differ for children with reading difficulties and normally-achieving readers. Moreover, these results support previous findings that the best predictors of reading skills may differ for samples of children with normal reading levels and those with reading difficulties.*

## INTRODUCTION

Children with reading difficulties tend to name visually presented items, including numbers, colors, pictures of common objects, and letters, more slowly than normally-achieving readers. This skill, now commonly referred to as "rapid automatized naming" (RAN)(Denckla, 1972; Denckla & Rudel, 1976; Wolf, Bowers, & Biddle, 2000), is a well-established correlate of reading performance. Although the genetic etiology of reading disability has been well-established (DeFries & Alarcón, 1996), less is known regarding the genetic and environmental etiologies of individual differences in performance on tests of rapid naming (RN) and the extent to which these influences on rapid naming are shared with those found for reading. In order to explore this new area, we conducted a twin study of reading performance, rapid naming, and their covariation. In this report, we review evidence for the association between reading and rapid naming, assess the genetic influence on both reading performance and rapid naming, and explore the degree to which the same genetic influences affect both variables. We also compare the etiology of the relationship between reading performance and rapid naming in two groups of children: those who score lower on tests of reading performance (low-range) and those who score higher on tests of reading performance (normal-range).

Denckla (1972) provided some of the earliest evidence for a correlation between reading and rapid repetitive naming of colors in severely dyslexic boys. Subsequently, Spring and Capps (1974) examined two groups of boys (poor readers and normal readers) between the ages of 8 and 13 years who were presented with visual stimuli including randomly sequenced digits, color patches, and common objects. The investigators concluded that boys from the poor reading group performed this naming task more slowly than boys from the normal reading group and that this difference was larger for digits than for colors and pictures. A number of studies by Denckla and others have since confirmed that children with reading disability often experience difficulties when attempting to name a series of items rapidly (e.g., Denckla & Rudel, 1976; Blachman, 1984; Wolf, 1986; Cornwall, 1992; Badian, 1993; Korhonen, 1995; Snyder & Downey, 1995; Wolf et al., 2000).

Denckla and Rudel (1976) found that performance on RAN tasks differentiated children with reading difficulties, normally-achieving readers, and children who were nondyslexic but otherwise learning-disabled. They tested 128 children with learning disabilities and 120 normal-range children between the ages of 7 and 13 years on rapid naming of numbers, colors, objects, and letters. Results revealed a significant relationship between reading deficits and the speed of verbal responses to visual stimuli.

Snyder and Downey (1995) also reported the utility of rapid naming tasks in differentiating children with reading disability from normally-achieving peers using measurements of serial rapid naming. Participants in the Denver Reading Study were tested on their ability to name the color and shape of 36 colored geometrical figures as quickly as possible. Subjects' responses were audiotaped and analyzed online for reaction time, production duration, total time, and accuracy. The authors reported that although levels of accuracy were not significantly different for children with reading difficulties and normally-achieving readers, reaction times and production durations were significantly longer for children with evidence of reading problems.

Deficits in rapid naming experienced by children with reading disability seem to be apparent long before the children are introduced to reading. Results from a study of 98 children tested for three consecutive years from kindergarten to second grade indicated that children with later reading difficulties could be differentiated from children without evidence of reading problems on the basis of prereading rapid naming performance (Wolf, 1986). Further, deficits in rapid naming may persist into later childhood and early adulthood (Wolf, 1986; Snyder & Downey, 1995; Korhonen, 1995). Korhonen (1995) followed nine children with reading and rapid naming deficits from age 9 to 18 years and found that deficits in RN, as well as in reading and spelling, persisted into early adulthood.

Rapid naming may correlate more highly with measures of reading performance in samples of children with reading difficulties than in samples without evidence of reading problems. For example, McBride-Chang and Manis (1996) found that rapid naming tasks were significantly associated with word reading in a sample of poor readers ($r = -.32$ to $-.52$), but not significantly associated with word reading for good readers ($r = .16$ to $-.11$). Similarly, studies by Meyer, Wood, Hart, and Felton

(1998) and Scarborough (1998) also suggest that the most important predictors of later reading performance may differ for children with and without reading difficulties. In both studies, rapid naming significantly improved prediction of later reading performance for children with reading difficulties but did not add predictive power for children without evidence of reading problems in which the best predictor of later reading performance was earlier literacy scores.

Results of these previous studies suggest that the phenotypic, or observed, relationship between reading performance and rapid naming differs for children with and without reading difficulties. In the present study, we explore the genetic and environmental etiology of the relationship between rapid naming and reading performance among children with reading difficulties and among normally achieving readers. Twin pairs with and without evidence of reading difficulties were examined using a multivariate model-fitting analysis of data collected in either the Colorado Reading Project (DeFries, 1985) or the Colorado Learning Disabilities Research Center (DeFries et al., 1997). In this report, we assess the phenotypic correlation between reading performance and rapid naming and partition this correlation to assess genetic and environmental contributions to the relationship between these measures. We also assess the magnitude of genetic influence on rapid naming as well as the degree to which the same genetic influences affect both reading performance and rapid naming. Last, we compare the etiology of the relationship between reading performance and rapid naming in two groups of children: those who score lower on tests of reading performance (low-range) and those who score higher on tests of reading performance (normal-range).

## METHOD

### PARTICIPANTS

In order to reduce the possibility of ascertainment bias, school administrators from 27 cooperating school districts in the State of Colorado identified all twin pairs within a school without regard to reading status. Parental permission was then sought to examine the twins' school records for evidence of reading problems (e.g., low reading achievement test scores, referral to a reading therapist, reports by classroom teachers or school psychologists, and so on). Two broad subsamples of twins were then defined that differed substantially in mean reading performance: A "low-range" group in which at least one twin of each pair had a positive school history of reading disability; and a "normal-range" group in which there was no school history for reading disability in either twin of each pair, although some of these twins had low reading scores when tested in the laboratory.

The analysis sample consisted of 324 (164 male; 160 female) monozygotic (MZ; identical) and 263 (143 male; 120 female) same-sex dizygotic (DZ; fraternal) twin pairs in which at least one member of each pair exhibited a positive school history of reading problems (low-range; LR), and a comparison sample of 221 (97 male; 124 female) monozygotic (MZ) and 139 (72 male; 67 female) same-sex dizygotic (DZ) normal-range (NR) twin pairs in which neither member had any school history of reading problems. The age of the sample ranged from 7.9 years to 20.4 years (92 percent of the sample was less than 16 years of age), with a mean age of 11.7 years (MZLR mean ages: males = 11.7 years ± 2.6, females = 11.8 years ± 2.8; DZLR mean ages: males = 11.5 years ± 2.7, females = 11.6 years ± 2.7; MZNR mean ages: males = 11.9 years ± 2.4, females = 11.7 years ± 2.8; DZNR mean ages: males = 11.9 years ± 2.8, females = 11.5 years ± 2.6). All twin pairs included in this analysis were reared in predominantly middle-class, English-speaking homes. Zygosity (i.e., identical versus fraternal) was determined by selected items from the Nichols and Bilbro (1966) questionnaire which has a reported accuracy of 95 percent compared to zygosity determined by blood or buccal samples. However, in the case of doubtful zygosity, twin pairs were genotyped using DNA markers.

## MEASURES

Twin pairs in which at least one member demonstrated evidence of reading problems, as well as matched normal-range pairs, were invited to laboratories at the University of Colorado to complete an extensive battery of psychometric tests measuring various cognitive abilities. This battery included the reading recognition (REC), reading comprehension (COMP), and spelling (SPELL) subtests of the *Peabody Individual Achievement Test* (PIAT; Dunn & Markwardt, 1970), and the numbers (NUM), colors (COL), pictures (PIC), and letters (LET) subtests of the rapid naming paradigm (RN; version derived from Denckla & Rudel, 1976). Using the rapid naming paradigm, subjects were presented with a series of stimuli (either numbers, colored circles, pictures, or letters) and then asked to identify the items orally as quickly as possible. Each subtest has a maximum time allowance of 15 seconds. Scores for the variables included in the present analysis were age-adjusted and standardized separately within the low-range and normal-range group. Unstandardized mean reading performance and rapid naming scores for the low-range and normal-range groups are presented in table I. Selection of low-range and normal-range subjects resulted in two groups that differed on both reading and rapid naming measures.

Table I.   Unstandardized Mean Reading Performance[1] and Rapid Naming[2] Scores (± SD) of Identical and Same-sex Fraternal Twin Pairs in Low-range and Normal-range Groups.

| Measure | Group | |
|---|---|---|
| | Low-range (*n* = 587 pairs) | Normal-range (*n* = 360 pairs) |
| **Reading** | | |
| REC | 93.10 ± 10.63 | 106.78 ± 8.42 |
| COMP | 95.74 ± 11.50 | 109.53 ± 9.36 |
| SPELL | 91.81 ± 10.92 | 105.02 ± 10.52 |
| **RN** | | |
| NUM | 32.09 ± 7.78 | 35.24 ± 7.74 |
| COL | 21.45 ± 5.41 | 24.03 ± 5.36 |
| PIC | 18.99 ± 3.76 | 20.95 ± 3.91 |
| LET | 28.99 ± 8.16 | 33.82 ± 7.55 |

[1] Peabody Individual Achievement Test standard scores.
[2] Number of items read in 15 seconds.

The rapid naming paradigm used in the present study is an alternate version of the traditional rapid automatized naming (RAN) paradigm developed by Denckla and Rudel (1976). In the traditional RAN test, participants are presented with a series of stimuli similar to those used in the alternate version (numbers, colored circles, pictures, or letters) and then asked to identify orally all 50 items in each category without an imposed time restriction of 15 seconds. Items in each category are presented to the subject 10 times in random order. Results from a recent commonality analysis (Compton, Olson, & DeFries, under review) indicate that both rapid naming tasks accounted for a considerable amount of the explained variance in word reading skills. However, the alternate version of the rapid naming paradigm explained significantly more unique variance in word reading skills than the traditional rapid automatized naming test, particularly in subjects with reading difficulties.

# ANALYSES

## PHENOTYPIC ANALYSES

Four 14 x 14 covariance matrices (REC, COMP, SPELL, NUM, COL, PIC, and LET for each twin in a pair) were computed using the SPSS statistical package (SPSS-X, 1988): one each for MZ low-range pairs, DZ low-range pairs, MZ normal-range pairs, and DZ normal-range pairs. The phenotypic factor structure among the reading and rapid naming performance variables was initially analyzed separately for low-range and normal-range groups by fitting a bivariate factor model with two correlated factors (READ and RN) (figure 1) to the data using the Mx statistical modeling package (Neale, 1999). A residual for each of the measured variables was included to account for specific influences not due to the factors. Model fit (i.e., how well the specified model fit the data) and submodel comparisons were evaluated using the chi-square ($\chi^2$) statistic, with low values representing the best fit; however, because the sample size is large and the $\chi^2$ is dependent on sample size (Neale & Cardon, 1992), Root Mean Squared Error Approximation (RMSEA: values between .05 and .10 indicate a good fit, and values below .05 indicate a very good fit; Neale, 1999) was also employed as an alternative goodness-of-fit test.

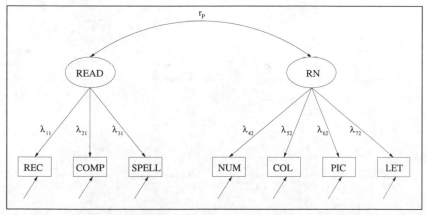

*Figure 1.    Phenotypic path model of the factor structure among measures of reading and rapid naming (RN) performance.*

## GENOTYPIC ANALYSES

The correlation between members of monozygotic twin pairs is expected to include all of the additive genetic (i.e., heritable) variance ($a^2$) and all of the shared environmental (i.e., environ-mental influences common to members of a twin pair) variance ($c^2$) associated with a trait, i.e., $r_{MZ} = a^2 + c^2$. In contrast, the correlation between members of dizygotic twin pairs is expected to include half of the additive genetic variance (because DZ twins share 50 percent of their segregating genes, on average) and all of the shared environmental variance ($c^2$) associated with a trait, i.e., $r_{DZ} = \frac{1}{2}(a^2) + c^2$. Therefore, the additive genetic and shared environmental influences associated with one trait (univariate) may be estimated using twin data, and this methodology may be easily generalized to the bivariate case. In the present study, this concept is utilized in a model-fitting approach (Neale & Cardon, 1992). A full genetic-environmental bivariate model (figure 2) that partitioned the phenotypic factor structure into additive genetic ($a^2$), shared environmental ($c^2$), and nonshared environmental ($e^2$) influences separately for low-range and normal-range groups was also fitted to the data using the Mx statistical modeling package (Neale, 1999).

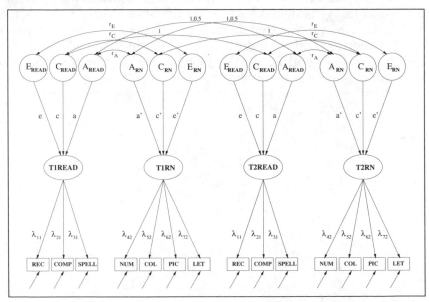

*Figure 2.   Partitioning of the phenotypic model into genetic, shared environmental, and nonshared environmental factors.*

In figure 2, additive genetic, shared environmental, and nonshared environmental factors influencing reading performance are represented by $A_{READ}$, $C_{READ}$, and $E_{READ}$, respectively, and those factors influencing rapid naming performance are represented by $A_{RN}$, $C_{RN}$, and $E_{RN}$, respectively. Correlations between the READ and RN factors are depicted by $r_A$, $r_C$, and $r_E$ for the additive genetic, shared environmental, and nonshared environmental correlations, respectively. Because monozygotic twin pairs share all their genes, the additive genetic correlation between members of a twin pair for the same trait (e.g., READ or RN) is assumed to be 1.0. Similarly, because the coefficient of relationship between members of dizygotic twin pairs is one half, the corresponding correlation is 0.50. The shared environmental correlation is 1.00, and nonshared environmental influences (those environmental influences that are independent of the sibling relationship) are uncorrelated between members of a twin pair. The influences of $A_{READ}$, $C_{READ}$, and $E_{READ}$ are represented by a, c, and e, respectively, and those of $A_{RN}$, $C_{RN}$, and $E_{RN}$ are represented by a', c', and e', respectively. As in the phenotypic model, factor loadings for each observed variable are depicted using the symbol $\lambda$, and each observed variable is also allowed a residual.

# RESULTS

## PHENOTYPIC RESULTS

The full phenotypic model yielded separate parameter estimates for low-range and normal-range twin pairs (figure 3). Goodness-of-fit indices for the full model ($\chi^2$ = 292.63, df = 82, RMSEA = .011) indicated a reasonable fit to the data. In order to test the significance of specific parameters in the model, parameters were then dropped or equated for the low-range and normal-range groups. Although parameter estimates for the low-range and normal-range groups are similar, they could not be equated as a whole without significant deterioration of model fit; nor could reading parameters alone. However, RN parameters alone could be equated for the two groups without significant decrease in model fit. Further, the phenotypic correlation between READ and RN latent, or underlying, factors for the low-range sample (.58, CI = .52 − .63) was significantly greater ($\Delta\chi^2$ = 24.30, df = 1, $p \leq .001$) than that for the normal-range sample (.32, CI = .23 − .41).

## GENOTYPIC RESULTS

Twin correlations, variances, and covariances for the observed reading performance and rapid naming measures are presented

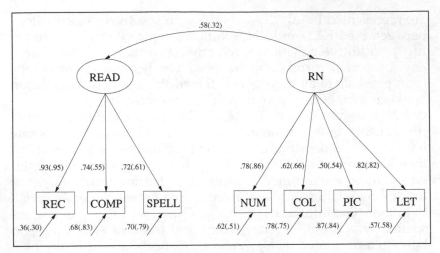

Figure 3.    Observed phenotypic factor structure among measures of
reading and rapid naming performance for low-range and
normal-range groups. Estimates for the normal-range
group are shown in parentheses.

in tables II and III for the MZ and DZ low-range samples, respectively, and in tables IV and V for the MZ and DZ normal-
range samples, respectively. MZ twin correlations are
substantially higher than DZ twin correlations for both groups,
suggesting that individual differences in these measures are due
at least in part to heritable influences.

Results of the genetic analysis presented in figure 4 confirm
substantial contributions of genetic and nonshared environmental influences to the variances in READ and RN. The propor-
tions of phenotypic variance due to genetic ($a^2$), shared
environmental ($c^2$), and nonshared environmental ($e^2$) sources
of variation in READ and RN, estimated from the full genetic

Table II.    Twin Correlations for Identical Twin Pairs in the Low-range
Sample. Twin Pair Correlations Are on the Diagonal, Cross-correlations Are
above the Diagonal, and Covariances Are below the Diagonal.

|       | REC  | COMP | SPELL | NUM  | COL  | PIC  | LET  |
|-------|------|------|-------|------|------|------|------|
| REC   | **0.72** | 0.51 | 0.49  | 0.22 | 0.17 | 0.16 | 0.35 |
| COMP  | 0.45 | **0.52** | 0.33  | 0.17 | 0.22 | 0.15 | 0.26 |
| SPELL | 0.42 | 0.29 | **0.56**  | 0.21 | 0.19 | 0.18 | 0.32 |
| NUM   | 0.21 | 0.16 | 0.19  | **0.48** | 0.30 | 0.22 | 0.43 |
| COL   | 0.16 | 0.20 | 0.17  | 0.29 | **0.50** | 0.33 | 0.35 |
| PIC   | 0.15 | 0.14 | 0.16  | 0.21 | 0.32 | **0.43** | 0.24 |
| LET   | 0.32 | 0.23 | 0.29  | 0.41 | 0.33 | 0.23 | **0.50** |

Table III. Twin Correlations for Fraternal Twin Pairs in the Low-range Sample. Twin Pair Correlations Are on the Diagonal, Cross-correlations Are above the Diagonal, and Covariances Are below the Diagonal.

| | REC | COMP | SPELL | NUM | COL | PIC | LET |
|---|---|---|---|---|---|---|---|
| REC | **0.28** | 0.22 | 0.19 | 0.18 | 0.13 | 0.09 | 0.22 |
| COMP | 0.24 | **0.26** | 0.14 | 0.11 | 0.09 | 0.05 | 0.14 |
| SPELL | 0.21 | 0.15 | **0.22** | 0.20 | 0.12 | 0.06 | 0.20 |
| NUM | 0.19 | 0.12 | 0.20 | **0.35** | 0.19 | 0.15 | 0.31 |
| COL | 0.14 | 0.10 | 0.12 | 0.19 | **0.25** | 0.16 | 0.18 |
| PIC | 0.10 | 0.06 | 0.06 | 0.15 | 0.16 | **0.16** | 0.14 |
| LET | 0.24 | 0.15 | 0.21 | 0.31 | 0.19 | 0.15 | **0.32** |

Table IV. Twin Correlations for Identical Twin Pairs in the Normal-range Sample. Twin Pair Correlations Are on the Diagonal, Cross-correlations Are above the Diagonal, and Covariances Are Below the Diagonal.

| | REC | COMP | SPELL | NUM | COL | PIC | LET |
|---|---|---|---|---|---|---|---|
| REC | **0.59** | 0.42 | 0.52 | 0.26 | 0.16 | 0.11 | 0.32 |
| COMP | 0.41 | **0.46** | 0.35 | 0.13 | 0.12 | 0.10 | 0.16 |
| SPELL | 0.54 | 0.35 | **0.62** | 0.22 | 0.15 | 0.07 | 0.27 |
| NUM | 0.27 | 0.13 | 0.23 | **0.49** | 0.41 | 0.31 | 0.45 |
| COL | 0.16 | 0.12 | 0.16 | 0.44 | **0.54** | 0.37 | 0.39 |
| PIC | 0.12 | 0.10 | 0.07 | 0.34 | 0.40 | **0.50** | 0.32 |
| LET | 0.34 | 0.16 | 0.29 | 0.48 | 0.42 | 0.36 | **0.50** |

Table V. Twin Correlations for Fraternal Twin Pairs in the Normal-range Sample. Twin Pair Correlations Are on the Diagonal, Cross-correlations Are above the Diagonal, and Covariances Are below the Diagonal.

| | REC | COMP | SPELL | NUM | COL | PIC | LET |
|---|---|---|---|---|---|---|---|
| REC | **0.31** | 0.27 | 0.22 | 0.04 | 0.07 | 0.05 | 0.12 |
| COMP | 0.27 | **0.31** | 0.09 | 0.01 | -0.02 | 0.03 | 0.02 |
| SPELL | 0.20 | 0.09 | **0.28** | 0.09 | 0.08 | -0.03 | 0.12 |
| NUM | 0.04 | 0.01 | 0.08 | **0.18** | 0.09 | 0.09 | 0.18 |
| COL | 0.06 | -0.02 | 0.07 | 0.09 | **0.12** | 0.10 | 0.12 |
| PIC | 0.04 | 0.03 | -0.03 | 0.07 | 0.09 | **0.26** | 0.10 |
| LET | 0.11 | 0.02 | 0.11 | 0.16 | 0.11 | 0.08 | **0.21** |

model, are summarized in table VI. In order to ensure identification of the model, the variances of the latent variables were constrained such that $a^2 + c^2 + e^2 = 1$ and $a'^2 + c'^2 + e'^2 = 1$. High heritability estimates were obtained for both READ ($a^2 = .84$ and .76 for low-range and normal-range groups, respectively), and RN ($a^2 = .57$ and .62 for low-range and normal-range groups, respectively).

The path coefficients in figure 4 indicate that 86 percent of the phenotypic correlation ($r_p = .58$) between READ and RN latent factors in the low-range group was accounted for by additive genetic influences (($a \times r_A \times a'$)/$r_p$ = (.92)(.71)(.76)/.58 = .86), and 13 percent (($c \times r_C \times c'$)/$r_p$ = (.02)(1.0)(.42)/.58 = .13) was accounted for by shared environmental influences. For the normal-range group, 71 percent of the phenotypic correlation

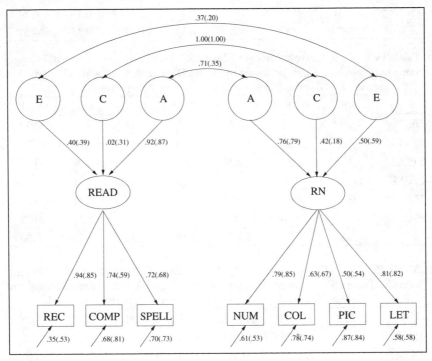

*Figure 4.*   *Genetic and environmental factor structures among measures of reading and rapid naming performance for low-range and normal-range twin pairs (shown for one twin only). Estimates for the normal-range group are shown in parentheses.*

Table VI.   **Genetic and Environmental Contributions to the Variance in READ and RN Estimated from the Full Genetic Model.**

| Measure | Low-range | | | Normal-range | | |
|---|---|---|---|---|---|---|
| | $a^2$ | $c^2$ | $e^2$ | $a^2$ | $c^2$ | $e^2$ |
| READ | .842 | .000 | .157 | .757 | .094 | .150 |
| RN | .572 | .178 | .249 | .620 | .033 | .348 |

$(r_p = .34$, estimated from the full genetic model) between READ and RN latent factors was accounted for by additive genetic influences, and 16 percent was accounted for by shared environmental influences.

Although genetic parameter estimates did not differ significantly between the low-range and normal-range samples for either READ or RN, the genetic correlations between READ and RN (.71, CI = .57 – .92, and .35, CI = .00 – .62, for low-range and normal-range samples, respectively) for the two groups were significantly different. In addition, genetic influences could not be dropped without a significant deterioration of model fit. Shared environmental parameter estimates, both excluding and including the shared environmental correlation, were not significantly different for low-range and normal-range groups, even with genetic parameters constrained to be equal. Moreover, shared environmental estimates could be dropped altogether for both the low-range and normal-range groups without significant reduction in model fit. Nonshared environmental parameter estimates, both excluding and including the nonshared environmental correlation, were not significantly different for low-range and normal-range groups, even with genetic and shared environmental estimates constrained to be equal, or with genetic estimates constrained to be equal and shared environmental estimates dropped from the model. Therefore, the most parsimonious model to fit the data is one in which all shared environmental paths have been dropped and all estimates are equated to be equal for the low-range and normal-range groups, with the exception of the genetic correlation between READ and RN.

## DISCUSSION

In the present study, we examined the genotypic and environmental etiologies of reading performance and rapid naming (RN), as well as their covariation, using a multivariate model-fitting approach. We assessed the phenotypic correlation between reading performance and rapid naming and partitioned this correlation to examine genetic and environmental aspects of the relationship between these measures. We also explored the genetic influences on both reading performance and rapid naming, as well as the degree to which the same influences affect these latent variables. Last, we compared the etiology of the relationship between reading performance and rapid naming in two groups of children: those who score lower on tests of reading performance (low-range) and those who score higher on tests of reading performance (normal-range).

Results from the phenotypic analysis indicated that the correlation between reading and rapid naming performance for the low-range sample (.58) was significantly higher than that for the normal-range sample (.32), suggesting that the relationship between reading performance and rapid naming may differ for children with reading difficulties and normally-achieving readers. This is consistent with previous findings that rapid naming may have greater predictive value for children with reading problems (McBride-Chang & Manis, 1996; Meyer et al., 1998; Scarborough, 1998).

When the phenotypic model was partitioned to include estimates of additive genetic ($a^2$), shared environmental ($c^2$), and nonshared environmental ($e^2$) contributions to the variance in READ and RN factors, results indicated that both latent variables are highly heritable in low-range and normal-range twin pairs ($a^2_{READ}$ = .84 and .76 for low-range and normal-range groups, respectively, and $a^2_{RN}$ = .57 and .62 for low-range and normal-range groups, respectively). However, the genetic correlation between READ and RN ($r_A$) was significantly higher for children with reading difficulties (.71) than for the normal-range group (.35). Similarly, 86 percent of the phenotypic correlation between READ and RN was accounted for by genetic influences in the low-range sample, compared with 71 percent for the normal-range sample. Therefore, the extent to which genetic and environmental factors influence the relationship between reading and rapid naming may differ for children with reading disabilities and children without evidence of reading problems. Moreover, these results suggest that the finding that rapid naming tasks provide a better index of later reading skills for children with reading difficulties than for children in the normal-range group (McBride-Chang & Manis, 1996; Meyer et al., 1998) may be due, at least in part, to genetic influences.

Similar results were obtained when data from reading level matched subsamples of the original participants (209 monozygotic (MZ) and 162 same-sex dizygotic (DZ) twin pairs between the ages of 10 and 19 years in which at least one member of each pair exhibited a positive school history of reading problems (low-range), and a comparison sample of 135 MZ and 89 same-sex DZ normal-range twin pairs between the ages of 7 and 12 years in which neither member had any school history of reading problems were analyzed. As expected, the phenotypic analysis indicated that the correlation between reading and rapid naming performance for the low-range sample (.55) was significantly higher than that for the normal-range sample (.27), suggesting that the relationship between reading performance and rapid naming differs for children with reading difficulties and normally-achieving readers and is not just a function of absolute reading level. When the phenotypic model was partitioned to include estimates of additive genetic ($a^2$), shared environmental ($c^2$), and nonshared environmental ($e^2$) contributions to the variance in the latent factors, results indicated that reading performance is highly heritable in both the low-range and normal-range samples ($a^2_{READ}$ = .85 and .88 for low-range and normal-range groups, respectively), but heritability estimates were somewhat lower for the RN latent factor ($a^2_{RN}$ = .48 and .30 for low-range and normal-range groups, respectively). The genetic correlation between READ and RN ($r_A$) also was substantially higher for children with reading difficulties (.72) than for the normal-range group in the reading level matched subsample (.42); however, this difference was only marginally significant ($p$ = .07), possibly due to loss of power as a result of reduced sample size.

In conclusion, results of this study indicate that there are significant genetic influences on individual differences in reading performance and rapid naming in both low-range and normal-range reading samples, but the correlation between reading performance and rapid naming is significantly higher in the group with reading difficulties. Moreover, because the genetic correlation between READ and RN latent factors in the two groups also differs significantly ($r_A$ = .71 and .35 for low-range and normal-range groups, respectively), the differential predictive validity of rapid naming tasks for later reading performance in children with reading difficulties and normally-achieving readers may be due at least in part to genetic influences. Future analyses will focus on identifying specific genes related to both reading disability and rapid naming skill.

## ACKNOWLEDGMENTS

This work was supported in part by program project and center grants from the National Institute of Child Health and Human Development (HD-11681 and HD-27802) to J. C. DeFries. This report was prepared while C. J. Davis was supported by

NIMH training grant MH-16880 and V. S. Knopik was supported by NICHD training grant HD-07289. The invaluable contributions of staff members of the many Colorado school districts from which our sample of twins was ascertained, and of the families who participated in this study, are gratefully acknowledged.

Address correspondence to: Chayna Davis, Institute for Behavioral Genetics, University of Colorado, Boulder, CO 80309-0447, Telephone 303-492-2817, Fax 303-492-8063. e-mail: davisc@colorado.edu

## References

Badian, N. A. (1993). Phonemic awareness, naming, visual symbol processing, and reading. *Reading and Writing: An Interdisciplinary Journal, 5*, 87–100.

Blachman, B. A. (1984). Relationship of rapid naming ability and language analysis skills to kindergarten and first-grade reading achievement. *Journal of Educational Psychology, 76*, 610–622.

Compton, D. L., Olson, R. K., & DeFries, J. C. (under review). Are all RAN created equal? Comparing the relationships among two different formats of alphanumeric RAN and various word reading skills in normally achieving and reading disabled individuals.

Cornwall, A. (1992). The relationship of phonological awareness, rapid naming, and verbal memory to severe reading and spelling disability. *Journal of Learning Disabilities, 25*, 532–538.

DeFries, J. C. (1985). Colorado reading project. In D. B. Gray & J. F. Kavavagh (eds.), *Biobehavioral measures of dyslexia* (pp. 107–122). Parkton, MD: York Press.

DeFries, J. C., & Alarcón, M. (1996). Genetics of specific reading disability. *Mental Retardation and Developmental Disabilities Research Reviews, 2*, 39–47.

DeFries, J. C., Filipek, P. A., Fulker, D. W., Olson, R. K., Pennington, B. F., Smith, S. D., & Wise, B. W. (1997). Colorado Learning Disabilities Research Center. *Learning Disabilities: A Multidisciplinary Journal, 8*, 7–19.

Denckla, M. B. (1972). Color-naming defects in dyslexia boys. *Cortex, 10*, 186–202.

Denckla, M. B., & Rudel, R. G. (1976). Rapid "automatized" naming (r.a.n.): Dyslexia differentiated from other learning disabilities. *Neuropsychologia, 14*, 471–479.

Dunn, L. M., & Markwardt, F. C. (1970). *Examiner's manual: Peabody individual achievement test.* Circle Pines, Minnesota: American Guidance Service.

Korhonen, T. T. (1995). The persistence of rapid naming problems in children with reading disabilities: A nine-year follow-up. *Journal of Learning Disabilities, 28*, 232–239.

Mcbride-Chang, C., & Manis, F. R. (1996). Structural invariance in the associations of naming speed, phonological awareness, and verbal reasoning in good and poor readers: A test of the double deficit hypothesis. *Reading and Writing: An Interdisciplinary Journal, 8*, 323–339.

Meyer, M. S., Wood, F. B., Hart, L. A., & Felton, R. H. (1998). Selective predictive value of rapid naming in poor readers. *Journal of Learning Disabilities, 31*, 106–117.

Neale, M. C. (1999). *Mx: Statistical modeling*, 5th edition. Box 126 MCV, Richmond, VA, 23298: Department of Psychiatry.

Neale, M. C., & Cardon, L. R. (1992). *Methodology for genetic studies of twins and families*. Boston: Kluwer Academic Publishers.

Nichols, R. C., & Bilbro, W. C. (1966). The diagnosis of twin zygosity. *Acta Genetica et Statistica Medica, 16*, 265–275.

Scarborough, H. S. (1998). Predicting the future achievement of second graders with reading disabilities: Contributions of phonemic awareness, verbal memory, rapid naming, and IQ. *Annals of Dyslexia, 48*, 115–136.

Snyder, L. S., & Downey, D. M. (1995). Serial rapid naming skills in children with reading disabilities. *Annals of Dyslexia, 45*, 31–49.

Spring, C., & Capps, C. (1974). Encoding speed, rehearsal, and probed recall of dyslexic boys. *Journal of Educational Psychology, 66*, 780–786.

SPSS-X. (1988). Statistical package for the social sciences (3rd ed.) [computer program]. Chicago: SPSS Inc.

Wolf, M. (1986). Rapid alternating stimulus naming in the developmental dyslexias. *Brain and Language, 27*, 360–379.

Wolf, M., Bowers, P. G., & Biddle, K. (2000). Naming-speed processes, timing, and reading: A conceptual review. *Journal of Learning Disabilities, 33*, 322–324.

# The Effects of Phonological Transparency on Reading Derived Words

*Joanne F. Carlisle*

*C. Addison Stone*

*Lauren A. Katz*

University of Michigan
Ann Arbor, Michigan

*The purpose of this study was to determine whether poor readers have more pronounced problems than average-reading peers reading derived words the base forms of which undergo a phonological shift when a suffix is added (i.e., shift relations as in "natural"), as compared to derived words whose forms are phonologically and orthographically transparent (i.e., stable relations, as in "cultural"). Two computer-based word recognition tasks (Naming and Lexical Decision) were administered to children with reading disability (RD), peers with average reading ability, and adults. Across tasks, there was an effect for transparency (i.e., better performance on stable than shift words) for both child groups and the adults. For the children, a significant interaction was found between group and word type. Specifically, on the naming task, there was an advantage for the stable words, and this was most noteworthy for the children with RD. On the lexical decision task, trade-offs of speed and accuracy were evident for the child reader groups. Performances on the nonwords showed the poor readers to be comparable to the average readers in distinguishing legal and illegal nonwords; further analyses suggested that poor readers carried out deeper processing of derived*

Annals of Dyslexia, Vol. 51, 2001
ISSN 0736-9387

*words than their average reading peers. Additional study is needed to explore the relation of orthographic and phonological processing on poor readers' memory for and processing of derived words.*

## INTRODUCTION

Current literature abounds with documentation of a relationship between phonological awareness and reading development, with extensive evidence to suggest that reading disabilities arise from underlying phonological deficits (Liberman, Shankweiler, & Liberman, 1989; Stanovich, 1986). While studies have shown that children with reading disabilities have significant problems with word reading accuracy and speed (Compton & Carlisle, 1994), such studies have generally focused on words of one morpheme. Of considerable interest is whether morphological structure plays a role in word reading speed and accuracy, and whether students with reading disabilities have greater problems reading morphologically complex words than morphologically simple words. Moreover, studying morphology as it relates to reading in the school-age years is important because of its educational relevance. Nagy, Anderson, Schommer, Scott, and Stallman (1989) found that after the fourth grade, over 60 percent of the words that children encounter through reading are morphologically complex. Employing an alphabetic strategy for reading morphologically complex words is bound to be only partially successful in providing access to meaning, as the addition of one or more suffixes often results in phonological changes in the base word (e.g., *revise* to *revision*), and the pronunciation of the suffix is not the sum of the parts (e.g., *-sion*).

There is evidence that the phonological properties of words affect morphological processing, and phonological aspects of morphological processing are related to reading achievement (Carlisle & Nomanbhoy, 1993; Fowler & Liberman, 1995; Shankweiler et al., 1995; Singson, Mahoney, & Mann, 2000; Windsor, 2000). The demands of phonological processing are most evident on tasks that include morphologically complex words that undergo a shift in pronunciation when a derivational suffix is added to the base form. For example, the long vowel sound in *nature* is shortened when the suffix *-al* is added to the base word to make *natural*. Recognizing that children with reading disabilities have difficulty with the phonological aspects of reading, we might suspect that they encounter particular difficulties reading derived words whose base forms may be obscured by such phonological shifts.

Shankweiler et al. (1995) found reading disabled children to be deficient in generating morphologically complex forms in an oral production task. These researchers found strong correlations between phonological skills and morphological skills. Their results suggested that underlying phonological deficits could be largely responsible for these children's difficulties in generating derived forms. Furthermore, children's facility with words that reflected shifts in pronunciation from base to derived form (e.g., *five/fifth*) more clearly separated poor readers from normal readers than words for which pronunciation remained stable (e.g., *four/fourth*). Similarly, Fowler and Liberman (1995) found that poor readers differed from good readers in the oral production of words that undergo phonological shifts and that students' sensitivity to morphologically complex words on an oral production task was related to their reading and spelling abilities. Additionally, Champion (1997) and Leong (1989) both contrasted good and poor readers. Leong showed that poor readers and spellers were slower at producing derived and base word forms than good readers/spellers, particularly when the words involved both phonological and orthographic changes from base to derived form. Champion found that while poor readers differed from good readers in awareness of the semantic and syntactic aspects of derived forms, the differences were more pronounced on reading than on oral tasks. These studies provide evidence for the importance of phonology as it relates to morphological processing, and they show connections between impairment in one or both of these processes and below average skills in reading.

A limitation of these studies is that they did not include a direct measure of reading aloud morphologically complex words. One study that did include such a measure was carried out by Elbro and Arnbak (1996). These researchers asked Danish teenage dyslexics and younger normal readers to read a set of complex words that were semantically transparent and nontransparent; the set included compounds as well as inflected and derived words. The dyslexic students read morphologically transparent words faster and more accurately than nontransparent words. These researchers suggested that morpho-semantic transparency may be a compensatory mechanism in word decoding and comprehension for dyslexic adolescents and may be more important for dyslexics than for reading-age matched controls.

Differences in reading phonologically transparent and non-transparent words have been found for normally achieving readers. Carlisle (2000) compared third and fifth graders' reading of derived words. Performance on words for which the pronunciation between corresponding base and derived forms was stable (e.g., *enjoy/enjoyment*) was compared to performance on words for which there were shifts in pronunciation (e.g., *nature/ natural*), matched for word length and frequency (base and surface forms). Both third and fifth graders were significantly more accurate on reading transparent than shift words. We would expect this difference to be more pronounced for students with reading disabilities.

Questions remain about how to assess the effects of phonological transparency on students' reading of morphologically complex words. A word naming task can be used to investigate the extent to which morphological processing is used in reading morphologically complex words. This task requires pronunciation of the words aloud. Consequently, if reading derived words of transparent and shift relations, matched for word length and frequency, differs in speed or accuracy, the difference would reflect the relative ease with which the phonological representation of the base word facilitates recognition and pronunciation of the complex word form. Such facilitation would not take place if the complex word form was not decomposed morphologically. Thus, if transparent words are not read more quickly and accurately than shift words, a likely interpretation would be that the words were not processed with regard to their morphological structure. Further, evidence suggests that children with reading disabilities demonstrate difficulties in naming, which presumably include accessing the phonological representation in memory, and preparing and delivering the speech act of naming the word (Denckla & Rudel, 1976). Naming problems may be an important contributor to difficulties reading aloud derived words, along with other aspects of phonological processing. For this reason, the gap between performance on transparent and shift words might be greater for students with RD than for their average-achieving peers

Because poor readers might have specific naming problems, it seemed desirable to include a second task that did not require an oral response, namely, a lexical decision task. Lexical decision tasks have shown that morphological structure affects word recognition (e.g., Cole, Beauvillain, & Segui, 1989; Stoltz & Feldman, 1995), but these results have come from studies of adults with average reading skills. With the exception of Gordon

(1989), who used flashcards to record accuracy of lexical decisions with five- through nine-year olds in order to explore a model of word formation, we are not aware of other studies that have utilized this task for studying morphology in children.

The lexical decision task requires students to make a judgment about whether a letter string is or is not a word. Presumably, the decision is made on the basis of whether the student does or does not find the string of letters stored as a word in memory. Models of word recognition indicate that finding a word in memory entails processing not only the orthographic representation but also the phonological and semantic representations (Besner, 1999). Thus, performance on the task might indicate whether phonological complexity influenced the speed and accuracy of processing shift as compared to stable words. However, studies of adults gave us reason to expect morphological composition to play a role in word recognition on this task as well. Performance on lexical decision tasks with priming have shown an effect for morphological structure that cannot be explained by orthographic, phonological, or semantic properties of the words (e.g., Stolz & Feldman, 1995). Furthermore, studies have shown that both high school students and adults make use of orthographic information in analyzing the morphological structure of words (Derwing, Smith, & Wiebe, 1995; Templeton & Scarborough-Franks, 1985). If middle school students (with and without reading problems) also decompose words in the process of visual word recognition, we might expect to find an interference effect for derived words whose base forms undergo a sound shift, but not for base forms whose phonological representation is fully incorporated in the derived counterpart.

An added value of the lexical decision task was its potential for exploring the extent to which orthographic processing of the letter string affects the reading of words and nonwords differently for poor and average achieving readers. One issue is the level of orthographic awareness of students with reading disabilities. Results of previous studies have suggested that poor readers are sensitive to the "legality" of letter strings (i.e., combinations or patterns of letters found in English orthography) (Siegel, Share, & Geva, 1995). As a result, they would not be expected to differ from their peers in rejecting nonwords constructed of letter combinations that are not permissible in English. However, poor readers are less efficient in developing a full representation of words (including orthographic and phonological characteristics) than their peers and so might be slower and/or less accurate at recognizing legal letter strings as nonwords (Ehri, 1997). Readers make connections between graphemes and phonemes in the words that they encounter through print; with repeated exposures, these words are stored in memory and become sight words. Through experience with text, readers abstract orthographic rules about permissible letter patterns that are important for reading (Perfetti, 1992). The ease with which a reader forms connections between letter patterns and their corresponding phonological representations affects the process of learning to read over time (Berninger & Abbott, 1994). Thus, for example, Manis (1985) found that disabled readers were slower and less accurate than normal readers in processing unfamiliar real words (e.g., *scaup*), and it took more exposures to words before the disabled readers could recall them accurately.

The present study explored the difficulties that students with reading disabilities have reading derived words that undergo phonological shifts. Two experimental word recognition tasks (Word Naming and Lexical Decision) were presented to compare the speed and accuracy with which poor and average readers respond to shift words, as compared to stable words, when all of the words are orthographically transparent. Longer response latencies and less accurate responses to shift (e.g., *natural*) in comparison to stable words (e.g., *cultural*) would suggest that the phonological representation of base words is accessed and causes some amount of interference in the processing of the derived form. Differences in responses to the Naming and Lexical Decision tasks might indicate whether the requirement of an overt pronunciation particularly affected poor readers (i.e., greater difference between shift and stable words on the Naming than the Lexical Decision task). In addition, we included a group of adult readers to determine whether the effect for shift words would be found for adult readers as well. We expected poor readers to be less accurate and slower on both word types and both tasks than average achieving readers because of less efficient processing of the orthographic representation and greater difficulty accessing orthographic and phonological representations from memory. However, we expected differences in performance on stable and shift words to be more pronounced for poor than average readers because of the likelihood that poor readers have difficulties learning complex phonological relations.

In addition to the comparison of derived forms that were orthographically transparent but different in phonological transparency, the study included analysis of the speed and accuracy of students' recognition of orthographically legal and illegal nonwords that resembled derived forms. This analysis provided a way to assess the role of orthographic sensitivity in word recognition. Specifically, as foils for the shift words and stable words in the lexical decision task described above, nonwords that ended in common suffixes (e.g., -ic, -ize) were presented. One-half of these nonwords consisted of legal orthographic sequences (e.g., *hodropic, deromity*), and one-half consisted of illegal letter sequences (e.g., *reflsiber, oprbodity*).

The research questions were

1. Do poor readers differ from average achieving readers on speed and accuracy of naming derived forms with and without phonological shifts?

2. Is the same pattern of performance on the two types of derived words found on a lexical decision task?

3. Do adults also perform more accurately and rapidly on stable than shift words?

4. Do poor readers differ from average achieving readers on speed and accuracy of responses to legal and illegal nonword letter strings?

5. To what extent does speed of responding to legal and illegal nonword letter strings contribute to speed of recognizing derived words (shift and stable) for the two child reader groups?

# METHOD

## SUBJECTS

Three groups of subjects were included in the study: two groups of children and a group of normal adult readers. All child subjects were attending one of two schools for children with learning problems and were in Grades 4 to 9. Their ages ranged from 10.75 years to 15.75 years. There were two groups of children, defined in terms of *Wide Range Achievement Test III (WRAT)* Reading scores (Wilkinson, 1993). The Poor Readers (PR: $N = 18$) had WRAT Reading scores below 90. The Average Readers (AVR: $N = 33$) had WRAT scores of 90 or above. Children in both groups had receptive vocabulary at least in the Low Average range on the *Peabody Picture Vocabulary Test III (PPVT > = 79)* (Dunn & Dunn, 1997).

Descriptive statistics for the two groups of children are presented in table I. The two groups did not differ in mean age. However, there were significant differences in verbal ability

(PPVT), $t(49)$ = 3.58, $p$ <.001, in word reading (WRAT), $t(49)$ = 8.25, $p$ < .001, and in word attack on the *Woodcock Reading Mastery Test, Revised (WRMT)*, $t(46)$ = 4.40, $p$ <.001 (Woodcock, 1987).

Table I.  Differences Between the Two Child Reader Groups on Descriptive Measures.

| Measure | Poor Readers | | Average Readers | | t-test (df = 49) |
|---|---|---|---|---|---|
| Age | 13.62 | (1.28) | 13.31 | (1.47) | .74 |
| PPVT | 95.83 | (10.65) | 108.27 | (12.47) | 3.58* |
| WRAT Reading | 83.39 | (5.75) | 98.76 | (6.66) | 8.25* |
| WRMT Word Attack | 88.50 | (6.22) | 98.20 | (8.00) | 4.40* |

*Note: Ages are mean age in years, and others are mean standard scores. Numbers in parentheses are standard deviations.
  p < .01

The adult readers (AR) were 19 undergraduate or first-year graduate students with normal reading skills. Ages ranged from 18 to 27 years ($M$ = 20.61, $SD$ = 2.89). AR scores on the WRAT Reading subtest averaged 115.21 ($SD$ = 4.91).

## TASKS

Three tasks were administered to all subjects: two experimental word recognition tasks and a measure of simple choice reaction time, all presented on a microcomputer.

The Choice Reaction Time task was part of the Computerized Academic Assessment System (CAAS) (Royer & Sinatra, 1994). Subjects were shown a series of stimuli consisting of three asterisks or plus signs, appearing in the center of the screen. For each trial, the subject had to respond by naming the stimulus (i.e., "star" or "plus"). Accuracy was recorded by the examiner (using a button box interface), but the major dependent variable was reaction time, recorded automatically by the computer using a voice-activated relay attached to a headset microphone. Subjects' scores were percent correct and mean reaction time. To minimize the influence of aberrant trials, in calculating the reaction times, the computer automatically removed any individual item score that was more than 2 standard deviations from the subject's overall mean across trials.

For the two experimental word recognition tasks, subjects responded to letter strings appearing on the computer screen. The two tasks differed in processing and output demands. In the Naming task, subjects were asked to read each word aloud as quickly as possible into a headset microphone. In the Lexical Decision task, subjects were asked merely to indicate (by pressing one of two response buttons on an interface box) whether or not each letter sequence constituted a real word. For both tasks, accuracy was entered directly into the data base by the examiner using a button box. Reaction time was recorded automatically by the computer. As for the Choice Reaction Time task, aberrant reaction times were removed by the computer during the calculation of the task averages for that student.

Three types of items were included in both word recognition tasks: shift, stable, and foils. The shift list consisted of 13 derived words containing a phonological shift in the base word with the addition of the suffix (e.g., *natural, majority*). The stable list consisted of 13 similar derived words without a phonological shift (e.g., *cultural, maturity*). The two word groups were matched for type of suffix (i.e., *-al, -ity, -ence, -ce,* or *-tion*), orthographic patterns, number of syllables (3.62 for shift and 3.46 for stable words), base word frequency (49.08 for shift and 50.28 for stable), and surface frequency (43.90 for shift and 44.92 for stable). The frequency figures are the Standard Frequency Index, representing frequency of word use in written texts through Grade 9 (Carroll, Davies, & Richman, 1971). See Appendix A for a complete list of the target words. The foils on the Naming task consisted of 19 derived words (e.g., *suitable*) that were comparable to the target words in length and frequency, but that differed in morphological endings (e.g., *-ly, -able, -ful*). These words were interspersed randomly among the target words in order to reduce the likelihood that the subject would notice patterns in word endings. The foils on the Lexical Decision task consisted of the 19 foils from the Naming task plus 40 nonwords. The nonwords ended in common suffixes (e.g., *-ic, -ity*) and were comparable in length to the target words (3 to 4 syllables; $M = 3.5$). One half of these words consisted of legal orthographic sequences (e.g., *hodropic, deromity*), and one-half consisted of illegal letter sequences (e.g., *infsioble, zrenderize*).

## PROCEDURES

The students took the standardized measures and completed the computer tasks in two sessions. In one session, all three standardized tests were administered; then the student completed the Naming task. In the second session, the student completed the Choice Reaction Time and Lexical Decision tasks. The experimental tasks were presented on a microcomputer. Each item consisted of a series of visual stimuli (displayed individually on the computer screen) to which the subject made a speeded response (by means of a button box or a voice-activated relay). The words on each task were presented in a random order for each subject. Subjects responded to all target and foil words. Only the shift and stable words were used in analyses of the Naming task, whereas analysis of performance on the Legal and Illegal nonwords was carried out for the Lexical Decision task in addition to analyses of the shift and stable words. Response latencies to both correctly and incorrectly named and recognized words were included so that the performance of groups could be compared on the basis of responses to the same number of words of each type.

# RESULTS

## GROUP DIFFERENCES IN CHOICE REACTION TIME

Possible differences in choice reaction time between the two child groups were examined using analysis of variance. Because of scheduling difficulties and computer malfunctions, these data were available for only a subset of each group (PR: $N = 15$; AVR: $N = 23$). As expected, the mean reaction times for these two groups did not differ significantly, $F(1, 36) = 1.74$, $p = .20$ (PR: $M = .689$, $SD = .176$; AVR: $M = .754$, $SD = .130$), indicating that children in these two groups were equally skilled at recognition and labeling of simple stimuli on response-choice tasks.

## EFFECTS OF PHONOLOGICAL TRANSPARENCY AND TASK DEMANDS FOR THE CHILD READER GROUPS

The accuracy and speed data from the two experimental word recognition tasks were analyzed in two separate Group × Task × Transparency ANOVAs; the results are shown in tables II and III.

There were significant differences as a function of group, task demand, and phonological transparency for both accuracy and speed of word recognition. Significant Group x Task Demand and Group x Transparency interactions indicated that the effect of task demands was greater for the PR group than for the AVR group and that the effect of phonological transparency was also greater for the PR group. Tables IV and V show descriptive statistics on speed and accuracy of responses on the Naming and Lexical Decision tasks.

For speed of word recognition, group differences as a function of phonological transparency were much more pronounced on the Naming task than on the Lexical Decision task. This differential effect was less pronounced for accuracy and was not statis-

**Table II. Effects of Child Reader Group, Task Demands, and Phonological Transparency on the Accuracy of Word Recognition.**

| Source | Degrees of Freedom | Mean Square | F Value |
|---|---|---|---|
| Group (G) | 1 | .797 | 18.9*** |
| Error | 49 | .042 | |
| Task Demand (TD) | 1 | 1.050 | 62.3*** |
| G x TD | 1 | .259 | 15.4*** |
| Error | 49 | .017 | |
| Transparency (T) | 1 | 1.087 | 94.9*** |
| G x T | 1 | .079 | 6.9* |
| Error | 49 | .011 | |
| TD x T | 1 | .472 | 38.1*** |
| G x TD x T | 1 | .000 | .01 |
| Error | 49 | .012 | |

*p < .05; ***p < .001

**Table III. Effects of Child Reader Group, Task Demands, and Phonological Transparency on the Speed of Word Recognition.**

| Source | Degrees of Freedom | Mean Square | F Value |
|---|---|---|---|
| Group (G) | 1 | 2.459 | 9.4** |
| Error | 49 | 2.595 | |
| Task Demand (TD) | 1 | 13.963 | 26.6*** |
| G x TD | 1 | 8.507 | 16.2*** |
| Error | 49 | .524 | |
| Transparency (T) | 1 | 7.649 | 33.3*** |
| G x T | 1 | .940 | 4.1* |
| Error | 49 | .230 | |
| TD x T | 1 | 3.627 | 21.7*** |
| G x TD x T | 1 | 1.631 | 9.8** |
| Error | 49 | .167 | |

*p < .05; **p < .01; ***p < .001

tically reliable. These findings remained the same when variation in receptive vocabulary or in choice reaction time was controlled.

## TRANSPARENCY AND TASK EFFECTS FOR THE ADULT READERS

Although there were effects of phonological transparency in the adult readers, there was no evidence of a differential effect of

Table IV.   Accuracy of Word Recognition in the Three Reader Groups as a Function of Task Demands and Phonological Transparency.

| Reader Group | Naming Task | | Lexical Decision Task | |
|---|---|---|---|---|
| | Shift Words | Stable Words | Shift Words | Stable Words |
| PR | 46.0   (19.2) | 75.6  (16.5) | 78.7  (15.2) | 87.9  (11.7) |
| AVR | 70.8   (17.5) | 91.9  (11.3) | 88.3  (12.9) | 89.5  (11.6) |
| Adult Readers | 98.4   (3.2) | 100.0  (0) | 98.8  (3.9) | 100.0  (0) |

*Note:* Entries are mean percent correct. Numbers in parentheses are standard deviations. PR= Poor readers; AVR = Average readers.

Table V.   Speed of the Three Reader Groups as a Function of Task Demands and Phonological Transparency.

| Reader Group | Naming Task | | Lexical Decision Task | |
|---|---|---|---|---|
| | Shift Words | Stable Words | Shift Words | Stable Words |
| PR | 3.106  (1.937) | 2.093  (.982) | 1.665  (.794) | 1.584  (.747) |
| AVR | 1.625  (1.092) | 1.270  (.569) | 1.413  (.654) | 1.242  (.550) |
| Adult Readers | .691  (.11) | .660  (.130) | .655  (.126) | .621  (.115) |

*Note:* Entries are mean reaction times in seconds. Numbers in parentheses are standard deviations. PR= Poor readers; AVR = Average readers.

phonological transparency as a function of task demands, as tables IV and V show. Because the adults made no errors naming the stable words, statistical analysis would not be appropriate. For the reaction time data, ANOVA revealed a significant effect of Transparency, $F(1,18) = 7.23$, $p = .015$, but no effect of Task Demand, $F(1, 18) = 1.59$, $p = .22$, and no significant interaction, $F(1, 18) = .02$, $p = .90$.

## THE ROLE OF SENSITIVITY TO ORTHOGRAPHIC PATTERNS

A question of some importance in interpreting the results of the Naming and LD tasks is the extent to which sensitivity to orthographic composition affected performance. An initial analysis of reader group differences in sensitivity to orthographic legality was conducted on the data for the two child reader groups by contrasting reaction times for rejecting legal versus illegal nonword letter strings. In terms of response latencies, the results of a Group (RD, AVR) × Legality (legal, illegal) ANOVA indicated a significant effect of Legality, $F(1, 49) = 48.0$, $p < .001$, but no difference as a function of reading group, $F(1, 49) = .19$, $p = .67$, and no significant interaction, $F(1, 49) = .92$, $p = .34$. In terms of accuracy, there was again a significant effect for Legality, $F(1, 49) = 125.96$, $p < .001$, but no difference between reading groups, $F(1, 49) = 2.71$, $p = .11$, and no significant interaction,

$F(1, 49) = 2.50$, $p = .12$. Responses to illegal and legal nonwords are summarized in table VI.

Table VI.   Speed and Accuracy of Responses to Legal and Illegal Non-Words for the Poor Reader and Average Reader Groups.

| | Legal | | Illegal | |
|---|---|---|---|---|
| Group | Accuracy | Speed | Accuracy | Speed |
| PR | 70.4 | 1.96 | 92.7 | 1.43 |
| | (13.8) | (.92) | (10.4) | (.81) |
| AVR | 78.9 | 1.74 | 95.2 | 1.36 |
| | (14.0) | (1.00) | (8.4) | (.75) |

*Note:* Standard deviations are given in parentheses; accuracy is mean percent correct, while speed is mean reaction time in seconds. PR= Poor readers; AVR = Average readers.

We assumed that speed of responding to illegal words reflects ease of recognizing letter combinations that are not permissible in English, a relatively superficial level of orthographic awareness. In contrast, speed of responding to legal nonwords involves integration of the orthographic and phonological representations of a letter string, as well as semantic processing to determine lexical status. This represents a more complex and time-consuming process. Both levels of orthographic processing might play a role in the recognition of stable and shift real words, but the two levels may contribute to word recognition in different ways for students who are PR and AVR. To explore this possibility, we carried out four parallel hierarchical regression analyses. For each analysis, we entered the measure of rate of responding to illegal words first in the prediction, followed by the measure of rate of responding to legal nonwords. These analyses were run separately for the two reader groups. For each group, we ran one analysis predicting speed of response to shift words and one analysis predicting speed of response to stable words. In order to normalize the data distributions, these analyses were conducted using log-transformed reaction time measures. The results from these analyses are summarized in tables VII and VIII.

Overall, the role of the two orthographic processing measures in predicting speed of response to the real words was similar for the shift and stable words, but the pattern of predictors was different for the two groups. For both groups, when speed of response to illegal nonwords was entered as the sole predictor variable, it played a powerful role in predicting speed of response to shift words (Beta values of .89 and .88 for the PR and AVR groups, respectively). However, when speed of response to

Table VII.   Differential Contribution of Levels of Orthographic and Phonological Processing to Recognition of Shift and Stable Words for the Poor Reader Group.

| Regression Step/ Predictor | Multiple $R^2$ | Beta | $R^2$ Change | F-test/t-test |
|---|---|---|---|---|
| **Shift Words** | | | | |
| Step 1 | .799 | | | 63.70*** |
| Illegal Nonwords | | .894 | | 7.98*** |
| Step 2[a] | .959 | | .159 | 57.78*** |
| Illegal Nonwords | | .085 | | .72 |
| Legal Nonwords | | .902 | | 7.60*** |
| **Stable Words** | | | | |
| Step 1 | .797 | | | 62.87*** |
| Illegal Nonwords | | .893 | | 7.93*** |
| Step 2[a] | .949 | | .152 | 44.81*** |
| Illegal Nonwprds | | .103 | | .78 |
| Legal Nonwords | | .881 | | 6.69*** |

[a] The F-test reported for step 2 is the F to enter. ***$p < .001$.

Table VIII.   Differential Contribution of Levels of Orthographic and Phonological Processing to Recognition of Shift and Stable Words for the Average Reader Group.

| Regression Step/ Predictor | Multiple $R^2$ | Beta | $R^2$ Change | F-test/t-test |
|---|---|---|---|---|
| **Shift Words** | | | | |
| Step 1 | .779 | | | 109.48*** |
| Illegal Nonwords | | .883 | | 10.46*** |
| Step 2[a] | .792 | | .012 | 1.77 |
| Illegal Nonwords | | .605 | | 2.69* |
| Legal Nonwords | | .299 | | 1.33 |
| **Stable Words** | | | | |
| Step 1 | .803 | | | 126.71*** |
| Illegal Nonwords | | .896 | | 11.26*** |
| Step 2[a] | .806 | | .002 | .35 |
| Illegal Nonwords | | .776 | | 3.57** |
| Legal Nonwords | | .129 | | .59 |

[a] The F-test reported for step 2 is the F to enter. *$p < .05$; **$p < .01$; ***$p < .001$.

legal nonwords was added to the predictive equation in a second step, this measure became the main predictor for the PR group (Beta = .90), reducing the contribution of the illegal nonword measure to nonsignificance (Beta = .09). In contrast, for the AVR group, the legal nonword measure played no significant predictive role (Beta = .30); instead, speed of response to illegal nonwords remained the important predictor (Beta = .60). A similar pattern was evident for the stable words (see table VIII).

In addition, it is interesting to note that the orthographic processing variables accounted for more of the variance in the speed of recognizing shift and stable words for the PR than the AVR group: for PR, 96 percent of the variance in shift words and 97 percent of the variance in stable words; for AVR, 79 percent of the variance in shift words and 81 percent of the variance in stable words.

## DISCUSSION

This study was undertaken to determine whether students with word reading disabilities had more pronounced problems than their average-reading peers in the reading of derived words whose base forms undergo a phonological shift (e.g., *nature, natural*), in comparison to words whose base forms are phonologically transparent (i.e. stable relations as in *culture* and *cultural*). Comparison of performance on these word types should help us determine the extent to which students with reading disabilities have particular difficulties processing the complex phonological relations that characterize so many derived forms. The results of previous studies have shown that the phonological complexities of morphologically complex words are related to the word reading skill of students with reading disabilities, but this has been determined on the basis of correlations of oral morphological awareness tasks with performance on general word reading tests (e.g., Fowler & Liberman, 1995; Singson, Mahoney, & Mann, 2000). We had reason to expect that both average-achieving and poor readers would perform less well on shift than stable derived words. Earlier work (Carlisle, 2000) had shown that average third and fifth graders read transparent derived words more accurately than shift derived words, but we also had reason to expect that poor readers would be relatively weaker at naming shift and stable words than their peers. For example, Windsor (2000) found that for students with language-learning disabilities, phonological complexities of derived words posed particular problems for performance in reading.

### TRANSPARENCY EFFECTS ACROSS TASKS

Overall, our results showed that for all three reader groups, the effect for transparency was evident on both naming and lexical decision tasks. Our investigation was particularly focused on the children who were poor readers, and the results confirmed the expectation that poor readers have less difficulty reading stable than shift words. These results provide support for Elbro and

Arnbak's (1996) argument that morpho-semantic processing may be a particular advantage for poor readers. The average-achieving readers showed a similar pattern of responses, but the difference in performance on the two word types was far less pronounced in their case. The effect of transparency was significant for the capable adult readers as well, when performance on shift and stable words was collapsed across tasks.

Performance on the Naming task showed a stronger effect for phonological transparency than on the Lexical Decision task. In fact, for the Lexical Decision task, interpretation of the results is somewhat problematic. The poor readers were less accurate on shift than stable words, but their response latencies to the two word types were very similar; on the other hand, average-achieving readers were equally accurate identifying shift and stable words as words, but they were slower on the shift words. Overall, poor readers showed a greater advantage for stable words than their peers, but this effect was noteworthy only when they were asked to pronounce words aloud. These results did not change when group differences in speed of naming simple stimuli and vocabulary knowledge were controlled.

To interpret the results, it is important to remember that the shift and stable words were presented without any reference to their base forms. In addition, these word types did not differ in word length or frequency. For both shift and stable words, the spelling contains almost all of the base form—for some words among the shift and stable word set, a final e (or, for one word, y) is dropped to add the suffix (e.g., *intense, intensity* and *sincere, sincerity*). The orthographic redundancy of base and derived forms is considerable, and it is comparable for the two word types. Thus, it is not the orthographic representation of the base word that provides an advantage for recognition of the stable words. More likely, it is the phonological match of the base in the derived form that makes stable words easier than shift words. The longer response latencies and less accurate responses to shift than stable words are attributable to difficulties accessing the phonological representation of the word by means of the phonology of the subword morphological units.

Differences in responses to shift and stable words by poor and average-achieving readers underscore difficulties learning the rule-governed phonological form of some base morphemes. However, students evidently engaged in morphological analysis; had they not done so, performance on the shift and stable words would not have differed significantly for either group. Note that in figures 1a and 1b, both the poor and average-achieving readers had more difficulties with the shift than the stable words, especially in comparison to the adults. The difference between the children reader groups is a matter of degree, not of kind. Nonetheless, the poor readers' very slow reading of the shift words, in particular, is striking.

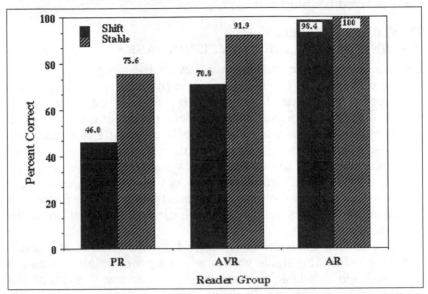

*Figure 1a.   Accuracy of naming words on the Word Naming task.*

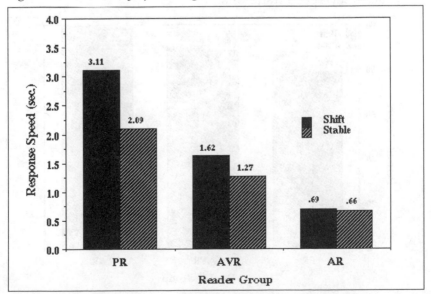

*Figure 1b.   Speed of naming words on the Word Naming task.*

The important point may be that the weaker readers' poor performance on derived words whose base forms have a different phonological form suggests difficulties with a particular aspect of morphological learning, the mastery of systematic relations or allomorphs in the representation of base forms in their derived counterparts.

## DIFFERING STRATEGIES FOR NAMING VERSUS LEXICAL DECISION TASKS

On the Naming task, one explanation for the slower and less accurate responses to the shift words is that the students process the word for pronunciation by noticing first the base form (e.g., *nature*). The time course of subsequent processing of the word may be such that the reader is mentally preparing to pronounce the base form before he or she has fully processed the affix and the stress pattern of the whole word, which in the case of *natural* would involve the shortening of the vowel. In effect, prolonged focus or reliance on the base form interferes with the process of accessing or constructing the phonological representation of the derived word.

The lexical decision task offered a comparison of performance on shift and stable words when a pronunciation was not required. On this task, the transparency effect was evident but subtle, as figures 2a and 2b show. As noted earlier, there appear to be accuracy-speed trade-offs.

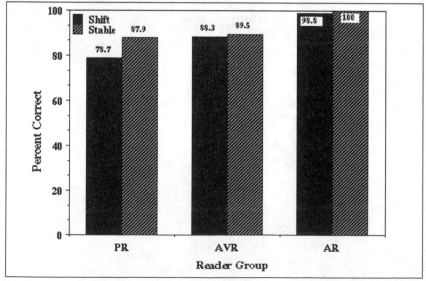

*Figure 2a.   Accuracy of recognizing words on the Lexical Decision task.*

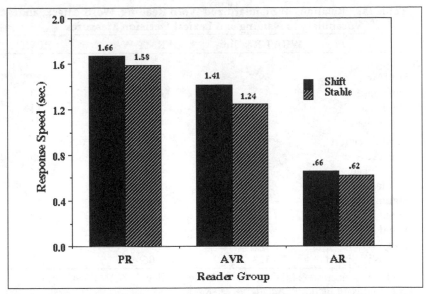

*Figure 2b.   Speed of recognizing words on the Lexical Decision task.*

The child readers took about twice as long as the adult readers to respond to the words. The average-achieving child readers were reasonably accurate (88 percent to 90 percent correct for shift and stable words), whereas the poor readers' accuracy on the two word types was lower (79 percent and 88 percent for shift and stable words). The poor readers were more accurate on the stable than the shift words, but their response latencies were similar on the two word types. The average-achieving readers, on the other hand, were quite accurate at identifying shift and stable words as words, but they were slower at responding to the shift than the stable words. For both groups, the effect of transparency is less pronounced than it was on the naming task. Interestingly, the response latencies of the adult readers, shown in Figure 2a and 2b, were similar to those of adults on other types of lexical decision tasks (about 600 to 700 ms) (e.g., Stolz & Feldman, 1995).

The data from the lexical decision task raise questions about the difficulty of the words for the fourth- through ninth-grade readers, as well as the nature of the processing and the basis for decision-making they used. Additional concerns about interpretation of the results of the lexical decision task stem from the relationship between lexical decision responses and performances on the WRAT Reading and the WRMT Word Attack, shown in table IX.

**Table IX.   Relations of Standardized Word Reading, Word Attack, and Vocabulary to Naming and Lexical Decision Measures.**

|  | WRAT Reading | WRMT WA | PPVT |
|---|---|---|---|
| **Naming** | | | |
| Shift Ac | .59*** | .46*** | .37** |
| Shift Speed | −.43*** | −.31* | −.13 |
| Stable Ac | .57*** | .43*** | .14 |
| Stable Speed | −.45*** | −.34* | −.24 |
| **Lexical Decision** | | | |
| Shift Ac | .39** | .31* | .25 |
| Shift Speed | −.25 | −.09 | −.12 |
| Stable Ac | .23 | .24 | .15 |
| Stable Speed | −.35* | −.24 | −.16 |
| Legal NW Ac | .23 | .18 | .09 |
| Legal NW Speed | −.17 | −.07 | −.003 |
| Illeg NW Ac | .17 | .27* | .11 |
| Illeg NW Speed | −.12 | −.06 | .02 |

*Note:* Ac = accuracy; NW = nonword; Illeg = illegal; WA= Word Attack; PPVT = *Peabody Picture Vocabulary Test-R.*

$^*p < .05, ^{**}p < .01, ^{***}p < .001$

Standardized word reading measures were significantly related to *accuracy* of responses to words (shift and stable) on the Naming and Lexical Decision tasks, whereas standardized reading measures were significantly related to *speed* of responding to words on the Naming but not the Lexical Decision task. Further, performances on the standardized measures were generally not related to nonword lexical decision responses (speed or accuracy). We were particularly surprised to find that accuracy of responses to legal nonwords was only weakly related to WRMT Word Attack performance ($r = .27, p < .05$). A strong relation was expected because both measures involve legal nonwords.

These results suggest that the presence of both legal and illiegal nonwords on the lexical decision task directed attention to aspects of orthographic representation. As Balota (1990) pointed out, the lexical decision task is not an identification task but rather a discrimination task. Characteristics of both the target words and the nonword foils may influence the readers' basis for distinguishing words from nonwords (see Besner, 1999).

## DIFFERENCES IN DEPTH OF PROCESSING IN WORD RECOGNITION

Performance on the nonword items of the lexical decision task provided some information about the processing of the letter strings that students engaged in on their way to making a lexical decision. The two reader groups responded more rapidly and accurately on illegal than legal nonwords, as we had expected. However, the groups did not differ in speed or accuracy. These results support Siegel et al.'s (1995) conclusion that poor readers are able to distinguish legal from illegal letter strings as well as their peers. The relative speed of responses suggests that legal nonwords required more thorough processing; illegal words were responded to in less than one and one-half seconds, whereas legal nonwords were responded to in close to two seconds. Correct identification of illegal nonwords involves awareness of permissible orthographic letter combinations and positions in English. For example, *amhpasritic* might be rejected quickly because of the *amhp-* at the beginning; more complete processing of the letter string might not be necessary. In contrast, orthographic processing of legal nonwords might involve going beyond a superficial orthographic analysis to the formation of a phonological representation (Balota, 1990; Perfetti, 1992). In order to reject *deromity*, for example, the reader needs to determine that no such word is found in his or her mental dictionary. This decision involves phonological and semantic as well as orthographic processing. Because of the presence of illegal nonwords, the students may have adopted an approach of checking letter strings for sequences that are not permissible in English (whether consciously or not). As noted earlier, the nature of the task may have predisposed the students to focus on the orthographic characteristics of the items.

Further examination of the processing of words and nonwords was carried out to determine whether depth of processing of the illegal and legal nonwords would account for speed of recognition of the target words (shift and stable). For the poor reader group, the results showed that speed of processing of the legal nonwords accounted for a very large portion of the variance in speed of responding to both the real shift and stable words. In contrast, for the average-achieving reader group, only speed of responses to illegal nonwords was related to performance on the shift and stable words. In addition, nonword performance (in total) accounted for a smaller portion of the variance in word recognition than was the case for the poor readers. Thus, for the poor readers, the close relation between speed of processing real words and legal nonwords suggests activation of both orthographic and phonological representations, whereas the average readers appear to have used a surface-level orthographic processing approach on this task. The poor readers may processed the real derived words as if they were not familiar words for which they have an easily accessed representation in memory.

There are several possible explanations for these results. One is that developing ready access to orthographic and phonological codes in memory is a challenge for poor readers (e.g., Manis, 1985). Another possibility is that poor readers have less experience reading complex words because they tend to read easier books and to read less overall than their peers (Stanovich, 1986). Derwing et al. (1995) raised the possibility that orthographic awareness of the structure of derived words may come from educational experiences. However, because both the poor and the average-achieving readers in this study attended the same schools, and these were schools that taught systematic phonics, we cannot attribute the pattern of results for the reader groups to differences in word-reading instruction. In short, the nature of our study does not provide a basis for determining why the two child reader groups differed in the depth of processing of words and nonwords.

Although the results from the lexical decision task suggest possible differences in word recognition approaches, it is not clear that performance on this task provides a trustworthy measure of phonological processing of shift and stable words. We recommend further studies that employ different methodologies such as lexical decision tasks with a very short exposure of the words or priming tasks. These might shed light on the role of phonological interference in the processing of complex words (see Balota, 1990; Fowler, Napps, & Feldman, 1985).

One limitation of the present study is that we did not include a group of younger children matched to the poor readers in reading ability. This is because younger children (second or third graders) would not have had experience with many of the words used for purposes of studying phonological shifts of derived words. Very high-frequency derived words tend not to be characterized by the systematic phonological shifts found in less common words like *majority*. Furthermore, high-frequency derived words (e.g., *happiness*) may be processed as single lexical items without regard for morphological structure (Gordon, 1989). Nonetheless, the results of an earlier study (Carlisle & Stone, in press) suggest that the poor readers would be likely to resemble a reading-age matched group, at least in their reading of the transparent words.

## EDUCATIONAL IMPLICATIONS

While it may be premature to consider educational implications of our results in any depth, at this point the findings seem to suggest that poor readers experience difficulties learning the complex phonological representation of base forms of derived counterparts. In addition, to pronounce derived words aloud, poor readers may need to carry out more deliberate analysis of the word form than average readers. Accessing the full representation of a letter string (i.e., both orthographic and phonological codes) is a slow process for many poor readers. Such problems can be addressed by instructional programs that include word study beyond basic phonics.

Instructional programs should provide guidance in understanding complex phonological relations and a variety of strategies for working out the pronunciation of complex words, one of which involves looking for ways to use known morphemes to help arrive at the pronunciation of an unfamiliar word. For example, a program developed by Lovett, Lacerenza, and Borden (2000) includes "peeling off" as a strategy for morphological decomposition. In addition, guided experiences recognizing base morphemes that have undergone phonological and orthographic changes (e.g., *decide/decision; strong/strength*) may sensitize students to morphological relations. Morphological family members can be used to remember unexpected spellings and pronunciations of words (e.g., *muscle/muscular*).

As others have shown, poor readers need ample experience in order to develop trustworthy mental representations of words (e.g., Manis, 1985), and this principle is bound to hold for reading complex as well as simple words. Programs should include sufficient practice to ensure that the particular words students are learning are recognized rapidly and accurately. In addition, decoding strategies should become a well-engrained habit so that they are used spontaneously to assist in the analysis of unfamiliar words. It is probably not possible to overemphasize the need to make sure that students are experiencing success when it comes to using strategies to work out the pronunciation of unfamiliar words (see Lovett, et al., 2000).

Word study that focuses on morphemes not only facilitates the development of decoding strategies but also helps students acquire a strategy for figuring out word meanings. Instructional programs in morphological analysis skills, therefore, can provide valuable links between word reading and comprehension. Rationale and guidelines for morphological instruction can be found in Henry (1988), Moats (2000), and Carreker (1999).

## ACKNOWLEDGMENTS

This project was made possible by a research grant from the International Dyslexia Association. We are grateful for their support and for the interest and participation of students and staff at the Cove School in Northbrook, Illinois, and Dunnabeck School in Amenia, New York.

Address correspondence to Joanne F. Carlisle, University of Michigan, School of Education, 610 E. University Avenue, Ann Arbor, MI 48109; telephone (734) 615–1267.

*References*

Balota, D. A. (1990). The role of meaning in word recognition. In D. A. Balota, G. B. Flores d'Arcais, & K. Rayner (eds.), *Comprehension processes in reading* (pp. 9–32). Hillsdale, NJ: Lawrence Erlbaum Associates.

Berninger, V. W., & Abbott, R. D. (1994). Multiple orthographic and phonological codes in literacy acquisition: An evolving research program. In V. W. Berninger (ed.), *The varieties of orthographic knowledge I: Theoretical and developmental issues* (pp. 277–319). Dordrecht, The Netherlands: Kluwer Academic Publishers.

Besner, D. (1999). Basic processes in reading: Mulitple routines in localist and connectionist models. In R. M. Klein, & P. McMullen (eds.), *Converging methods for understanding reading and dyslexia* (pp. 413–458). Cambridge, MA: MIT Press.

Carlisle, J. F. (2000). Awareness of the structure and meaning of morphologically complex words: Impact on reading. *Reading and Writing, 12(3–4),* 169–190.

Carlisle, J. F., & Nomanbhoy, D. (1993). Phonological and morphological development. *Applied Psycholinguistics, 14,* 177–195.

Carlisle, J. F., & Stone, C. A. (in press). The effects of morphological structure on children's reading of derived words. In E. Assink & D. Santa (eds.), *Reading complex words: Cross-language studies*. Kluwer.

Carreker, S. (1999). Teaching reading: Accurate decoding and fluency. In J. R. Birsh (ed.), *Multisensory teaching of basic language skills* (pp. 141–182). Baltimore: Paul H. Brookes.

Carroll, J. B., Davies, P., & Richman, B. (1971). *Word frequency book.* NY: American Heritage Publishing Company.

Champion, A. H. (1997). Knowledge of suffixed words in reading and oral language contexts: A comparison of reading disabled and normal readers. *Annals of Dyslexia, 47,* 29–55.

Cole, P., Beauvillain, C., & Segui, J. (1989). On the representation and processing of prefixed and suffixed derived words. *Journal of Memory and Language, 28,* 1–13.

Compton, D. L., & Carlisle, J. F. (1994). Speed of word recognition as a distinguishing characteristic of reading disabilities. *Educational Psychology Review, 6,* 115–140.

Denckla, M. B., & Rudell, R. G. (1976). Naming of objects by dyslexic and other learning-disabled children. *Brain and Language, 3,* 1–15.

Derwing, B. B. L., Smith, M. L., & Wiebe, G. E. (1995). On the role of spelling in morpheme recognition: Experimental studies with children and adults. In L. B. Feldman (ed.), *Morphological aspects of language processing* (pp. 3–27). Hillsdale, NJ: Lawrence Erlbaum Associates.

Dunn, L. M., & Dunn, L. M. (1997). *Peabody picture vocabulary test, 3rd edition.* NY: American Guidance Service.

Ehri, L. C. (1997). Sight word learning in normal readers and dyslexics. In B. Blachman, (ed.), *Foundations of reading acquisition and dyslexia* (pp. 163–189). Hillsdale, NJ: Lawrence Erlbaum Associates.

Elbro, C., & Arnbak, E. (1996). The role of morpheme recognition and morphological awareness in dyslexia. *Annals of Dyslexia, 46,* 209–240.

Fowler, A. E., & Liberman, I. Y. (1995). The role of phonology and orthography in morphological awareness. In L. B. Feldman (ed.), *Morphological aspects of language processing* (pp. 157–188). Hillsdale, NJ: Lawrence Erlbaum Associates.

Fowler, C., Napps, S., & Feldman, L. B. (1985). Relations among regular and irregular morphologically related words in the lexicon as revealed by repetition priming. *Memory and Cognition, 13,* 241–255.

Gordon, P. (1989). Levels of affixation in the acquisition of English morphology. *Journal of Memory and Language, 28,* 519–530.

Henry, M. K. (1988). Beyond phonics: Integrated decoding and spelling instruction based on word origin and structure. *Annals of Dyslexia, 38,* 259–275.

Leong, C. K. (1989). Productive knowledge of derivational rules in poor readers. *Annals of Dyslexia, 39,* 94–115.

Liberman, I. Y., Shankweiler, D., & Liberman, A. M. (1989). The alphabetic principle and learning to read. In D. Shankweiler & I. Y. Liberman (eds.), *Phonology and reading disability* (pp. 1–34). Ann Arbor, MI: University of Michigan Press.

Lovett, M., Lacerenza, L., & Borden, S. L. (2000). Putting struggling readers on the PHAST track: A program to integrate phonological and strategy-based remedial reading instruction and maximize outcomes. *Journal of Learning Disabilities, 33,* 458–476.

Manis, F. R. (1985). Acquisition of word identification skills in normal and disabled readers. *Journal of Educational Psychology, 77(1),* 78–90.

Moats, L. (2000). *Speech to print: Language essentials for teachers.* Baltimore: Brookes.

Nagy, W. E., Anderson, R., Schommer, M., Scott, J. A., & Stallman, A. C. (1989). Morphological families and word recognition. *Reading Research Quarterly, 24,* 262–282.

Perfetti, C. A. (1992). The representation problem in reading acquisition., In P. B. Gough, L. C. Ehri, & R. Treiman (eds.), *Reading acquisition* (pp. 145–174). Hillsdale, NJ: Lawrence Erlbaum Associates.

Royer, J. M., & Sinatra, G. M. (1994). A cognitive-theoretical approach to reading diagnostics. *Educational Psychology Review, 6,* 81–113.

Shankweiler, D., Crain, S., Katz, L., Fowler, A. E., Liberman, A. M., Brady, S. A., Thornton, R., Lundquist, E., Dreyer, L., Fletcher, J. M., Stuebing, K. K., Shaywitz, S. E., & Shaywitz, B. A. (1995). Cognitive profiles in reading disabled children: Comparison of language skills in phonology, morphology, and syntax. *Psychological Science, 6(3),* 149–156.

Siegel, L. S., Share, D., & Geva, E. (1995). Evidence for superior orthographic skills in dyslexics. *Psychological Science, 6(4),* 250–253.

Singson, M., Mahoney, D., & Mann, V. (2000). The relation between reading ability and morphological skills: Evidence from derivational suffixes. *Reading and Writing: An Interdisciplinary Journal, 12,* 219–252.

Stanovich, K. E. (1986). Matthew effects in reading: some consequences of individual differences in the acquisition of literacy. *Reading Research Quarterly, 21,* 360–406.

Stoltz, J. A., & Feldman, L. B. (1995). The role of orthographic and semantic transparency of the base morpheme in morphological processing. In L. B. Feldman (ed.), *Morphological aspects of language processing* (pp. 109–129). Hillsdale, NJ: Lawrence Erlbaum Associates.

Templeton, S., & Scarborough-Franks, L. (1985). The spelling's the thing: Knowledge of derivational morphology in orthography and phonology among older students. *Applied Psycholinguistics, 6,* 371–390.

Wilkinson, G. (1993). *Wide range achievement test, 3rd edition.* Wilmington, DE: Wide Range Inc.

Windsor, J. (2000). The role of phonological opacity in reading achievement. *Journal of Speech, Language, and Hearing Research, 43,* 50–61.

Woodcock, R. M. (1987). *Woodcock reading mastery test – revised.* Circle Pines, MN: American Guidance Service.

# APPENDIX A

List of Words Used in the Two Word Recognition Tasks

| STABLE | SHIFT |
| --- | --- |
| Cultural | Natural |
| Maturity | Majority |
| Security | Severity |
| Intensity | Serenity |
| Confession | Convention |
| Confusion | Precision |
| Conformity | Finality |
| Dependence | Confidence |
| Stupidity | Sincerity |
| Activity | Mortality |
| Oddity | Locality |
| Classical | Colonial |
| Difference | Preference |

# PART V
## Dyslexia and Math

Readers of *Annals of Dyslexia* may note that math achievement has received relatively little attention in relation to other aspects of dyslexia. Yet, many individuals with dyslexia have difficulties with some mathematical tasks and especially with the language of math and the reasoning processes necessary for understanding mathematical concepts. The two articles in Part IV address these math difficulties in unique ways, including the use of structured interviews with children or math teachers. In the first paper, C. K. Leong and his colleague describe results of a study they conducted on math word problems. In the second paper, T. R. Miles and his colleagues examine the extent to which individuals with dyslexia have difficulties with math and how their problems differ from those of underachievers and nondyslexic peers. In both papers the authors utilize interview data to complement their group analyses.

The article by C. K. Leong and Wendy Jerred provides two language-based attributes of math word problems: The effects of "consistent" and "inconsistent" language and the inclusion of redundant information. In their study of 3rd, 4th, and 5th graders grouped by ability, they found that word problems that contain inconsistent information were more difficult than those with consistent information and that there were substantial individual differences in the children's recognition of redundant information. Through structured interviews with a subsample of the children, they draw inferences about the children's problem-solving strategies.

T. R. Miles and his colleagues report some new findings from the British Births Cohort Study (see reference in their article in this issue) which has followed the development of a sample of over 12,000 10-year olds born in England, Scotland, and Wales on a particular week in 1970. Using well-defined criteria, they divided the students into groups by severity of their reading problems and examined their math performance on math problem-solving tasks. The test, a copy of which is included as an Appendix to the article, was constructed by several mathematics specialists and included a wide range of skills. Their findings indicate that the students identified as dyslexic had lower scores than normal achievers and an underachieving group. Seeking to explain the students' difficulties, the authors scrutinized those questions that showed large discrepancies in scores between the students with dyslexia and the others and then interviewed the test raters ("judges").

# Effects of Consistency and Adequacy of Language Information on Understanding Elementary Mathematics Word Problems

*Che Kan Leong*

*Wendy D. Jerred*

Department of Educational Psychology & Special Education
University of Saskatchewan
Saskatoon, Canada

*Two types of elementary mathematics word problems involving different linguistic structures were devised to examine the understanding and solution of these problems by 91 Grade 3, 4, and 5 children divided into "more able" and "less able" subgroups. One task consisted of 12 consistent and 12 inconsistent language problems on the basic processes of addition, subtraction, multiplication and division. Another task consisted of a total of 36 word problems with 12 items each containing adequate, inadequate, and redundant information, respectively, for problem solution. Subsidiary tasks of general ability, vocabulary, reading comprehension, mathematics concepts, reflection on mathematics learning, and working memory were also administered to provide estimates of the contribution of these "nonmathematics" tasks to the solution of elementary mathematics problems. Analyses of variance and covariance of group data showed significant main effects of grade, consistency, and adequacy of linguistic*

Annals of Dyslexia, Vol. 51, 2001
ISSN 0736-9387

*information in problem solution. Word problems containing incon-*
*sistent information were more difficult than those with consistent in-*
*formation. Further, word problems containing inadequate and*
*redundant information were more difficult to classify, and for the*
*children to explain, than those items with just enough information.*
*Interviews with 12 individual children provided further insight into*
*their strategies for problem solutions. Both cognitive and develop-*
*mental perspectives are important for mathematics learning and*
*teaching for children with or without learning disabilities.*

Of the overlapping subgroups of learning disabilities, it is generally agreed that those with developmental dyslexia constitute
the largest subgroup and are relatively well researched,
whereas those with mathematics disabilities are less well researched. The situation is changing, however, because of important studies on children's mathematical development and
learning by such researchers as Geary (1993, 1996), Ginsburg
(1977), McCloskey (1992), Miles and Miles (1992), Nunes and
Bryant (1996), Rivera (1997), Schoenfeld (1985), and Verschaffel
(1994), among others.

## ENGAGING STUDENTS IN "MATHEMATICS THINKING"

More than 20 years ago, Ginsburg (1977) explained that mathematics learning and teaching should emphasize building relationships among knowledge among declarative knowledge
(facts about mathematics), procedural knowledge (rules, algo-
rithms, procedures to solve mathematics tasks), and conceptual knowledge (connected web of information). Students
must understand the nature of the mathematical problems and
use their knowledge of facts such as numbers, units of lengths,
and money to operate on the different pieces of information.
Each of the interrelated aspects of knowledge is critical to developing "mathematical literacy" (Goldman, Hasselbring, &
the Cognition and Technology Group at Vanderbilt [CTGV],
1997). The CTGV group envisions engaging students in
"mathematics thinking" in solving numerical problems, especially with the help of multimedia technology. These cognitive
perspectives are consistent with the goals and directions of the
National Council of Teachers of Mathematics (NCTM) (1989)
in emphasizing broader mathematical reasoning away from

the narrow focus of computation. This broader approach to instruction and curriculum development by engaging students in problem-solving strategies applies to students with or without learning disabilities (Thornton, Langrall, & Jones, 1997).

The present study was motivated by the cognitive information approach (e.g., McCloskey, 1992) and elementary school children's reasoning of mathematical relations and systems (e.g., Geary, 1993, 1996; Nunes & Bryant, 1996). McCloskey's modular functional architecture in representing numeral and verbal information has been influential in both cognitive and neuropsychological studies. In essence, abstract internal representation of numbers constitutes the core and is connected with input and output modules. The input consists of both numeral comprehension (e.g., five times four) and verbal comprehension (e.g., five times four, and the output consists of numeral production (e.g., 20) and verbal production (e.g., twenty). Mediating between the input and the output modules and acting on the abstract semantic quantity representation are the calculating procedures of using number facts to act on mathematical concepts. It would appear that McCloskey's (1992) formal modular model interfaces the declarative, procedural, and conceptual knowledge discussed in mathematics learning more than 20 years ago and reemphasized in both the recent learning and learning disabilities literature. What is also important is that the McCloskey model explains well several types of number processing disabilities and the dissociation between number facts and number procedures in different number processing modules. This modular approach should serve well as a theoretical framework in working with children with or without disabilities in mathematics learning.

The central core of "abstract internal representation" in number processing in the modular functional model of McCloskey (1992) is reiterated by Geary (1993, 1996) in his notion of "semantic structure" in understanding mathematical problems. Semantic structure "refers to the meaning of the statements in the problem and their interrelationships" (Geary, 1996, p. 98). Different types of arithmetic problems on addition and subtraction are conceptualized as involving "combine," "change," "compare," and "equalize;" similar general categories also apply to multiplication and division (Geary, 1996, Chapter 3). The keynote of this notion of semantic structure is that students should match their problem-solving strategies to the structure of the problem. Geary also stresses the need to study developmental patterns in children's understanding and representing mathematical concepts in their solution of arithmetic word problems. Even children just beginning to add and subtract have concepts about mathematics, and they progressively elaborate on these concepts to attain full understanding of mathematics reasoning as they grow and develop (Nunes & Bryant, 1996). These authors also emphasize the interrelationship of logical invariance and transformation, mathematical systems and connections in mathematics reasoning and, in particular, the role of the family and school within a cultural context as critical in acquiring mathematical knowledge.

The purpose of the present study was to examine the way 91 Grades 3, 4 and 5 children understand and solve elementary mathematics word problems. In particular, we studied the effects of two aspects of linguistic information on their performance: consistency or inconsistency of language and the adequacy or inadequacy of linguistic information embedded in the word problems. We also studied the effects of some cognitive and memory tasks on the children's performance. In addition to group results, we interviewed 12 individual children in order to learn about the verbal strategies they used to solve these "simple" arithmetic word problems.

## CONSISTENCY AND ADEQUACY IN LANGUAGE INFORMATION IN MATHEMATICS WORD PROBLEMS

The general idea of *consistency* of language is that the order of information presentation is in keeping with the order that problem-solvers prefer and that inconsistency of language presents a conflict with the order or an inverse relationship (Verschaffel, 1994). As an example, consistent language problems are of the kind: "Paul has 5 books, Len has 2 more books than Paul. How many books does Len have?" The unknown variable (i.e., books that Len has) in relation to the second sentence is consistent with the expected operation of addition. An example of inconsistent language is: "John can run 5 km in one day. This is 3 km less than the distance that Pete can run in one day. How far can Pete run in one day?" Briars and Larkin (1984) and Verschaffel (1994) found that inconsistent language problems could be attributed more to the understanding of the problems than their solution and that comprehension errors are much more likely to occur when the order of the problem is incongruent with the schema the children have developed for the problems presented.

Word problems with too much or "not needed" (NN) information in terms of level of *adequacy* are of the kind: "What is the area of a rectangular park if one side is 60 meters and the other side is 20 meters, and there is a path one meter surrounding the park?" This more than adequate information may violate the logical structure schemata for some children (Low & Over, 1993). Conversely, Low and Over pointed out that some children experience difficulties with problems containing inadequate or "not enough" (NE) formation such as "What is the area of the rectangle if one side has 3 meters?" The above two examples are typically from 3-string structure so as to minimize the working memory component (Cooney & Swanson, 1990). An example of "just enough" (JE) information is: "Saskatoon is 440 km from Calgary. Dean's dad went to Calgary on a business trip and he returned to Saskatoon the next day. How far did he drive in all?"

# METHOD

## PARTICIPANTS, TASKS, AND PROCEDURE

The participants consisted of 32 Grade 3 students (15 boys and 17 girls) with a mean age of 108 months (SD 3.25 months); 32 Grade 4 students (18 boys and 14 girls) with a mean age of 120 months (SD 3.78 months); and 27 Grade 5 students (19 boys and 8 girls) with a mean age of 133 months and an SD of 4.66 months. These 91 children came from two "average" schools in a western Canadian city. They were first administered a series of "subsidiary" tasks in small groups: General Ability (*British Ability Scales* or *BAS Matrix D*, Elliott, Murray, & Pearson, 1978); Reading Comprehension (*Canadian Test of Basic Skills* or *CTBS Level 10*, King, 1982); Vocabulary (CTBS Level 10); Mathematics Concepts (e.g., "Which numeral is nearest in value to 9,000—8,998, 9,998, 8,008, or 9,119?") (CTBS Level 10); modified Reflection on Mathematics Learning with 20 items on a 5-point scale (e.g., "Math problems can be done correctly in only one way" (Schoenfeld, 1989); and Working Memory span in two parts with two, three, four, and five unrelated declarative sentences from Leong's (1999) adaptation of Swanson (1992). The general idea of administering these subsidiary tasks was to estimate or rule out the contribution of these nonmathematical tasks to the solution of simple arithmetic word problems. The means and standard deviations by grade for these subsidiary tasks are shown in table I.

Table I.  Means (M) and Standard Deviations (SD)
for the Subsidiary Tasks by Grade.

| Task | | Grade 3 | Grade 4 | Grade 5 | Total |
|---|---|---|---|---|---|
| BAS Matrix D | M | 105.50 | 101.72 | 108.11 | 104.95 |
| | SD | 10.24 | 11.30 | 14.43 | 12.13 |
| CTBS Reading | M | 31.16 | 31.69 | 37.70 | 33.29 |
| Comprehension | SD | 7.17 | 7.48 | 7.91 | 7.96 |
| CTBS Vocabulary | M | 22.63 | 29.13 | 30.30 | 27.19 |
| | SD | 6.48 | 5.23 | 4.79 | 6.49 |
| CTBS Mathematics | M | 16.34 | 22.19 | 23.96 | 20.66 |
| Concepts | SD | 4.25 | 5.35 | 3.37 | 5.48 |
| Reflection on | M | 69.63 | 64.72 | 66.70 | 67.03 |
| Mathematics | SD | 6.85 | 6.96 | 6.38 | 7.00 |
| Working Memory A | M | 20.38 | 21.13 | 23.70 | 21.63 |
| | SD | 5.63 | 5.34 | 6.05 | 5.77 |
| Working Memory B | M | 19.81 | 21.22 | 21.19 | 20.71 |
| | SD | 7.13 | 4.96 | 5.24 | 5.86 |
| Working Memory | M | 40.19 | 42.34 | 44.89 | 42.34 |
| Total | SD | 11.72 | 8.70 | 10.55 | 10.45 |
| *n* | | 32 | 32 | 27 | 91 |

The consistent/inconsistent language information task consisted of 12 consistent and 12 inconsistent word problems requiring the operations of addition, subtraction, multiplication, and
division. All the items were designed with real situations in mind
and were pretested with a small sample of children. Further examples of inconsistent items were: "Jason has half as much money
as Paul. If Jason has $20.00, how much money does Paul have?"
(multiplication problem), and "Anita has read 24 books. She has
read twice as many books as her friend Carla. How many books
has Carla read?" (division problem). All the items (see Appendix
A) were administered in small groups to the 91 children in a quiet
room in the schools. They were required to show their calcula-
tions in the space provided, and were given credit for correct representation of the problems, even though the actual calculation
may have been incorrect. The means and standard deviations of
the consistent and inconsistent language problems by ability subgroups and total for each of Grades 3, 4, and 5 are shown in table
II. The same information is shown graphically in figure 1.

The adequacy/inadequacy language information task consisted of 12 problems containing just enough (JE) information, 12 problems with insufficient or not enough (NE) information, and 12 problems with redundant or not needed (NN)

**Table II.  Means (M) and Standard Deviations (SD)
for the Consistency of Language Problems for Less Able,
More Able Subgroups and Total for Each of Grade 3, 4, and 5 Students.**

| Type of Language (12 Items Each) | | Grade 3 | | | Grade 4 | | | Grade 5 | | |
|---|---|---|---|---|---|---|---|---|---|---|
| | | Less Able (LA) and More Able (MA) Subgroups and Total Each Grade | | | | | | | | |
| | | LA | MA | Total | LA | MA | Total | LA | MA | Total |
| Inconsistent | M | 5.47 | 7.31 | 6.22 | 7.13 | 8.81 | 7.97 | 8.00 | 8.08 | 8.04 |
| | SD | 2.22 | 3.12 | 2.73 | 3.12 | 2.95 | 3.11 | 2.86 | 1.71 | 2.33 |
| Consistent | M | 8.79 | 9.23 | 8.97 | 9.69 | 10.25 | 9.97 | 10.21 | 10.38 | 10.30 |
| | SD | 1.87 | 2.49 | 2.12 | 1.49 | 1.57 | 1.53 | 2.86 | 1.26 | 2.20 |
| | *n* | 19 | 13 | 32 | 16 | 16 | 32 | 14 | 13 | 27 |

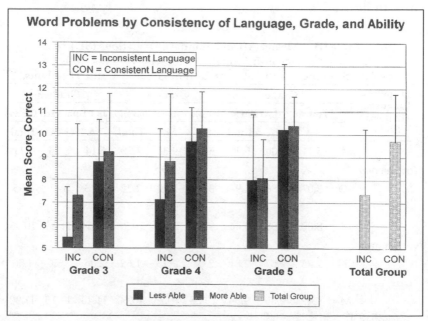

*Figure 1.    Means and standard deviations of performance on word
problems by consistency of language information, general
ability for Grade 3, 4, and 5 students.*

information, as explained earlier (see full list in Appendix B). Again, all the items were pretested and found to be of appropriate difficulty level. There were nine practice examples with discussion. Sets of three items containing each of the JE, NE, and NN types in random order were given at a time to small groups of about four children each with the aid of overhead illustrations for each item. The children were required to classify each problem as JE, NE, or NN, and to justify their answers where appropriate. Specifically, if the problem was classified as having not needed (NN) information, the children were asked to cross out the redundant sentence or phrase. If the problem was classified as containing not enough (NE) information, the children were asked to write down in a few words the needed information for the solution of the problem. If the problem had just enough (JE) information the children were asked to give the solution. This differential method of scoring the three types of language information items provided insight into the children's thinking. The means and standard deviations of this task by ability subgroups and the total for each of Grades 3, 4, and 5 are shown in table III. The same information is displayed graphically in figure 2.

**Table III.  Means (M) and Standard Deviations (SD)**
**for the Adequacy of Information Problems for Less Able,**
**More Able Subgroups and Total for Each of Grade 3, 4, and 5 Students.**

| Type of Language (12 Items Each) | | Grade 3 | | | Grade 4 | | | Grade 5 | | |
|---|---|---|---|---|---|---|---|---|---|---|
| | | Less Able (LA) and More Able (MA) Subgroups and Total Each Grade | | | | | | | | |
| | | LA | MA | Total | LA | MA | Total | LA | MA | Total |
| Not Needed | M | 5.11 | 6.00 | 5.47 | 6.19 | 9.38 | 7.78 | 6.14 | 8.15 | 7.11 |
| | SD | 3.07 | 2.86 | 2.97 | 3.33 | 2.22 | 3.22 | 4.28 | 3.41 | 3.95 |
| Not Enough | M | 8.00 | 9.08 | 8.44 | 9.81 | 10.75 | 10.28 | 10.64 | 11.31 | 10.96 |
| | SD | 2.75 | 2.87 | 2.81 | 2.04 | 1.13 | 1.69 | 2.06 | .63 | 1.56 |
| Just Enough | M | 9.47 | 9.69 | 9.56 | 10.25 | 10.75 | 10.50 | 11.43 | 11.15 | 11.30 |
| | SD | 1.98 | 2.75 | 2.29 | 1.73 | 1.24 | 1.50 | .85 | .69 | .78 |
| *n* | | 19 | 13 | 32 | 16 | 16 | 32 | 14 | 13 | 27 |

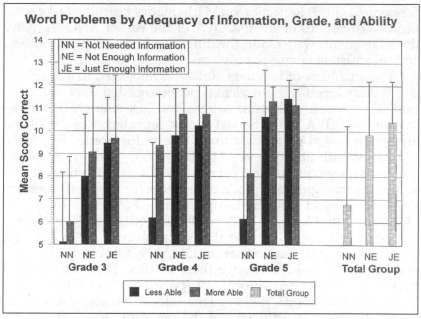

*Figure 2.    Means and standard deviations of performance on word problems by adequacy of language information, general ability for Grade 3, 4, and 5 students.*

## RESULTS

### GROUP ANALYSES

The scaled scores of the BAS Matrix task were used to divide the children in each grade into "more able" (MA) and "less able" (LA) ability subgroups. A 3 (grade) × 2 (ability) × 2 (problem type: consistent or inconsistent) ANOVA with the last factor repeated showed significant main effects for grade, $F(2, 85)$, = 4.32, MSE = 8.81, $p < .05$ and consistency of language facilitating more correct answers, $F(1, 85) = 96.49$, MSE = 2.44, $p < .001$. Further, the results showed significant grade differences for the consistent language problems, $F(2, 88) = 3.78$, $p < .05$. In pair-wise comparisons, the consistent language problems showed a significant difference between Grades 3 and 5, $t(88) = 2.59$, $p < .05$, and the inconsistent language problems showed significant difference between Grades 3 and 4, $t(88) = 2.53$, $p < .05$, and between Grades 3 and 5, $t(88) = 2.52$, $p < .05$.

The four variables of CTBS Vocabulary, CTBS Reading Comprehension., CTBS Mathematics Concepts, and modified

Schoenfeld (1989) Reflection on Mathematics Learning tasks were used as covariates in an ANCOVA of the earlier ANOVA. After the adjustments were made, the difference between the consistent and inconsistent language problems remained significant.

The adequacy of language data was subjected to a 3 (grade) $\times$ 2 (ability level) $\times$ 3 (problem type: not needed (NN) information, not enough (NE) information, and just enough (JE) information) ANOVA with the last factor repeated. Results of the analysis showed significant main effects for grade, $F(2, 85) = 10.02$, $p < .001$, ability level, $F(1, 85) = 7.35$, $p < .01$, and adequacy of information, $F(2, 170) = 84.33$, $p < .001$. Further, the results showed significant grade differences for the total scores on the Adequacy of Information problems, $F(2, 88) = 10.30$, $p < .001$, the JE problems, $F(2, 88) = 7.90$ $p < .001$, the NE problems $(F2, 88) = 11.49$, $p < .001$, and the NN problems, $F(2, 88) = 3.96$, $p < .05$. Similar to the first set of data, ANCOVA with the various covariates did not change these results. The ANOVA also revealed a significant problem type interaction with ability level, $F(2, 170) = 4.93$, $p < .05$. This interaction suggests that in some instances, the difficulty of the problem types varies with the abilities of the students.

We further reasoned that the adequacy/inadequacy of linguistic information should contribute to the variation in understanding mathematics concepts. Accordingly, we carried out a stepwise multiple regression analysis in which the CTBS Mathematics Concepts task was used as the criterion measure and the total consistency/inconsistency task, the total adequacy/inadequacy task, BAS Matrix, CTBS Vocabulary, Reading Comprehension, Reflection on Mathematics Learning and Working Memory tasks and chronological age were entered as predictor variables. As hypothesized, the adequacy/inadequacy linguistic information task was the most predictive of mathematics concept, with a multiple $R$ of .764, accounting for 58.3 percent of the variation. This was followed by chronological age with an additional 7.2 percent, consistency/inconsistency of language information with a further 5.8 percent, and BAS Matrix with yet another 1.4 percent. The total contribution of 73 percent of these variables seemed to buttress the claim of the utility of the level of adequacy of linguistic information in understanding and solving elementary mathematics problems.

## ANALYSES FROM INTERVIEWS

Following the suggestion of Ginsburg (1997) and Montague (1997), clinical interviews were conducted with 12 (6 more able and 6 less able) of the 91 children to gain some insight into their cognitive processes involved in solving the 24 consistent/inconsistent linguistic information word problems and the 36 elementary mathematics word problems varying in degrees of adequacy of linguistic information. Verschaffel's (1994) retelling technique was used which requires the student to construct the mental representation generated after reading the word problem and before choosing an arithmetic operation. Some excerpts of the interviews are shown in the following paragraphs.

In answer to the inconsistent addition problem of "Bill scored 15 baskets in the game on Saturday. This was 10 fewer baskets than he had scored on Wednesday. How many baskets did he score on Wednesday?" A less able Grade 5 student insisted that the word "fewer" meant subtraction and gave the answer of "5 baskets." On the other hand, a less able Grade 4 student was able to self-correct his error after some prompting as shown in this exchange to the problem: "The temperature in Saskatoon is 20 degrees. This is 6 degrees warmer than the temperature in Regina. What is the temperature in Regina?"

> Student: 20 plus 6 – that's 26
>
> Researcher: Why did you add?
>
> Student: Because it says that it is 6 degrees warmer than the temperature in Regina and . . . oh, just wait . . . mmm . . . maybe . . . 20 take away 6 and that's 14 (degrees).

While prompting from the interviewer would help, some students needed to understand the relationship between subsets within a larger set of quantities. In answer to the problem: "One half of the flowers in the garden were tulips. If there were 12 tulips in the garden, how many flowers were in the garden?" a less able Grade 4 student verbalized this way:

> Student: 12, I'm pretty sure.
>
> Researcher: 12 flowers in total?
>
> Student: Yeah. No, not 12, yeah.
>
> Researcher: So that means all of the flowers were tulips?
>
> Student: No. Half of them were tulips in the garden and the other half were flowers.
>
> (After further discussion, the student said "24 [flowers])."

Structured interviews with appropriate prompts with the students showed their progressive level of sophistication even though they might arrive at a correct answer. For the inconsistent language division problems such as: "Julie can run three times farther now than when she first started running. If she can run 9 km now, how far could she run when she first started running?" some students arrived at the answer by adding 3 + 3 + 3 instead of dividing 9 by 3. Similar answers were given by a more able Grade 5 student and a less able Grade 4 student as shown below. At some point in the interview, they realized the need to revise their mental representation.

Student: I'd probably say 9 take away 3 or something like that. . . . It's hard.

Researcher: What does 3 times farther mean? What arithmetic operation (step) is needed?

Student: Multiplication.

Researcher: Do you want to multiply 9 by 3?

Student: Ummm . . . No.

Researcher: Why not?

Student: 'Cause that's more than she's running right now and she has to find less.

(After some more discussion, the student said "divide" and came to the answer of "3" [km]).

There were similar patterns of responses from the interviews on the adequacy of language information items. In some cases, students might classify correctly the levels of adequacy of language information but gave the wrong verbal answers. In more extreme cases, less able students had difficulties in understanding the information and operating on it. This is shown by a less able Grade 3 student in answer to this adequacy/inadequacy language information word problem: "Jean ate 10 marshmallows for a contest. Fred ate 4 times as many marshallows as Jean. How many marshmallows did they eat altogether?"

Student: It'd be 10 − 10 . . . umm . . . 10 plus 4 . . .

Researcher: But did Fred eat 4 marshmallows?

Student: Mmm . . .

Researcher: He ate . . .

Student: 4 times as many marshmallows as Jean. That's 8.

The interviews showed that the "not enough" word problems were sources of difficulty for both classifying the level of adequacy of information and the computation based on incorrect premises. In answer to the NE word problem of: "There were 14 children swinging in the playground. Some children jumped off to go to the slide. Soon 6 more children came to swing. How many children are now swinging?" Those who classified the problem as containing enough information invariably gave 14 + 6 or 20 (children) as the answer. For the "not needed" kinds of problems, many students classified them as having just enough information but some needed help in arriving at the classifying and the correct answers. The following was the excerpt of the interview with a less able Grade 5 student in answer to the problem: "Heather sold 5 of her 10-cent comic books. Before she sold them, she had 43 comic books. How much did Heather make when she sold her 5 comic books?"

Student: JE (just enough information).

Researcher: What about the second sentence? Would you still say JE?

Student: Yeah.

Researcher: Did you use that second sentence?

Student: Ymm . . . oh . . . NN. You wouldn't need that. Before she sold them she had 43 comic books.

## DISCUSSION

The group analyses and the interview data are discussed in the context of the literature on early mathematics learning and mathematics disabilities. It is recognized that the present study was limited to the understanding of elementary mathematics word problems with a rather circumscribed focus on the consistent/inconsistent and adequate/inadequate language information and that early mathematics learning is both complex and many-faceted. However, the emphasis on "mathematics thinking" is in keeping with notions put forward by Ginsburg (1977), Geary (1993, 1996), and Goldman and her colleagues at the Cognition and Technology Group at Vanderbilt (CTGV) (Goldman et al., 1997).

On both kinds of language information tasks there was the expected grade differences in performance. It would appear that Grade 3 seems to be the sensitive stage where children learn more complex mathematical problems and have to bring their declarative, procedural, and conceptual knowledge to bear on the solution of these problems. The significant difference between the more able and less able students on the basis of the BAS Matrix task for only the adequacy of language information task may be explained by the more complex and varied demand of this task placed on the students. The considerably larger standard deviation in relation to the mean for the inconsistent than the consistent items may be due to the children's difficulty in grasping the inverse relationship between language and mathematics reasoning. Similarly, there are larger individual differences for the "not needed" items in terms of adequacy of language information as compared with the "not enough" and the "just enough" items. It seems some children have not picked up certain principles about logical relationship and the needed information to arrive at solutions of problems.

The interview data complement those from the group analyses. The excerpts of exchanges show that problem-solvers will do well to follow the suggestions of Montague (1997) and NCTE (1989) in taking broader views rather than narrowly focusing on computation. Montague (1997) suggests that the interrelated steps of read, translate, transform (e.g., using diagrams and visuals), estimate, compute, and verify should serve all students well. This step-by-step approach is particularly useful to those with disabilities as they can see how one step feeds into another. Moreover, students should be encouraged to discuss in class the nature of a problem and to justify their procedures in arriving at a solution (Thornton et al., 1997). They need to separate relevant from irrelevant information and to use multiple ways to represent and communicate mathematics information (Goldman et al., 1997). Goldman et al. also point out that when both declarative and procedural knowledge is in place, students with disabilities often fail to apply their knowledge in meaningful ways. These researchers have further shown how the use of multimedia technology can provide both concrete and meaningful contexts for problem solution. In a recent paper, Bransford and his colleagues at CTGV discuss their current thinking about designing learning environments that invite and sustain mathematical thinking in middle school years (Bransford, Zech, Schwartz, Barron, Vye, & the Cognition and Technology Group at Vanderbilt [CTGV], 2000). These learning environments are organized around a series of videodiscs and CD-ROM-based adventures known as Jasper Woodbury Problem Solving Series. The aim is to help students focus on mathematical modeling as a way to think visually as well as symbolically, and to create solutions.

Ginsburg (1997) and Nunes and Bryant (1996) further remind us that a developmental perspective is needed to understand early mathematics learning and that informal learning of "street mathematics" should complement "school mathematics."

In the context of disabilities and dyslexia research, Badian (1999) has raised several important issues in her fairly comprehensive follow-up study of "persistent low school achievers" from about 1,000 children in each of Grades 1 to 8. She emphasizes the need to study those children with a disability only in reading or in arithmetic only, and those with disabilities in both subject areas. It has been estimated that there are as many children with mathematics disabilities as there are those with reading disabilities and that both disabilities co-occur in many children (Ackerman & Dykman, 1995).

Defining children with mathematics disabilities (MD) as those with low mathematics achievement test scores combined with low-average IQ, Geary, Hoard, and Hamson (1999) studied 90 first graders classified as those with MD, those with reading disabilities (RD), those with MD and RD, and "normal" children on their counting, number and arithmetic skills, and some of the cognitive and neuropsychological systems. Their general finding was that the children at risk for MD suffered from difficulties in retrieving basic number facts and mathematics information from long-term memory, and they used improper or immature problem-solving procedures. In a subsequent longitudinal study of 84 children consisting of similarly constituted groups plus a "variable" group, Geary, Hamson, and Hoard (2000) confirmed their earlier findings. Those children with MD/RD committed more retrieval errors than did the other four groups. This finding was thought to relate to the inefficient inhibition of irrelevant information. There was also a developmental trend in that the retrieval deficits are more persistent. These various studies raise the need for more in-depth studies in the diagnosis, remediation, and prevention of arithmetic disabilities. The problem-based approach to learning early mathematics and the need to help those children with difficulties are the challenges in research, pedagogy, and clinical practice.

## ACKNOWLEDGMENT

We thank the students, teachers, and parents in the two schools in Saskatoon, Canada, for their cooperation in this study. We also thank the two anonymous reviewers and the editor for their insightful comments. Any shortcomings are necessarily our own.

Address correspondence to Dr. Che Kan Leong, Department of Educational Psychology & Special Education, University of Saskatchewan, Saskatoon, Sask., Canada. S7N 0X1, Telephone: (306) 966-5257, FAX: (306) 966-7719, e-mail: leong@sask.usask.ca

## References

Ackerman, P. T., & Dykman, R. A. (1995). Reading-disabled students with and without comorbid arithmetic disability. *Developmental Neuropsychology, 11*, 351–371.

Badian, N. A. (1999). Persistent arithmetic, reading, or arithmetic and reading disability. *Annals of Dyslexia, 49*, 45–70.

Bransford, J., Zech, L., Schwartz, D., Barron, B., Vye, N., & the Cognition and Technology Group at Vanderbilt (CTGV). (2000). Designs for environments that invite and sustain mathematical thinking. In P. Cobb, E. Yackel, & K. McClain (eds.), *Symbolizing and communicating in mathematics classrooms: Perspectives on discourse, tools, and instructional design* (pp. 275–324). Mahwah, NJ: Lawrence Erlbaum Associates.

Briars, D. J., & Larkin, J. H. (1984). An integrated model of skill in solving elementary word problems. *Cognition and Instruction, 1*, 245–296.

Cooney, J. B., & Swanson, H. L. (1990). Individual differences in memory for mathematical story problems: Memory span and problem perception. *Journal of Educational Psychology, 82*, 570–577.

Elliott, C. D., Murray, D. J., & Pearson, L. S. (1978). *British ability scales: Manual 3; Directions for administration and scoring/Manual 4: Tables of abilities and norms.* Windsor, Berks: National Foundation for Educational Research.

Geary, D. C. (1993). Mathematical disabilities: Cognitive, neuropsychological, and genetic components. *Psychological Bulletin, 114*, 345–362.

Geary, D. C. (1996). *Children's mathematical development: Research and practical applications.* Washington, DC: American Psychological Association.

Geary, D. C., Hamson, C. O., & Hoard, M. K. (2000). Numerical and arithmetic cognition: A longitudinal study of process and concept deficits in children with learning disability. *Journal of Experimental Child Psychology, 77*, 236–263.

Geary, D. C., Hoard, M. K., & Hamson, C. O. (1999). Numerical and arithmetic cognition: Patterns of functions and deficits in children at risk for a mathematical disability. *Journal of Experimental Child Psychology, 74*, 213–239.

Ginsburg, H. P. (1977). *Children's arithmetic: The learning process.* New York: D. van Nostrand.

Ginsburg, H. P. (1997). Mathematics learning disabilities: A view from developmental psychology. *Journal of Learning Disabilities, 30*, 20–33.

Goldman, S. R., Hasselbring, T. S., & the Cognition and Technology Group at Vanderbilt (1997). Achieving meaningful mathematics literacy for students with learning disabilities. *Journal of Learning Disabilities, 30*, 198–208.

King, E. M. (Ed.). (1982). *Canadian tests of basic skills: Multilevel edition: Levels 9-12/Forms 5 & 6.* Toronto: Nelson.

Leong, C. K. (1999). Phonological coding and children's spelling. *Annals of Dyslexia, 49*, 195–220.

Low, R., & Over, R. (1993). Gender differences in solution of algebraic word problems containing irrelevant information. *Journal of Educational Psychology, 85*, 331–339.

McCloskey, M. (1992). Cognitive mechanisms in numerical processing: Evidence from acquired dyscalculia. *Cognition, 44*, 107–157.

Miles, T. R., & Miles, E. (Eds.). (1992). *Dyslexia and mathematics*. London: Routledge.

Montague, M. (1997). Cognitive strategy instruction in mathematics for students with learning disabilities. *Journal of Learning Disabilities, 30,* 164–177.

National Council of Teachers of Mathematics (1989). *Curriculum and evaluation standards for school mathematics.* Reston, VA: Author.

Nunes, T., & Bryant, P. (1996). *Children doing mathematics.* Oxford, UK: Blackwell.

Rivera, D. P. (Ed.). (1997). Mathematics education and students with learning disabilities: Introduction in the special series (Special series Part I & II). *Journal of Learning Disabilities, 30 (1 & 2).*

Schoenfeld, A. H. (1985). *Mathematical problem solving.* New York: Academic Press.

Schoenfeld, A. H. (1989). Explorations of students' mathematical beliefs and bahavior, *Journal for Research in Mathematics Education, 20,* 338–355.

Swanson, H. L. (1992). Generality and modifiability of working memory among skilled and less skilled readers. *Journal of Educational Psychology, 84,* 473–488.

Thornton, C. A., Langrall, C. W., & Jones, G. A. (1997). Mathematics instruction for elementary students with learning disabilities. *Journal of Learning Disabilities, 30,* 142–150.

Verschaffel, L. (1994). Using retelling data to study elementary school children's representations and solutions of compare problems. *Journal for Research in Mathematics Education, 25,* 141–165.

# APPENDIX A

## CONSISTENT LANGUAGE ADDITION PROBLEMS

1. Andy has $25.00. Beth has $12.00 more than Andy. How much money does Beth have?
2. Carl weighs 8 pounds more than Tim. If Tim weighs 78 pounds, how much does Carl weigh?
3. The cost of a skateboard increased by $2.00. If the original cost of the skateboard was $25.00, how much does the skateboard cost now?

## CONSISTENT LANGUAGE SUBTRACTION PROBLEMS

1. The tempersture decreased by 12 degrees overnight. If the temperature wss 25 degrees last night, what was the temperature in the moming?
2. Sarah has 23 compact discs in her collection of music. Joe has 3 fewer compact discs than Sarah. How many compact discs does Joe have?
3. Sharon is studying for exams, so she watches 5 hours less television per week than she used to. If she used to watch 16 hours of television per week, how many hours per week does she watch now?

## CONSISTENT LANGUAGE MULTIPLICATION PROBLEMS

1. Yellowknife, N.W.T. gets 4 times as many hours of daylight in the summer than in the winter. If Yellowknife gets 5 hours of daylight in the winter, how many hours of daylight does it get in the summer?
2. Last year, Debbie hit 12 home runs. This year, she hopes to hit twice as many home runs as she did last year. How many home runs does she hope to hit this year?
3. We spent $50.00 on groceries this week. Last week, we spent twice as much on groceries as we did this week. How much money did we spend on groceries last week?

## CONSISTENT LANGUAGE DIVISION PROBLEMS

1. Tom told his dad that he would cut half of the grass. If the area of the grass is 20 square meters, how much grass does Tom have to cut?
2. One half of the monkeys in the cage were swinging by their tails. If there were 8 monkeys in the cage, how many monkeys were swinging by their tails?
3. There are 10 children at the swimming pool. If one half of these children are taking swimming lessons, how many children are taking swimming lessons?

## INCONSISTENT LANGUAGE ADDITION PROBLEMS

1. Billy scored 15 baskets in the game on Saturday. This was 10 fewer baskets than he had scored on Wednesday. How many baskets did he score on Wednesday?
2. While training for a race, Sue ran 15 km each day. Sue ran 5 km less each day than Fay ran How far did Fay run each day?
3. Bill weighs 92 pounds. This is 4 pounds less than he weighed last month. How much did Bill weigh last month?

## INCONSISTENT LANGUAGE SUBTRACTION PROBLEMS

1. If Mark had $2.00 more he would have $10.00. How much does Mark have now?
2. Paul wants to buy a toy for $12.00. He only has $4.00. How much more money does he need?
3. The temperature in Saskatoon is 20 degrees. This is 6 degrees warmer than the temperature in Regina. What is the temperature in Regina?

## INCONSISTENT LANGUAGE MULTIPLICATION PROBLEMS

1. Jason has half as much money as Paul. If Jason has $20.00, how much money does Paul have?
2. One half of the flowers in the garden were tulips. If there were 12 tulips in the garden, how many flowers were in the garden?
3. There are 20 children at the swimming pool. If this is one half of the number of children who are at the roller skating rink how many children are at the roller skating rink?

## INCONSISTENT LANGUAGE DIVISION PROBLEMS

1. Julie can run three times farther now than when she first started running. If she can run 9 km now, how far could she run when she first started running?
2. Anita has read 24 books. She has read twice as many books as her friend Carla How many books has Carla read?
3. Melissa delivered twice as many flyers on Saturday than she did on Friday. If she delivered 40 flyers on Saturday, how many did she deliver on Friday?

# APPENDIX B

## JUST ENOUGH INFORMATION PROBLEMS

1 . There were 2 puppies in each basket. There were 3 baskets. If each puppy had 5 spots, how many spots were there in all?
2. There were 16 balls on the playground Five of the balls were basketballs and 4 were softballs. All of the other balls were kickballs. How many kickballs were there?
3. Nicole makes 8 cents on esch school newspaper she sells. She has sold 4 newspapers so far. How much more money does she need to earn to buy a pen that costs $1.00?
4. Carl bought a small box of popcorn for 90 cents and a small drink for 70 cents. He paid with 2 loonies. How much change did Carl get?
5. Jean ate 10 marshmallows for a contest. Fred ate 4 times as many marshmallows as Jesn. How many marshmallows did they eat altogether?
6. Saskatoon is 440 km from Calgary. Dean's dad went to Calgary on a business trip and he returned to Saskatoon the next day. How far did he drive in all?
7. A building has 6 stories, each of the same height. It takes 10 seconds for the elevator to get from the first floor to the third floor. How many seconds does it take for the elevator to get from the first floor to the sixth floor?

8. Grace, Lee, and Patty went to the beach. Each of them collected 27 seashells. How many seashells did they collect in all?
9. Jean earns 3 cents for each flyer that she delivers. If she delivers 40 flyers a night for 5 nights, how much money does she earn?
10. Pogs were on sale for 5 cents each. How much did one dozen pogs cost?
11. The theatre can seat 292 people. One day, 197 children and 88 adults came to see the show. How many theatre seats were empty?
12. Marcy made 13 cups of coffee. She drank 2 cups herself, Joy drank 4 cups, and Sheila drank 3 cups. How many cups of coffee were left?

## NOT ENOUGH INFORMATION PROBLEMS

1. There were 14 children swinging in the playground. Some children jumped off to go to the slide. Soon 6 more children came to swing. How many children sre now swinging?
2. Lou bought a sandwich for 50 cents and a lemon drink for 25 cents. How much change did she get back?
3. An office building has 3 large elevators. Each elevator can hold the same number of people. One morning all 3 elevators were filled to the limit. How many people were on the 3 elevators altogether?
4. Tom's classroom has 5 rows of desks. There are 24 children in class today. How many seats are empty?
5. Jason had $15.00. He bought a present for his mother. He earned $9.00 washing cars. How much money does he have now?
6. Mom, Dad, and the twins went to a movie. For each adult, it costs $4.75 and for each child, it costs $2.75. They each bought a box of popcorn How much did the family spend altogether?
7. One Saturday, Lori cleaned her room for 25 minutes. Then she worked in the garden for 45 minutes. What time did she finish her work?
8. Carol earns $2.00 more on Saturdays than on weekdays. Last month she worked 10 weekdays and 3 Saturdays. How much money did she eam?
9. The students at the school are having a picnic at Pike Lake. There will be 300 students and 10 teachers going to

the picnic. How many buses will be needed to take the students and the teachers to Pike Lake?

10. Linda expects 40 people for a barbecue. She wants to have enough hamburger meat so that each person will have 2 hamburgers. How many grams of hamburger meat should she buy?

11. Russell skated laps for a skate-a-thon. He collected 5 cents a lap from his brother and 10 cents a lap from his father. How much money did Russell collect in all?

12. When Chris takes a bath, he uses about 150 liters of water. When he takes a shower, he uses about 8 liters of water per minute. How much water does Chris save when he takes a shower instead of a bath?

## NOT NEEDED INFORMATION PROBLEMS

1. Jill spent $6.89 to buy weiners and $2.25 to buy buns. She also spent $4.10 to buy juice. How much did it cost Jill to make hotdogs?

2. There are 3 posters. Each poster has 6 flags on it and each flag has 2 stars on it. How many stars are on one poster?

3. Heather sold 5 of her 10 cent comic books. Before she sold them she had 43 comic books. How much did Heather make when she sold her 5 comic books?

4. A bookshelf has 6 shelves. Each shelf holds 15 books. Each shelf is 40 cm high. How tall is the bookshelf7

5. At Funland, there are 4 rides that cost 20 cents each. Each ride lasts 5 minutes. How much does it cost to ride all the rides one time?

6. Bob wanted to collect 100 bottles. He filled 5 cases with 6 bottles each. How many bottles has Bob already collected?

7. Sue is on page 142 of her library book. Her book is 260 pages long. She has to read 25 more pages before bedtime. What page will she be on when she goes to bed?

8. Steve bought a go-kart ticket for $1.75. He was able to go around the track 3 times for one ticket. Then he bought another go-kart ticket. How much money did Steve spend?

9. Jill took her brother and her sister to a matinee show. Tickets were $2.50 for the matinee show. Tickets were $4.00 for the evening show. How much did Jill pay the cashier?

10. A regular jet can carry 210 people. A jumbo jet can carry 515 people. How many people can 3 regular jets carry?

11. The Parkview Tollway charges 50 cents for a car, 75 cents for a bus, and $1.00 for a truck. If 10 cars and 5 buses get on the tollway, how much money is collected?

12. Jason bought a baseball for $5.99 and a baseball glove for $29.99. He paid for the items with a $50.00 bill. How much did Jason pay for the ball and the glove?

# The Mathematical Abilities
# of Dyslexic 10-Year-Olds

*T. R. Miles*

School of Psychology, University of Wales,
Bangor, United Kingdom


*M. N. Haslum*

Department of Psychology, University of the West of England
Bristol, United Kingdom


*T. J. Wheeler*

Chester College of Higher Education
Chester, United Kingdom

*Seventy-two items testing various aspects of mathematics were given to 12,131 ten-year-old children. Criteria for specific developmental dyslexia (SDD) and for other groupings are specified. Despite the absence of differences in intelligence level, the mean score on the mathematics test for the dyslexics was not only lower than that of the normal achievers but lower also than that of underachievers believed not to be dyslexic.*

*On some of the 72 items, there was little difference in percentage pass rate between the groups; on others, however, there were wide differences. On the basis of ratings carried out "blind" by a panel of experienced teachers of dyslexic children, and in the light of other considerations, some tentative suggestions are put forward as to what*

Annals of Dyslexia, Vol. 51, 2001
ISSN 0736-9387

*it is about certain mathematical items that makes them relatively hard or easy for children with dyslexia.*

## INTRODUCTION

In this paper, the word "dyslexia" should be understood to mean "specific developmental dyslexia," an identifiable syndrome earlier described by Hinshelwood (1917) as "word-blindness" and by Orton (1937/1989) as "strephosymbolia" (although the theoretical implications of both these expressions now need to be discounted). Evidence supporting the idea of dyslexia as a syndrome also will be found in many more recent writers including Critchley (1970, 1981), Naidoo (1972), Thomson (1991), Miles (1993), Nicolson and Fawcett (1995), Frith (1997), and Galaburda (1999). This definition of dyslexia is important since there are still those who equate the term simply with "reading disability," and this has led to confusion.

The recognition that dyslexic children, in this sense, have difficulties in mathematics goes back at least as far as Hermann (1959) and Ansara (1973). Research that systematically compares dyslexic and nondyslexic children on mathematical tasks has been reported by Joffe (1981), Steeves (1983), Miles (1993), Turner Ellis, Miles, and Wheeler (1996), and Leong and Jerred (2001). The balance of evidence suggests, not that some dyslexics are weak at mathematics in general and others not, but that all of them are weak at certain aspects of mathematics. Miles (1993) found that in a sample of 80 dyslexics aged nine to twelve, 96 percent were unable to recite the 6×, 7×, and 8× tables without stumbling. A review of the evidence on dyslexia and mathematics up to the early 1990s will be found in Miles (1992). The neurological bases of mathematical reasoning are outside the scope of this paper, but interested readers should consult Butterworth (1999).

The present paper reports on the results of a mathematics test given to 12,131 ten-year-olds. We asked the following four questions:

1. Are dyslexic ten-year-olds weaker in general at mathematics than suitably matched controls?

2. Do they differ in this respect from others with literacy problems who are not typically dyslexic?

3.  If they perform worse than these others, does this mean that they are weaker "across the board"; that is, weaker at all aspects of mathematics, or only at some?

4.  If there are items that dyslexics tend to find extra difficult, how can these difficulties best be explained?

# PARTICIPANTS AND METHOD

## THE BRITISH BIRTHS COHORT STUDY

The participants were drawn from all those children born in England, Wales, and Scotland between April 5 and 11, 1970. They had been examined at birth and again in 1975 when they were age five. The present data were obtained as part of a follow-up study in 1980 when they were age 10. Further details of the study will be found in Miles, Haslum, and Wheeler (1998). At this stage, in addition to undergoing a medical examination, they were given a variety of educational tests. Those that are relevant to the present paper will be described: 12,905 children were studied at this stage.

## MEASURES

The children were given a test of single-word recognition, a reading comprehension test (the *Edinburgh Reading Test*, 1985), a spelling test, two tests of intelligence (the Similarities and Matrices tests from the *British Ability Scales*) (Elliott, Murray, & Pearson, 1979, 1983), and four so-called "supplementary" tests aimed at picking out dyslexics in the sense of those with specific developmental dyslexia (SDD). In the Similarities test, the children were presented with three words (horse, cow, and sheep); they then had to say how the three were alike and give a fourth example of the same kind. In the Matrices test, they were required to identify the correct pattern (from a choice of nine) that correctly filled a given space. The four supplementary tests comprised the Recall of Digits item from the British Ability Scales (Elliott, Murray, & Pearson, 1979, 1983) and three items later published as part of the *Bangor Dyslexia Test* (Miles, 1982, 1997), viz. Left-Right, Months Forward, and Months Reversed. More information on these three tests will be found in the Appendices to Miles, Haslum, and Wheeler (1998), and this paper also gives reasons as to why these particular test items were chosen.

## GROUP CRITERIA

Scores on the word recognition and spelling tests were standardized so as to give a mean of 100 and a standard deviation of 15; they were not normalized. The Similarities and Matrices results were combined so as to provide a single score, taken to be a measure of intelligence; this, too, was standardized in the same way.

Full details as to how the groups were selected will be found in Miles, Haslum, and Wheeler (1998). In brief, where there was no mismatch between their word recognition score or their spelling score and their intelligence as judged by their combined score on the Similarities and Matrices tests, the children were described as "normal achievers" ($N = 6338$, 49.11%). Where there was a slight mismatch (1 to 1.5 standard deviations below prediction), the children were described as "moderate underachievers" ($N = 1703$, 24.20%), and if there was a large mismatch (more than 1.5 standard deviations below prediction), they were described as "severe underachievers" ($N = 907$, 7.04%). Those whose scaled score was below 90 on the Similarities and Matrices tests were treated as a separate group called "low ability children" ($N = 3200$, 24.80%); this was done on the grounds that factors connected not with dyslexia as such but with low all-round ability might be distorting our results. There were 757 children (5.87%) who, because of insufficient data, could not be assigned to any of the groups (see the footnote to table II).

The intention in the case of the supplementary items was to specify operations for picking out from the full total of 907 severe underachievers those showing typical signs of dyslexia in the SDD sense. The responses to each question or set of questions were scored as "plus" (dyslexia positive), "zero" (marginal), or "minus" (dyslexia negative). Those severe underachievers with two or more "pluses" or three or more "zeros" were classed as "underachievers A" ($N = 269$, 2.08%); those with two "zeros" or one "plus" and one "zero" were classed as "underachievers B" ($N = 221$, 1.71%), and those with no more than one "plus" or one "zero" as "underachievers C" ($N = 417$, 3.23%). On the basis of only four items it is not possible to claim that dyslexia was assured in the case of all of those children in the underachievers A group or that it was firmly excluded in the case of all those assigned to the underachievers C group. We claim only that the underachievers A group contained a larger proportion of typically dyslexic (SDD) children than did underachievers C, with underachievers B occupying an intermediate position. For convenience, we shall refer in what follows to underachievers A as the "dyslexics," to underachievers B as the "buffer" group (since they occupied an intermediate position, not classifiable with assurance either as dyslexic or as nondyslexic), and to underachievers C as the "nondyslexic underachievers." The qualification that the underachievers A group contained *mostly* dyslexics and the underachievers C group *mostly* nondyslexics should always be borne in mind.

## THE MATHEMATICS TEST

As part of the British Births Cohort Study, a test was devised to assess knowledge, concepts, and applications in all aspects of mathematics taught in primary schools in Britain in 1980. The survey team sought help in the construction of a suitably wide-ranging test from two specialists, Colin Appleton and John Kerley, who were working with a London inner city mathematics program designed to interest less able children in mathematics. It was suggested that the items should be highly pictorial with an emphasis on cartoon presentation. They sampled a wide range of skills and included items on number, time, length, area, volume, capacity, temperature, mass, money, shape, angles, coordinates, statistical tables, and graphs.

More than 200 items were created, split into two parallel tests, and piloted on 400 ten-year-old children. Item analysis was undertaken, with considerable effort made to maintain a variety of items within each major area of assessment.

The final version of the test was presented to the children in the main survey as the "Friendly Maths Test" and it will be referred to in what follows as the FMT. Although the FMT was not originally designed for researching into dyslexia, we decided that the wide range of the items in it made it a valuable tool for answering a variety of questions about the mathematical strengths and weaknesses of 10-year-old dyslexics. We know of no other study of mathematics and dyslexia that has been carried out on this scale.

There were 72 items in all. A small-scale reproduction is shown in figure 1. The original test form contained three items to one A4 page (21 cm. by 29.7 cm.).

It will be seen from this figure that the items were in multiple-choice format, five boxes being provided for each item. The children were instructed to put a line through the box outside which was the correct answer. This meant that for

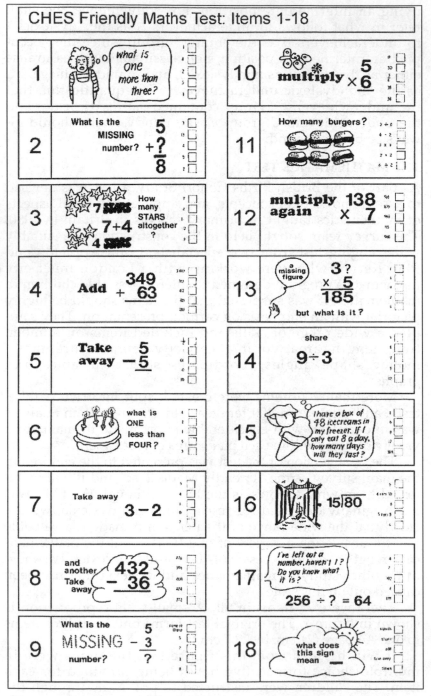

*Figure 1.    Items of the Friendly Mathematics Test.*

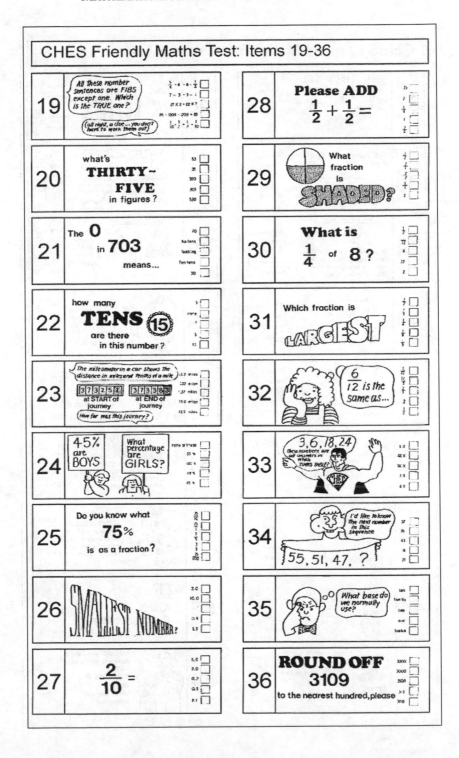

# CHES Friendly Maths Test: Items 37-54

**37** "What's the time, please mister?"
- 6 o'clock
- between 1 and 2
- 12 o'clock
- 3 past 6
- 5 past 12

**38** Your train is due at 10.52. It is now 9.05. How long do you have to wait?
- 47 mins
- 1 hr 47 mins
- 1 hr 37 mins
- 57 mins
- 1 hr 2 mins

**39** If you left on the 9.50 train from King's Cross, how long would it take you to reach BRADFORD EXCHANGE?
- 2 hrs 20 mins
- 17 hrs 10 mins
- none of these
- 2 hrs 50 mins
- 3 hrs 10 mins

**40** Which line is shortest?
- a
- b
- c
- d
- e

**41** Estimate the HEIGHT of your CLASSROOM DOOR.
- 2 centimetres
- 2 millimetres
- 2 kilometres
- 2 hectometres
- 2 metres

**42** please tell me please, which is a unit of AREA please!
- kilometre
- cubic metre
- metre
- square metre
- millimetre

**43** What's the AREA of this RECTANGLE? 4cm 3cm
- 4 cm²
- 12 cm²
- 7 cm²
- 14 cm²
- 3 cm²

**44** What UNITS do we use to measure the CAPACITY of the bottle? Cola
- kilograms
- milligrams
- litres
- grams
- metres

**45** How many of these CENTICUBES would fit into this box? MINE
- 8
- 2
- 4
- 6
- 12

**46** UNIT OF VOLUME
- kilometre
- square metre
- metre
- cubic metre
- millimetre

**47** BUTTER costs £1 per kilogram. How much is this pack? 250g
- 50p
- £2.50p
- £5
- £4
- £?

**48** How heavy are the apples?
- 200 kg
- 2 kg
- 1 kg
- 20 kg
- 2000 kg

**49** The bird bath has FROZEN. How cold is it?
- 100°C
- -5°C
- 10°C
- 28°C
- 5°C

**50** 10p CONES! You have these coins: ② ② ② ② 2 5 ⑤ ⑤ 2① © ⑤ Which others do you need to buy a cone?

**51** PEDISWLAND £1.00 = $2.31. If ONE POUND is worth 2.31 DOLLARS, how many DOLLARS would you get for £3?
- $64.10
- $ 0.49
- $ 0.65
- $ 0.77
- $ 6.93

**52** What is the least number of coins you could use to make 38p?
- 7
- 4
- 6
- 38
- 1

**53** IF A = 3, B = 4, C = 5 what is A+B+C?
- ABC
- 12
- none of these
- 345
- 60

**54** AMANDA ate TWICE as many lollies as WAYNE. If they ate 6 altogether, how many did WAYNE eat?
- 3
- 1
- 2
- 5
- 4

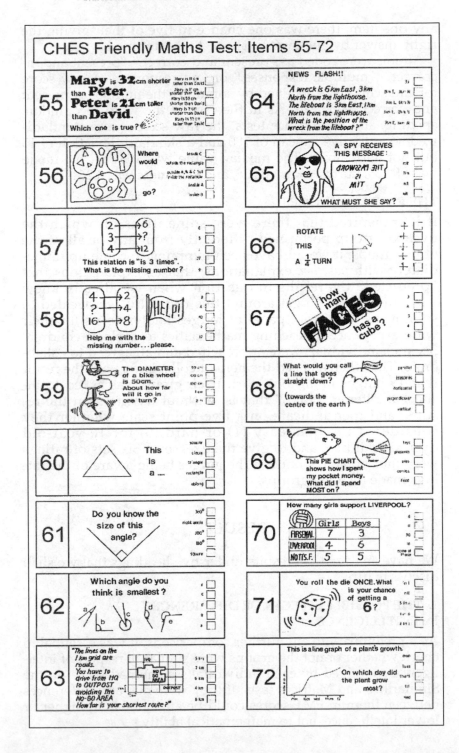

# CHES Friendly Maths Test: Items 55-72

any one item, there was one chance in five of their giving the right answer by guesswork. The test was untimed.

Items were coded as "present and correct," "present and incorrect," "multiple responses," or "no response." A raw score for each child was obtained by summing the number of present and correct responses. As in the case of the word recognition, spelling, and intelligence tests, the raw scores were standardized so as to give a mean of 100 and a standard deviation of 15 but not normalized. The median value was 100.357, the mode was 99.135, kurtosis was –0.228, and skewness was 0.261.

## THE PANEL OF JUDGES

If it transpired that there were some items on which the dyslexic group performed differently from any or all of the other groups, it would have been tempting to come up immediately with *post hoc* explanations; that is, explanations that "predicted" the results in question when we already knew what they were. To get around this difficulty, we decided to submit the items to a panel of judges known to us for their wide experience in teaching mathematics to dyslexic children. Six such individuals were approached and all agreed to collaborate. They then enlisted the help of colleagues, with the result that 19 judges in all took part. Each group was asked to inspect the items "blind," that is, without having seen the results, and then indicate on a five-point scale whether they considered the item easy (1) or hard (5) for 10-year-old dyslexic children, and to give their reasons. Six sets of ratings were thus obtained, none of the judges being aware of the ratings made by other groups.

# RESULTS

We have analyzed the results under five headings that we shall discuss in turn.

## 1. THE POSSIBLE EFFECTS OF DIFFERENCES IN INTELLIGENCE

As a preliminary to any further comparisons, it was essential to check whether or not the groups were similar in respect of intelligence as judged by each individual's combined score on the Similarities and Matrices tests. If they were not, any differences between them in FMT scores could be attributable to higher or lower intelligence, not to mathematical ability *per se*.

Table I gives the mean scores (Similarities and Matrices combined) for the six groups into which the cohort was divided, along with the standard deviations and standard errors.

**Table I.   Combined Scores (scaled) on Similarities and Matrices Broken Down by Group.**

| Group | N | Mean | Standard Deviation | Standard Error |
|---|---|---|---|---|
| Normal achievers | 6,338 | 106.51 | 10.14 | 0.127 |
| Moderate underachievers | 1,703 | 107.79 | 10.58 | 0.256 |
| Underachievers A | 269 | 106.18 | 10.44 | 0.476 |
| Underachievers B | 221 | 106.24 | 10.35 | 0.0.696 |
| Underachievers C | 417 | 107.97 | 9.70 | 0.637 |
| Low ability children | 3,200 | 80.48 | 8.01 | 0.142 |
| Unclassifiable | 757 | | | |
| TOTAL | 12,905 | | | |

Analysis of variance revealed absence of homogeneity in the data, $F(5, 12,142) = 3485.73$, $p < 0.001$. Post hoc tests (Tamhane) showed (not surprisingly, since this was an artefact of our selection procedure) that the mean score of the low ability children was significantly lower than that of all the other groups ($p < 0.001$). The mean score of the normal achievers was significantly lower than that of the moderate underachievers (106.51 compared to 107.79, $p < 0.001$) and significantly lower than that of the nondyslexic underachievers (106.51 in comparison with 107.97, $p < 0.05$). Since these differences were very small, and in any case did not favor the normal achievers, it was decided that they could safely be discounted. All other differences were nonsignificant. Importantly, there was no significant difference between the dyslexics and the normal achievers ($p > 0.05$).

## 2. COMPARISONS OF THE FMT SCORES OF THE DIFFERENT GROUPS

The next stage of the analysis was to compare the FMT scores of the different groups. These are set out in table II. In the case of this table, we judged it more informative to present the raw scores rather than the scaled scores.

Analysis of variance revealed absence of homogeneity in the data, $F(5, 12,125) = 1249.67$, $p < 0.001$. Post hoc tests (Tukey) showed significant differences between all the groups ($p < 0.001$) except that the differences between the nondyslexic

underachievers and the buffer group, and between the dyslexics
and the buffer group, were nonsignificant ($p > 0.05$).

Table II.   Raw Scores on the Mathematics Test Broken Down by Group.

| Group | N | Mean | Standard Deviation | Standard Error | Missing Data |
|---|---|---|---|---|---|
| Normal achievers | 6,333 | 49.02 | 9.56 | 0.12 | 5 |
| Moderate underachievers | 1,700 | 47.18 | 10.72 | 0.26 | 3 |
| Underachievers A | 269 | 39.13 | 11.96 | 0.52 | None |
| Underachievers B | 221 | 40.95 | 9.81 | 0.66 | None |
| Underachievers C | 417 | 42.46 | 10.66 | 0.73 | None |
| Low ability children | 3,191 | 32.44 | 9.84 | 0.84 | 9 |
| Unclassifiable | 757* | | | | |
| Missing data | 17 | | | | |
| TOTAL | 12,905 | | | | |

* In our previous paper (Miles, Haslum, & Wheeler, 1998) 1,101 cases were
reported as unclassifiable. Among them, however, were 344 children in the low-
ability group for whom FMT scores were available (though some other information was lacking), and there was no reason for not including these scores in the
present paper. If we then take into account the 17 children (see column 6) for
whom other data were available but not FMT scores, this gives a figure of 774
cases missing, which constitutes 5.87 percent of the original cohort of 12,905.

## 3. THE INFLUENCE OF READING ON THE FMT SCORES

Now, it is clear that the items in the FMT call for considerable
skill in reading. It is possible, therefore, that the differences between the groups are the consequence of the poorer reading
ability of the underachievers. Dyslexia was, in fact, diagnosed
by a complicated combination of criteria, but since poor reading
was one criterion among others, it is prima facie possible that
the weaker performance of the dyslexics on the FMT was not
due to lack of mathematical skill as such but to their relative
difficulty in reading the questions.

If this were the case, however, there would be no reason to
expect any difference in mean score between the dyslexics and
the nondyslexic underachievers, whereas such a difference was
in fact found. As a further safeguard, however, we carried out
an analysis of covariance in which we used the *Edinburgh
Reading Test* ( 1985) as the covariate. Scores on this test had not
been employed as part of the original definition of dyslexia, and
its use in the present context enabled us to check what proportion of the variance in the FMT scores could be explained in
terms of poor reading comprehension. We found that this

percentage was 5.6, from which it may be concluded that the FMT to a large extent was measuring skills other than reading comprehension.

## 4. PERCENTAGE PASS RATES FOR THE DIFFERENT ITEMS

Appendix 1 contains the percentage pass rates for four of the six groups: normal achievers, underachievers A, underachievers B, and underachievers C. (We did not include percentages for the moderate underachievers or for the low-ability children because no reference is made to either of these groups in the analysis which follows.) To make comparisons between the groups on any individual FMT item, readers may find it helpful to subtract the percentage pass rate of one group from that of the other.

## 5. THE JUDGES' RATINGS AND THEIR COMMENTS

A full record of the ratings by the groups of judges for each of the 72 items is given in Appendix 2. Kendall's tau (the coefficient of concordance between the six sets of ratings) was found to be $W = 0.7647$, chi-squared (df 71) = 318.0757, $p < 0.00001$ (the matrix of ranks used was $6 \times 72$). This represents a high degree of consensus overall.

To save space we have limited ourselves to extracting from the judges' comments those which refer to items 3, 5, 8, 12, 13, 15, 26, 30, 31, 32, 65, and 68. These are the items to which we shall be referring in the discussion section. In each case, we have presented the number of the question, a reminder of what was asked (though not the picture as shown in figure 1), and, in brackets, the rating(s) given by the group of judges who made the comment(s). Hyphens indicate disagreement between judges within the same group. Readers who so wish may attempt their own ratings by referring to figure 1; they may then like to compare them with those of the judges, which are given in Appendix 2.

Q. 3. (7 + 4 – how many stars altogether?) "Manageable numbers + actual stars to count if necessary" (1).

Q. 5 (Take away: 5 – 5) "Numbers are small - 'Take away' is familiar language" (1).

Q. 8 (432-36) "Decomposition is unusually difficult for dyslexics" (3). "Borrowing in two columns difficult" (5). "The cloud is confusing" (4).

*Q.* 12 (138 X 7) "7 times table is one of the most difficult tables. Memory difficulties – remembering stages and at the same time the size of the numbers" (4-5) "Lots of procedures to remember" (4).

*Q.* 13 (Thirty something times 5 = 185) "Dyslexics usually find this difficult because there is a lot to keep track of and they easily get lost" (4).

*Q.* 15 (48 ice creams, eat 6 a day) "A lot of steps" (5). "A dyslexic would have difficulty in extracting the essential information from the language" (5). "8 times table is difficult" (5).

*Q.* 26 (Smallest number, including decimals) "Dyslexic children very confused by decimal places. They will look at the zeros and be confused or count them" (3). "We think few 10-year-olds would have met this" (5).

*Q.* 30 (What is 1/4 of 8?) "Easy. This is a manageable everyday fraction" (1). "Straightforward" (3). "Understanding the term 'of' is problematic" (5). "Probably not experienced this. Concept and language demands are high" (5).

*Q.* 31 (Which fraction is largest?) "Many dyslexics find concept of largest fraction, smallest denominator difficult" (5). "Some, with good concept of 'easier' fractions will be OK. Others will go for one sixth" (2-3-4).

*Q.* 32 (6/12 is the same as ...) "Straightforward" (3). "Dyslexics find fractions fairly difficult at the age of 10" (4) "Almost impossible" (5).

*Q.* 65 (decoding mirror writing) "We disagreed on this. SC felt that MIT was manageable (1). The question is written in capital letters but the answer choices are in lower case – confusing. Once over this – the question is straightforward" (2). "Mirror writing is too difficult for a dyslexic 10-year-old to understand" (5).

*Q.* 68 (knowledge of "perpendicular") "Graphic looks like a Christmas pud" (3). "A 10-year-old would not know what this means or be able to read the words given as answer choices" (5).

## DISCUSSION

We are now in a position to suggest some possible answers to the four questions raised at the start of this paper.

1. *Are dyslexic ten-year-olds weaker in general at mathematics than suitably matched controls?*  This question can be answered with an unequivocal "yes." The mean score for the dyslexics on the FMT was lower than that for the normal achievers (see table II).

2. *Do they differ in this respect from others with literacy problems who are not typically dyslexic?*  Again the answer to this question is "yes." The mean score for the nondyslexic underachievers was higher than that for the dyslexics, with the buffer group occupying an intermediate place. The results are, therefore, compatible with two hypotheses which are interlinked: 1) that the "dyslexic" group did indeed contain the largest proportion of dyslexics in the SDD sense, that the buffer group contained the next largest, and that the nondyslexic underachievers group contained the smallest; and 2) that dyslexics tend to have more problems with mathematics than those who are underachieving at literacy for other reasons.

Since there are these differences in score and since these groups were differentiated by reason of their performance on the supplementary items, our results provide further evidence that the supplementary items—originally chosen on the basis of clinical observation—yield data that, whatever one's theoretical position, require explanation.

3. *If they perform worse than these others, does this mean that they are weaker "across the board"; that is, weaker at all aspects of mathematics or only at some?*  It is clear from Appendix 1 that when the dyslexics are compared with the normal achievers (the comparison on which we shall be concentrating), there are large differences in percentage pass rate in the case of some items but only small differences in the case of others. All the differences were in favor of the normal achievers except in the case of item 1, where the difference in favor of the dyslexics was minimal.

In 17 other items (if we discount nos. 39, 59, and 72,* which were clearly too hard for both groups), the difference in pass rate was under 10 percent. (nos. 2, 6, 7, 9, 10, 14, 18, 20, 22, 23, 28, 35, 36, 45, 61, 62, and 71). In the case of 13 items, however (nos. 8, 12, 13, 15, 16, 17, 26, 30, 31, 32, 42, 65, and 68), the difference was

---

*It is interesting that in item 59 the dyslexics' pass rate was 8.18%, which is considerably *lower* than might have occurred by chance—a result which we find hard to explain.

over 20 percent. There were also differences, though not as large, between the dyslexics and the other two groups of underachievers, mostly in favor of the latter. It is therefore clear that there were some items that were presenting the dyslexics with distinctive difficulty and others where the results were not all that different from those of the normal achievers.

**4. If there are items that dyslexics tend to find extra difficult, how can these difficulties best be explained?** The judges' comments were many and varied. It is possible, however, to impose some order on them if we consider them under two heads, those referring to the need to memorize and those referring to what the children may or may not have experienced. A few further comments will then be added.

First, the comments on questions 8, 12, 13, and 15 make very clear that memory problems seriously impede the progress of dyslexics in mathematics (e.g. "borrowing in two columns difficult," "lots of procedures to remember," "remembering stages and at the same time the size of the numbers," "there is a lot to keep track of and they easily get lost"). The importance of memory for some aspects of mathematics was also emphasized by Steeves (1983). That the great majority of dyslexics have problems of immediate memory is now well established and is probably a consequence of their phonological difficulties, their slowness in processing speech sounds. Our data show very clearly how these difficulties affect their performance in mathematics.

One way of compensating for a poor memory is to make use of concrete aids such as one's fingers or marks on paper (compare Miles, 1993). A reason why question 3 was easy, as one judge pointed out, was that the stars could easily be counted, and it makes sense to suppose that counting physical objects saves the dyslexic from having to memorize number facts.

One judge said that the cloud in question 8 was confusing, while another said that the graphic in question 68 "looks like a Christmas pud [pudding]." The fact that many of the items in the FMT were presented as cartoons created a considerable amount of redundant information, and one must suppose that deciding which parts of the information supplied are relevant presents dyslexics with an extra "cognitive load" (for further evidence on this point, see Leong and Jerred, 2001).

Second, the judges regularly raised the question of whether a certain concept was or was not within a 10-year-old dyslexic's experience (e.g. "'Take away' is familiar language"). Now, as was pointed out at the start of this paper, the aim of those who devised the FMT was to test children on items that were being taught to 10-year-olds in schools at the time. What seems likely, therefore, is that dyslexics can be exposed to language which does not "register" with them as it does with nondyslexics; thus, unfamiliar words are not being brought into association with other things in their experience.

There is, in fact, good evidence that dyslexics are weak at paired associate learning (Done & Miles, 1978; Vellutino, 1979); this means, in effect, that they require more "exposures" before it is clear that a name is remembered and the concept associated with it is available for use. Although "take away" (question 7) was understood by most of the dyslexics, relatively few of them understood "perpendicular" (question 68). It is presumably part of the same limitation that dyslexics require more exposures to the same stimulus than nondyslexics before their responses become automatic (Nicolson & Fawcett, 1990).

This kind of consideration also makes sense of their difficulties with fractions and decimals. It seems likely that there are few or no skills, mathematical or other, that are downright impossible for dyslexics if they are given sufficient time and practice. At a given age, however, it is likely that they will not have "absorbed" as much as their nondyslexic peers.

Question 65, which involves the reading of mirror writing, is interesting for two reasons. In the first place, it was suggested by Orton (1937/1989) that some dyslexics might actually be extra strong at reading words in a mirror; yet our data suggest that this is not so. Secondly, question 65 led to one of the largest disagreements among the judges. All five categories of difficulty were used; one group of judges gave the response "unsure," while another group of judges within a single school disagreed among themselves. Experience suggests that the reading of mirror writing is not all that easy for anyone, and this makes sense of the fact that the dyslexics in the present study found it extra difficult.

Finally, it is possible that some of the children in the cohort may have been affected by disorders in their awareness of space. This would be a kind of analogue to the difficulties which occur as a result of acquired injury as described, for instance, by Hecaen (1962). Hecaen speaks of "dyscalculia of the spatial type (inability to work out sums from neglect of part of the figures or from wrong positioning of these figures while retaining the principle of calculation)" (p. 235). It seems possible to us that children with this type of disability continue to be confused when they have to subtract a larger number from a smaller one, as for example in question 8. The same confusion could also occur when they had to say which is the larger of two fractions or decimals, and it is possible that the difficulty which many of the dyslexics in this study experienced with the spy message (question 65) could be explained in the same way.

In this connection, it is interesting to note that Hermann and Norrie (1958) suggested that word-blindness (their term for dyslexia) might be a type of Gerstmann syndrome. The chief manifestations of this syndrome are left-right confusion, disorders of the body-schema, including finger agnosia, and, significantly, problems with calculation. This is in line with Hecaen's "dyscalculia of the spatial type." It is also in line with a claim by Karadi et al. (2001) that there can be spatial dysfunction in 9-year-old dyslexic children. This whole area is a fascinating one and calls for systematic further research.

## CONCLUDING REMARKS

This paper is in effect a sequel to Miles, Haslum, and Wheeler (1998). Both papers report on the British Births Cohort Study and use the same criteria for dyslexia. In both papers a central aim was to try to show that the concept of SDD, operationalized in terms of literacy difficulties in the context of specified responses to the four supplementary items—left-right, months forward, months reversed, and recall of digits—provides the basis for a useful taxonomy.

If a concept is to be accepted as valuable by the scientific community, those who propose it are committed to showing that interesting things can be done with it that could not have been done without it. In the case of SDD, we showed in the 1998 paper that it led to a different gender ratio for dyslexics from that provided by the concept of "reading disability," and one more in line with what the early pioneers such as Hinshelwood and Orton believed. In the present paper our main aim has been to show that in some mathematical tasks SDD children perform worse than normal achievers and worse than those underachievers in whom the typical signs of SDD are absent. We have made suggestions as to why they may have these distinctive difficulties.

# ACKNOWLEDGEMENTS

We are grateful to the judges for all the time they gave to doing their ratings and providing comments. The organizers were Steve Chinn, Sula Turner Ellis, Mary Kibel, John Temby, Michael Thomson, and Patience Thomson. We are also grateful to Keith Mitchell for his help in the preparation of figure 1.

Address correspondence to Professor T. R. Miles, School of Psychology, Brigantia Building, Penrallt Road, Bangor, Wales, United Kingdom, LL57 2AS. Telephone and fax: +44/(0) 1248 383842. e-mail: t.r.miles@bangor.ac.uk

*References*

Ansara, A. (1973). The language therapist as a basic mathematics tutor for adolescents. *Bulletin of the Orton Society, 23*, 119–139.

Butterworth, B. (1999). *The mathematical brain*. London: Macmillan.

Critchley, M. (1970). *The dyslexic child*. London: Heinemann.

Critchley, M. (1981). Dyslexia: An overview. In G. Th. Pavlidis & T. R. Miles (eds.), *Dyslexia research and its applications to education* (pp. 1–11). Chichester: Wiley.

Done, D. J., & Miles, T. R. (1978). Learning, memory and dyslexia. In M. M. Gruneberg, P. E. Morris, & R. N. Sykes (eds.) *Practical aspects of memory* (pp. 553–560). London: Academic Press.

*Edinburgh reading test*. (1985). London: Hodder & Stoughton.

Elliott, C. D. , Murray, D. J., & Pearson, L. S. (1979, 1983). *The British ability scales.* Windsor: NFER-Nelson.

Frith, U. (1997). Brain, mind and behaviour in dyslexia. In C. Hulme & M. J. Snowling (eds.), *Dyslexia: Biology, cognition and intervention* (pp. 1–19). London: Whurr.

Galaburda, A. M. (1999). Developmental dyslexia: A multilevel syndrome. *Dyslexia: An International Journal of Research and Practice, 6(4)*, 183–191.

Hecaen, H. (1962). Clinical symptomatology in right and left hemispheric lesions. In V. B. Mountcastle (ed.), *Interhemispheric relations and cerebral dominance* (pp. 215–263). Baltimore: The John Hopkins Press.

Hermann, K. (1959). *Reading disability*. Copenhagen: Munksgaard.

Hermann, K., & Norrie, E. (1958). Is word-blindness a type of Gerstmann syndrome? *Psychiatrica ac Neurologica*, 136–159.

Hinshelwood, J. (1917). *Congenital word-blindness*. London: H. K. Lewis.

Joffe, L. S. (1981). School mathematics and dyslexia. Aspects of the interrelationship. Unpublished doctoral thesis, University of Aston in Birmingham, United Kingdom.

Karadi, K., Kovaks, B., Szepesi, T., Szabo, I., & Kallai, J. (2001). Egocentric mental rotation in Hungarian dyslexic children. *Dyslexia: An International Journal of Research and Practice, 7(1)*, 3–11.

Leong, C. K., & Jerred, W. D. (2001). Effects of consistency and adequacy of language information on understanding elementary mathematics word problems. *Annals of Dyslexia*, this volume.

Miles, T. R. (1982, 1997). *The Bangor dyslexia test.* Wisbech, Cambridge: Learning Development Aids.

Miles, T. R. (1992). Some theoretical considerations. In T. R. Miles & E. Miles (eds.), *Dyslexia and mathematics* (pp. 1–22). London: Routledge.

Miles, T. R. (1993). *Dyslexia: The pattern of difficulties* (2nd ed.). London: Whurr.

Miles, T. R., Haslum, M. N., & Wheeler, T. J. (1998). Gender ratio in dyslexia. *Annals of Dyslexia, 48,* 27–55.

Naidoo, S. (1972). *Specific dyslexia.* London: Heinemann.

Nicolson, R. I., & Fawcett, A. J. (1990). Automaticity: A new framework for dyslexia research. *Cognition, 35,* 158–182.

Nicolson, R. I., & Fawcett, A. J. (1995). Dyslexia is more than a phonological disability. *Dyslexia: An International Journal of Research and Practice, 1(1),* 19–36.

Orton, S. T. (1937, 1989). *Reading, writing and speech problems in children and selected papers.* Austin, Tx: PRO-ED.

Steeves, K. J. (1983). Memory as a factor in the computational efficiency in dyslexic children with high abstract reasoning power. *Annals of Dyslexia, 33,* 141–152.

Thomson, M. E. (1991). *Developmental dyslexia* (3rd ed.). London: Whurr.

Turner Ellis, S. A., Miles, T. R., & Wheeler, T. J. (1996). Speed of multiplication in dyslexics and non-dyslexics. *Dyslexia: An International Journal of Research and Practice, 2(2),* 121–139.

Vellutino, F. R. (1979). *Dyslexia: Theory and research.* Cambridge, MA: MIT Press.

## APPENDIX 1

# Percentage Pass Rates on Each Item of the FMT for Four of the Six Groups

| Mathematics Test | Normal Achievers Mean | Under-achievers A Mean | Under-achievers B Mean | Under-achievers C Mean |
|---|---|---|---|---|
| Item 1 | 97.95% | 98.88% | 98.64% | 98.08% |
| Item 2 | 96.07% | 92.94% | 91.86% | 94.24% |
| Item 3 | 99.23% | 98.14% | 98.64% | 98.56% |
| Item 4 | 94.07% | 83.27% | 89.59% | 88.97% |
| Item 5 | 99.27% | 97.03% | 98.19% | 98.08% |
| Item 6 | 99.29% | 99.26% | 96.83% | 97.84% |
| Item 7 | 98.17% | 96.28% | 96.83% | 96.40% |
| Item 8 | 81.97% | 58.36% | 62.44% | 68.35% |
| Item 9 | 81.81% | 81.41% | 77.83% | 77.70% |
| Item 10 | 97.55% | 91.08% | 94.12% | 94.24% |
| Item 11 | 91.92% | 78.44% | 81.45% | 81.06% |
| Item 12 | 76.78% | 38.29% | 47.96% | 51.56% |
| Item 13 | 54.21% | 26.77% | 27.15% | 36.69% |
| Item 14 | 92.54% | 84.01% | 83.71% | 87.29% |
| Item 15 | 83.46% | 60.22% | 61.54% | 65.47% |
| Item 16 | 65.45% | 40.89% | 39.37% | 49.16% |
| Item 17 | 44.45% | 23.79% | 27.60% | 27.58% |
| Item 18 | 98.93% | 97.03% | 98.19% | 97.12% |
| Item 19 | 36.64% | 21.19% | 20.81% | 26.62% |
| Item 20 | 98.41% | 91.82% | 92.76% | 93.53% |
| Item 21 | 79.66% | 59.11% | 59.73% | 64.03% |
| Item 22 | 97.43% | 94.80% | 97.74% | 95.20% |
| Item 23 | 40.41% | 32.71% | 23.53% | 31.18% |
| Item 24 | 57.59% | 36.43% | 40.72% | 41.01% |
| Item 25 | 53.41% | 36.43% | 36.20% | 43.88% |
| Item 26 | 49.76% | 28.25% | 31.67% | 34.29% |
| Item 27 | 30.51% | 18.59% | 19.46% | 18.94% |
| Item 28 | 83.67% | 76.95% | 74.21% | 76.02% |
| Item 29 | 89.49% | 76.21% | 76.47% | 84.41% |
| Item 30 | 74.22% | 52.04% | 49.77% | 55.88% |
| Item 31 | 69.77% | 45.72% | 54.30% | 53.96% |
| Item 32 | 56.30% | 31.60% | 32.13% | 40.29% |
| Item 33 | 84.35% | 69.89% | 71.95% | 77.70% |
| Item 34 | 95.00% | 81.41% | 90.50% | 88.97% |

*continued*

*Appendix 1: continued*

| Mathematics Test | Normal Achievers Mean | Under-achievers A Mean | Under-achievers B Mean | Under-achievers C Mean |
|---|---|---|---|---|
| Item 35 | 51.45% | 44.98% | 46.61% | 45.80% |
| Item 36 | 45.58% | 37.92% | 38.01% | 38.13% |
| Item 37 | 84.55% | 70.26% | 76.92% | 76.98% |
| Item 38 | 53.36% | 36.80% | 38.46% | 43.65% |
| Item 39 | 23.79% | 19.70% | 17.65% | 18.47% |
| Item 40 | 94.04% | 82.16% | 90.05% | 88.73% |
| Item 41 | 78.18% | 63.20% | 65.61% | 71.70% |
| Item 42 | 58.79% | 28.25% | 38.01% | 42.69% |
| Item 43 | 40.41% | 21.19% | 21.27% | 29.98% |
| Item 44 | 84.60% | 66.17% | 70.59% | 71.46% |
| Item 45 | 53.69% | 49.07% | 48.42% | 51.56% |
| Item 46 | 37.05% | 21.56% | 22.17% | 26.62% |
| Item 47 | 33.81% | 15.61% | 18.55% | 17.03% |
| Item 48 | 34.21% | 20.82% | 17.65% | 19.90% |
| Item 49 | 40.68% | 27.14% | 28.51% | 28.78% |
| Item 50 | 92.60% | 75.46% | 80.54% | 83.93% |
| Item 51 | 77.37% | 57.62% | 59.28% | 67.63% |
| Item 52 | 53.22% | 41.64% | 40.72% | 39.33% |
| Item 53 | 91.75% | 77.32% | 86.88% | 82.97% |
| Item 54 | 53.88% | 36.06% | 38.01% | 40.53% |
| Item 55 | 28.57% | 14.50% | 18.10% | 23.02% |
| Item 56 | 79.90% | 69.14% | 75.11% | 77.94% |
| Item 57 | 81.73% | 63.94% | 72.40% | 72.66% |
| Item 58 | 65.13% | 45.72% | 57.47% | 54.44% |
| Item 59 | 10.65% | 8.18% | 7.24% | 9.83% |
| Item 60 | 96.77% | 86.62% | 93.21% | 93.05% |
| Item 61 | 56.22% | 49.07% | 51.58% | 51.08% |
| Item 62 | 70.76% | 62.83% | 68.33% | 67.63% |
| Item 63 | 46.53% | 33.46% | 35.29% | 35.01% |
| Item 64 | 31.75% | 16.73% | 21.27% | 23.50% |
| Item 65 | 82.08% | 48.33% | 62.44% | 64.51% |
| Item 66 | 45.41% | 34.94% | 38.91% | 35.49% |
| Item 67 | 80.36% | 60.97% | 68.78% | 71.46% |
| Item 68 | 54.59% | 31.97% | 35.29% | 36.69% |
| Item 69 | 94.41% | 76.21% | 81.90% | 83.21% |
| Item 70 | 85.69% | 71.75% | 74.66% | 75.06% |
| Item 71 | 31.70% | 29.00% | 26.70% | 31.89% |
| Item 72 | 23.52% | 17.10% | 18.55% | 19.18% |

## APPENDIX 2

# Summary of Judges' Ratings

| | Question and Judges' Ratings[*] | | | | |
|---|---|---|---|---|---|
| 1. | 1,1,2,1,3,1 | 25. | 3,3,2,3-4,5,5 | 49. | 4,3,2,5,3,1 |
| 2. | 3,1,3,1,3-4,3 | 26. | 3,4,3,4,4,5 | 50. | 2,2,2,3,3,2 |
| 3. | 2,1,1,1,1,1 | 27. | 3,3,2,4,5,4 | 51. | 5,3,4,5,5,5 |
| 4. | 2,1,2,4,5,3 | 28. | 1,1,2,2,3,2 | 52. | 3,4,4,3-4,5,5 |
| 5. | 1,1,1,1,1-2,1 | 29. | 2,1,2,2,2,1 | 53. | 3,2,2,3,4,3 |
| 6. | 2,2,1,3,3,5 | 30. | 2,1,3,5,4,5 | 54. | 4,4,5,4,5,5 |
| 7. | 1,1,1,1,1,1 | 31. | 5,4,3,4,5,2-3-4 | 55. | 5,4,5,4,5,5 |
| 8. | 3,3,4,4,5,5 | 32. | 3,4,3,4,5,4 | 56. | 2-3,,3,2,5,1 |
| 9. | 2,1,1,1,3,2 | 33. | 4, 2-3,3,3,3,5,4 | 57. | 3, 2,3,2,3,3 |
| 10. | 3,2,2,2,3,1 | 34. | 3,3,2,4,4,5 | 58. | 2,3,3,2-3,4,3 |
| 11. | 3,2,1,3,3,5 | 35. | 5,4,4,4,5,5 | 59. | 5,5,4,4,5,5 |
| 12. | 4,4,3,4-5,5,5 | 36. | 4,4,3,4,4,3 | 60. | 1,1,1,1,1,1 |
| 13. | 5,4,5,5,5,5 | 37. | 2,2,4,4,4,3 | 61. | 2,2,2,2,2,1 |
| 14. | 1,2,1,2,4,2 | 38. | 4,4,4,5,5,5 | 62. | 3,1,2,1,3,1 |
| 15. | 5,5,5,4,5,5 | 39. | 5,5,5,5,5,5 | 63. | 3,1,3,2,5,1 |
| 16. | 5,4,5,5,5,5 | 40. | 2,1,1,1-2,2,1 | 64. | 5,5,5,5,5,5 |
| 17. | 5,5,5,5,5,5 | 41. | 2,2,1,4,2,1 | 65. | 3,unsure, 3,2,5,1 |
| 18. | 1,1,1,2,4,1 | 42. | 3,4,4,4,4,2 | 66. | 2,2,2,3,3,4 |
| 19. | 5,4,4,5,5,5 | 43. | 3,2,2,2,4,3-4-5 | 67. | 3,2,1,3,2,2 |
| 20. | 1,1,2,1,2,1 | 44. | 3,3,3,4,4,2 | 68. | 4,4,3,4,5,5 |
| 21. | 2,2,3,3,4,3 | 45. | 3,2,3,4,4,4 | 69. | 1,1,3,2,2,1 |
| 22. | 2,2,3,4,3,1 | 46. | 4,4,4,3,5,4 | 70. | 2,2,2,1,3,4 |
| 23. | 5,5,5,5,5,5 | 47. | 3,3,4,4,5,4 | 71. | 3,2,3,4,4,2 |
| 24. | 4,2,3,4,4,2-3-4 | 48. | 3,2,2,3,5,4 | 72. | 3,1,4,4,5,5 |

[*] Where numbers are joined by hyphens, this indicates disagreement or uncertainty within the same group of judges.

# Index

*(Page numbers in italics indicate material in figures or tables.)*